MW00736833

TRAVEL & LEISURE

Washington, D.C.

*by Joe Brown
with Elise Hartman Ford
and Theodore Fischer*

Macmillan • USA

MACMILLAN TRAVEL
A Simon & Schuster Macmillan Company
1633 Broadway
New York, NY 10019

Find us online at **http://www.mgr.com/travel** or on
America Online at Keyword: **Frommer's**

ISBN 0-02-860692-2
ISSN 1088-4785

Map Editor: Douglas Stallings
Design by Amy Peppler Adams—designLab, Seattle
Digital Cartography by Ortelius Design
Illustrations on pages 34, 65, 107, 112, 113, 119, 131, 143,
and 145 by Giselle Simons.

SPECIAL SALES

Bulk purchases (10+ copies) of Frommer's and selected
Macmillan travel guides are available to corporations,
organizations, institutions, and charities at special discounts,
and can be customized to suit individual needs. For more
information write to Special Sales, Macmillan General
Reference, 1633 Broadway, New York,
NY 10019.

Manufactured in Singapore

Contents

LIST OF MAPS

About the Author

Joe Brown signed on to edit and revise this guidebook as a way of taking one last long, loving look at Washington, D.C., the city he lived in for 15 years. A former staff writer for the *Washington Post,* specializing in arts, entertainment, and lifestyle stories, he has moved to the opposite side of the country to San Francisco, where he recently wrote Frommer's *San Francisco by Night* (Macmillan USA) and is (apprehensively) awaiting his first earth-shaking experience.

Elise Hartman Ford is a freelance features and travel writer, whose pieces have appeared in the *Washington Post,* the *Ladies' Home Journal,* and *Washingtonian* magazine. She is the author of a popular guide to unusual party and meeting sites, *Unique Meeting Places in Greater Washington,* recently released in its fourth edition.

Theodore Fischer, a freelance writer and Washington-area transplant, is the author of the Cheap/Smart series of guidebooks and *Frommer's Irreverent Guide to Washington, D.C.*

An Additional Note

Please be advised that travel information is subject to change at any time—and this is especially true of prices. We therefore suggest that you write or call ahead for confirmation when making your travel plans. The author, editor, and publisher cannot be held responsible for the experiences of readers while traveling. Your safety is important to us, however, so we encourage you to stay alert and be aware of your surroundings. Keep a close eye on cameras, purses, and wallets, all favorite targets of thieves and pickpockets.

INTRODUCTION

MUCH OF MY FIRST 15 YEARS IN D.C. WAS SPENT AS A staff writer for the *Washington Post,* covering popular culture, entertainment, and the arts. This gave me unusual entree to both the official and unofficial sides of the city. In those 15 years—I arrived as a 21-year-old college graduate just in time to witness the pomp of Ronald Reagan's inauguration, and left just as the 1996 presidential campaigns were gathering steam (that's another word for "hot air")—I shook hands with 3 presidents, watched the city change, and shared its pleasures and growing pains.

During those years, I saw D.C. begin to take itself less seriously (admittedly, it's still got a long way to go). It seemed as though the city was beginning to remember that it was a place to live, as well as a place to work. I witnessed the revitalization of once-lovely inner-city neighborhoods, outpourings of homegrown arts and culture, and a new appreciation of food and comfort.

Now, when I think about D.C. (I've recently moved to San Francisco), I first envision the same iconic images that probably come to mind for you—the white marble monuments, the priceless, fascinating clutter of the Smithsonian museums, the wide avenues and low skyline. . . .

But my mind and heart always return to the livable and lived-in side and sights of the city, especially the blessed green expanses of Rock Creek Park and the National Mall, and the funky, funny, only-in-Washington pockets in neighborhoods like Dupont Circle and Adams Morgan.

I will not miss the weather, particularly the notorious D.C. summers. But this "capital city" will always have a cherished place in my heart.

My hope is that this book will help make you feel like an insider, too. I've tried to share information and ideas, to encourage you to find a fresh way of looking at the familiar sights, to suggest a way of seeing Washington with independence and curiosity.

Along with the essentials of getting around and staying in D.C., you'll find a concise history of the capital city, an armchair tour of the many famous landmarks, buildings, monuments, and attractions; and bite-sized reviews of D.C.'s most distinctive restaurants for all tastes and budgets. I've also filed an insider's report on the town's active arts, nightlife, sports, and shopping scenes.

So with this book in hand, feel free to ramble the streets and savor the distinct neighborhood flavors of our capital city: The cobblestone-and-honky-tonk incongruity of Georgetown; kaleidoscopic Adams Morgan; grand, gracious Logan Circle; embassy-lined Kalorama; and Capitol Hill, perhaps the most "Washington-esque" of all the neighborhoods.

Take a walk through Rock Creek Park, Washington's jewel, or explore one of the many neighborhoods by bike or Rollerblades. Or take the immaculate, dependable Metro subway system out of town—say to Old Town Alexandria's King Street stop and walk down the quaint boutique-and-restaurant-packed main drag to the waterfront.

If money's no object, take a Potomac River dinner cruise (a 3-hour tour) on the luxurious, futuristic-looking, new Odyssey cruise ship.

Or get over your "I'm NOT-a-tourist" attitude and take the Old Town Trolley Tour around the city in an open-air green and orange car—the guides are funny and it's a good way to catch all the monuments. Your secret's safe with us.

Whatever you do, please enjoy this grand city while you're here. Heck, you paid for it!

WASHINGTON, D.C.
TODAY

M OST FOLKS GET THEIR FIRST AND MOST LASTING impression of Washington, D.C. from the movies and TV.

Think *Mr. Smith Goes to Washington. All the President's Men. JFK* and *Nixon. Dave* and "Murphy Brown."

Many Americans have come to think of the District of Columbia as a sort of marble Disneyland, where all the characters actually exist, and all the stories are true. (Well, most of them.)

Washington takes itself rather more seriously. This is a place that likes to call itself Powertown without irony. Business comes first here.

It's a city of Northern charm and Southern efficiency, as President Kennedy once famously put it. It's also a city of transients. As the saying goes: If you've lived here more than 4 years (the life span of most presidential administrations), you qualify as a native.

As a result, life here has its peculiarities: Most residents don't even look up when a limousine and motorcycle motorcade goes screeching by the main avenues, speeding some head of state to another meeting.

Media-saturated Washingtonians are more likely to cross the street to avoid Sam Donaldson or his ilk doing a standup on the halogen-lit sidewalk, than to try and sneak into the shot for a "Hi Mom!"

And the first question a Washingtonian is likely to ask in conversation is "What do you do?" (instantaneously assigning you a ranking based on your GS [government service] level).

It's hard to forget, when you see the white dome and obelisk that dominate the low skyline, that this provincial southern town is weighed down by its self-important main industries: government, reporting on government, and law. As a result, not much changes around here—except for the guy sitting in the Oval Office.

In the past decade, a see-America/buy-American tourist boom has made out-of-towners the area's leading industry. There's got to be some reason why more than 10 million visitors each year make the pilgrimage to this most American city (population 700,000).

In the 1990s, Washington entered a golden age. Never before has this city been so vibrant, lively, cosmopolitan, and civilized. It retains its classical dignity, its exquisite monuments and majestic perspectives, but it has acquired chic tastes, international habits, and a new joie de vivre. The city's learning how to have fun.

Washington is waking up and smelling the coffee—and savoring the sights and sounds and styles, the restaurants, the clubs, the shopping, the day-trips and hikes, the sports and lively arts.

Washington is discovering its own quality of life.

It's certainly got all the necessary raw ingredients, starting with a beautifully designed city plan, with wide streets and low buildings, which makes it a pleasant place to live (except perhaps during its notoriously humid summers!). City residents have easy access to vibrant neighbors on the Northeast Corridor: Baltimore, Philadelphia, and New York. There's good food, too—what D.C. lacks in indigenous tastes or trend-setting style, it makes up for with an abundance of expense-account restaurants and a richness of international cuisines.

The importance of the arrival of coffee culture—which began in 1994 with the invasion of the Starbucks chain and its imitators—should not be overestimated, as it has changed this workaholic, self-important city's temperament as much as it has its urban landscape. While simultaneously speeding Washington up with caffeine infusions (what DID we do for coffee before the latté revolution?), the cafe revolution has paradoxically taught overly serious citizens how to slow down, chat, hang out.

Throw in a culture and arts scene that continues to have impact beyond the official halls of the Smithsonian and Kennedy Center, a rabidly loyal fan base for the Redskins and other sports teams, and a truly international ambiance (sparked by the presence of all those embassies, diplomats, and immigrants), and you've got a city that's a work of art, a place that deserves to be called "a Capital City."

Orientation

Central Washington is laid out on a grid radiating out from the Capitol. To the north and south, the streets run alphabetically (omitting the letters J, X, Y, and Z), while to the east and west they are numbered. This divides the whole city into 4 quadrants: northwest (NW), northeast (NE), southwest (SW), and southeast (SE). Addresses must always bear these designations, or confusion reigns as there are four 1st streets, four A streets, and so on.

Avenues, named after states (Connecticut, Wisconsin, Massachusetts, etc.), cut diagonally across the street grid. Once you grasp the system, this is an easy city in which to find your way around.

The 4 quadrants are fairly distinct in character. Northwest is where the president lives, along with most of the city's middle-class population, black and white, Asian and Hispanic. Affluence does not cover the whole area, however, and a few poorer neighborhoods remain. Downtown Northwest contains most of the city's tourist attractions, hotels, restaurants, and places of entertainment.

The Mall, lined with prestigious museums and public buildings, straddles the northwest and southwest sections. The small southwest area, once filled with slums, has been redeveloped on a large scale and now houses a middle-class community. Southeast and northeast are predominantly poor areas with a mainly black population, except for the middle-class enclave of Capitol Hill. The Maryland and Virginia suburbs are home to good hotels and dazzling shopping malls. Otherwise the immediate environs have little of interest to visitors, except for isolated attractions such as Arlington National Cemetery, the old town of Alexandria and George Washington's country estate at Mount Vernon (see "Excursions").

At the center of the cluster of communities that makes up the Washington metropolitan area is the District of Columbia. The District itself is an area of about 69 square miles (179km²), stretching along the northeast side of the Potomac River and incorporating a slice of land to the southeast of the Anacostia River.

The main core of Washington is the area nestling in the fork of the 2 rivers. Originally the District was a regular diamond-shaped area straddling the Potomac, but in 1846 the inhabitants of the territory to the

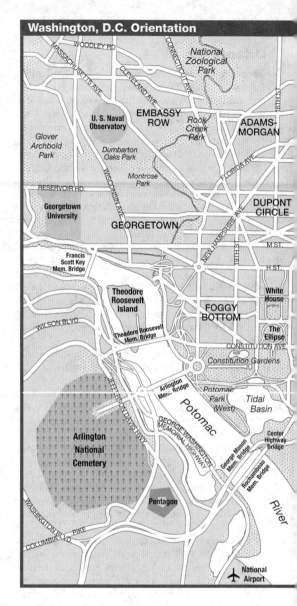

Washington, D.C. Orientation

southwest of the river opted to return to Virginia. Even a current map will show that the county boundaries on the Virginia side are still based on the old District line. Metropolitan Washington is ringed by the famous Capitol Beltway (Interstate 495).

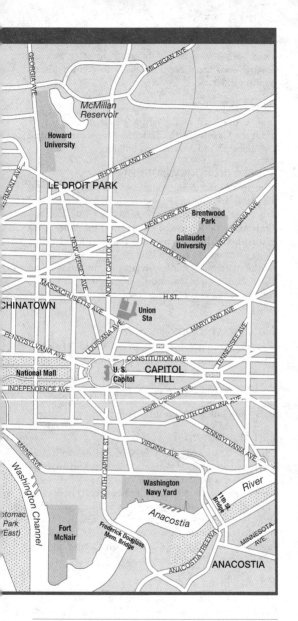

Washington, D.C.'s Neighborhoods

Washington, unlike Paris, London, or Boston, is not a city of small, distinct villages. But it does have neighborhoods of widely differing character. The following areas are those most likely to come within a visitor's itinerary.

The Mall

This is the heart of the city, a 2-mile stretch of park from the **Capitol** to the **Lincoln Memorial,** flanked by museums and government buildings.

West End/Foggy Bottom

The area to the north, south, and west of Washington Circle is a commercial, government, residential, and academic district that includes George Washington University, the **Kennedy Center** and the **Watergate Complex.** These surround a neighborhood called Foggy Bottom, so named because of the miasmic fogs that once engulfed this low-lying, swampy ground. The West End area, to the north of Washington Circle, incorporates a cluster of big new luxury hotels, but not much else.

New Downtown

The district to the northwest of the **White House** is bounded roughly by N Street, 16th Street, Pennsylvania Avenue, and New Hampshire Avenue. This is now the focus of commercial life in Washington, and boasts many new office buildings, smart shops, and expensive restaurants, but not a great deal of charm.

Old Downtown

This district runs east from the White House to within a few blocks of the splendidly restored **Union Station.** After a period of decay, most parts of the area have undergone a remarkable renaissance. It now contains department stores, museums, theaters, restaurants, smart shops, small galleries, luxury hotels, and some fine old buildings that have been renovated. On its north side is the **Washington Convention Center** and the new Techworld Trade Center.

Capitol Hill

This comprises the Capitol complex and the residential area to the east, as far as Lincoln Park, and extending roughly from E Street in the south to E Street in the north. An area of charming, tree-lined streets, some of which are still poor and crime-ridden, Capitol Hill is being colonized by a United Nations of young professionals, many of whom work on the Hill, of course.

Southwest

The entire area south of the Mall is dominated by government departments, high-rise apartment blocks, and new townhouses. The main sites of tourist interest are the Mall itself and the colorful (and, um, fragrant) Waterfront area, which has some good seafood restaurants.

Georgetown

Between **Rock Creek Park** and Georgetown University, Georgetown is, in part, a charming tree-lined enclave of the Establishment, who live in elegantly restored historic houses with inflated real-estate values. The other part, radiating out from Wisconsin Avenue and M Street, is a brasher, livelier world of discotheques, jazz clubs, cafes, boutiques, and other haunts of the young, loud, and trendy.

Dupont Circle

With Georgetown, this is the closest that Washington has to a Left Bank. In addition to a relaxed yet lively atmosphere and a youngish gay and lesbian residential population, Dupont Circle has some fine architecture and many small businesses: bookstores, art galleries, cafes, small bars, and restaurants. Just to the northwest of Dupont Circle is a dense colony of embassies, many occupying gracious houses along Massachusetts Avenue, now nicknamed "Embassy Row."

Adams Morgan

In northwest Washington, in the fork between Connecticut and Florida avenues, is a colorful, international (though mainly Hispanic) enclave with a mixture of yupscale, bohemian, and ethnic elements and a correspondingly wide variety of restaurants.

Upper Northwest

This covers most of the city above Georgetown and northwest of Rock Creek Park. Here can be found the **National Zoological Park, Washington National Cathedral,** the **U.S. Naval Observatory,** some pleasant leafy suburbs, and many interesting restaurants on Connecticut and Wisconsin avenues.

Northeast of the White House

The area stretching northeast from the White House to Logan Circle contains a rich potpourri of fine architecture in various styles. Bordering a poor district to the east, it is becoming less dilapidated as more affluent families move in and renovate, and there are now a number of recommended hotels in the area. For years, 14th Street and its environs were rife with prostitution and pornography. While the sex industry is not dead, big business is currently redeveloping 14th Street into a steel-and-glass office building corridor.

DINING

L ET'S FACE IT: D.C.'S NOT ANYONE'S IDEA OF A FOOD town. Not like restaurant-obsessed San Francisco, New York, or Los Angeles, anyway. It's got other things on its mind, like power, sex, and scandal.

D.C. is still a town of transients, who come here to get things done, make a mark, add a few paragraphs to their resume, and go on their way. This is not exactly conducive to the development of an indigenous food style or food culture.

On the plus side, even the coldest-blooded lobbyist has to eat, and much of the city's business gets done over lunch and dinner. Washington is truly an international city, thanks to both the high-profile embassies and the recent waves of immigrants from countries such as Ethiopia, El Salvador, and Vietnam. This has contributed immeasurably to the rich variety of the city's dining experience.

Lines of taste have been shifting around town. While Georgetown still has the popular, almost-mythical reputation as *the* place to hang out and dine, the heat has really moved to Adams Morgan, where the trendy and international restaurants compete with dance clubs. The what-passes-for-bohemian neighborhood of Dupont Circle and the "new Downtown" are also undergoing a restaurant renaissance of sorts. Maybe it's all those well-traveled Washingtonians returning home and saying, "Hey, why can't we have that quality of life thing here?"

The D.C. scene has produced a few culinary stars; Provencal was named 1995 Restaurant of the Year by Esquire magazine; Galileo's Roberto Donna, Jean-Louis Palladin of the Watergate, and Francesco Ricchi of i Ricchi are just a few of the chefs you might recognize if you keep up with gourmet magazines.

You can't go wrong with dining at the major hotels—many of the city's better chefs are working in hotels, in such restaurants as Nicholas at the Mayflower, Coeur de Lion at the Henley Park, the Colonnade at the ANA, the Bristol Grill at the Wyndham-Bristol, Chardonnay at the Radisson Mark Terrace, and Celadon at the J. W. Marriott.

If you're sore from sightseeing or just don't feel like going out, many D.C. and suburban eateries deliver (often for free, sometimes for a small surcharge; be sure to ask if there is a minimum order). Or call **Takeout Taxi** (☎ 202/986-0111) or **A La Carte Express** (☎ 202/546-8646), which deliver full menu selections from many area restaurants right to your door.

The price key is based on a meal including entree and dessert. Not included in this estimate are appetizers, drinks, desserts, gratuity (15% recommended) or D.C.'s 9% tax.

STAR RATINGS The stars—none, one and two—are a subjective overall rating, reflecting the entire experience—ambiance,

Price Chart	
$	= Under $15
$$	= $15–$25
$$$	= $25–$35
$$$$	= $35 plus

service, food taste, quality, and presentation. Remember, even the unstarred places are recommended.

Restaurants by Neighborhood

Adams Morgan
Argentine Grill. **$$**
Cafe Lautrec. **$$**
★ Cashion's Eat Place. **$$$**
Cities. **$$/$$$**
★ Coppi's. **$**
The Grill From Ipanema. **$$**
I Matti. **$$**
★ Las Cruces. **$**
Perry's. **$$**
Peyote Cafe/Roxanne. **$$**
Polly's Cafe. **$**
Red Sea. **$**
Tom Tom. **$$**

Capitol Hill
America. **$/$$**
American Café. **$/$$**
Bullfeathers. **$/$$**
La Brasserie. **$$**
★ Two Quail. **$$**

Downtown
★ Bombay Club. **$$**
Bombay Palace. **$$**

Cafe Mozart. **$$**
★ Capitol City Brewing Company. **$$**
Ciao Baby. **$$**
★ Coco Loco. **$$**
Dixie Grill. **$**
★ Georgia Brown. **$$$**
★★ Gerard's Place. **$$$**
★ Hunan Chinatown. **$/$$**
★ Jaleo. **$$**
★ Legal Sea Foods. **$$**
★★ Le Lion d'Or. **$$$$**
★★ Maison Blanche. **$$$$**
★ Marrakesh. **$$$**
★ Mr. Yung's. **$**
★ Muer's Seafood. **$$**
★ Notte Luna. **$$**
★★ Occidental/Occidental Grill. **$$$**
★ Old Ebbitt Grill. **$$**
★★ Prime Rib. **$$$**
Red Hot and Blue. **$**
★★ Red Sage. **$$$**

Tony Cheng's Mongolian
Restaurant. **$$**

Dupont Circle
★ Bacchus. **$$**
El Bodegon. **$/$$**
Carmella Kitty's. **$$**
★ City Lights of China.
$$
Food for Thought. **$**
★★ Galileo. **$$$$**
Il Radicchio. **$$**
★ i Ricchi. **$$$**
★★ Jockey Club. **$$$**
★★ Nora. **$$$**
★★ Obelisk. **$$$**
★ The Palm. **$$$**
★ Pizzeria Paradiso. **$$**
Saigon Gourmet. **$**
★ Sam & Harry's. **$$**
★ Tabard Inn. **$$**
★ Vidalia. **$$$**
Zorba's Cafe. **$**

Foggy Bottom/West End
★ Garden Cafe. **$$**
★★ Jean-Louis at the
Watergate. **$$$$**
★ Kinkead's. **$$$**

Georgetown
American Café. **$/$$**
Au Pied du Cochon. **$/$$**
Austin Grill. **$$**
★ Citronelle. **$$$**
Clyde's. **$$**
Martin's Tavern. **$$**
★ Music City Roadhouse.
$$
★ Sarinah Satay House. **$$**
Sequoia. **$$**
★★ 1789. **$$$**

Upper Northwest
Dancing Crab. **$$**
★ Dolce Finale. **$$**
★ Germaine's. **$$**
★ Lebanese Taverna. **$$**
★ Mrs. Simpson's. **$$**
★ New Heights. **$$$**

Maryland Suburbs
★ Inn at Glen Echo. **$$**
★★ Old Angler's Inn. **$$$$**
★ Parkway Deli. **$**

Virginia Suburbs
★ L'Auberge Chez Francois.
$$$

Restaurants by Cuisine

American
America. **$/$$**
American Café. **$/$$**
Bullfeathers. **$/$$**
★ Capitol City Brewing
Company. **$$**
Clyde's. **$$**
Martin's Tavern. **$$**
★ Old Ebbitt Grill. **$$**
Polly's Cafe. **$**
★ Tabard Inn. **$$**

Argentine
Argentine Grill. **$$**

Barbecue/Chili
★ Music City Roadhouse.
$$
Red Hot and Blue. **$**

Brazilian
The Grill From Ipanema. **$$**
★ Coco Loco. **$$**

Cajun
Carmella Kitty's. **$$**

Chinese
★ City Lights of China. **$$**
★ Hunan Chinatown.
$/$$
★ Mr. Yung's. **$**
Tony Cheng's Mongolian
Restaurant. **$$**

Deli
★ Parkway Deli. **$**

Dessert
★ Dolce Finale. **$$**

Eclectic
Cities. **$$/$$$**
Tom Tom. **$$**

Ethiopian
Red Sea. **$**

French
Au Pied du Cochon. **$/$$**
Cafe Lautrec. **$$**
★★ Gerard's Place. **$$$**
★★ Jean-Louis at the
Watergate. **$$$$**
★ L'auberge Chez Francoise.
$$$
La Brasserie. **$$**
★★ Le Lion d'Or. **$$$$**
★★ Maison Blanche. **$$$$**

German
Cafe Mozart. **$$**

Greek
Zorba's Cafe. **$**

Indian
★ Bombay Club. **$$**
Bombay Palace. **$$**

Indonesian
★ Sarinah Satay House. **$$**

Italian
Ciao Baby. **$$**
★ Coppi's. **$**
★★ Galileo. **$$$$**
Il Radicchio. **$$**
I Matti. **$$**
★ i Ricchi. **$$$**
★ Notte Luna. **$$**
★★ Obelisk. **$$$**

Japanese
Perry's. **$$**

Lebanese
★ Bacchus. **$$**
★ Lebanese Taverna. **$$**

Moroccan
★ Marrakesh. **$$$**

New American
★ Cashion's Eat Place. **$$$**
★ Citronelle. **$$$**
★ Garden Cafe. **$$**
★ Inn at Glen Echo. **$$**

★★ Jockey Club. **$$$**
★ Kinkead's. **$$$**
★ Morrison-Clark Inn
★ Mrs. Simpson's. **$$**
★ New Heights. **$$$**
★★ Nora. **$$$**
★★ Occidental/Occidental
Grill. **$$$**
★★ Old Angler's Inn.
$$$$
Sequoia. **$$**
★ 1789. **$$$**
★ Two Quail. **$$**
★ Vidalia. **$$$**

Pan-Asian
★ Germaine's. **$$**

Pizza
★ Pizzeria Paradiso. **$$**

Seafood
Dancing Crab. **$$**
★ Legal Sea Foods. **$$**
★ Muer's Seafood. **$$**

Southern
Dixie Grill. **$**
★ Georgia Brown. **$$$**

Southwestern
Austin Grill. **$$**
★ Las Cruces. **$**
Peyote Cafe/Roxanne. **$$**
★★ Red Sage. **$$$**

Spanish
El Bodegon. **$–$$**
★ Jaleo. **$$**

Steak
★ The Palm. **$$$**
★★ Prime Rib. **$$$**
★ Sam & Harry's. **$$**

Vegetarian
Food for Thought. **$**

Vietnamese
Saigon Gourmet. **$**

Critic's Choice

After Midnight Can't sleep? Here are a few spots to
satisfy late-night cravings. **Soho Tea & Coffee** (2150
P St. NW; 202/463-7646) is the hippest for all-nighters

(closed 4–6am for cleaning). Old Georgetown stand-bys include **Au Pied du Cochon** (1335 Wisconsin Ave. NW; 202/333-5440) and **Bistro Francais** (3128 M St.; 202/338-3830), and if grease is the word, there's always the **Georgetown Cafe** (1623 Wisconsin Ave. NW; 202/338-0215). And **Kramerbooks & Afterwords** bookstore/cafe (1517 Connecticut Ave. NW; 202/387-1462) now stays open 24 hours Friday and Saturday for binging and book-browsing.

Alfresco   Outdoor dining is one of the bonuses of living in Washington when the weather permits—and it sometimes surprises us with 70° days in January!—every restaurant tries to drag a table or two out on the sidewalk. The most popular outdoor decks are at **Perry's** (1811 Columbia Rd. NW; 202/234-6218) and **Kramerbooks & Afterwords** (1517 Connecticut Ave. NW; 202/387-1462). And up on the roof at the **Sky Terrace** at the Hotel Washington (15th St. and Pennsylvania Ave. NW; 202/638-5900), close by the White House, you can enjoy cocktails and hors d'oeuvres while taking in the best views of the monuments and federal buildings.

Asian   You can head to Chinatown and take your pick of a score of restaurants, or you can head for the heart of town, where a quintet of Asian restaurants, a "virtual Chinatown" in the Dupont Circle area, often outshine the Chinatown mainstays: **City Lights of China** (1731 Connecticut Ave. NW; 202/265-6688), **Pan-Asian Noodles & Grill** (2020 P St. NW; 202/872-8889), **Bua Thai** (1635 P St. NW; 202/265-0828), **Sala Thai** (2016 P St. NW; 202/872-1144), and **Cafe Japone** (2032 P St. NW; 202/223-1573), which also has sumo videos or karaoke.

Bagels, Etc.   Somewhere back there, the bagel seems to have replaced the hot dog as our national food. Holiest of holeys is **Whatsa Bagel** (3513 Connecticut Ave. NW; 202/966-8990), which always has long lines for its special flavored bagels, from sun-dried tomato to chocolate chip. We're purists ourselves. Bagel hounds also flock to **Chesapeake Bagel Bakery** (215 Pennsylvania Ave. NW, Capitol Hill, 202/546-0994; and 1636 Connecticut Ave. NW, 202/328-7985) and **Georgetown Bagelry** (3245 M St. NW; 202/965-1011). You can get heaping bagel sandwiches at 2 chain delis: **Schlotzky's** (Dupont Underground; beneath Dupont Circle at Connecticut Ave. NW), and Krupin's (4620 Connecticut Ave. NW;

202/686-1989), a northern outpost of the popular Florida deli/restaurant.

Big Food   Those hankerin' for heapin' helpin's should head for the Chevy Chase branch of the national **Cheesecake Factory** chain (Chevy Chase Pavilion, 5345 Wisconsin Ave. NW; 202/364-0500): You could make 3 big meals from the mountainous Santa Fe Salad, for instance. (But try to save room for cheesecake.) The restaurant is incredibly popular, so try to go at off-hours. Other favorites with the doggie-bag set: For years, Georgetown students have survived on the humongous sandwiches at **Booeymonger** (3265 Prospect St. NW; 202/333-4810); and the meat and potatoes reach Flintstones-sized proportions at **Sam & Harry's** (1200 19th St. NW; 202/296-4333).

Breakfast/Brunch   Sure, you can have your fancy brunch at any of the area's hotels, but why, when you can eat yer fill at The Patsy Cline Memorial Brunch at **Las Cruces** (1524 U St. NW; 202/328-3153). Seven days a week, early risers line up for the hearty, traditional eggs-pancakes-and-bacon breakfast at the **Original Pancake House** (7700 Wisconsin Ave., Bethesda; 301/986-0285). A great way to start the downtown day is sitting in the sunny glass-enclosed atrium at **Kramerbooks & Afterwords** (1517 Connecticut Ave. NW; 202/387-1462), which is on the pricey side for breakfast, but very good. And there's always **Bob's Big Boy.** No kidding, we love the awesome all-you-can-eat breakfast bar at the Bob's (2601 Virginia Ave. NW; 202/965-2700) in the Howard Johnson's Motor Lodge across from the Watergate.

Coolest Crowd   Go figure: The same hipper-than-thou bunch that will frost you in a nightclub will later eat out at **Las Cruces** (1524 U St. NW; 202/328-3153), where the friendliness is as genuine as the Southwestern food. **Dante's** (1522 14th St. NW; 202/667-7260) draws a colorful they-only-come-out-at-night crowd of punks, actors, and artists.

Date City   For a blind date, head to **Kramerbooks & Afterwords** (1517 Connecticut Ave. NW; 202/387-1462), where you can browse the books if conversation runs out.

For a dream date, you've got a choice: the cute, quaint **Two Quail** (320 Massachusetts Ave. NE; 202/543-8030); casually elegant **Nora** (2132 Florida Ave. NW; 202/462-5143); or the **Tabard Inn** (1739 N St.

NW; 202/833-2668), where you can cuddle on the parlor couch before your candlelit dinner.

Dessert   Skip dinner and get right to the jewel-like pastries at Georgetown's quaint indoor-outdoor **Cafe La Ruche** (1039 31st St. NW; 202/965-2684). A secret treasure in the former wine cellar at Petitto's restaurant, Dolce Finale (2653 Connecticut Ave. NW; 202/667-5350) serves *only* homemade desserts— think tiramisu and cheesecake—plus specialty coffees and liqueurs. And there are more than 30 varieties of cheesecake (none of them low-fat, alas) at the **Cheesecake Factory** (Chevy Chase Pavilion, 5345 Wisconsin Ave. NW; 202/364-0500).

Food Courts   On the plus side, food courts take you around the world in a day, and everyone gets to eat what they want. On the minus side: Almost everything is high-fat and high-calorie, and haute cuisine they're not. Among our favorites is the bazaarlike **Post Office Pavilion** (1100 Pennsylvania Ave. NW. Metro: Federal Triangle: Blue/Orange), developed by the folks who designed Baltimore's snazzy Harborplace and Boston's Faneuil Hall. When you've decided between sushi, souvlakis, or sky-high deli sandwiches, bring your meal to a table under the vast, vaulted atrium. The **Circle Underground** food court recently opened in long-abandoned trolley tunnels under Dupont Circle, and you can get bagels, pizza, Indian food, coffee—and backrubs!—in the trolley-shaped boutiques. Located at the business district central Metro stop, **Connecticut Connection** (downstairs at Connecticut Ave. and L St. NW) is your basic mess hall for suits, with a Sbarros, a McDonald's, and lots of harried-looking business-people. **Union Station** (50 Massachusetts Ave. NW; 202/484-7540) is a now full-fledged destination, with a massive international food court, plus lots of shops and a movie multiplex.

Ice Cream   A few of these decadent calorie palaces remain. Among the best are **Bob's Famous Ice Cream** (236 Massachusetts Ave. NE, near Union Station, 202/546-3860; and 3510 Connecticut Ave. NW, 202/ 244-4465), the original home of Oreo ice cream, and quite a few other exotic flavors. You can sample flavors like Decadence and Ecstasy at **Larry's Ice Cream** (1633 Connecticut Ave. NW; 202/234-2690), which also sells cookies and espresso, neatly wrapping up 2 decades of impulse-eating trends. Don't be afraid: They also cater to the vanilla crowd.

Joints   There's nothing like a good joint to get the feel of a city—greasy food, sassy waitresses, a sense of history, and if you play your cards right, some tips and gossip from the locals.

The cranky waitresses at **Sherrill's Bakery** (233 Pennsylvania Ave. SE; 202/544-2480) were the subject of an Oscar-nominated short film. If you like this kind of punishment, you can also try these legendary neighborhood hangouts: **Trio** (1537 17th St. NW; 202/232-6305) and **Tune Inn** (331½ Pennsylvania Ave. SE; 202/543-2725), a Capitol Hill dive par excellence, with surly waitresses serving great burgers and cheap beer.

A beer-drinker's nirvana, the **Brickskeller** (1523 22nd St. NW; 202/293-1885) has for some reason adopted buffalo meat burgers as its staple, but after a few tall ones from the hundreds of international brews in bottles, cans, and on tap, they start looking pretty good. The **Childe Harolde** (1610 20th St. NW; 202/483-6700) is open late and has an "Upstairs/Downstairs" thing going on. The main floor is a traditional (but casual) dining room, and below is a friendly brick-walled basement pub. Claim to fame: Bruce Springsteen and Emmylou Harris both played here early in their careers. The **Post Pub** (1422 L St. NW; 202/628-2111) will never make anyone's Ten Best List (or even 50 Best, or 100 Best), but it's got a certain basic bar-and-grill appeal. (How basic? Budweiser is the only beer on tap.) The Post Pub gets what little glamour it has from its kitty-corner location from the the *Washington Post,* so it's a good place to spot journalists lunching on the awesome cheeseburgers.

Tourist buses make a beeline for **Scholl's Colonial Cafeteria** (1990 K St. NW; 202/296-3065; closed Sun) for the unpretentious, homestyle food, and maybe you will, too, if you're feeling homesick. In Adams Morgan, the relatively young **Toledo Lounge** (2435 18th St. NW; 202/986-5416) feels like it's been around forever—this is the place to go for red meat, hard liquor, and neighborhood characters. **American City Diner** (5532 Connecticut Ave. NW; 202/244-1949) is a loving re-creation of an old-style shiny-aluminum 1950s diner with tabletop jukeboxes and a Coke machine. Open round the clock, for when nothing but a grilled cheese sandwich and a chocolate shake will do. The beloved **Tastee Diner** is the real, decades-old thing 24 hours a day (8516 Georgia Ave., Silver Spring, MD; 301/589-8171).

Downtown & Capitol Hill Dining

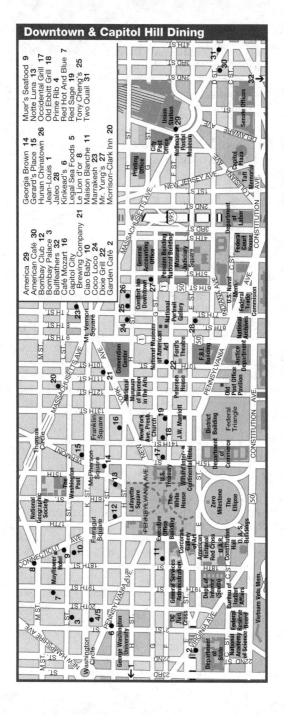

America 29
American Café 30
Bombay Club 12
Bombay Palace 3
Bullfeathers 32
Café Mozart 16
Capitol City
  Brewing Company 21
Ciao Baby 10
Coco Loco 24
Dixie Grill 22
Garden Café 2

Georgia Brown 14
Gerard's Place 15
Hunan Chinatown 26
Jean-Louis 1
Jaleo 28
Kinkead's 6
Legal Sea Foods 5
Le Lion d'or 8
Maison Blanche 11
Marrakesh 23
Mr. Yung's 27
Morrison-Clark Inn 20

Muer's Seafood 9
Notte Luna 13
Occidental Grill 17
Old Ebbitt Grill 18
Prime Rib 4
Red Hot And Blue 7
Red Sage 19
Tony Cheng's 25
Two Quail 31

Mexican/Salvadorean   Burrito Brothers was the first to bring the San Francisco Mission District–style taqueria to D.C., and the inexpensive concept has expanded into 3 always-busy locations in Georgetown (3273 M St. NW; 202/965-3963), Dupont Circle (1524 Connecticut Ave. NW; 202/332-2308) and Capitol Hill (205 Pennsylvania Ave. NW; 202/543-6835). At the **Burro** (1621 Connecticut Ave. NW; 202/483-6861) you can design your own burritos, or opt for the Burro, a big rolled sandwich stuffed with smoked turkey or guacamole and black olives. For good, cheap, filling food, **El Tamarindo** (1785 Florida Ave. NW; 202/328-3660) is the ticket. If you order the Mexican pizza appetizer, you can hold off on ordering an entree. Good place for pitchers of sangria or margaritas. Another tacky, loud, fun spot is Capitol Hill's **Tortilla Coast** (400 1st St. SE; 202/546-6768).

Museum Quality   If you're making a day of the Smithsonian or art galleries, best to eat before you go, or bring lunch along with you. Most of the Smithsonian cafeterias are mediocre, but there are a few options: The underground, skylit cafe between the East and West wings of the National Gallery of Art is always busy, but still very lovely and tranquil, with good soups, salads, and specialty coffees. Kids will like the cafeteria at the National Air and Space Museum, which sends ready-made plates and appetizers spinning via a big conveyor belt, just like in "The Jetsons." The National Museum of American Art and the National Portrait Gallery share a cafe; the food may not be suitable for framing, but you can take a tray out into the charming enclosed courtyard.

Pizza   Sure, you could go the lemming route and order from Domino's, Pizza Movers, or Pizza Hut. But why, when you can have the real thing? **Pizzeria Paradiso** (2029 P St. NW; 202/223-1245) and **Cafe Petitto** (1724 Connecticut Ave. NW; 202/462-8771) are the spots for chic, grownup gourmet pizza with exotic toppings. Many Washingtonians swear by **Listrani's** (5100 MacArthur Blvd. NW; 202/363-0619), which is in a rather remote but charming neighborhood. But they gladly deliver, if they're not too busy. Ask for the pizza with the sliced potatoes, and order a Caesar salad to go.

In town, the choices are **Gepetto's** (1917 M St. NW; 202/333-2602) or **Luigi's** (1132 19th St. NW; 202/331-7574), both romantic candlelit spots (remember the spaghetti scene in *Lady and the Tramp?*) with that checkered tablecloth thing going on. If you don't mind a bit of a drive, you can have a formative experience for many Washingtonians: the unusual rectangular pizza at **Ledo** (2420 University Blvd. E., Hyattsville, MD; 301/422-8622). On the chain side, there's **Bertucci's Brick Oven Pizzeria** (in the mall at 2000 Pennsylvania Ave. NW; 202/296-2600), which offers gourmet pizza and other Italian specialties; and the downtown branch of the **California Pizza Kitchen** (1250 Connecticut Ave. NW; 202/331-4020), with dozens of boutique pizzas and awesome salads.

Seafood   You have to be ready to travel to find a good seafood spot. **Crisfield** is arguably *the* place for seafood (and people will argue with you about it). There are really 2 Crisfields: The funky original (8012 Georgia Ave., Silver Spring, MD; 301/589-1306), with Formica counters, and waitresses as crabby as the blue crabs. The new yuppified version (around the corner at 8606 Colesville Rd., Silver Spring, MD; 301/588-1572) has tablecloths, but the same attitude. Whichever you chose, be prepared to wait. And it ain't cheap. And they don't take credit cards, either.

It's fun to visit the open-air fish market in the Southwest quadrants (we're not implying that "open-air" means "smells good"). There are several big fish-factory/tourist-mills nearby, including **Hogate's** (9th St. and Maine Ave. SW; 202/484-6300), noted for its sticky sweet roll appetizers and for its dangerously tasty snapping turtle soup. On a smaller, cozier scale, the **Gangplank** (600 Water St. SW; 202/554-5000) is a jaunty little nautical-themed restaurant, where you get a good view of the comings and goings of tourist boats like the *Odyssey*, and the *Spirit of Washington*.

Southern/Soul Food   D.C.'s still a Southern town, of course. First stop on the soul food circuit is the **Florida Avenue Grill** (1100 Florida Ave. NW; 202/265-1586. Metro: U St./Cardozo), made famous in the now-forgotten flick *D.C. Cab.* (What? You didn't see it?) The Grill features all the down-home Southern must haves—scrapple, home fries, grits and greens, and sassy waitresses, too. **Ben's Chili Bowl** (1213 U St. NW, U St.; 202/667-0809. Metro: Cardozo) is open for breakfast, too—if you can you deal with a heaping chili dog before noon. Denzel Washington filmed a scene from *The Pelican Brief* at this venerable greasy spoon, and Bill Cosby's a fan, too. It's right next door to the historic and recently resurrected Lincoln Theatre, a birthplace of black vaudeville. And if you're thirsty afterwards, wander into **Manute Bol's Spotlight** (1211 U St. NW; 202/265-5833)—if you're lucky, you'll catch a glimpse of the 7-foot-2-inch basketball player who owns the bar and grill. He's pretty hard to miss.

Turista   There's a Hard Rock Cafe and Planet Hollywood here, just as in every big city. But if you want the look and feel of the real Washington, try the **Old Ebbitt Grill** (675 15th St. NW; 202/347-4800). While you're visiting, grab a bite at the Senate or Supreme Court cafeterias, where you might just catch a glimpse of one of the Supremes slurping soup between sessions.

Washington D.C.'s Restaurants A to Z

America

Union Station. ☎ 202/682-9555. AE, DC, MC, V. Reservations advised. Wheelchair accessible. Metro: Union Station (Red). AMERICAN. **$/$$**.

If you don't know what you want to eat, this enormous, noisy restaurant is the place to go. (On the other hand, if you're a slow orderer, this place could be a nightmare for your companions.) Like its namesake, it's a big place, with something for everyone—America seats 700 people inside and out, and features more than 150 items on its melting-pot menu, from grilled pork chops and mashed potatoes to Fluffernutter sandwiches. The food is generally good if you stick to the standard American fare and steer clear of the more exotic sounding items. Save room for Death by Chocolate.

American Café

227 Massachusetts Ave. NE, ☎ 202/547-8500, Metro: Union Station (Red); 13th St. and F St. NW, ☎ 202/626-0770, Metro: Metro Center (Red, Blue/Orange); 1211 Wisconsin Ave. NW, ☎ 202/944-9464; 5252 Wisconsin Ave. NW, ☎ 202/363-5400, Metro: Friendship Heights (Red); 1200 19th St. NW, ☎ 202/223-2121, Metro: Farragut North (Red). AE, M, V. Reservations accepted. All locations closed Christmas, Thanksgiving. AMERICAN. **$/$$**.

This all-purpose, all-American chain has a dozen locations in the Washington area, all in commuter-friendly locations and shopping/tourist venues. Dishes rotate seasonally, but the food is basically light, standard American fare. It varies in quality, but pasta, quiches, and salads, especially the chicken and tarragon chicken salad, are always good bets. The wines are all American. Ownership has changed hands several times but AmCaf remains dependable, and keeps up with the dining trends—the emphasis lately has been on healthy eating and fresh ingredients. We like the Arizona Veggie Chili and

the Thai Chicken Combo.
Takeout available at market
entrance.

Argentine Grill

2433 18th St. NW. ☎ 202/
234-1818. MC, V. Reservations
accepted. Wheelchair accessible.
Closed: Mon. Metro: Dupont
Circle (Red Line). ARGENTINE/
ITALIAN. **$$**.

Reflecting its multiethnic
neighborhood, this restaurant
is a marriage of cultures. A
good, off-the-beaten-path
choice, especially if you like
meat. Argentine staples (char-
grilled sweetbreads, grilled
fish, chorizo, filet mignon
with green chimichurri
sauce) are complemented by a
few decorative Italian touches.
It's a literal marriage, too—
the owner/chefs are an
Argentine-Italian couple.

★ L'Auberge Chez Francois

332 Springvale Rd., Great Falls,
VA. ☎ 703/759-3800. AE, DC,
MC, V. Reservations required,
2 weeks to 1 month in advance.
Closed: Mon, Christmas, New
Year's Day. FRENCH. **$$$**.

Nestled about 15 miles
(22.5km) up the Potomac
River from central Washington, this atmospheric Alsatian
country inn has a long-
standing and devoted
following. Once inside the
warm and inviting setting,
you'll find the menu is prix
fixe only, with a choice of such
entrees as peppered swordfish
steak, salmon soufflé, and duck
choucroute. Reservations are
essential (so are the snails, foie
gras, and frog legs!).

Au Pied du Cochon

1335 Wisconsin Ave. NW.
☎ 202/333-5440. AE, MC, V.
No reservations. Open daily
24hrs. FRENCH. **$/$$**.

Many locals will tell you
they've never seen the inside
of this amiable, durable,
round-the-clock French bistro
by the light of day. For a long
time it was one of the only
Washington boîtes open after
midnight, and it remains a
wee-hours catchall for an
international assortment of
funky-to-elegant night people.
Au Pied gained a touch of
notoriety when Vitaly
Yurechenko, a KGB defector
to the CIA, abandoned his
meal here to defect back to
the Soviet Union. Specialties
include such passable-to-fine
French-style comfort foods as
coq au vin and onion soup,
and ratatouille comes with
every order. And great French
fries. Au Pied shares a
restaurant with its seafood-
serving sister restaurant Aux
Fruit De Mer (1329 Wisconsin
Ave. NW; 202/333-2333),
next door—the live lobster
tank in the Wisconsin Avenue
window marks the spot.

Austin Grill

2404 Wisconsin Ave. NW
(Georgetown), ☎ 202/
337-8080, (not near Metro);
801 King St., Alexandria, VA,
☎ 703/684-8969, Metro: King
St. (Yellow/Blue). AE, D, DC,
MC, V. No reservations.
SOUTHWESTERN. **$$**.

Fun Tex-Mex is the byword of
this roadhouse-chic standby,
which rounds up the usual
south-of-the-border suspects—
tacos, burritos, fajitas, etc. But
check out the specialties, like
quesadillas with crabmeat or
chorizo, chopped all-meat chili
(red beef or green chicken),
pork loin enchilada, and the
daily $4.95 blue plate specials.

★ Bacchus

1827 Jefferson Place (between
M and N sts.) NW, ☎ 202/

785-0734. Metro: Dupont Circle
(Red); 7945 Norfolk Ave.,
Bethesda, MD, ☎ 301/
657-1722. AE, MC, V.
Reservations recommended.
Closed: Sun, major holidays.
LEBANESE. **$$**.

Both locations of this small,
elegant Lebanese restaurant
serve consistently good food.
You might begin with mezza,
a platter of 2-bite appetizers,
and move on to the zucchini
pancakes and stuffed eggplant,
and ouzi—lamb served on
a bed of spiced rice with
minced meat, almonds, and
pine nuts.

El Bodegon

1637 R St. NW. ☎ 202/
667-1710. AE, MC, V.
Reservations accepted but not
necessary. Closed: Sun. Metro:
Dupont Circle. SPANISH. **$/$$**.

Flamenco dancing is the
appetizer for this somewhat
tacky, but still charming
Madrid-styled taberna, where
hams and garlands of garlic
and dried peppers hang from
the ceiling. Aficionados nibble
on the traditional bar snacks
called tapas, selecting from
a changing list of up to 40
dishes. In the main room,
such staple Spanish recipes as
seafood paella and zarzuela are
understandable favorites.

★ Bombay Club

815 Connecticut Ave. NW.
☎ 202/659-3727. AE, DC, MC,
V. Reservations recommended.
Metro: Farragut North (Red).
INDIAN. **$$**.

With its slowly-revolving
ceiling fans, giant palms, and
wicker chairs, the Bombay
Club looks like something out
of a late-late-show epic about
the Fall of Empire. Introduce
yourselves to the Indian palate
with a "thali," a sampler of
representative dishes. Good
stuff: Tandoori-marinated

roasted salmon, grilled
scallops, and lamb curried
with dried apricots. Vegetarian
dishes are available in full or
appetizer portions. Adding to
that late-movie feel is the
piano bar at happy hour. Our
choice for the best Indian food
in town.

Bombay Palace

1835 K St. NW. ☎ 202/
331-0111. AE, DC, MC, V.
Reservations accepted. Metro:
Farragut West (Blue/Orange).
INDIAN. **$$**.

Regulars willingly stand in
line for up to an hour for the
bargain all-you-can-eat
weekend brunches at this
outpost of the international
chain, which is less expensive
than the Bombay Club.
Descend from street level past
brass figurines in lighted
niches, into a series of large
basement rooms in pale green,
rose, and pink, with a few
vaguely Art Moderne filigrees,
no doubt left over from an
earlier tenant. Tandoori breads
and fowl and, of course,
curries lead the charge. We
love the Butter Chicken:
Tandoor-roasted, then
simmered in a decadent
tomato-butter bath. While
prices are higher than most
ethnic eateries, they are a relief
compared to the expense
account palaces of nearby
K Street.

La Brasserie

239 Massachusetts Ave. NE.
☎ 202/546-6066. AE, MC, V.
Reservations accepted. Metro:
Union Station (Red). FRENCH.
$$.

A teeny townhouse with
charm to spare, La Brasserie
offers nouvelle and country
French cuisine, exquisitely
prepared in tiny portions.
The decor is intimate and
recherché, with outdoor

Adams-Morgan & Dupont Circle Dining

tables in season. They serve breakfast, too.

Bullfeathers

401 South St. SE. ☎ 202/543-5005. AE, MC, V. No reservations. Metro: Capitol South (Blue/Orange). AMERICAN. **$/$$**.

If there was a real-life counterpart to the newshounds-and-politicos hangout for the "Murphy Brown" gang, this comfy Capitol Hill saloon would be the place. It takes its name from Teddy Roosevelt's favored euphemism—and with its heavy roll call of Hill People regulars, the joint is often echoing with bull. Which makes it a Washington must. Oh yeah, the food: Passable burgers and salads, but conversation (and gossip) is the main course here.

Cafe Lautrec

2431 18th St. NW. ☎ 202/265-6436. AE, MC, V. No reservations. Metro: Dupont Circle (Red). FRENCH. **$$**.

One of the friskiest spots in the already plenty-frisky Adams Morgan district, this neighborhood institution is a French bistro, a jazz bar and a tap dance studio. An explanation is in order: On Friday nights, the place is packed to watch tap dancer Johne Forget tippy-tap the night away atop the wooden bar. The food is so-so, but dark, noisy, and ancient-looking Lautrec has got beaucoup atmosphere. Weather permitting, the outdoor seating allows a ringside seat for the parade of browsers and parking-spot extortionists.

Cafe Mozart

1331 H St. NW. ☎ 202/347-5732. AE, MC, V. Reservations accepted. Closed: Thanksgiving, Christmas, New Year's Day. Metro: Metro Center (Red, Blue/Orange); McPherson Square (Blue/Orange). GERMAN. **$$**.

The charming Cafe Mozart is the spot for excellent Deutsche food at reasonable prices (best of the wurst: the wurst sampler, allowing you to taste up to 5 sausages). The *Sound of Music* atmosphere is enriched by live piano or oom-pah-pah accordion tunes. Good pastries, too.

★ Capitol City Brewing Company

1100 New York Ave. NW. ☎ 202/628-2222. AE, MC, V. No reservations. Wheelchair accessible. Metro: Metro Center (Red, Blue/Orange). AMERICAN SALOON. **$$**.

What? *What??*WHAT??? Oh, sorry—couldn't hear you: We've arrived at the Capitol City Brewing Company at peak time. Actually, any time after 7pm is peak time at this noisy, cavernous cash-in on the national microbrew craze. It's located in the old Greyhound bus station, and the building's New York Avenue entrance retains the Art Deco entrance and a marble mosaic hallway, and has added a copper-topped bar surrounding huge copper fermenting vats. When you finally get a seat (try for one of the cozy red leatherette booths by the windows), you'll find yourselves screaming away at each other, too. You get a big bowl of warm pretzels (both soft and hard) before placing your orders—hearty he-man portions of consistently high-quality saloon-style food like ribs, burgers, and chili. Check out what's brewing on the big production schedule on the wall. Try one of the half-dozen house-made brews on offer (including the annual

Inaugurale); you can get a sampler with four small glasses (they also have a three-pack sampler of the Sausages of the Day, if you dare).

Carmella Kitty's

1602 17th St. NW. ☎ 202/ 667-5937. AE, MC, V. Reservations accepted. Metro: Dupont Circle (Red). CAJUN/ CREOLE. **$$**.

Since you'll probably have to wait for a table anyway, head straight for the teeny basement lounge, an enjoyably seedy slice of the French Quarter, where you can try a Cajun Martini, Louisiana Lemonade, Hurricane, or Blackened Voodoo Beer, and probably lose your appetite on spicy appetizers. The food doesn't quite approach the piquant flavor of its New Orleans inspiration, but the sampling of shrimp po' boys, muffaletlas, gumbos, and beiguets, gets the *bon temps* rolling.

★Cashion's Eat Place

1819 Columbia Rd. NW. ☎ 202/ 797-1819. MC, V. Reservations suggested. Closed: Mon. Metro: Dupont Circle or Woodley Park/ Zoo (Red). NEW AMERICAN. **$$$**.

A newcomer at press time, chef Ann Cashion's new Eat Place was getting the hip crowd tasting and talking. Cashion was the original chef at the still-hot Austin Grill, i Ricchi, and Jaleo, and her own place is a homey, honey-colored paean to comfort food, with family photos on the walls, and rich seafood gumbo and crabcake platters on the meat-lover's menu.

Ciao Baby

1736 L St. NW. ☎ 202/ 331-1500. AE, MC, V. Reservations accepted. Wheelchair accessible. Metro: Farragut North (Red). ITALIAN. **$$**.

Say hello to Ciao Baby at happy hour: A free, fabulous antipasti buffet is spread on the marble bar, with garlic potatoes, green beans, pastas, olives, and salami. The look: Sunset-sponged walls, baskets of dried flowers and Italian tunes. The Look: Euro-chic.

Cities

2424 18th St. NW. ☎ 202/ 328-7194. AE, DC, MC, V. Reservations suggested. Wheelchair accessible. Metro: Dupont Circle (Red). ECLECTIC. **$$/$$$**.

Cities is the restaurant equivalent of one of those 1980s-era New York nightclubs like Area that changed themes from month to month. Chef Mary Richter keeps things interesting for herself and keeps customers coming back by rotating cuisines (and decors) to reflect a different city every few months. We've seen Moscow, Sicily, Paris, Mexico City, Havana, and L.A. (almost a foreign country). Who knows where you'll be when you get here. Downstairs glass fronted "garage doors" roll up to create an open-to-the-street dining room bar, in what was once an auto service shop. Since the cuisine changes along with the restless decor, we can't predict what you'll find. Standards include tasty gourmet pizza, risottos, grilled meats, and seafood.

★ Citronelle

3000 M St. NW (in the Latham Hotel). ☎ 202/265-2150. AE, D, DC, MC, V. Reservations recommended. Metro: Foggy Bottom (Blue/Orange). NEW AMERICAN. **$$$**.

The chef of this garden-graced grownup restaurant is Martial

Noguier, who worked for years at founder Michel Richard's original Citrus in L.A. But the real star is the glass-fronted kitchen, where you can watch Noguier's 6 chefs in action, creating the gorgeous entrees—roasted lobster, saddle of rabbit with chanterelles, wild mushroom napoleon, and other representatives of creative American cooking. Maybe you'll decide it all looks good, and make a meal of appetizers—white tuna carpaccio with ginger vinaigrette, sauteed fois gras with chanterelles, crab cannelloni, and more.

★ City Lights of China

1731 Connecticut Ave. NW.
☎ 202/265-6688. AE, D, DC, MC, V. Reservations recommended. Wheelchair accessible. Metro: Dupont Circle (Red). CHINESE. **$$**

Mick Jagger's favorite Chinese restaurant—in Washington, D.C., anyway. No kidding: Jagger and Jerry Hall liked the Szechuan lamb and tinkling bells pork so much they brought the rest of the Stones along on another night. Considered the city's best Chinese restaurant outside Chinatown, this surprisingly bright and roomy underground warren on busy Connecticut Avenue is a neighborhood favorite, too, because of its consistently well-prepared Szechuan-Hunan standards and specialties.

Clyde's

3236 M St. NW. 202/333-9180. AE, D, DC, MC, V. Reservations accepted but not necessary. AMERICAN. **$$**

Chili is the signature dish of this friendly Georgetown saloon—it's even canned and sold in the Britches

preppy-clothes catalog. There are 4 outposts of these atmospheric chophouses, but the Georgetown institution is the neighborhood's original scene bar. Standard American dishes such as hamburgers and fried chicken are highly recommended.

★ Coco Loco

810 7th St. NW. ☎ 202/289-2626. AE, DC, MC, V. Reservations recommended. Metro: Chinatown (Red). TAPAS/BRAZILIAN. **$$**

This sexy see-and-be-seen restaurant/club, tapas bar/all-you-can-eat churrasqueria is a good bet for a hot date. Chef/owner Yannick Cam's tropical fantasia attracts a chic crowd. Free salsa lessons on Monday, and dancing to Latin-spiced music Thursday through Saturday.

★ Coppi's

1414 U St. NW. ☎ 202/319-7773. AE, MC, V. No reservations. Wheelchair accessible. Metro: U St./Cardozo (Green). ITALIAN/PIZZA. **$**

This Italian trattoria is decorated with old family photos and vintage bicycle-race memorabilia. You might think you're in New York's Little Italy or San Francisco's North Beach. The menu is simple—mostly wood-fired pizza, pastas, and salads—but there are lots of unusual and creative variations. Coppi's also has the warmest service in town (and we're not just saying that because of the wood-burning stove, which keeps the room glowing).

Dancing Crab

4611 Wisconsin Ave. NW.
☎ 202/244-1882. AE, MC, V. Reservations accepted. Closed: Christmas. Metro: Tenleytown (Red). SEAFOOD. **$$**

Steamed-and-spiced blue crabs—served whole, with corn on the cob and ice-cold beer—are a summer tradition around D.C., thanks to the proximity of the Chesapeake Bay. If you don't want to make the day-trip drive to the Eastern Shore, this seriously informal restaurant is the next best thing, and you can go year-round. Come prepared to roll up your sleeves to attack steamed and Old Bay-spiced crabs (your server will teach you how it's done) on brown paper tablecloths, with all the fried clams and shrimp, corn on the cob, hush puppies, and of course, cole slaw, you can ingest. And you can make as much mess as you like!

Dixie Grill

518 10th St. NW. ☎ 202/628-4800. AE, DC, MC, V. Reservations accepted for 6 or more. Wheelchair accessible. Metro: Metro Center (Red, Blue/Orange). SOUTHERN. **$**

That Clinton-fueled "Southern Invasion" everyone predicted never really materialized, but the Dixie Grill is one of the survivors. It's hard to decide whether to list it under "restaurant" or "nightclub." The theme is sleepy-Southern-town circa 1963 (a kitschy-cool in-joke on Southern culture and Washington's Southern roots), and the multiroom upstairs bar comes complete with all-Southern jukebox, 20 Southern soft drinks (including NuGrape, HOKO, and Barq's Root Beer), weekend slot-car racing (bring-your-own), and a big-screen TV that is frequently vrooming with NASCAR races. But since the food downstairs is so dang finger-lickin' good (and such big portions!), we decided it's a restaurant.

Have a heapin' helpin' of their milk-fried chicken, catfish fingers, and, of course, chicken-fried steak and red beans and rice. Don't miss Saturday and Sunday brunch—and take our word for it: Schedule time for a nap afterwards.

★ Dolce Finale

2653 Connecticut Ave. NW (below Petitto's). ☎ 202/667-5350. AE, CB, D, DC, MC, V. Metro: Woodley Park/Zoo (Red). DESSERT. **$$**

Your humble guide's idea of a perfect restaurant: ALL DESSERTS! Formerly the wine cellar of the upstairs Italian restaurant, this grappa bistro/espresso bar is a charmer. Let me count the ways: chocolate fudge custard pear tart, chocolate hazelnut cheesecake, homemade chocolate amaretto ice cream, grapes soaked in grappa, and, of course, tiramisu, which just may be the best in town.

Food for Thought

1738 Connecticut Ave. NW. ☎ 202/797-1095. AE, V, MC. No reservations. Wheelchair accessible. Metro: Dupont Circle (Red). VEGETARIAN. **$**

This earthy, mostly vegetarian restaurant is unlike any place in Washington. In fact, the regulars—many of them pierced and tattooed—come here to forget they are in Washington. If it resembles anything, it's Berkeley, circa 1972, a bit on the dim, grungy side. Seat yourself, if you want—the punky wait staff is irritatingly or amusingly casual, depending on how hungry or hurried you are. Try the Tiik burger (named after the chef, who moonlights as a folksinger), and sprout salad, which is buried under a mushroom cloud of sprouts—

the lemon-tahini salad dressing is definitive.

★★ Galileo

1110 21st St. NW. ☎ 202/ 293-7191. AE, CB, D, DC, MC, V. Reservations required. Wheelchair accessible. Metro: Farragut West (Blue/Orange), Farragut North (Red). ITALIAN. **$$$$**.

Galileo himself would have approved of this small, gracious, perennially popular restaurant that has attained a national reputation for authentic northern Italian cuisine, prepared by chef and owner Roberto Donna from Turin. You might want to try the 3-course pasta sampler or the 4- or 5-course *menu de gustacione*.

★ Garden Cafe

2117 E St. NW. ☎ 202/ 861-0331. AE, MC, V. Reservations accepted. Wheelchair accessible. Metro: Foggy Bottom (Blue/Orange). NEW AMERICAN. **$$**.

Here's a state secret: a fetching little restaurant, where State Department officials and George Washington University professors like to lunch on the standard American salads and sandwiches. Outdoor tables are available in good weather. Because the restaurant is part of the State Plaza Hotel, the kitchen is open for early breakfasts as well as fashionably late dinners.

★ Georgia Brown

950 15th St. NW. ☎ 202/ 638-0950. AE, CB, DC, MC, V. Reservations recommended. Wheelchair accessible. Closed: Sat lunch, Sun. Metro: McPherson Square (Blue/ Orange). SOUTHERN. **$$$**.

Excellent updated Haute-Southern cooking (think gumbo, she-crab soup)

in a snazzy, sophisticated, up-to-date setting, convenient to both Old and New Downtown. Gorgeous shrimp and crab dishes with specials such as braised rabbit and wild mushrooms all come with enormous biscuits and Tabasco-cheddar crackers that do the South proud. Live jazz on Saturday nights!

★★ Gerard's Place

915 15th St. NW. ☎ 202/ 737-4445. AE, MC, V. Reservations recommended. Closed: Sun. Wheelchair accessible. Metro: McPherson Square (Blue/Orange). FRENCH. **$$$**.

This stark and simple room—perfect for a business lunch or other intimate conversation—is a reflection of the character of its excellent and unpretentious young chef, Gerary Pangaud.

★ Germaine's

2400 Wisconsin Ave. NW. ☎ 202/965-1188. AE, DC, MC, V. Reservations recommended. PAN-ASIAN. **$$**.

Fun fact: Located 2 blocks from the Russian Embassy complex, this is where double agent Aldrich Ames finally told his wife that he had peddled state secrets to the Russians. This famous pan-Asian restaurant, presided over by Germaine herself, sensitively and imaginatively blends influences from Vietnamese, Korean, Japanese, Filipino, Indonesian, Thai, Chinese, Burmese, and French cuisines.

The Grill from Ipanema

1858 Columbia Rd., NW. ☎ 202/986-0757. AE, DC, MC, V. No reservations. Wheelchair accessible. Metro: Dupont Circle. BRAZILIAN. **$$**.

With a name like that, it's gotta be fun, and it is. This

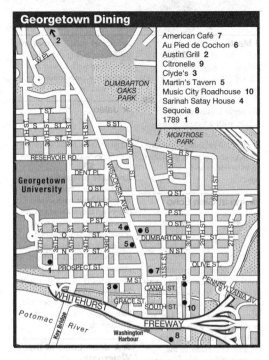

Georgetown Dining

American Café	**7**
Au Pied de Cochon	**6**
Austin Grill	**2**
Citronelle	**9**
Clyde's	**3**
Martin's Tavern	**5**
Music City Roadhouse	**10**
Sarinah Satay House	**4**
Sequoia	**8**
1789	**1**

DUMBARTON OAKS PARK

MONTROSE PARK

RESERVOIR RD.

Georgetown University

DENT PL.

VOLTA PL.

PROSPECT ST.

WHITEHURST

GRACE ST.

CANAL ST.

SOUTH ST.

OLIVE ST.

PENNSYLVANIA AV.

Potomac River

Key Bridge

FREEWAY

Washington Harbour

---

sleek, dark, handsome Brazilian boîte specializes in feijoada, Brazil's cassouletlike national dish (served on Wed and Sun only—get there early). Other offerings include marinated grilled shrimp and spicy shellfish and stews in coconut sauces. Expect lots of beef—we like carne del sol, beef roast; salted, grilled and thinly sliced. While you wait, get into the carnival spirit with a caipirinha, Brazilian's potent answer to the daiquiri.

★ Hunan Chinatown

624 H St. NW. ☎ 202/ 783-5858. AE, MC, V. No reservations. Closed: major holidays. Metro: Gallery Place/ Chinatown (Red). CHINESE. **$/$$**.

If you've time for only one restaurant in D.C.'s dense 1-block Chinatown enclave, this is the one to visit. Decorated in placid brown and beige, its only concession to the usual Chinatown decorative conceits is a fierce ceramic dragon near the door. The clientele is usually rather sedate. One of the pricier dishes is also one of the kitchen's best: Crispy Whole Fish, a sea bass in tangy Hunan sauce.

Il Radicchio

1509 17th St. NW. ☎ 202/ 986-2627. AE, CB, MC, V. No reservations. Metro: Dupont Circle (Red). ITALIAN. **$$**.

Concept Italian: At chef Roberto Donna's lower-cost alternative to his pricey Galileo, you choose the type of spaghetti you want for $6, then choose from a palette of 20-something sauces, from $2.50. It's all you can eat, and the locals love it, so try showing up early or late.

I Matti

2436 18th St. NW. ☎ 202/
462-8844. AE, CB, MC, V.
Reservations suggested.
Wheelchair accessible. Metro:
Dupont Circle (Red). ITALIAN. **$$**.

Roberto Donna pops up
again, with a bright, stylish,
informal Adams Morgan
trattoria at reasonable prices.
Donna stresses such specialties
as osso bucco and game
specials.

★ Inn at Glen Echo

6119 Tulane Ave., Glen Echo,
MD. ☎ 301/229-2280. AE, MC,
V. Reservations suggested.
Wheelchair accessible. NEW
AMERICAN. **$$**.

This delightful old-fashioned
country home, complete with
slamming screen door and a
big old front porch, is suitable
for sittin' and sippin'. The walls
are decorated with pictures of
a defunct amusement park
nearby. The plates in the
warren of little dining rooms
are decorated with creative
interpretations of American
dishes.

★ i Ricchi

1220 19th St. NW. ☎ 202/
835-0459. AE, CB, DC, MC, V.
Reservations suggested.
Wheelchair accessible. Closed:
Sat lunch, Sun. Metro: Dupont
Circle (Red). ITALIAN. **$$$**.

President Bush and the First
Lady anointed Francesco
Ricchi's Tuscan restaurant by
attending a party here shortly
after the Bush inaugural. The
spare interior of quarry tiles
and suggestions of arches has as
its focal point an exhibition
kitchen with an imported
woodburning oven. In an age
of culinary hyperbole, it
produces dishes of gratifying
simplicity. An example is the
appetizer called la fettunta,
garlic bread heaped with white
beans. Many of the main

courses are merely herbed and
grilled, including the baby
goat chops with lemon and
rosemary. Reservations 2 or 3
days ahead are wise.

★ Jaleo

480 7th St. NW. ☎ 202/
628-7949. AE, CB, D, DC, MC,
V. Reservations accepted. Metro:
Gallery Place/Chinatown (Red).
SPANISH. **$$**.

The name translates in Spanish
as "jamboree." And Jaleo lives
up to the buzz with loud
colors on the walls and plates,
conversation-starting tapas
(cauliflower flan, poached
octopus!), sangrias, sherries,
and Spanish wines, and spirited
chatter from the sassy, stylish
crowd, many of whom might
be going to or from a
performance at the estimable
Shakespeare Theatre around
the corner.

★★ Jean-Louis at the Watergate

Watergate Hotel, 2650 Virginia
Ave. NW. ☎ 202/298-4488. AE,
CB, D, DC, MC, V. Reservations
required. Metro: Foggy Bottom/
GWU (Blue/Orange). FRENCH.
$$$$.

Washington's most famous
address (well, after the White
House) is also home to
Washington's most celebrated
chef, Jean-Louis Palladin, who
conjures up southern France
in this tiny, exquisite underground room, which has been
called one of the most expensive (also one of the best)
restaurants in the country (the
all-truffle dinner costs $150). A
good way to go: The 4-course
prix-fixe dinner, which is $45
if you dine before 6:15pm.

★★ Jockey Club

Ritz Carlton Hotel, 2100
Massachusetts Ave. NW.
☎ 202/659-8000, AE, CB, D,
DC, MC, V. Reservations

suggested. Wheelchair accessible. Metro: Dupont Circle (Red). NEW AMERICAN. **$$$**.
One of Washington's prestige restaurants, this is a place to see and be seen in. Prices are predictably high, but so is the standard of food. The menu is sophisticated French-Continental, with a touch of nouvelle. Italian-trained Japanese chef Hide Yamamoto is strong on fresh seafoods, some imported from France. The decor has the wood-paneled coziness of an English country inn. The walls are hung with horse-racing prints.

★ Kinkead's

2000 Pennsylvania Ave. NW.
☎ 202/296-7700. AE, D, DC, MC, V. Reservations required. Metro: Foggy Bottom/GWU (Blue/Orange). NEW AMERICAN. **$$$**.
Chef/owner Bob Kinkead has created a location for all occasions. The steet-level takeout features soup, salad, and great sandwiches. You can indulge in the authentic New England seafood chowder at the downstairs cafe, or dress up for the splendid New American cuisine in the handsome upstairs dining room.

★ Las Cruces

1524 U St. NW. ☎ 202/328-3153. AE, MC, V. No reservations. Closed: Mon. Metro: U St./Cardozo (Green). SOUTHWESTERN. **$**.
This authentic and genuinely friendly New Mexican cantina is the home of Washington's only (maybe the world's only) Elvis Happy Hour, which starts at 5:43pm daily (don't ask) and goes until whenever, with bartender Donnie mixing the margaritas. (On Sat and Sun, pile up your plate at the $10.95 Patsy Cline Memorial Brunch.) Owner/chef Mark Boudreau, a native of Las

Cruces, flies in beans, peppers, and other ingredients from his home state; and his burritos, tamales, and enchiladas are the real thing. So is the atmosphere—a yard-sale jumble of dinette-set tables and chairs; menus sandwiched between real New Mexico license plates. You know it's gonna be a charmed night if you're seated at the table for two underneath the Elvis Shrine.

★ Lebanese Taverna

2641 Connecticut Ave. NW.
☎ 202/265-8681. AE, CB, D, DC, MC, V. Reservations recommended. Wheelchair accessible. Metro: Woodley Park/Zoo (Red). LEBANESE. **$$**.
This is a friendly, family-run restaurant where guests play backgammon and other games while waiting for a front room table. The main dining room is lovely, with its vaulted ceiling and romantic haze of honey amber light. For an overview, try mezza, a shared meal of appetizer-sized portions— think Middle Eastern tapas.

★ Legal Sea Foods

2020 K St. NW. ☎ 202/496-1111. AE, CB, D, DC, MC, V. Reservations accepted. Wheelchair accessible. Metro: Farragut North (Red). SEAFOOD. **$$**.
The Cambridge-based legendary Leviathan of a seafood palace splashed into D.C. last fall. Legal regularly offers more than 40 different varieties of fish. Signature dishes include smoked bluefish pâté, clam chowder, mussels au gratin, and a New England clambake (a combination of lobster, mussels, steamers, and clam chowder). Ask for the Marion Berrie Cobbler, which has been added for the Washington market.

★★ Le Lion d'Or

1150 Connecticut Ave. NW.
☎ 202/296-7972. AE, CB, D,
DC, MC, V. Reservations
suggested. Wheelchair
accessible. Closed: Sat lunch,
Sun, most major holidays. Metro:
Farragut North (Red). FRENCH.
$$$$.

The inconspicuous location of
this restaurant downstairs in a
large office building does not
prepare you for the château-
style elegance and comfort of
its decor nor for the superb,
impeccably French cuisine,
generally rated among the best
of its kind in Washington. Le
Lion d'Or was D.C.'s first
national-class restaurant,
serving French haute cuisine
with some interesting
innovations, such as duck
sausages, as well as standard
dishes, always prepared with
great finesse and subtlety
of flavoring. Reserve in
advance.

★★ Maison Blanche

1725 F St. NW. ☎ 202/
842-0070. AE, CB, D, DC,
MC, V. Reservations suggested.
Wheelchair accessible. Closed:
Sun, some major holidays. Metro:
Farragut West (Blue/Orange).
FRENCH. **$$$$**.

Where you are seated at this
restaurant can be more
important than what you eat—
it's a haunt of politicians,
lobbyists, and White House
staffers. The decor re-creates
old-world elegance, with
tapestries and crystal
chandeliers. The food is best
described as modern French,
classical with some innovative
touches.

★ Marrakesh

617 New York Ave. NW. ☎ 202/
393-9393. No credit cards.
Reservations necessary.
Wheelchair accessible. Closed:
lunch, Thanksgiving. Metro:
Gallery Place/Chinatown (Red).
MOROCCAN. **$$$**.

At this colorful corner of
Morocco in D.C.'s Old
Downtown, a belly-dancer
will visit your table between
courses. Designed for large
dining parties, Marrakesh
makes a memorable, sybaritic
dining adventure, as diners
recline on pillows and low
couches with pillows, and
indulge in course after course
of fragrantly spiced chicken,
lamb, and vegetable dishes, all
of it meant to be eaten with
the hands.

Martin's Tavern

1264 Wisconsin Ave. NW.
☎ 202/333-7370. AE, D, DC,
MC, V. Reservations accepted.
Closed: Christmas. AMERICAN.
$$.

Look for mentions of this cozy
corner in Margaret Truman's
popular Washington-themed
mystery novels. This Georgetown bar-restaurant has
a welcoming wood-paneled
interior decorated with
sculptures and English racing
prints from President
Madison's collection. Opened
in 1933 on the very day
Prohibition was repealed,
Martin's is locally renowned
for its hearty meat dishes and
civilized breakfasts.

★ Mrs. Simpson's

2915 Connecticut Ave. NW.
☎ 202/332-8300. AE, DC,
MC, V. Reservations suggested.
Wheelchair accessible. Metro:
Woodley Park/Zoo. NEW
AMERICAN. **$$**.

This sweet, white-linen
trysting spot is discreetly
tucked into a handsome
apartment building on
Connecticut Avenue. A block
before the zoo, this elegant
little restaurant lives up to its
romantic connotations. The
gems on its brief menu include

crab cakes, Chinese-spiced duck breast, and calf's liver.

★ Mr. Yung's

740 6th St. NW. ☎ 202/ 628-1098. AE, D, DC, MC, V. No reservations. Metro: Gallery Place-Chinatown. CHINESE. **$**. Highly recommended by local critics (including myself), and frequented by visiting overseas Chinese, Mr. Yung's serves Cantonese and Hong Kong dishes. A full dim sum menu is available daily; try the specials, such as whole fresh fish or the barbeque platter with roast duck, roast pork and soy-glazed chicken. A short walk from the National Museum of American Art.

★ Muer's Seafood

1101 Connecticut Ave. NW. ☎ 202/785-4505. AE, D, DC, MC, V. Reservations accepted. Wheelchair accessible. Closed: lunch Sat–Sun. Metro: Farragut North (Red). SEAFOOD. **$$**. Formerly known as Charley's Crab, this handsomely remodeled, sprawling seafood restaurant is located in the middle of the busy New Downtown area, within an office and shopping complex linked to the Farragut North Metro station. A good lunch or dinner stop for clam chowder, crabmeat cakes, broiled fish, superb mussels, and other seafood. The food here isn't exceptional, but it's some of the best seafood you'll find downtown.

★ Music City Roadhouse

1050 30th St. NW (in the Old Foundry complex). ☎ 202/ 337-4444. AE, D, DC, MC, V. Reservations accepted. Wheelchair accessible. BARBEQUE/CHILI. **$$**. Music City Roadhouse is a carefully designed, cool roadside joint, gaining a reputation for "family-style"

servings of big food: For $10.95, you'll be brought endless platters of ribs, pot roast, fried chicken and catfish, lumpy-to-chunky mashed potatoes, sweet potatoes, and fantastic greens. "Anyone caught eating chicken with a knife and fork will be thrown out," says the sign over the dining room. Taking a cue from the Hard Rock Cafe, the restaurant offers live entertainment (including a Sunday Gospel brunch with Brother Luke and the Sensational Stars) and some sorta-celebrity paraphernalia, including lots of autographed country-and-western album jackets and a pair of Tanya Tucker's well-worn jeans.

★ New Heights

2317 Calvert St. NW. ☎ 202/ 234-4110. AE, DC, MC, V. Reservations suggested. Metro: Woodley Park/Zoo (Red). NEW AMERICAN. **$$$**. Overlooking Rock Creek Park (ask for a window seat), this converted townhouse is a favorite date spot for locals. If you're staying at the Omni Shoreham or Sheraton Washington, it's a pleasant stroll for the lovely desserts alone. The food is eclectic and adventurous, with a splash of Louisiana style: Poblano chillis stuffed with rabbit and red beans, seared duck breast with coarse grits.

★★ Nora

2132 Florida Ave. NW. ☎ 202/ 462-5143. No credit cards. Reservations recommended. Wheelchair accessible. Metro: Dupont Circle (Red). NEW AMERICAN. **$$$**. Nora is one of the healthiest, and arguably the most romantic, restaurants in D.C. Organic before organic was

Nora Restaurant

cool, owner Nora grows much of her own produce and raises additive-free animals. The sweet corner spot is even surrounded by a thriving herb and edible-flower garden (the green glider in the garden is a secret moon-gazing and makeout spot). You'll want to linger over dinner here.

★ Notte Luna

809 15th St, NW. ☎ 202/ 408-9500. AE, CB, DC, MC, V. Reservations recommended. ITALIAN. **$$**

This is a colorful, noisy, fun Italian bistro, with tables spilling out onto the sidewalk in warm weather. The food is as bright and brash as the decor: grilled swordfish with black olive pesto, a dozen pizzas (including a "bagel pizza," with gravlax, dill mascarpone, red onion, and caviar), and saffron fettucini with grilled salmon and fennel.

★★ Obelisk

2029 P St. NW. ☎ 202/ 872-1180. DC, MC, V. Reservations suggested. Metro: Dupont Circle (Red). ITALIAN. **$$$**.

In this tiny, chic room (it seats just 30 or so), Chef Peter Pastan offers a prix-fixe menu with only 2 or 3 choices per course. Try the artichokes with goat cheese, followed by grilled seafood or a thick soup or pasta with veal, fish, or game bird. A 4-course meal costs around $33. If that seems too dear, try Pastan's friendly, fun (and much less pricey) Pizzeria Paradiso across the street.

★★ Occidental/ Occidental Grill

1475 Pennsylvania Ave. NW. ☎ 202/783-1475. AE, CB, DC, MC, V. Reservations recommended. Wheelchair accessible. Closed: major holidays. Metro: Metro Center (Red, Blue/Orange), Federal Triangle (Blue/Orange). NEW AMERICAN. **$$$**

Save this one for special occasions. Adjacent to the Willard Inter-Continental hotel, but independently managed, it's a grand reminder of a more courtly (and comfy) age. At street level is a popular white-linen bar and grill, where dressy informality is the rule. Part of the fun is trying to identify the media and government bigwigs in scores of framed photos. Up the stairs is a vast pillared room with a soaring ceiling, etched glass, dark paneling, crimson drapes, and tufted red-velvet booths. Here the walls are graced with gilt-framed portraits of former presidents. The ample menu is supplemented by a long roster of daily specials, which tests the memory banks of the well-trained service staff. Appetizers can easily serve as light entrees. For instance, the signature charred rare tuna with orange and ancho chili vinaigrette; the marlin with banana, green peppercorns, and rum, topped with mango relish; all arrive in attractive, not precious, presentations.

★★ Old Angler's Inn

10801 MacArthur Blvd., Potomac, MD. ☎ 301/365-2425. AE, DC, MC, V. Reservations necessary. Wheelchair accessible. Closed: Mon. NEW AMERICAN. **$$$$**

You're treating? The sky's the limit? OK, let's go to the Old Angler's Inn. The beautiful site lives up to its name—an old-fashioned inn above the Potomac, with a crackling fireplace in the downstairs parlor bar and a cluster of small dining rooms upstairs—weather permitting, the stone terrace is also open. The menu can be on the staid side—fillets of fresh fish, rack of lamb, lobster, rabbit sausage—but the daily specials are paeans to chef Jeffrey Tomchek's imagination as he's at his most inventive with his vegetarian entrees, such as butternut squash ravioli and 2 mixed salads with truffles. Ask him to surprise you with a 5- or 7-course menu—you just tell him what you don't like.

★ Old Ebbitt Grill

675 15th St. NW. ☎ 202/347-4800. AE, CB, DC, MC, V.

Reservations suggested. Wheelchair accessible. Closed: Christmas. Metro: Metro Center (Red). AMERICAN. **$$**

This power nexus is located a dinner roll's throw from the White House and is fitted out in style with brass-and-glass opulence, borrowing the stuffed owls and brass bar rails from the now-demolished Back Bay–styled original restaurant of the same name. Roomier, lighter, and convenient to the National Theater, the National Press Club, the Willard Inter-Continental hotel, and the White House, it is much patronized by the young executive class. But as we still live in a democracy, ties and T-shirts are seated side by side.

★ The Palm

1225 19th St. NW. ☎ 202/293-9091. AE, DC, MC, V. Reservations suggested. Wheelchair accessible. Metro: Dupont Circle (Red). STEAK. **$$$**

The walls of this see-and-be-scene steakhouse (the first outpost of the famous original N.Y.C. Palm) are lined with caricatures of the rich, famous, and infamous from the worlds of politics, finance, media, and sports; the tables are crammed with briefcase–big-shots, with fat cigars and attendant blondes. The menu is a delicious, screamingly unhealthy throwback: lobsters by the pound, sliced sirloin with grilled sweet peppers and onions, jumbo shrimp cocktails, and heavenly creamed spinach and fries.

★ Parkway Deli

8317 Grubb Rd., Silver Spring, MD. ☎ 301/587-1427. AE, V, MC. No reservations. Directions: Take 16th St. NW north all the way to East-West Hwy., turn left on East-West, then left on Grubb. DELI. **$**.

How can a city call itself "the most powerful in the world" without a decent deli? It's a Capitol crime. Luckily, just over the district line, in Maryland, is the Parkway, a treasure tucked into a Silver Spring shopping center. You'll find those eyes-are-bigger-than-your-stomach sandwiches, real egg creams, and even a pickle bar (free after 4pm). Those in the know get here early on weekends—you're looking at a (well-worth-it) hour-long wait, at least.

Perry's

1811 Columbia Rd. NW. ☎ 202/234-6218. AE, DC, MC, V. No reservations. Metro: Dupont Circle (Red). JAPANESE. **$$**.

The former site of several beloved discos is now a restaurant with one of the city's most coveted roof decks—people arrange to meet here even if they don't care for Japanese food. The cuisine is Japanese/Californian, with a touch of Tex-Mex. If the weather's bad or the wait's too long for the deck, the high-style, always-changing dining room, with its enormous Palladian windows, is always an alternative. For the adventurous, check out the Sunday drag brunch, with breakfast served by fabulous self-made women.

Peyote Cafe/Roxanne

2319 18th St. NW. ☎ 202/462-8330. AE, D, MC, V. Reservations suggested for Roxanne. Metro: Dupont Circle (Red). SOUTHWESTERN. **$$**.

This upstairs/downstairs combo shares a chef. Roxanne is fancier, with a heated rooftop terrace bar and cafe. Downstairs is the teeny

basement-level Peyote Cafe, dishing up Tex-Mex staples, good chips and salsas, and your choice of 24 tequilas, including Dos Gusanos, delivered to your table in a personal-sized bottle complete with 2 worms—one for each of you!

★ Pizzeria Paradiso

2029 P St. NW. ☎ 202/223-1245. DC, MC, V. No reservations. Metro: Dupont Circle (Red). PIZZA. **$$**.

Chic pizza in one of the coolest and coziest rooms in town. The tiny room, with maybe a dozen tables, is always crowded, so try to come at off-peak hours. Sit at the bar and look up at the trompe l'oeil mural, which depicts the ceiling bursting open to let in the blue sky, or gaze into the wood-burning stove, where the specialty pizzas (our favorite is potato and pesto) bake. The panini sandwiches are fantastic, too—you'll never look at a tuna sandwich the same way again. Ditto the fresh lemonade.

Polly's Cafe

1342 U St. NW. ☎ 202/265-8385. D, DC, MC, V. No reservations. Metro: U St./Cardozo (Green). AMERICAN. **$**.

One of the pioneers in the funky-but-chic renaissance neighborhood now known as "the new U," this basement-level restaurant-bar brings in a crowd of hungry, grungy locals, who love to gossip by the fireplace. It's a rustic, hearty approach to sandwiches, burgers, and salads, plus fine specialties like herb marinated broiled trout. Breakfast is especially inviting, especially if you've been out all night at one of U Street's wilder dance bars.

★★ Prime Rib

2020 K St. NW. ☎ 202/
466-8811. AE, CB, DC, MC, V.
Reservations recommended
Closed: Sat lunch, Sun. Metro:
Farragut West (Blue/Orange).
STEAK. **$$$**.

This 1940s-style supper club
and power-lunch place is one
of the staples along the K
Street "expense account
corridor." The piano-bass
duo is big on Cole Porter and
suit-and-tie required. Ebony
walls with brass accents are
backdrops for pictures of
1920s flappers languishing
on settees and in inglenooks.
Even with reservations, there
is almost certain to be a wait
in the crowded bar, at least
at night. Appetites are thus
whetted for manly salads
and 20-ounce portions of
prime beef, plus equally
fine lobster and crab
imperial. Patrons are
overwhelmingly men on
the gray side of 40.

Red Hot and Blue

1120 19th St. NW (also 2
locations in Md. and Va. suburbs).
☎ 202/466-6731. MC, V. No
reservations. BARBECUE/CHILI. **$**.
Come for the best pork ribs in
town—either wet (rubbed and
sauced) or Memphis-style dry
(smoked and rubbed) in half
or full slabs. There are also
sandwiches of pulled pork
shoulder or pulled chicken,
with slaw, beans, and bread.
This casual, slick, and clever
place was a favorite of the
controversial late Republican
master media-manipulator
Lee Atwater, and he lingers
on in the blues-themed
memorabilia.

★★ Red Sage

605 14th St. NW. ☎ 202/
638-4444. AE, DC, MC, V.
Reservations required for dining
room. Wheelchair accessible.

Metro: Metro Center (Red, Blue/
Orange). SOUTHWESTERN.
$$$.
Superstar chef Mark Miller
brought D.C. into the era of
Restaurant as Theater with
Red Sage, the culinary
equivalent of an Andrew Lloyd
Webber musical extravaganza.
It's a $5 million design
production with a new wave
take on Santa Fe style,
fancifully designed, from the
cast-iron lizard door handles to
the plaster cloud ceiling (watch
for occasional flashes of
lightning). If you're lucky
enough to get a reservation,
gather in the street-level
lobby/chili bar and sip a
microbrew or margarita. When
your name is called, descend to
the main stage, where each
table is the best table, situated
near a fireplace or some other
picturesque detail. The food
lives up to the setting: Check
out the cinnamon-smoked
quail with wild rice, sausage of
the day (from venison, duck,
rabbit, wild boar . . .), the
Indian flatbread veggie pizza
with chili pesto and jalapeno-
decorated corn-and-molasses
bread. After 2 years, this is still
the hottest ticket in town, but
if you're willing to eat early or
late, you may be able to get
around the reservations racket.

Red Sea

2463 18th St. NW. ☎ 202/
483-5000. MC, V. Metro: Dupont
Circle (Red). ETHIOPIAN. **$**.
Disregard the unappealing,
timeworn exterior: Red Sea
was the first, and remains the
foremost Ethiopian eatery in
the Adams Morgan neighborhood (other good bets include
Fasika's and Meskerem). Eating
Ethiopian is a rare treat—
you're allowed to—supposed
to, even—eat with your
hands. Tear off a wedge of
injera (spongy discs of thin

unleavened bread) and scoop up an assortment of mild-to-spicy stews called wats, choosing from lamb, chicken, beef, and vegetables. To be really authentic, cool your palate with a glass of just-sweet-enough Ethiopian honey wine. The food is tasty enough to make it worth a repeat visit after the novelty of "hands-on" dining wears off.

Saigon Gourmet

2635 Connecticut Ave. NW. ☎ 202/265-1360. MC, V. Reservations recommended. Wheelchair accessible. Metro: Woodley Park/Zoo (Red). VIETNAMESE. **S**.

Washington enjoys a preponderance of Vietnamese restaurants, and Saigon Gourmet is the best (you might also check out the "Little Vietnam" row in nearby Va. suburb of Clarendon). Good bets include cinnamon beef, skewer-grilled marinated pork wrapped in rice crepes, and quail roasted in coconut juice.

★ Sam & Harry's

1200 19th St. NW. ☎ 202/296-4333. AE, CB, DC, MC, V. Reservations and jackets recommended. Wheelchair accessible. Metro: Dupont Circle (Red). STEAK. **SS**.

After a hard day of handshaking and backstabbing, lawyers and lobbyists coverge on Sam & Harry's (modeled after Morton's of Chicago) for their man-sized portions of meat and salads. Even the salads are jumbo here. Dine on 2-inch thick New York strip and veal T-bones in a men's club ambiance of dark woods and jazz music. Expect the biggest, if not the best steak in town. Yes, you can split meals (bet you'll still need a doggie bag).

★ Sarinah Satay House

1338 Wisconsin Ave. NW. ☎ 202/337-2955. AE, DC, MC, V. Reservations suggested. INDONESIAN. **SS**.

Now, here's something you may not have tried before. Leaving the hubbub of Georgetown, you pass through a nondescript door on Wisconsin Avenue, descend a staircase, and find yourself in a romantic subterranean garden: It's like falling into the rabbit-hole with Alice. The Indonesian menu is exotic and theatrical. I recommend the customized dozen-dish sampler dinner called rijsttafel (about $22.95 for two), the à la carte seafood dumplings, and chicken with a chili-spiked peanut dipping sauce. Our pick for the best Indonesian cuisine in town.

Sequoia

Washington Harbour, 3000 K St. NW. ☎ 202/944-4200. AE, DC, MC, V. Reservations recommended. Wheelchair accessible. Metro: Foggy Bottom (Blue/Orange). NEW AMERICAN. **SS**.

Whether you're eating indoors or out, Sequoia offers an unbeatable waterfront view. Named after the presidential yacht, the vast restaurant easily accommodates both the after-work drop-bys and the more formal, special-occasion diners. And the melting pot menu is almost comically huge, with everything from Italian to Cajun to Tex-Mex to French. . . . Of course, they do some things better than others—if you ask, the reliable and personable staff will steer you away from the losers.

★ 1789

1226 36th St. NW. ☎ 202/965-1789. AE, DC, MC, V. Reservations recommended, jacket required. Metro: Foggy Bottom (Blue/Orange). AMERICAN. **$$$**.

Escape the modern world in this museum-quality Federal townhouse in Georgetown, and imagine yourself dining fireside at Mount Vernon with George and Martha. Taking its cues from the seasonable availability of regional game and seafood, the menu walks the line between classic traditional—roasted rack of American lamb with creamy feta potatoes and merlot sauce—and adventurously modern—seared tuna with curried bulgar salad, lemon, mint, and fava beans.

★ Tabard Inn

1739 N St. NW. ☎ 202/833-2668. MC, V. Reservations recommended. Metro: Dupont Circle (Red). AMERICAN. **$$**.

Half the fun of going to the Tabard Inn for dinner is waiting for your table. Really! In the anachronistic, Agatha Christie–esque fireplace-lit library you can snuggle into the beat-up old couches and sip a drink beforehand. The restaurant itself is as modern as they come, with airy open parlors in California-style unpainted wood and bright local artwork. The menu changes daily but the food remains fresh, and tasty. Entrees you might find include saffron linguine with fish and shellfish in tomato-caper fumet or grilled salmon fillet with orange-ginger glaze and Asian noodle salad. One of the more romantic spots in town.

Tom Tom

2333 18th St. NW. ☎ 202/588-1300. AE, CB, D, DC, MC, V. Reservations accepted. Wheelchair accessible. Metro: Dupont Circle (Red). ECLECTIC. **$$**.

Trendy Tom Tom is one of several restaurants in town that try to combine the art and eating experiences. The owners hire local artists and craftspeople as human center-pieces, and situate them around the restaurant, where they paint, sculpt, weave, and field comments from diners. One guy creating an anatom-ically correct male sculpture served as the icebreaker for the whole restaurant one night. There's outdoor dining in a number of settings—on the patio in front, on the balcony, and on the rear roof deck. The menu, fresh and always chang-ing, free-ranges from creative tapas to wood-fired pizzas making it worth the visit even without the artist-model scene.

Tony Cheng's Mongolian Restaurant

619 H St. NW. ☎ 202/842-8669. AE, MC, V. No reservations. Metro: Gallery Place/Chinatown (Red). CHINESE. **$$**.

The gimmick here is you get to cook your own dinner. Actually, you scoop portions of beef, chicken, seafood, vegetables, and sauces from the salad bar–styled buffet and hand them over to the chef, who stir-fries them all together on an enormous round slab of a grill at the center of the restaurant. It's fun and relatively inexpensive ($6 for 1 serving, $14 for all you can eat, last time we looked). But to tell the truth, everything comes out tasting sort of the same no matter what ingredients or sauces you choose.

★ Two Quail

320 Massachusetts Ave. NE. ☎ 202/543-8030. AE, CB, D,

DC, MC, V. Reservations recommended. Metro: Union Station (Red). NEW AMERICAN. **$$**.

Head to the Hill for a can't-miss romantic dinner. In this converted townhouse, every table is a different, Victorian tableau, with adorably kitschy ornaments and lamps and mismatched china and silver. Save this for tête-à-tête: The room is set up for parties of two; larger groups seem to confuse the staff and kitchen. Menu offerings might include scallops with black olive pesto over fettucini, chicken stuffed with cornbread and pecans, and smoked peppered bluefish.

★ Vidalia

1990 M St. NW. ☎ 202/659-1990. AE, DC, MC, V. Reservations recommended. Wheelchair accessible (through office building elevator). Metro: Dupont Circle, Farragut North (Red). Closed: Sun. NEW AMERICAN. **$$$**.

Escape the fast-food frenzy of the downtown business district in this vision from the pages of *Martha Stewart Living*. The food is every bit as pretty and welcoming as the homey Southern surroundings. The first-course salads are sizable, and the imaginative daily specials often win out over the other offerings. Menu choices may include pan roasted sweetbreads with fresh morels, sautéed shrimp with creamed grits, and crab cakes served with sweet pepper and cabbage.

Zorba's Cafe

1612 20th St. NW. ☎ 202/387-8555. No credit cards. Reservations not required. Wheelchair accessible. Metro: Dupont Circle (Red). GREEK. **$**.

Get your gyros, hummus, falafel, and tabouli here. There are fancier places, but Zorba's dishes out dependable, basic Middle Eastern/Greek/Italian fast food. Place your order at the counter, and grab one of the coveted front patio seats, where you can watch the kaleidoscopic Dupont Circle scene in true Mediterranean style (complete with cheesy music). But don't spill your food! There was a big local flap when the grouchy owner refused to replace a customer's food after she accidentally dropped her tray.

ACCOMMODATIONS

by Theodore Fischer

Introduction

Most Washington hotels fit within a triangle that begins north of the National Mall at Union Station and fans out in a northwesterly direction as far as Georgetown and Woodley Park. Within the hotel zone, great differences exist between neighborhoods in terms of safety, charm, nighttime activity, and rates.

Most of the hotels that claim **Capitol Hill** locations are actually at the bottom of The Hill, immediately southwest of Union Station. Capitol Hill deluxe and bargain properties offer proximity to the Capitol, government agencies headquartered on the east end of the Mall, and Mall museums. Most restaurants are in the hotels, and safety becomes an issue once day-workers head home.

The Washington **Convention Center** (9th and H streets) is flanked by everything from mega convention properties to boutique charmers and historic B&Bs. They are reasonably near the Mall attractions, but there's no nightlife and danger lurks north of the Massachusetts Avenue border.

Hotels within the **White House–K Street** axis have history, elegance, high-voltage Washington electricity, proximity to big business, and important attractions. Rates are high, nights are quiet, and security forces patrolling the area keep it safe. Hotels around Scott Circle (16th and N streets) swap some panache for affordability.

Lodging in **Dupont Circle,** a lively residential neighborhood of bars, restaurants, shops, and all-hour sidewalk traffic, runs from the Ritz to family-friendly all-suite bargains. With embassies on all sides, Dupont Circle is within walking distance of many business and leisure attractions and right on top of a Metro station.

Foggy Bottom is a residential and academic (George Washington University) enclave between the office canyons of K Street and the bright lights of Georgetown. Many Foggy Bottom hotels are converted apartment buildings where suites with kitchens cost no more than standard rooms elsewhere. Zero nightlife, but you can walk to Georgetown and Dupont Circle along safe streets. A more commercial area of newer business-class hotels and good restaurants along M Street on the north edge of Foggy Bottom has been dubbed **West End.**

The streets of **Georgetown,** Washington's oldest neighborhood, are safe at all hours and quiet, away from the main drags, Wisconsin Avenue and M Street. Rates in its few hotels are generally high, but they're within walking distance of Georgetown's many restaurants, bars, and clubs.

Woodley Park, a safe, upper–middle-class residential neighborhood beside Rock Creek Park, has 2 large convention hotels and a handful of B&Bs. Plenty of restaurants are clustered nearby on Connecticut Avenue, near the Metro station, and even more are in nearby **Adams–Morgan.**

The price and availability of Washington hotel rooms varies dramatically throughout the year. The time you go will largely determine the difficulty of finding rooms as well as their costs.

One major factor is the season. April, May, and June, the time of cherry blossom festivals, school trips, and family spring vacations, are high seasons, when rates soar and rooms are scarcest. High season continues to expand in both directions, with occupancy rates steadily climbing in March and July. August is slower than July, although the weather is no more hot or humid. Business and pleasure travel pick up in September and October. Since few vacationers arrive from November through February, rates are lowest and bargain packages abound.

Another factor is the day of the week. Since Washington is essentially a business-travel weekday destination, rates decline and sometimes plummet on weekends. As a rule, the grander the property the steeper the weekend discount. In addition, weekend packages may include free meals, free city tours or shows, free parking, free rooms for kids—whatever it takes to fill empty spaces. Some weekend rates extend to Thursday and Sunday, but most are Friday and Saturday only. Check out ads in the travel sections of the *New York*

Times, Boston Globe, Chicago Tribune, and *Washington Post* for deals.

Other factors that determine price and availability include the congressional calendar: Occupancy rates are higher when Congress is in session. Washington is also a major convention site, and big conventions fill hotel rooms throughout the area.

Reservations

First call the toll-free telephone numbers listed for most hotels. Many of these numbers access centralized reservation services for the hotel chain, but some go directly to the hotel itself. If you don't like what a central reservation operator tells you (and even if it sounds alright), it may be worth paying the price to talk the hotel itself. Sometimes hotels run specials the chain doesn't know about; sometimes reservationists have license to haggle. In any event, you'll be surprised at how often the rates provided by the central reservation number and the hotel differ. Another option is to call a travel agent, who may have access to lower rates.

Whomever you talk to, don't fail to mention any conceivable affiliation. AAA, AARP, employer, union, trade association, professional society, frequent flyer club—all may qualify you for a discount. In fact, your Washington-based association, society, or union might have some kind of arrangement with a local hotel; ask member services.

As in most U.S. cities, Washington hotels are in a constant state of renovation and redecoration. Renovated rooms and rooms with views are available for the asking, sometimes at the same price as unrenovated, viewless rooms, and sometimes at a premium.

Washington is big on nonsmoking rooms and floors—and getting bigger each year. As hotels continue to increase smoke-free inventories, smokers and nonsmokers alike must remember to state their preferences when they book.

Most hotels provide guest parking—but at a price. Unless listings indicate free parking or no parking, expect to pay $7 to $15 a night.

If the price *is* definitely an object—and Washington hotel rates are among the highest in the United States—contact a hotel discounter that books Washington hotels. Hotel discounters are allowed to sell rooms at steeply reduced rates—as much as 65% below the rack rates—as long as they do so with some discretion.

Discounters can also be helpful for last-minute reservations. When you call, most hotel discounters will offer 4 or 5 hotels in your price-range and preferred location. The service is free, but each discounter has its own procedures for guaranteeing and canceling reservations.

Hotel discounters serving the Washington area (D.C. and suburban Maryland and Virginia) include: **Capitol Reservations,** ☎ 800/847-4832 or 202/452-1270; **Washington, D.C. Accommodations,** ☎ 800/554-2220 or 202/289-2220; **Accommodations Express,** ☎ 800/444-7666; **Hotel Reservation Network,** ☎ 800/964-6835; **Quikbook,** ☎ 800/789-9887; **RMC Travel,** ☎ 800/782-2674; and **Room Exchange,** ☎ 800/846-7000.

Bed & Breakfast reservation services book guests into private homes, apartments, or small inns all over the area. Accommodations vary widely in terms of price, comfort level, degree of child-friendliness, and location, but reservation services attempt to forge an ideal match. Tell them what you need and they'll mail or fax back detailed descriptions of listings.

B&B reservation services include: **Bed & Breakfast Accommodations, Ltd.,** ☎ 202/328-3510, fax: 202/332-3885, e-mail: bnbaccom@aol.com.; **Bed & Breakfast League-Sweet Dreams & Toast,** ☎ 202/483-9191.

If you arrive by train at Union Station, the courtesy board beside Gate G offers direct phone connections to a variety of area hotels, including many low-priced motels and B&B inns.

Prices

Prices are based on a standard double room (weekday, high season), not including local sales and hotel taxes (13% plus $1.50/room/night in D.C.; 5% plus 1–10% local increments in Maryland; 5.5% plus various local increments in Virginia).

Price Chart		
$	=	Under $100
$$	=	$100–$150
$$$	=	$151–$200
$$$$	=	$201–$250
$$$$$	=	Over $250

Hotels by Neighborhood

Capitol Hill
★ Bellevue. **$$**
Capitol Hill Suites. **$$$**
Hyatt Regency Washington on Capitol Hill. **$$$$**
★ Phoenix Park. **$$$**
Washington Court on Capitol Hill. **$$$**

Convention Center
Comfort Inn. **$**
★ Henley Park. **$$$**
★ Morrison-Clark. **$$$**
Renaissance Washington. **$$$$**

White House/K Street
Capital Hilton. **$$$$**
★ Carlton. **$$$$$**
Crowne Plaza. **$$$**
Doubletree Park Terrace. **$$$**
Governor's House. **$$**
★ Grand Hyatt Washington. **$$$$$**
★ Hay-Adams. **$$$$$**
★ Holiday Inn Central. **$**
J.W. Marriott. **$$$$**
★ Jefferson. **$$$$$**
Madison. **$$$$$**
★★ Renaissance Mayflower. **$$$$$**
Washington. **$$$**
Washington Vista. **$$$$**
★★ Willard Inter-Continental. **$$$$$**

Southwest
Loews L'Enfant Plaza. **$$$**

Foggy Bottom/West End
★ ANA. **$$$$$**
Howard Johnson Lodge. **$**
Inn at Foggy Bottom. **$$**
★ Lombardy. **$$**
★ One Washington Circle. **$$$**
★ St. James. **$$**
Watergate. **$$$$$**
★ Westin. **$$$$**

Dupont Circle
Barceló Hotel Washington. **$$$**
Canterbury. **$$$**
★ Embassy Inn/Windsor Inn. **$**
★ Embassy Row. **$$**
Embassy Square Suites. **$$**
★ H. H. Leonards Mansion. **$$$**
Normandy Inn. **$$**
★★ Ritz-Carlton. **$$$$$**
Sofitel. **$$$$**
★ Tabard Inn. **$/$$**
Washington Hilton & Towers **$$$**

Georgetown
★ Four Seasons. **$$$$$**
★ Georgetown Dutch Inn. **$$**
Georgetown Inn. **$$$**
Latham. **$$$**

Woodley Park/Adams-Morgan/Upper Northwest
Embassy Suites–Chevy Chase Pavilion. **$$$**
Kalorama Guest House. **$**
Omni Shoreham. **$$$$**
Sheraton Washington. **$$$**

Suburban Virginia
★★ Morrison House. **$$$$$**

National Airport
Ritz-Carlton Pentagon City. **$$$$**
Sheraton Suites. **$$$**

Dulles Airport
Holiday Inn Express. **$**
Washington Dulles Airport Marriott. **$$**

Baltimore-Washington International Airport
Hampton Inn. **$**
Sheraton International at BWI Airport. **$$**

Critic's Choice

Choose the **Hay-Adams** or **Renaissance Mayflower** to stride corridors of rawest Washington power, but the **Jefferson** for a more subtle sense of authority. The **Willard Inter-Continental** is the best place to time-travel back in Washington history. The post–Civil War era **Morrison-Clark** is romantic enough to make you feel far away from downtown Washington. To find out if proximity to power really is an aphrodisiac, check into the **Ritz-Carlton.** Try the **Bellevue** for funky film-noirish trysts. Family travelers will enjoy the space and rates at **Embassy Square Suites;** for a few dollars more, the **J.W. Marriott** close to the Mall has a family-sized indoor pool and a panoply of fast-food options under the same roof. The staff at **Embassy Inn/Windsor Inn** win the Congeniality Award. The **Holiday Inn Central** and **Georgetown Dutch Inn** are the best deals. If you hate convention hotels but have to attend a convention, the serene **Henley Park** lets you forget the Washington Convention Center is 2 blocks away. If you love convention hotels, the **Grand Hyatt** and **Washington Hilton & Towers** will make you most happy. **Tabard Inn** appeals to guests who regard "the sixties" with affection—even if they weren't around yet to enjoy them. The health club in the **ANA** is the biggest and has the fanciest toys, but the facilities at **Four Seasons** aren't far behind. Washington's strangest hotel is **H. H. Leonards Mansion:** trust us on this.

Washington D.C.'s Hotels A to Z

★ ANA

2401 M St. NW, Washington, DC 20037. ☎ 202/429-2400; 800/262-4683; fax: 202/457-5010. 415 rooms. Metro: Foggy Bottom, Dupont Circle. AE, D, DC, MC, V. **$$$$$**.

This East Coast outpost of Japan's All Nippon Airways (ANA) boasts a vast foliage-filled lobby thronged with top-rung international businesspeople. Except for the Japanese breakfast on the menu of the informal the Bistro restaurant, there's no sign of the Japanese connection in this 12-year-old former Westin. Rooms are traditional, formulated to suggest a stately embassy. It has the biggest and snazziest fitness center in the city: the Schwarzenegger/Shrivers and Jesse Jackson use it when they come to town. *Amenities:* Executive floor, 2 restaurants, large fitness center, indoor pool, squash and racquet-ball courts, rooms for disabled travelers, in-room data ports.

Barceló Hotel Washington

2121 P St. NW, Washington, DC 20037. ☎ 202/293-3100; 800/333-3333; fax: 202/331-9719. 298 rooms. Metro: Dupont Circle. AE, D, DC, MC, V. **$$$**.

Renowned for sun-and-sand Mediterranean resorts, Spain's Barceló Hotels' first U.S. venture aims at cost-conscious international business travelers. The former OmniGeorgetown is located in the Dupont Circle area, not far from the edge of Georgetown. The rooms of the converted circa-1968 apartment house are so large (500–550 square feet) that guests get either 1 king- or 2 queen-sized beds. Gabriel, its Spanish-Caribbean-Mexican-Southwestern restaurant, has innovative cuisine and a popular cocktail hour. *Amenities:* Restaurant, small exercise room, outdoor pool, rooms for disabled travelers, in-room data ports.

★ Bellevue

15 E St. NW, Washington, DC 20001. ☎ 202/638-0900; 800/327-6667; fax: 202/638-5132. 144 rooms. Metro: Union Station. AE, D, DC, MC, V. **$$**.

Several factors combine to make the Bellevue our favorite hotel in Capitol Hill: public areas and large individualized rooms that seem little changed since its 1928 opening as an apartment building; a prime Capitol Hill location near Union Station, the Capitol, the Labor Department, and federal courts; a complimentary buffet breakfast; and Packards. Old Packards serve as guest limos, ancient Packards as lobby sculpture, Packard paraphernalia as wall ornaments. Tiber Creek Pub serves yards of beer to happy-hour hordes of young congressional staffers. Free parking weekends. *Amenities:* Restaurant, free airport transportation.

Canterbury

1733 N St. NW, Washington, DC 20036. ☎ 202/393-3000; 800/424-2950; fax: 202/785-9581. 99 rooms. Metro: Dupont Circle. AE, D, DC, MC, V. **$$$**.

Every accommodation at the Canterbury is a "junior suite"—a largish room with an alcove kitchen or kitchenette. They're no bargains, but they're often available when every other place is full. Decor is Olde England, with 18thC reproduction furniture and walls adorned with hunting prints, but ownership is modern India, the Taj International chain. Chaucer's serves English specialties like shepherds pie and roast beef with Yorkshire pudding later in the day. *Amenities:* Restaurant, pub, free *Washington Post,* access to nearby health club and indoor pool, in-room data ports.

Capital Hilton

16th and K St. NW, Washington, DC 20036-5794. ☎ 202/393-1000; 800/HILTONS; fax: 202/639-5784. 543 rooms. Metro: Farragut North, McPherson Square. AE, D, DC, MC, V. **$$$$**.

The former Statler and Statler-Hilton has been a power-broker hive since it opened in 1943—the only major American hotel opened during World War II. The setting for the original (William Holden/Judy Holliday) version of *Born Yesterday* has undergone a succession of makeovers that sacrificed 250 rooms to make the remaining rooms larger than normal for Hilton. Nonetheless it's still just a serviceable big-shoulders American-style business hotel

D.C. Accommodations

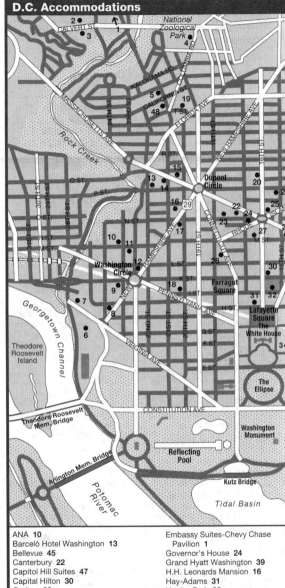

ANA **10**
Barceló Hotel Washington **13**
Bellevue **45**
Canterbury **22**
Capitol Hill Suites **47**
Capital Hilton **30**
Carlton **32**
Comfort Inn **41**
Crowne Plaza **33**
Doubletree Park Terrace **25**
Embassy Inn/Windsor Inn **20**
Embassy Row **15**
Embassy Square Suites **17**

Embassy Suites-Chevy Chase
  Pavilion **1**
Governor's House **24**
Grand Hyatt Washington **39**
H.H. Leonards Mansion **16**
Hay-Adams **31**
Henley Park **38**
Holiday Inn Central **21**
Howard Johnson Lodge **7**
Hyatt Regency Washington on
  Capitol Hill **44**
Inn at Foggy Bottom **8**
J.W. Marriott **36**

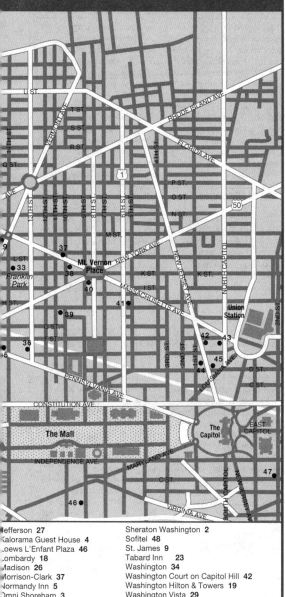

Jefferson **27**
Kalorama Guest House **4**
Loews L'Enfant Plaza **46**
Lombardy **18**
Madison **26**
Morrison-Clark **37**
Normandy Inn **5**
Omni Shoreham **3**
One Washington Circle **12**
Phoenix Park **43**
Renaissance Mayflower **28**
Renaissance Washington **40**
Ritz-Carlton **14**

Sheraton Washington **2**
Sofitel **48**
St. James **9**
Tabard Inn **23**
Washington **34**
Washington Court on Capitol Hill **42**
Washington Hilton & Towers **19**
Washington Vista **29**
Watergate **6**
Westin **11**
Willard Inter-Continental **35**

that happens to be 3 blocks from the White House. Another big change: Trader Vic and his parasoled cocktails are out; former Redskin Fran O'Brien's Steakhouse is in. *Amenities:* 2 restaurants, 24-hour room service, large health club and maps to "Monument Miles" (jogging courses between hotel and Mall monuments), rooms for disabled travelers, in-room data ports.

Capitol Hill Suites

200 C St. SE, Washington, DC 20003. ☎ 202/543-6000; 800/ 424-9165; fax: 202/547-2608. 105 rooms. Metro: Capitol South. AE, D, DC, MC, V. **$$$**.
This all-suite converted apartment house is over The Hill from other hotels that purport Capitol Hill locations, on a residential block opposite the Library of Congress (Madison Bldg.) and a block from House of Representatives office buildings. The only all-suite accommodation in the neighborhood has attractive Queen Anne–style furnishings, better equipment than most suite hotel kitchens, TVs and sprinkler systems, and frequent long-term congressional guests. *Amenities:* Complimentary continental breakfast, weekday happy hour, weekday *Washington Post*, access to health club.

★ Carlton

16th and K St. NW, Washington, DC 20006. ☎ 202/638-2626; 800/325-3535, fax: 202/ 638-4231. 197 rooms. Metro: Farragut North, McPherson Square. AE, D, DC, MC, V. **$$$$$**.
The lobby of the 70-year-old ITT Sheraton Luxury Collection property— encrusted with gilt, ornate ceilings, stressed-gold–

upholstered armchairs— is as overblown as the pretensions of any banana republic generalissimo or Washington lobbyist. The antiques and reproduction furniture in the guest rooms are a bit rococo for our democratic sensibilities, but if you get one the 13 suites with White House views, you won't look at them much. *Amenities:* 2 restaurants, afternoon tea in lobby, 24-hour room service, choice of complimentary newspaper, special amenities for Japanese guests, fitness center, pool privileges, tennis and golf privileges, rooms for disabled travelers, in-room data ports.

Comfort Inn

500 H St. NW, Washington, DC 20001. ☎ 202/289-5959; 800/ 221-2222; fax: 202/682-9152. 195 rooms. Metro: Gallery Place/ Chinatown. AE, D, DC, MC, V. **$**.
To be the only hotel in Washington's vest-pocket Chinatown is a distinction of dubious value, but this budget property is also close to the convention center, the National Building Museum, and, when it opens in fall 1997, MCI Center, where Washington's pro basketball team and hockey teams will play. All sleeping rooms were recently renovated, and guests can help themselves to fresh fruit in the lobby. *Amenities:* Restaurant, exercise room with sauna, free *USA Today*, rooms for disabled travelers.

Crowne Plaza

14th and K St. NW, Washington, DC 20005. ☎ 202/682-0111; 800/637-3788; fax: 202/ 682-9525. 318 rooms. Metro: McPherson Square. AE, D, DC, MC, V. **$$$**.
Washington's newest hotel (opened June 1996) is actually

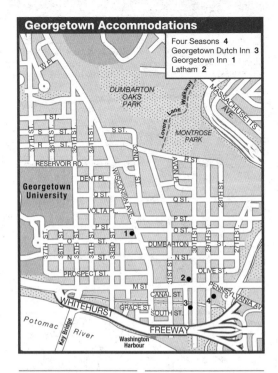

Georgetown Accommodations

Four Seasons **4**
Georgetown Dutch Inn **3**
Georgetown Inn **1**
Latham **2**

DUMBARTON OAKS PARK

MONTROSE PARK

Georgetown University

Potomac River

Washington Harbour

---

the transformed Hamilton hotel which was built in 1921 by the architect of the Jefferson hotel. The Hamilton peaked in the 1940s when Gene Autry (and steed Champion) used to play the Rainbow Room, but endured hard times as a Salvation Army women's shelter and federal office building. The building had been vacant for 13 years when it was taken over by Crowne Plaza, the upscale sister of Holiday Inn, which restored the original Beaux Arts–style grandeur and added 2 top floors for an executive level. With a prime site on the eastern portal of the K Street Corridor, the new Crowne is a boutique-sized hotel with big-hotel amenities and appealingly reasonable rates. *Amenities:* Executive floor, restaurant, espresso bar, 24-hour room

service, fitness center, in-room data ports.

Doubletree Park Terrace

1515 Rhode Island Ave. NW, Washington, DC 20005.
☎ 202/232-7000; 800/222-TREE; fax: 202/332-7152.
219 rooms. Metro: Dupont Circle, Farragut North. AE, D, DC, MC, V. **$$$**.

The transmogrified ex-Radisson is a crisply efficient relatively good deal on Scott Circle, a short walk from Massachusetts Avenue embassies, K Street business, and Dupont Circle pleasures. Built in 1960, the property was completely renovated by new owners who are so hands-on that they personally buy antiques for the restaurant and public areas. *Amenities:* Exercise room, in-room data ports, restaurant, complimentary newspaper.

★ Embassy Inn/ Windsor Inn

1627 16th St. NW, Washington, DC 20009; 1842 16th St. NW, Washington, DC 20009. ☎ 202/234-7800; 202/667-0300; 800/423-9111; fax: 202/234-3309. 38 rooms/45 rooms. Metro: Dupont Circle. **$**.

The 2 sister-hotels, a few blocks apart on 16th Street halfway between Dupont Circle and the burgeoning U Street nightlife district, started out in the lodging business as early 1920s boarding houses. Warm feelings abound between staff and guests who'd like to keep this Washington "find" all to themselves. Small rooms in Federalist-style Embassy Inn are best-suited for singles or couples. The Deco-style Windsor has larger rooms and 9 suites. Ask about the "green rate": You pay less money and they change your linen less often. No parking. *Amenities:* Complimentary breakfast and evening sherry, complimentary *Washington Post*.

★ Embassy Row

2015 Massachusetts Ave. NW, Washington, DC 20036. ☎ 202/265-1600; 800/424-2400; fax: 202/328-7526. 195 rooms. Metro: Dupont Circle. AE, D, DC, MC, V. **$$**

The 25-year-old independent Dupont Circle property, opposite the Indonesian embassy and down the block from India's, offers guests the "invisible security" of the embassies' private guardians. Coups have been plotted in the lobby; Vaclav Havel stayed in the Presidential Suite here. The location is every bit as good as the Ritz (a half-block away), rooms are even bigger, but room rates are less than half. It also has an outdoor rooftop pool and rooftop bar,

a rarity in Washington. Bistro 2150 mingles imaginative nouvelle American dishes with low-priced family-friendly fare (steaks, tacos, spaghetti). *Amenities:* fitness center, outdoor pool, restaurant, complimentary newspaper, in-room data ports.

Embassy Square Suites

2000 N St. NW, Washington, DC 20036. ☎ 202/659-9000; 800/424-2999; fax: 202/429-9546. 250 rooms. Metro: Dupont Circle. AE, D, DC, MC, V. **$$**

The 10-story Dupont Circle all-suite hotel attracts budget-minded families and long-term guests from developing nations. Options include simply furnished efficiencies, 1-bedroom suites, and 2-bedroom/2-bath suites—some with balconies. Efficiencies would cramp all but the closest families, but bedroom suites offer ample space. Complimentary breakfast can be taken beside the pool. *Amenities:* Complimentary breakfast, outdoor pool, small health club.

Embassy Suites–Chevy Chase Pavilion

4300 Military Rd. NW, Washington, DC 20015. ☎ 202/362-9300; 800/EMBASSY; fax: 202/686-3405. 198 rooms. Metro: Friendship Heights. AE, D, DC, MC, V. **$$$**

This is the only hotel located on Washington's answer to Rodeo Drive—amid a strip of chic stores (Saks, Neiman's, and the brand new Tiffany's) where Wisconsin Avenue crosses the border into Chevy Chase, Maryland. Embassy Suites offers its standard suite deals (bedroom units, kitchens, free breakfast, free cocktails) in an atrium above posh Chevy Chase Mall. You can reach the Metro for the (theoretically) 14-minute ride downtown without leaving the building. *Amenities:* Complimentary breakfast buffet, complimentary cocktails 5pm to 7pm, fully-equipped kitchens, restaurant plus other restaurants and food court in Pavilion, health club, indoor pool, VCR, in-room data ports.

Other Embassy Suites: **Embassy Suites-Washington** (1520 22nd St. NW, Washington, DC 20037; ☎ 202/857-3388; fax: 202/293-3173; Metro: Dupont Circle); **Embassy Suites-Alexandria-Old Town** (1900 Diagonal Rd., Alexandria, VA 22314; ☎ 703/684-5900; fax: 703/684-1403; Metro: King Street).

★ Four Seasons

2800 Pennsylvania Ave. NW, Washington, DC 20007. ☎ 202/342-0444; 800/332-3442; fax: 202/342-1673. 196 rooms. Metro: Foggy Bottom. AE, D, DC, MC, V. **$$$$$**.

Opened in 1979, the contemporary brick structure at the portal of Georgetown has rooms overlooking Rock Creek and the C&O Canal, some with balconies. The lobby has a rare Chippendale breakfront, odd sculpture by the chain-president's favorite artist, and plenty of lush foliage. Guest rooms are bright, furnished with antiques and reproductions, not overly spacious but apparently adequate for the king of Jordan and upper-crust business travelers. Highly rated—and perhaps somewhat overrated—it's the service and the 3-level fitness center with lap pool that command Washington's highest room rates. *Amenities:* Large fitness center, pool, 24-hour room service, complimentary limo service in D.C. area, 2 restaurants, rooms for disabled travelers, in-room data ports.

★ Georgetown Dutch Inn

1075 Thomas Jefferson St. NW, Washington, DC 20007. ☎ 202/337-0900; 800/388-2410; fax: 202/333-6526. 47 rooms. Metro: Foggy Bottom. AE, D, DC, MC, V. **$$**

Our favorite place to stay in Georgetown, the 7-story, red-brick, absolutely un-Colonial–style, all-suite hotel just off the C&O Canal is the closest thing to a bargain Georgetown has to offer. Options include tidy 1- or 2-bedroom suites, or 2-story penthouses, all with full kitchens (stoves, coffeemakers) and 2 TVs. It's particularly popular among Europeans and South Americans and hard to book any time of the year. Free, but limited, underground parking available. *Amenities:* Complimentary continental breakfast, exercise room.

Georgetown Inn

1310 Wisconsin Ave. NW, Washington, DC 20007. ☎ 202/333-8900; 800/424-2979; fax: 202/625-1744. 95 rooms. AE, D, DC, MC, V. **$$$**.

The 3-decade-old Georgetown Inn, a clubby place with 18thC American flavor, uses double-paned windows to insulate guests from the 20thC tumult just outside on Wisconsin Avenue. Georgetown University is nearby. The Georgetown Bar & Grill serves a popular breakfast buffet. *Amenities:* Fitness center, complimentary *Washington Post,* restaurant.

Governor's House

1615 Rhode Island Ave. NW, Washington, DC 20036. ☎ 202/296-2100; 800/821-4367; fax: 202/331-0227. 152 rooms. Metro: Farragut North, Dupont Circle. **$$**.

The tidy ex–Holiday Inn, 2 blocks from K Street and Dupont Circle, is a bargain for the location, especially popular with government travelers (who receive low per diem rates year-round) and visitors to the nearby embassies of Australia, Peru, and the Philippines. Rooms are large, kitchenette suites are ideal for families and long stays. Herb's attracts an arty crowd with the city's largest patio and American food faintly praised as "a good value." *Amenities:* Access to health club, outdoor pool, complimentary *Washington Post,* restaurant, in-room data ports.

★ Grand Hyatt Washington

1000 H St. NW, Washington, DC 20001. ☎ 202/582-1234; 800/233-1234; fax: 202/637-4781. 907 rooms. Metro: Metro Center. AE, D, DC, MC, V. **$$$$$**.

No D.C. hotel is closer to the Washington Convention Center and none has a taller atrium lobby: It starts below-ground at "lagoon level" and rises as far as height restrictions allow. Sleek cafes cling to the shores of the lagoon, and a gentleman clad in tuxedo plays a white grand piano enisled on a round islet in its center. Our favorite hotel in the shadow of the convention center, this place is grand even for a chain notorious for exuberant architectural flourishes. Unusually quiet guest rooms, renovated in 1994, have contemporary furnishings. An upscale sports bar, Grand Slam, is a local hangout for Duke fans. *Amenities:* Executive floor, 2-story health club with lap pool, 5 restaurants, 24-hour room service, rooms for disabled travelers, in-room data ports.

Hampton Inn

829 Elkridge Landing Rd., Linthicum, MD 21090. ☎ 410/850-0600, 800/HAMPTON; fax: 410/691-2119. 139 rooms. AE, D, DC, MC, V. **$**.

This shipshape 5-story budget property in the heart of the BWI business district sweetens an already good deal with a decent complimentary breakfast (the usual plus cereal, bagels, and fruit) and free Monday-through-Thursday happy hour (beer, wine, soft drinks). Best bargain in the BWI area. *Amenities:* Access to health club, free airport shuttle.

★ Hay-Adams

16th and H St. NW, Washington, DC 20006. ☎ 202/638-6600; 800/424-5054; fax: 202/638-3803. 137 rooms. Metro: McPherson Square, Farragut West. AE, D, DC, MC, V. **$$$$$**.

This dignified hotel on Lafayette Square was opened in 1927 to create "an island of civility in a sea of power." Our choice for best White House neighborhood address is so good that even totally clout-challenged guests feel like major Washington players. No hotel offers better White House views—especially from suites with balconies on the south side of the building. The lobby has classic Italian Renaissance architecture, but guest rooms look north to re-create the interior designs of 23 different English manor houses. *Amenities:* Restaurant, 24-hour room service, access to health club, complimentary daily newspaper, access to fitness center.

★ Henley Park

926 Massachusetts Ave. NW, Washington, DC 20001. ☎ 202/

638-5200; 800/222-8474; fax: 202/638-6740. 96 rooms. Metro: Metro Center. AE, D, DC, MC, V. **$$$**.

The Tudor-style 1918 converted apartment building offers the most understated English country elegance money can rent within 2 blocks from the Washington Convention Center. Guest rooms are furnished with 18thC English reproductions, including some 4-poster beds. Afternoon tea is served beside the fireplace. The highly rated Coeur de Lion restaurant serves Asian-accented continental specialties, with jazz and dancing on weekends. *Amenities:* 2 restaurants, 24-hour room service, access to exercise facilities, in-room data ports.

★ H. H. Leonards Mansion

2020 O St. NW, Washington, DC 20036. ☎ 202/496-2000, fax: 202/659-0547. 12 rooms. Metro: Dupont Circle. MC, V. **$$$**.

Small (12 rooms) and unobtrusive (no sign), the Mansion consists of 3 connected, 5-story, 1890s row houses on a quiet block near Dupont Circle. Rooms, each a figment of owner H. H. Leonards's artistic imagination, run from the Teddy Bear room, named after Teddy Roosevelt who used to play snooker here, to a 2-story log cabin suite. Every nook and cranny is filled with paintings, trinkets, and curios, and everything you see, except Teddy's pool table, is for sale. Many—ourselves included—find it more fun to talk about having stayed here than to stay here, but nobody forgets the "Mansion on O Street." *Amenities:* Complimentary breakfast, outdoor pool.

★ Holiday Inn Central

15th St. and Rhode Island Ave. NW, Washington, DC 20005. ☎ 202/483-2000; 800/248-0016; fax: 202/797-1078. 213 rooms. Metro: Dupont Circle, Farragut North. AE, D, DC, MC, V. **$**.

This Holiday Inn is a pleasant surprise. Totally rebuilt in 1991, it offers large, bright, cheerful rooms (some with balconies), free breakfast, a rooftop pool, and great rates for the location on Scott Circle. Families might (or might not) appreciate the game room and all-you-can-eat buffets in Avenue Cafe. *Amenities:* Complimentary continental breakfast, restaurant, fitness room, outdoor pool, in-room data ports.

Holiday Inn Express

485 Elden St., Herndon, VA 22070. ☎ 703/478-9777; 800/HOLIDAY; fax: 703/471-4624. 116 rooms. AE, D, DC, MC, V. **$**.

Three miles east of Dulles Airport, the 4-story exemplar of the Holiday Inn's budget line, with the basics, and extras like a free breakfast and free local calls. *Amenities:* Complimentary 24-hour airport shuttle, continental breakfast, access to health club, in-room data ports.

Other Holiday Inns: **Holiday Inn-Capitol** (550 C St. SW, Washington, DC 20004; ☎ 202/479-4000; fax: 202/479-4353; Metro: L'Enfant Plaza); **Holiday Inn-Capitol Hill** (415 New Jersey Ave. NW, Washington, DC 20001; ☎ 202/638-1616; fax: 202/638-0707; Metro: Union Station); **Holiday Inn Georgetown** (2101 Wisconsin Ave. NW, Washington, DC 20007; ☎ 202/338-4600; fax: 202/333-6113.

Howard Johnson Lodge

2601 Virginia Ave. NW, 20037.
☎ 202/965-2700; 800/
654-2000; fax: 202/965-2700,
ext. 7910. 192 rooms. Metro:
Foggy Bottom. AE, D, DC,
MC, V. **$**.

The hotel used as a staging
area by the Watergate plumbers
(rooms 419 and 723) is still a
strategically desirable bargain
close to the Mall, Kennedy
Center, and Georgetown. Like
HoJo's roadside properties,
rooms are large but relatively
charmless. Rooftop pool
and terrace has monument
views unavailable at snazzier
establishments. *Amenities:*
Outdoor pool, free parking,
restaurant, game room,
in-room data ports.

Hyatt Regency Washington on Capitol Hill

400 New Jersey Ave. NW,
Washington, DC 20001. ☎ 202/
737-1234; 800/233-1234; fax:
202/737-5773. 834 rooms.
Metro: Union Station. AE, D, DC,
MC, V. **$$$$**.

The largest hotel in the
Capitol Hill area caters to
people doing business with
Congress or the nearby
Departments of Labor,
Education, or Defense.
Inwardly, rooms overlook
the typically stunning Hyatt
atrium, but southside rooms
get views of the Capitol. The
Rooftop Capitol View Club (a
real private club for lunch) has
the city's best restaurant views.
Amenities: Executive floor, 2
restaurants, health club, indoor
pool, rooms for disabled
travelers, in-room data ports.

Inn at Foggy Bottom

824 New Hampshire Ave. NW,
Washington, DC 20037. ☎ 202/
337-6620; 800/426-4455; fax:
202/298-7499. 95 rooms. Metro:
Foggy Bottom. AE, E, DC, MC, V.
$$.

New owner George
Washington University has
installed a colonial
Williamsburg-inspired motif,
but the mid-1960s–era, 9-
story, white-brick building
doesn't look at all innlike. It's
unobtrusively located on a
quiet residential block near a
Metro station and the GWU
campus. The large rooms of
this converted apartment house
make handy temporary
quarters for visitors to the
State Department and
showfolk with Kennedy
Center gigs. *Amenities:*
Complimentary continental
breakfast, complimentary daily
Washington Post, restaurant,
access to health club.

★ Jefferson

16th and M St. NW, Washington,
DC 20036-3295. ☎ 202/
347-2200; 800/368-5966; fax:
202/331-7982. 100 rooms.
Metro: Farragut North. AE, D,
DC, MC, V. **$$$$$**.

Opened in 1923 as a near-the-
White-House residence for top
diplomats and social lions, the
Jefferson was drafted during
World War II to house visiting
soldiers. Since then, it's served
as a clubby, off-limelight
stopping place for celebrities
ranging from Ollie North
to Julia Roberts. Nothing
special from the outside, but
individually decorated guest
rooms display original art and
furniture design styles from
the 1920s to the present. The
Restaurant at The Jefferson,
a discreet power-lunch spot,
displays original documents
signed by TJ himself. *Amenities:*
restaurant, 24-hour room
service, access to health club
and indoor pool, in-room
CD players, in-room data ports.

J.W. Marriott

14th St. and Pennsylvania Ave.
NW, Washington, DC 20004.

☎ 202/393-2000; 800/
228-9290; fax: 202/626-6991.
773 rooms. Metro: Metro Center.
AE, D, DC, MC, V. **$$$$**
The behemoth on Pennsyl-
vania Avenue is part of the
block-square National Place
complex which includes the
National Press Club and Shops
at City Place mall. Pennsylvania Avenue–side rooms have
views of Mall monuments;
inside rooms view other wings
of the complex. Families will
like weekend deals, proximity
to museums on the capital
Mall, more than a dozen cheap
places to eat nearby, huge
indoor pool, and absence of
minibars. *Amenities:* Executive
floor, 4 restaurants, 24-hour
room service, large health club,
indoor pool, rooms for
disabled travelers, in-room data
ports.

Kalorama Guest House

Kalorama Park: 1854 Mintwood
Place NW, Washington, DC
20009. ☎ 202/667-6369; fax:
202/319-1262. 31 rooms. Metro:
Woodley Park. Woodley Park:
2700 Cathedral Ave. NW,
Washington, DC 20008. ☎ 202/
328-0860. 19 rooms. Metro:
Woodley Park. AE, MC, V. **$**.
This hotel in 2 distinct sections
is popular with representatives
of organizations long on
idealism but short on cash. The
Kalorama Park section consists
of 6 turn-of-the-century,
casually (rather than quaintly)
charming row houses on a
quiet back-street near the
raucous Adams Morgan
nightlife district. The 2 circa-
1920s buildings of the Woodley
Park offer brighter, larger
rooms and a more subdued
neighborhood. Half of the
Kalorama Guest House rooms
have private baths; none have
phones or TVs; furniture
comes from thrift shops.
Limited paid parking.

Amenities: Complimentary
continental breakfast.

Latham

3000 M St. NW, Washington, DC
20007-3701. ☎ 202/726-5000;
800/368-5922; fax: 202/337-
4250. 143 rooms. Metro: Foggy
Bottom. AE, D, DC, MC, V. **$$$**.
The red-brick structures
clinging to a slope between
Georgetown's M Street main
drag and the placid C&O
Canal offer an unusually rich
variety of accommodations:
regular rooms with canal, river,
or Georgetown "treetop"
views; bilevel carriage suites;
poolside bungalows; under-
ground, lower-priced,
windowless rooms with indoor
facades that mimic real
Georgetown town homes. Not
our first choice in George-
town—not enough pampering
to be a luxury hotel and not
cheap enough to be a
bargain—but jocks and
Europeans find it appealing.
The restaurant is the celebrity-
filled California-French
Citronelle. *Amenities:* Executive
floor, restaurant, health club
access, outdoor pool, in-room
data ports.

Loews L'Enfant Plaza

480 L'Enfant Plaza SW,
Washington, DC 20024. ☎ 202/
484-1000; 800/243-1166; fax:
202/646-4456. 370 rooms.
Metro: L'Enfant Plaza. AE, D, DC,
MC, V. **$$$**.
A concrete government-issue
facade conceals the marble and
chintz interior of the only
luxury hotel south of the Mall.
Yes, it has the ambiance of a
chain hotel, but that's a world
of personality more than the
government agencies—
Departments of Agriculture,
Energy, Housing and Urban
Development, and the U.S.
Postal Service, among others—
that encompass it. It's also the

closest place to stay near the National Air and Space Museum—the most popular museum in the world—and the Holocaust Memorial Museum. All guest rooms were recently refurbished; many have private balconies and most have monument views. *Amenities:* Executive floor, 4 restaurants plus coffee bar, large health club, rooftop all-season pool, located above a shopping arcade, rooms for disabled travelers, in-room data ports.

★ Lombardy

2019 I St. NW, Washington, DC 20006. ☎ 202/828-2600; 800/ 424-5486; fax: 202/872-0503. 126 rooms. Metro: Foggy Bottom, Farragut West. AE, D, DC, MC V. **$$**.

Peace Corps people stay here (if that's a recommendation) because the home office is around the corner and because the converted 1929 apartment building is loaded with retro charm. The ingratiating staff speaks 29 languages and operates the city's last remaining nonautomatic elevators. Rooms are large; some have Manhattan-sized kitchens and some have been renovated. Located on the cusp of K Street and Foggy Bottom, it is also convenient to World Bank, Eximbank, and George Washington University. *Amenities:* Restaurant, access to health club, in-room data ports.

Madison

15th and M St. NW, Washington, DC 20005. ☎ 202/862-1600; 800/424-8577; fax: 202/785-1255. 353 rooms. Metro: Farragut North, McPherson Square. AE, D, DC, MC, V. **$$$$$**

The exterior of this elegant business hotel, opened in 1963, fails to dazzle, but the lobby displays stunning oriental antiques and original paintings from the proprietors' own collection. Guest rooms contain some valuable custom-made furniture, blending English Regency, French Provincial, and Williamsburg styles, It's right across 15th Street from the *Washington Post,* which makes it convenient for reporters interviewing visiting heads-of-state who stay here. *Amenities:* Large fitness center, 2 restaurants, 24-hour room service, complimentary weekday *Washington Post.*

★ Morrison-Clark

11th St. and Massachusetts Ave. NW, Washington, DC 20001. ☎ 202/898-1200; 800/ 332-7898; fax: 202/289-8576. 54 rooms. Metro: Metro Center. AE, D, DC, MC, V. **$$$**.

Morrison and Clark were 2 merchants who built matching side-by-side, 4-story townhouses right after the Civil War. In 1923 their homes became the Soldiers, Sailors, Marines, and Airmen's Club offering servicemen quarter-a-night beds. In 1987 it became a much more costly bed-and-breakfast inn with a porch, public areas festooned with museum-quality photos, posters, and other curiosities, and tasteful antique-filled rooms trendily styled after lodgings in New Orleans or Provence, some with bay windows, others with fireplaces or sit-on porches. Two blocks north of the convention center (but just south of the danger zone), the Morrison-Clark staff can come off a bit snooty but at least they've got something to be snooty about. *Amenities:* Complimentary continental breakfast, restaurant, exercise room, newspapers, in-room data ports.

★★ Morrison House

116 S. Alfred St., Alexandria, VA
22314. ☎ 703/838-8000; 800/
367-0800; fax: 703/684-6283.
45 rooms. Metro: King Street.
AE, DC, MC, V. **$$$$$**.

One of Washington's finest
hotels, the Morrison House
is situated on a brick alley in
the Old Town section of
Alexandria, Virginia, one of
George Washington's stomping
grounds. Washington might
have stayed in a hotel like this,
but he didn't sleep here
because it wasn't built until
1985. Guest rooms amplify
the red-brick Federal Period
(1790–1820) exterior, with
2- and 4-poster beds,
fireplaces, and antique sconces
on every vertical surface, but
they don't stint on modern
indulgences like remote-
control TVs and bathroom
phones. The clublike Elysium
restaurant, with a Mediterranean menu, is a stand-out in
an area brimming with fine
restaurants; afternoon tea is
served beside the fireplace in
the parlor. *Amenities:*
Restaurant, 24-hour room
service, complimentary daily
newspaper, health club
privileges, in-room data ports.

Normandy Inn

2118 Wyoming Ave. NW,
Washington, DC 20008. ☎ 202/
483-1350; 800/424-3729; 202/
387-8241. 75 rooms. Metro:
Woodley Park, Dupont Circle. AE,
D, DC, MC, V. **$$**.

This unprepossessing 1960
building, originally a boarding
school dormitory, now houses
one of Washington's hotels
with the atmosphere of a well-
maintained but somewhat
austere European-style
pension. Despite a French-
sounding name, Normandy
Inn belongs to the Ireland-
based Irish Inns chain. Located
on a sedate residential street in

the Kalorama Heights district
near Dupont Circle and
Massachusetts Avenue
embassies, it has no restaurant
or bar but serves a non-
complimentary breakfast
in the Tea Room. *Amenities:*
Access to health club and
outdoor pool, in-room data
ports.

Omni Shoreham

2500 Calvert St. NW,
Washington, DC 20008. ☎ 202/
234-0700; 800/THE-OMNI; fax:
202/265-5333. 770 rooms.
Metro: Woodley Park. AE, D, DC,
MC, V. **$$$$**.

Built in 1930, this in-town
resort in the Woodley Park
neighborhood has put up (and
put up with) the Beatles and
Harry Truman's notorious
poker games. Every President
since FDR has held an
inaugural ball here. Oversized
guest-rooms were all renovated
in 1995; half overlook Rock
Creek Park, and a few have
fireplaces. Even if you're not
attending a convention, the
midtown sylvan setting has its
charm—as long as you can
avoid the newer plain-vanilla
100-room annex. Marquee
Lounge hosts improv groups
and the long-running satire of
Mrs. Foggybottom (Joan
Cushing). *Amenities:* 3 restau-
rants and nightclub, large
fitness center, 2 outdoor pools,
lighted tennis courts, rooms
for disabled travelers, in-room
data ports.

★ One Washington Circle

1 Washington Circle NW,
Washington, DC 20037. ☎ 202/
872-1680; 800/424-9671; fax:
202/887-4989. 151 rooms.
Metro: Foggy Bottom. AE, DC,
MC, V. **$$$**.

Five types of suites are available
in this converted Foggy
Bottom apartment house that

became Richard Nixon's post-Watergate Washington home (the 8th-floor Suite Grande Classe to be exact). Nixon didn't walk to K Street offices, the State Department, Dupont Circle, or the Mall, but other guests easily can. Suites, some of the most spacious and tastefully furnished in town, all have balconies and kitchens fully equipped down to coffee grinders and fresh beans. West End Cafe is a popular American bistro, and its Piano Room offers a lively nighttime scene, with lots of traveling musicians and theater people hanging out late. *Amenities:* Executive floor, restaurant, outdoor pool, access to health club, complimentary *Washington Post.*

★ Phoenix Park

520 N. Capitol St. NW, Washington, DC 20001. ☎ 202/638-6900; 800/824-5419; fax: 202/824-5419. 151 rooms. Metro: Union Station. AE, DC, MC, V. **$$$**.

You don't have to be Irish to appreciate Dan Coleman's brand of Irish hospitality (most guests aren't), but it has proven so captivating that in 1996 he had to open a 65-room addition. This is lace-curtain Irish hospitality, complete with Irish wool carpeting and Waterford crystal chandeliers, barmen who know the proper way to pour Guinness, and a staff comprised of 40% FBI (Foreign Born Irish). Opposite Union Station, it's close enough to the Capitol to host power breakfasts, lunches, and dinners; and diplomatic enough to lodge envoys from all sides in the Irish troubles. The Dubliner Pub, Coleman's original enterprise, is famed for Irish food, drink, and music. *Amenities:* Access to health club, 2 restaurants,

in-room data ports, rooms for disabled travelers.

★★ Renaissance Mayflower

1127 Connecticut Ave. NW, Washington, DC 20036. ☎ 202/347-3000; 800/HOTELS-1; fax: 202/466-9082. 659 rooms. Metro: Farragut North. AE, D, DC, MC, V. **$$$$$**.

The Mayflower opened in 1925, a block from K Street before K Street was K Street. Despite a few name and ownership changes (as it was acquired by Stouffer which was later acquired by Renaissance Hotels International), the granddaddy of power hotels still attracts the in-crowd. Starbuck's espresso bar in the gilded block-wide lobby is a prime spot for political people-watching; the Town and Country Lounge caters to operators who know what a good martini is. Rooms, all renovated under Stouffer, have customized furniture and marble bathrooms. With main-floor public areas teeming with convention traffic, this elegant old-shoe's no quiet charmer but it is the place to dive straight into the Washington mainstream. *Amenities:* 2 restaurants, coffee bar, 24-hour room service, large health club, complimentary coffee/newspaper, wake-up call, rooms for disabled travelers, in-room data ports.

Renaissance Washington

999 9th St. NW, Washington, DC 20001-9000; ☎ 202/898-9000; 800/228-9898; fax: 202/789-4213. 800 rooms. Metro: Gallery Place. AE, D, DC, MC, V. **$$$$**.

The glass-sided 16-story luxury convention hotel, opened in 1989, is directly across the street from the main entrance to Washington Convention Center. And it will be the hotel closest to the new convention center opening on the other side of Mount Vernon Square by the end of the century. The Grand Hyatt is our favorite convention center area mega-property, but the Renaissance is a strong runner-up. The dangling pagoda-topped lobby bar pays tribute to the near-Chinatown setting and to the present ownership, Hong Kong-based Renaissance Hotels. *Amenities:* Executive floor, 5 restaurants, 24-hour room service, large fitness center, indoor pool, rooms for disabled travelers, post office.

★★ Ritz-Carlton

2100 Massachusetts Ave. NW, Washington, DC 20008. ☎ 202/293-2100; 800/241-3333; fax: 202/293-0641. 206 rooms. Metro: Dupont Circle. AE, D, DC, MC, V. **$$$$$**.

Al Gore lived here when it was the Fairfax Hotel and his uncle owned it. Al's cousin Louise designed the clubby Jockey Club, Nancy Reagan's favorite lunch spot. In short, this Embassy Row landmark has good connections plus reasonably large rooms furnished with Federal and Empire antiques and reproductions, a dignified exercise room, and 2 floors of ultraluxury rooms with a private lounge that serves 5 meals a day. *Amenities:* Executive floors, restaurant, 24-hour room service, fitness center, tennis and golf privileges, complimentary newspapers, rooms for disabled travelers, in-room data ports.

Ritz-Carlton Pentagon City

1250 S. Hayes St., Arlington, VA 22202. ☎ 703/415-5000; 800/241-3333; fax: 703/415-5060. 345 rooms Metro: Pentagon City. AE, D, DC, MC, V. **$$$$**.

This 18-story hotel, 5 minutes from National Airport and 10 minutes from downtown D.C., has Virginia-horse-country decor and views of Washington you can't get in Washington. Public areas are filled with art and antiques; guest room furniture is inspired by Chippendale. The hotel is part of the Pentagon City Fashion Centre, a posh mall anchored by Nordstrom and Macy's, with some 150 stores and 6 movie screens. *Amenities:* Executive floor, restaurant, 24-hour room service, exercise room, lap pool, golf privileges, complimentary newspaper, in-room data ports, rooms for disabled travelers, free limo service to National Airport, Rosslyn, and Crystal City.

Sheraton International at BWI Airport

7032 Elm Rd., Baltimore, MD 21240. ☎ 410/859-3300; 800/325-3535; fax: 410/859-0565. 196 rooms. AE, D, DC, MC, V. **$$**.

The price is right at the only hotel on BWI grounds, a contemporary-style full-service property that does all it can to help you forget you're stuck in an airport. Our recommendation for BWI stays isn't connected to the terminal, but the terminal is only minutes away via free shuttles. Also free shuttle service to light rail (Baltimore Metro) to Baltimore. *Amenities:* Restaurant, 24-hour room service, exercise room, outdoor pool, jogging area, in-room data ports.

Sheraton Suites

801 N. St. Asaph St., Alexandria, VA 22314. ☎ 703/836-4700; 800/325-3535; fax: 703/548-4514. 249 rooms. A, D, DC, MC, V. **$$$**.

Not the cheapest hotel but best-for-the-buck near National Airport, all rooms in this red-brick high-rise are attractively furnished 2-room suites. Among the comforts of home are 2 phones, 2 TVs, a wet bar, fridge, and coffeemaker. It's located on the northern fringe of Alexandria, 2 miles south of National Airport. *Amenities:* Complimentary full breakfast buffet, exercise room, indoor pool, newspaper, in-room data ports, shuttles to airport and Old Town Alexandria.

Sheraton Washington

2600 Woodley Rd. NW, Washington, DC 20008. ☎ 202/328-2000; 800/325-3535, fax: 202/234-0015. 1,505 rooms. Metro: Woodley Park. AE, D, DC, MC, V. **$$$**

Washington's largest hotel, sprawling over 16 wooded acres of the Woodley Park neighborhood, 2 miles northwest of the White House, houses guests in 3 distinctive units. Request quarters in the 201-room, Deco-style Wardman Tower, which is a converted apartment building that 3 presidents (Hoover, Eisenhower, Lyndon Johnson) and 2 runners-up (Stevenson, Goldwater) have called home. Center Tower, with fountains and a sunny sprawling lobby that seems more Miami Beach than D.C., has 1,000 recently renovated rooms. Rooms in the Park Tower haven't been renovated but they cost less. Lots of discount packages, pools, parks, and proximity to the Metro and National Zoo make this a good deal for families, but when big conventions take over it's a zoo itself. *Amenities:* Executive floor, 2 restaurants and deli, 24-hour room service, fitness center, 2 outdoor pools, rooms for

disabled travelers, complimentary *USA Today*, in-room data ports.

Other Sheratons: **Sheraton City Centre** (22nd and M St. NW, Washington, DC 20037; ☎ 202/775-0800; fax: 202/331-9491; Metro: Foggy Bottom, Farragut North); **Sheraton National** (Columbia Pike and Washington Blvd., Arlington, VA 22204; ☎ 703/521-1900; fax: 703/521-2122); **Sheraton Premiere** (8661 Leesburg Pike, Vienna, VA 22182; ☎ 703/448-1234; fax: 703/893-8193); **Sheraton Reston** (11810 Sunrise Valley Dr., Reston, VA 22091; ☎ 703/620-9000; fax: 703/620-0696).

Sofitel Washington

1914 Connecticut Ave. NW, Washington, DC 20009. ☎ 202/797-2000; 800/424-2464; fax: 202/462-0944. 145 rooms. Metro: Dupont Circle. AE, D, DC, MC, V. **$$$$**

The elegant 1906 building above Dupont Circle spent 71 years as an apartment building before becoming the Highland Hotel, the Pullman, and since 1995, part of France's upscale Sofitel chain. Directly opposite the Washington Hilton & Towers—geographically and in spirit—the dignified and intimate Sofitel emphasizes service sufficiently attentive to please demanding French guests who occupy almost half the rooms and strain demand for 3 *chambres fumeurs* floors. *Amenities:* Restaurant, 24-hour room service, access to health club, in-room data ports.

★ St. James

950 24th St. NW, Washington, DC 200037. ☎ 202/457-0500; 800/852-8512; fax: 202/659-4492. 196 rooms. Metro: Foggy Bottom. AE, D, DC, MC, V. **$$$**

This all-suite Foggy Bottom hotel feels like home away from home, in part because it was an apartment building when it opened in the late 1980s. All units—studios and suites—have foyers, full-sized cook-in kitchens, and modern furniture you might actually buy for your own home. Half the rooms have balconies overlooking the pool. *Amenities:* Complimentary continental breakfast, fitness center, outdoor pool, in-room data ports.

★ Tabard Inn

1739 N St. NW, Washington, DC 20036. ☎ 202/785-1277; fax: 202/785-6173. 40 rooms, 25 with private bath. Metro: Dupont Circle. MC, V. **$/$$**.

The 3 contiguous Victorian townhouses on a quiet Dupont Circle street have been renting rooms since World War I. Of late it has turned into Washington's hippie hotel, its labyrinthine passages accessing rooms as quirkily furnished and configured as the guests. Largely thrift-minded envoys of leftish grass-roots organizations mingle in the cocktail lounge and in intimate de facto miniparlors, in nooks, and on landings. The restaurant features produce from Tabard Inn's own Virginia farm (meat and fish, too) plus homemade granola for breakfast. No room phones. No parking. *Amenities:* Restaurant, complimentary breakfast, access to health club.

Washington

15th St. and Pennsylvania Ave. NW, Washington, DC 20004. ☎ 202/638-5900; 800/424-9540; fax: 202/638-1595. 350 rooms. Metro: Metro Center, McPherson Square. AE, D, DC, MC, V. **$$$**.

Opened in 1918 and completely restored in 1988, the Washington is as close as most of us will ever get to sleeping in the White House. The Corner Bar sits at the end of a block-long big-city hotel lobby filled with ferns and inviting furniture groupings. Rooms have a traditional look, with marble baths, lace curtains and 2-poster beds; some have views of the Mall or White House grounds. Rates are moderate for the immediate President's neighborhood, but seem high for what you get. Sky Terrace, the city's only open-air rooftop restaurant, serves unexceptional light meals with a view, April through October. *Amenities:* Restaurant, rooftop in season, health club.

Washington Court on Capitol Hill

525 New Jersey Ave. NW, Washington, DC 20001. ☎ 202/628-2100; 800/321-3010; fax: 202/879-7918. 264 rooms. Metro: Union Station. AE, D, DC, MC, V. **$$$**.

One memorable feature of this Capitol Hill ex-Sheraton is a grand entrance that slopes down polished stairs to an atrium lobby. Another one is direct access from the lobby to the National Library of Education, one the largest of its kind. Rooms have bars or full kitchen and marble-appointed baths with phones and TVs. Some upper rooms have Capitol dome views. Not the best choice on Capitol Hill—character deficiencies—but a decent standard business-class hotel. *Amenities:* Restaurant, exercise center, complimentary daily newspaper, in-room data ports.

Washington Dulles Airport Marriott

333 W. Service Rd., Chantilly, VA 22021. ☎ 703/471-9500; 800/

228-9290; fax: 703/661-8714.
370 rooms. AE, D, DC, MC, V.
$$.

The best place to stay at Dulles Airport, 20 miles west of downtown, is the hotel closest to Dulles Airport—12 minutes to the terminal under ideal conditions. Tennis, swimming, basketball, volleyball, softball, and horseshoes are available on the premises, 21 acres of the rolling Virginia countryside. Golf, horseback riding, and indoor racquet sports available nearby. *Amenities:* Executive floor, restaurant, exercise room, indoor and outdoor pools, lighted tennis courts, free parking, free airport shuttle, in-room data ports.

Washington Hilton & Towers

1919 Connecticut Ave. NW, Washington, DC 20009. ☎ 202/483-3000; 800/445-8667; fax: 202/265-8221. 1,123 rooms. Metro: Dupont Circle. AE, D, DC, MC, V. **$$$**.

If you like the electricity and noise and bodies in motion of a big-time convention hotel, you will absolutely love this Hilton. This hilltop honeycomb above Dupont Circle has been the city's major convention site since it opened in 1965. Along with the city's largest ballroom (the one President Reagan was leaving when John Hinckley shot him on March 30, 1981) the Washington Hilton has decidedly unconventional, resort-hotel features such as a 25-meter outdoor pool with poolside cafe, tennis courts, and jogging track. If you haven't seen it since 1994, you won't recognize the place. A massive renovation project opened up the lobby, and transformed and renamed restaurants and bars. Guest rooms were renovated too, but

the rooms facing south still have Mall views. *Amenities:* Executive floor, large health club, outdoor pool, lighted tennis courts, 3 restaurants plus seasonal outdoor cafe, in-room data ports.

Washington Vista

1400 M St. NW, Washington, DC 20005. ☎ 202/429-1700; 800/847-8232; fax: 202/785-0786. 400 rooms. Metro: McPherson Square. AE, D, DC, MC, V. **$$$$**.

Opened in 1983 as the Vista International, its claim to notoriety came on January 18, 1990, when the FBI video-taped Mayor Marion Barry, Jr. smoking crack cocaine in room 727. Located on Thomas Circle, not far from the convention center, K Street, and the White House, its selling points include a foliage-filled lobby that sim-ulates a town square, suites designed by Hubert Givenchy, and a high level of luxury for the buck. *Amenities:* Executive floor, 3 restaurants, health club, 24-hour room service, rooms for disabled travelers, in-room data ports.

Watergate

2650 Virginia Ave. NW, Washington, DC 20037. ☎ 202/965-2300; 800/424-2736; fax: 202/337-7915. 235 rooms. Metro: Foggy Bottom. AE, D, DC, MC, V. **$$$$$**.

Heavy on pomp and name recognition, the hotel is part of the sawtooth complex that also includes an office building (once Democratic National Committee headquarters), condos (where Bob Dole lives), and a posh boutique mall. Down the hill from the State Department, next to Kennedy Center, and upriver from Water Gate where visiting dignitaries once disembarked from river craft, the hotel brims with the overstated elegance favored by upper-crust diplomats and industrialists. Large guest rooms offer river, Georgetown, or interior garden views, some from private balconies. The Watergate lost some allure in mid-1996 when it lost Michelin 2-star chef Jean-Louis Palladin and his 2 world-renowned eponymous restaurants, Jean-Louis at the Watergate and Palladin by Jean-Louis. *Amenities:* 2 restaurants, large fitness center, indoor pool, complimentary limo service weekdays, 24-hour room service, rooms for disabled travelers, complimentary newspaper, in-room data ports.

★ Westin

2350 M St. NW, Washington, DC 20037 ☎ 202/429-0100; 800/228-3000; fax: 202/857-0127. 263 rooms. Metro: Foggy Bottom, Dupont Circle. AE, D, DC, MC, V. **$$$$**.

This West End property was the Grand Hotel until early 1996. The former Westin that became the ANA Hotel in 1990 is across the street from the former Grand/present Westin. It was the most expensive hotel to build per room when it was built in 1984. Bathrooms are huge, marbled, absolutely fabulous, with vast steeping tubs and separate showers. The rest of the hotel and its service are catching up. At this point it's a toss-up between the Westin and ANA for best in the West End. *Amenities:* Outdoor pool, fitness center, 2 restaurants, 24-hour room service, rooms for disabled travelers, in-room data ports.

★★ Willard Inter-Continental

14th St. and Pennsylvania Ave. NW, Washington, DC 20004-1010. ☎ 202/628-9100; 800/327-0200; fax: 202/637-7326. 341 rooms. Metro: Metro Center. AE, D, DC, MC, V. **$$$$$**.

A block from the White House, the Willard looms large in Washington history. Julia Ward Howe composed "Battle Hymn of the Republic" here,

Willard Inter-Continental

and President Grant coined "lobbyists" to describe pests who assailed him with personal pleas in the lobby. That was the old Willard; the "new" one that replaced it in 1901 was where Martin Luther King, Jr. wrote his "I Have a Dream" speech. History notwithstanding, the hotel closed its doors in 1968 and didn't reopen—completely restored to original Beaux-Arts glory and under Inter-Continental management—until 1986. American history is all well and good but it is White House proximity and international-class service standards and business amentities that have lured some 60 heads of state (usually to State Department-vetted 6th-floor suites) since the reopening. Guest rooms are furnished with mahogany Queen Anne reproductions; some overlook the Mall (no White House views). Best place to stay by far is on the tourist side (Pennsylavania Ave.) of the White House, which is more fun than the business side (16th and K Streets). Round Robin Bar is a hangout for contemporary historians (i.e., reporters); local jazz musicians play the Nest Lounge. *Amenities:* 2 restaurants, 24-hour room service, complimentary newspaper, fitness center, access to indoor pool, rooms for disabled travelers, in-room data ports.

Sights & Attractions

How to Use This Section

On the following pages, Washington's top sights and places of interest are arranged in alphabetical order. They're classified by subject on pages 75 to 77. Bear in mind that certain less major sights do not have their own entries, but are mentioned as part of a district, such as **Georgetown,** or a walk in **Walks in Washington, D.C.** These sights can be found in the index at the end of this book.

We've given 2 stars (★★) to must-sees, 1 star (★) to places of special interest.

Entries without addresses and opening times are described more fully elsewhere in this guide.

For First-Time Visitors

Washington, D.C.'s top 10 major attractions:

The Capitol Building

Library of Congress

National Air and Space Museum

National Gallery of Art

National Museum of American History

Supreme Court

U.S. Holocaust Memorial Museum

Vietnam Veterans Memorial

Washington Monument

The White House

Orientation Tours

Washington/Arlington Cemetery Tour   The Tour-mobile (☎ 202/544-5100) offers sightseeing tours of Washington and Arlington Cemetery, as well as tours of the cemetery only. The combination tour stops at 15 different sights on or near the Mall and 3 sights at Arlington Cemetery: the Kennedy gravesites, the Tomb of the Unknowns, and Arlington House.

You can board a Tourmobile at 15 different loca-tions: the White House, the Washington Monument, the Arts and Industries Building/Hirshhorn Museum, the National Air and Space Museum, Union Station, the Capitol, the National Gallery of Art, the Museum of Natural History, the Museum of American History, the Bureau of Engraving and Printing/U.S. Holocaust Memorial Museum, the Jefferson Memorial, West Potomac Park, the Kennedy Center, the Lincoln Me-morial/Vietnam Veterans Memorial, and Arlington National Cemetery. You pay 1 fare when you first board the bus; during the course of the day, you can get on and off along the loop as much as you like. The buses serve each stop every 20 to 30 minutes. Well-trained narrators give commentaries about sights along the route and answer questions.

Tourmobiles operate daily year-round. From June 15 to Labor Day, they run from 9am to 6:30pm; after Labor day, 9:30am to 4:30pm. From April to Septem-ber, service to and from Arlington Cemetery starts at 8:30am and ends at 6:30pm; the rest of the year, hours are 8am to 4:30pm. A combination tour ticket is $10 for adults, $5 for children 3 to 11; for the cemetery tour only, it's $3 for adults, $1.50 for children. Kids under 3 ride free. From June 15 to Labor Day, you can buy a ticket after 4pm good for the rest of the after-noon and the following day ($12 for adults, $6 for chil-dren); the rest of the year, the same offer is available after 2pm.

Other Tourmobile Tours   Tourmobiles also run round-trip to Mount Vernon from April to October. Coaches depart from the Arlington National Cemetery visitors center and the Washington Monument at 10am and 2pm. The price is $17 for adults, $8.25 for chil-dren, including admission to Mount Vernon. A combi-nation tour of Washington, Arlington Cemetery, and Mount Vernon is $31 for adults, $15.50 for children—cheaper than the Gray Line equivalent.

The Frederick Douglass National Historic Site Tour runs from June 15 to Labor Day, and includes a guided tour of Douglass's home, Cedar Hill. Buses leave from Arlington National Cemetery and the Washington Monument at noon. Adults pay $5; children, $2.50. A 2-day combination Frederick Douglass and Washington–Arlington National Cemetery Tour is available at $20 for adults, $10 for children.

For both the Mount Vernon and Frederick Douglass tours, you must reserve at least an hour in advance.

Old Town Trolley Tours　A service similar to Tour-mobile's is the Old Town Trolley Tour of Washington (☎ 202/682-0079). For a fixed price, you can get on and off these green-and-orange vehicles as often as you like at 16 locations in the District, plus Arlington National Cemetery. Most stops are at or near major sightseeing attractions, including Georgetown. The trolleys operate 7 days a week: Memorial Day to Labor Day from 9am to 5pm; the rest of the year, 9am to 4pm. The cost is $16 for adults, $8 for ages 5 to 12, free for children under 5. The full narrated tour takes 2 hours, and trolleys come by each stop every 20 to 30 minutes. Stops are made at Union Station, the Hyatt Regency Hotel (near the National Gallery), the Pavilion at the Old Post Office, the Grand Hyatt (Chinatown), the FBI Building, the J. W. Marriott (near the Renwick and the Corcoran), the Hotel Washington (near the White House), the Capital Hilton (near the Geographic Society), the Washington Hilton (near the Phillips Collection and Adams Morgan restaurants), the Park Gourmet Washington (near the National Zoo), Washington National Cathedral, the Georgetown Park Mall, Washington Harbour, Lincoln Memorial, U.S. Holocaust Memorial Museum, the Holiday Inn Capitol Hill (near Mall museums), and the Libary of Congress. You can board without a ticket and purchase it en route.

Special-Interest Tours

Washington After Dark　Gray Line (☎ 202/389-1995) offers a 3-hour bus tour of the night-lit national monuments and federal buildings.

Spirit of Washington Cruises　Pier 4, at 6th and Water St. SW (☎ 202/554-8000). The *Spirit of Washington* offers daily harbor cruises from early March to December. The luxury harbor cruise ship is climate-controlled and has carpeted decks, 3 well-stocked bars, and huge panoramic windows designed for sightseeing. Lunch and dinner cruises include a 20-minute high-energy musical revue. Call for exact schedule and departure times, and to make advance reservations.

The Mount Vernon Cruise   This popular half-day excursion aboard the *Spirit of Washington*'s equally luxurious sister ship, the *Potomac Spirit,* takes in D.C. sights en route to Mount Vernon plantation, George Washington's beautiful estate on the Potomac. The trip is about $1^1/_2$ hours each way. The round-trip fare is $21.50 for adults, $19.25 for seniors, $12.75 for children 6 to 11, free for children 5 and under. Prices include entrance to Mount Vernon. It's a good idea to book in advance.

D.C. Ducks   This company offers unique land-and-water tours of Washington aboard a World War II–era amphibious army vehicle (basically a boat with wheels) that accommodates 30 passengers. Ninety-minute guided tours aboard the open-air canopied craft include the major sights—the Capitol, Lincoln Memorial, Washington Monument, the White House, and Smithsonian Museums—and a 30-minute Potomac cruise. Tours are offered from April to November, and leave from 1323 Pennsylvania Ave. NW. (☎ 202/966 3825). Departures are Monday to Friday at 10am, noon, 2pm, and 4pm; and Saturday and Sunday hourly between 10am and 4pm. Tickets are $16 for adults, $14 for seniors over 64, and $8 for kids under 13.

Scandal Tours   Gross National Product, D.C.'s brilliantly talented political-comedy group, offers a guided bus tour of Washington's sleaziest sites. Highlights include the White House, where the focus is on presidential sex scandals; the Old Executive Office Building, where Ollie North and Fawn Hall shredded their way into history; the Tidal Basin, where Former congressman Wilbur Mills and "Argentine firecracker" Fanne Foxe cavorted in the moonlight (she fell into the water; he got in hot water); the Capitol steps, scene of a night of passion for John and Rita Jenrette (congressman Jenrette was later entrapped by Abscam and, still later, caught shoplifting in a department store); the FBI ("Janet Reno" talks about J. Edgar Hoover, "another man in a dress"); the Washington Vista hotel, where Mayor Marion Barry repeatedly protested, "The bitch set me up"; Watergate (of course); and Gary Hart's townhouse, from which he emerged with Donna Rice one morning to find himself in the twilight of his political career. The 90-minute tours depart every Saturday at 1pm (call for reservations and departure point). The cost is $27 per person. Or you can buy "Scandal Tour In-A-Box" for $12.95 and take the tour yourself by car. To order or make your reservations, call 301/ 587-4291.

Best Bets for Kids

Capital Children's Museum

The Capitol Building

Dolls' House and Toy Museum

The Mall

National Air and Space Museum

National Aquarium

National Museum of Natural History

National Zoological Park

Washington Monument

The White House

Special Moments

The C&O Canal   Hike or bike along the scenic tree-lined canal towpath from Georgetown to Fletcher's Boat House (about 3 miles), where there are picnic tables and grills. Spend the day—bring kites, watercolors, a good book, whatever. Bikes can be rented from Big Wheels at 1034 33rd St. NW.

A Day in Alexandria   Just a short distance (by Metro or car) from the District is George Washington's Virginia hometown. Roam the quaint cobblestone streets, browse charming boutiques and antique stores, visit the boyhood home of Robert E. Lee and other historic sites, and dine in one of Alexandria's fine restaurants.

Afternoon Tea   Nothing is more totally self-indulgent than lingering over sweets in the middle of the day: fresh-baked scones with Devonshire cream, pastries, finger sandwiches, and more. Try Café Promenade at the Renaissance Mayflower hotel (☎ 202/ 347-3000).

The Lincoln Memorial After Dark   During the day, hordes of rambunctious schoolchildren detract from this monument's grandeur; at night, the experience is infinitely more moving.

D.C. Attractions

Experience the Earth Revolving   The Foucault Pendulum at the National Museum of American History proves empirically that the earth is actually revolving; don't miss it.

The Phillips Collection   Housed in a turn-of-the-century Georgian-Revival mansion, this museum is a gem, displaying many impressionist and modernist works in a charming residential setting. Plan your visit for the morning, have a relaxing tapas lunch at the elegant Gabriel nearby, and in the afternoon tour Anderson House, a palatial turn-of-the-century mansion filled with Belgian tapestries woven for Louis XIII, Ming Dynasty jade trees, and other treasures. It's open Tuesday through Saturday from 1 to 4pm.

Embassy Row   Head northwest on Massachussetts Avenue from Dupont Circle. It's a gorgeous walk along tree-shaded streets lined with beaux-arts mansions. Built by fabulously wealthy magnates during the Gilded Age, most of these palatial precincts today are occupied by foreign embassies.

Organizing Your Time

Washington's main sights are mostly concentrated in a relatively small area. The following are suggested 2-day and 4-day schedules.

Two-Day Visit

Day 1

Climb the **Washington Monument** in the morning for an introductory bird's-eye view of the city.

Visit one of a bewildering range of **Smithsonian** museums. Have lunch in the **Old Post Office Building** and, if stamina permits, climb the tower for another panoramic view.

Spend the afternoon in Georgetown and, if the season is right, take a boat trip on the **Chesapeake and Ohio Canal.**

Have dinner at one of **Georgetown's** numerous restaurants, concentrated along M Street and Wisconsin Avenue.

Day 2

First visit the **Capitol,** then take a Tourmobile tour of the **Mall.** You can stop off at any number of museums, but do not miss the **National Gallery of Art,** which, in addition to a superb collection, has several decent restaurants for lunch.

If time permits, visit the **National Archives,** immediately to the northwest, then have an early supper followed by a bus tour of Washington after dark, or go to the theater or a nightclub (see "The Arts" and "D.C. After Dark").

Four-Day Visit

Day 1
As per 2-day visit.

Day 2
In the morning, see the **Capitol** and the **Supreme Court.** In the afternoon, visit the **Library of Congress,** then take a Tourmobile to the **National Gallery of Art,** the **National Archives,** and any of the other museums on the North Mall.

In the evening, take a tour of the city by night. Alternatively, see an opera, ballet, or play at the **Kennedy Center,** dining at its rooftop restaurant.

Day 3
Spend the morning at the **National Air and Space Museum** and perhaps a few of the other museums on the South Mall.

Have lunch at one of the museum restaurants, then, if it's between March 15 and December 22, walk South to Pier 4 (6th and Water St. SW) and take the boat down to Mount Vernon (check beforehand when the boat is sailing, by calling Washington Boat Lines, ☎ 202/554-8000). A new 600-passenger ship serves meals, but there are also a number of recommended seafood restaurants on the waterfront.

If you have time after dinner, see a play at one of the theaters at the nearby and nationally-known **Arena Stage.**

Day 4
In the morning, take the Tourmobile to **Arlington National Cemetery** and visit **Arlington House.** You'll want to leave the cemetery by lunchtime, as there are no places to eat there.

Spend the afternoon exploring the quaint old town of **Alexandria,** and finish up with dinner in one of its many good restaurants.

Sights & Attractions by Category

Districts
Chinatown
Georgetown
Old Downtown

Federal Buildings
Bureau of Engraving and
  Printing
★★ Capitol

Congress
Executive Office Building
★ Federal Bureau of
   Investigation
★ National Archives and
   Records Administration
The Pentagon
State Department
★★ Supreme Court
Treasury Building

Galleries, Museums & Historic Houses

Anacostia Neighborhood
   Museum
Anderson House
Arlington House
★ Arthur M. Sackler Gallery
Arts Club of Washington
Arts and Industries Building
Blair-Lee House
B'nai B'rith Klutznick
   Museum
★ Capital Children's Museum
Columbia Historical Society
Corcoran Gallery of Art
Daughters of the American
   Revolution
Decatur House
Department of the Interior
   Museum
Dolls' House and Toy Museum
★ Dumbarton Oaks
Frederick Douglass House
Freer Gallery of Art
Hillwood
Hirshhorn Museum and
   Sculpture Garden
Historical Society of
   Washington, D.C.
House of the Temple
Islamic Center
Lillian and Albert Small Jewish
   Museum
Museum of Modern Art of
   Latin America
★★ National Air and Space
   Museum
National Building Museum
★★ National Gallery of Art
National Geographic Society
   Explorers Hall
★ National Museum of
   African Art
★ National Museum of
   American Art

★★ National Museum of
   American History
★ National Museum of
   Natural History
National Museum of Women
   in the Arts
★ National Portrait Gallery
The Octagon
Old Pension Building
Petersen House
The Phillips Collection
Renwick Gallery
Textile Museum
★★ U.S. Holocaust Memorial
   Museum
Washington Project for the Arts
★★ The White House
Woodrow Wilson House

Historic Theaters

Ford's Theatre
★ Kennedy Center for the
   Performing Arts

Libraries

Folger Shakespeare Library
★★ Library of Congress

Memorials & Monuments

★ Jefferson Memorial
★ Korean War Veterans
   Memorial
★ Lincoln Memorial
Marine Corps War Memorial
Navy Memorial
Police Memorial
★★ Vietnam Veterans Memorial
★ Washington Monument

Parks & Gardens

★ Dumbarton Oaks
Kenilworth Aquatic Garden
Lady Bird Johnson Park and
   Lyndon Baines Johnson
   Memorial Grove
Lafayette Square
★★ The Mall
Meridian Hill Park
National Arboretum
Potomac Park
★ Rock Creek Park
Theodore Roosevelt Island
   and Memorial
United States Botanic
   Garden

Religious Buildings

Church of the Epiphany
Mormon Temple
National Shrine of the
  Immaculate Conception
St. Matthew's Cathedral
★ Washington National
  Cathedral

Other Sights

Arlington National Cemetery
Chesapeake and Ohio Canal
Fort Leslie J. McNair
National Aquarium
★ National Zoological Park
Navy Yard

Organization of American
  States
Pierce Mill
Rock Creek Cemetery
Smithsonian Institution
  Building
Union Station
United States Naval
  Observatory
Voice of America
Washington Convention
  Center
Washington Harbour
  Complex
Washington Post
Watergate Complex

Sights & Attractions by Neighborhood

Adams Morgan

★ National Zoological Park
Rock Creek Cemetery
★ Rock Creek Park

Anacostia

Anacostia Neighborhood
  Museum
Frederick Douglass House

Capitol Hill

★ Capital Children's Museum
★★ Capitol
Folger Shakespeare Library
★★ Library of Congress
★★ Supreme Court
United States Botanic
  Garden

Chinatown

Chinatown
Washington Project for the
  Arts

Downtown

Church of the Epiphany
Old Downtown

Dupont Circle

B'nai B'rith Klutznick
  Museum
Fort Lesley J. McNair
Historical Society of
  Washington, D.C
House of the Temple
Islamic Center

The Phillips Collection
St. Matthew's Cathedral
Textile Museum
Woodrow Wilson House

Foggy Bottom/ West End

Arts Club of Washington
B'nai B'rith Klutznick
  Museum
Bureau of Engraving and
  Printing
Corcoran Gallery of Art
Daughters of the American
  Revolution
Department of the Interior
  Museum
Executive Office Building
★ Federal Bureau of
  Investigation
Ford's Theatre
★ Jefferson Memorial
★ Kennedy Center for the
  Performing Arts
★ Korean War Veterans
  Memorial
Lady Bird Johnson Park and
  Lyndon Baines Johnson
  Memorial Grove
Lafayette Square
Lillian and Albert Small Jewish
  Museum
★ Lincoln Memorial
Meridian Hill Park
Museum of Modern Art of
  Latin America
National Aquarium

★ National Archives and
   Records Administration
National Building
   Museum
★ National Museum of
   African Art
★ National Museum of
   American Art
National Museum of Women
   in the Arts
★ National Portrait
   Gallery
Navy Memorial
Navy Yard
The Octagon
Organization of American
   States
The Pentagon
Petersen House
Pierce Mill
Police Memorial
Potomac Park
Renwick Gallery
State Department
Treasury Building
Union Station
★★ U.S. Holocaust Memorial
   Museum
United States Naval
   Observatory
Voice of America
Washington Convention
   Center
★ Washington National
   Cathedral
Washington Post
Watergate Complex
★★ The White House

Georgetown
Chesapeake and Ohio Canal
Dolls' House and Toy Museum
★ Dumbarton Oaks
Washington Harbour Complex

The Mall
★ Arthur M. Sackler Gallery
Arts and Industries Building
Freer Gallery of Art
Hirshhorn Museum and
   Sculpture Garden
★★ The Mall
★★ National Air and Space
   Museum
★★ National Gallery of Art
★★ National Museum of
   American History
★ National Museum of
   Natural History
Smithsonian Institution
   Building
★★ Vietnam Veterans Memorial
★ Washington Monument

Upper Northwest
Hillwood

Maryland
Mormon Temple

Virginia
Arlington National Cemetary
Arlington House
Marine Corps War Memorial
Theodore Roosevelt Island
   and Memorial

Washington, D.C.'s Sights and Attractions A to Z

Anacostia Neighborhood Museum
1901 Fort Place SE, Washington, DC 20560. ☎ 202/287-3382 or
202/357-2700 for certain exhibitions. Open daily 10am–5pm. Closed:
Christmas. Admission free. Metro: Anacostia.

This lively museum on the southeast side of the
Anacostia River hosts temporary exhibits of works by
African-American artists and others. Established in 1967
as part of the Smithsonian Institution, the museum has
gained wide respect.

Arlington House (Custis-Lee Mansion)

Arlington National Cemetery, Arlington, VA 22211. ☎ 703/557-0613. Group tours by reservation. Open Apr–Sept 9:30am–6pm; Oct–Mar 9:30am–4:30pm. Admission free. Metro: Arlington Cemetery.

The view from the portico of this lovely mansion set on a hill in **Arlington National Cemetery** was claimed by L'Enfant, the designer of the city, to be the finest in the world. Don't miss it. Since 1955, the mansion has been a permanent memorial to Robert E. Lee, the Civil War Confederate commander who was widely admired both north and south of the Mason-Dixon line.

The house, with its massive Doric-columned portico, was built between 1802 and 1817 by George Washington Parke Custis, stepson of George Washington. Custis was an agriculturalist, painter, playwright, and orator. His portrait hangs over the fireplace in the family dining room, and some of his own paintings are also on view; for example, his dark hunting scenes in the center hall.

Custis's daughter, Mary, married Robert E. Lee in the family parlor in 1831, and the house was the Lee family home from then until the Civil War. Here, wrote Lee, "my affections and attachments are more strongly placed than at any other place in the world." It was here that he took his painful decision in 1861 to leave the U.S. Army and offer his services to Virginia. After that he never returned to the house.

During the Civil War the house was occupied by the Union Army of the North. It was later confiscated in lieu of property taxes, then won back by Lee's son through the Supreme Court and finally sold by him to the federal government.

The original atmosphere of a gracious Virginian family home has been painstakingly re-created, complete with staff dressed in 19thC costume. Some of the original furnishings have been returned, while others are similar period pieces or copies. The servants' quarters are on the south side of the circular drive. Across the garden is a small museum illustrating the history of the house and the life of Robert E. Lee.

Arlington National Cemetery

Arlington, VA 22211. ☎ 703/979-0690. Open Apr–Sept 8am–7pm; Oct–Mar 8am–5pm. Admission free. Accessible by Tourmobile. Metro: Arlington Cemetery.

A serene and dignified environment for a last resting place, the national military cemetery is approached by the Arlington Memorial Bridge with its dramatic gold statues at either end, and through the splendid gateway, built under President Franklin D. Roosevelt's Work Project Administration (WPA). The rolling, wooded slopes have row upon row of small, simple gravestones and white crosses, interspersed occasionally with larger and more imposing monuments. Burial here is now restricted to certain categories of people and their dependents: members of the armed forces who have served in a foreign war, Medal of Honor recipients, and important government or political figures.

The cemetery was formerly the estate of **Arlington House,** home of Robert E. Lee, which still dominates the area. The U.S. government took over the estate on the outbreak of the Civil War and in 1865 began using it as a national cemetery. It now honors the dead of both armies in the Civil War. A Confederate monument, in bronze and granite, surmounted by a female figure facing south, stands on the west side of the cemetery near McPherson Drive. To the south of the house, a huge granite sarcophagus marks a vault containing 2,111 unknown dead of the Civil War. Anonymous victims of more recent wars are commemorated by the Tomb of the Unknown Soldier, a chastely carved marble block standing before the Arlington Memorial Amphitheater, watched over constantly by soldiers of the Third Infantry who, in a fine display of military drill, change guard every half-hour during the day in summer and every hour in winter.

The most-visited graves are those of President John F. Kennedy and his wife Jacqueline Kennedy Onassis, which lie off Sheridan Drive on the slope below Arlington House. Marked by an eternal flame, JFK's famous grave is approached by a terrace with a curving wall inscribed with words from Kennedy's Inaugural Address. The modest grave of JFK's brother, Robert F. Kennedy, is nearby. A little farther up toward the house is the tablelike gravestone of Major Pierre L'Enfant, commanding a splendid view over the city that he planned.

★ Arthur M. Sackler Gallery

1050 Independence Ave. SW, Washington, DC 20560. ☎ 202/357-2700 (central Smithsonian information). Open 10am–5:30pm. Closed Christmas. Admission free. Metro: Smithsonian.

The focus of this new museum, which opened in 1987, is the art of the Near and Far East. New York psychiatrist and medical publisher Dr. Arthur M. Sackler pledged his collection of 1,000 Asian and Near Eastern works to the Smithsonian and donated $4 million toward the construction of an underground museum to house the collection. The museum is part of the handsome new Quadrangle complex behind the Smithsonian Castle, which also houses the **National Museum of African Art.** The Sackler Gallery complements the already strong Oriental collection of the neighboring **Freer Gallery of Art,** but has more 20thC works as well as visiting exhibitions. It shares the same curatorial and conservation staff, research facilities, and library. The library is open to the public Monday to Friday from 10am to 5pm (☎ 202/357-2091).

Arts Club of Washington

2017 I St. NW, Washington, DC 20006. ☎ 202/331-7282. Open Tues–Thurs 10am–5pm, Wed–Fri 2–5pm, Sat 10am–2pm, Sun 1–5pm. Closed: Mon; holidays. Admission free. Metro: Foggy Bottom, Farragut West.

This organization, whose aim is to support the arts in the greater Washington area, occupies 2 adjoining historic houses. Number 2017 was built between 1802 and 1805 and served for a time as the Executive Mansion under President James Monroe. Next door, number 2015 was built around 1870. Apart from their interest as period houses, the buildings house a permanent collection of works by Washington artists, as well as changing exhibitions of work by contemporary artists from Washington and elsewhere.

Arts and Industries Building

900 Jefferson Dr. SW, Washington, DC 20560. ☎ 202/357-2700 (central Smithsonian information). Open 10am–5:30pm. Closed Christmas. Admission free. Metro: Smithsonian.

A.K.A. "the Castle," this quintessentially Victorian structure (dig the turrets and polychromatic brickwork) is the second oldest of the Smithsonian buildings on the **National Mall.** It was completed in 1881, in order to house objects given to the Smithsonian from the U.S. International Exposition (held in 1876 to mark the centenary of Independence), and extensively restored in 1980.

Its 4 wings, radiating out from a central rotunda, and resplendent with fountain and potted plants, contain a startling selection of objects illustrating the wonders of 19thC inventiveness, brought from all over America and abroad. Pennsylvania is represented by objects as diverse as a railroad locomotive and a model of the Liberty Bell made out of sugar.

There is another Liberty Bell made of tobacco from North Carolina, a bale of cotton from Mississippi, optical instruments from Paris, and silverware from England. The growing pride in American industrial might that was felt in 1876 is reflected in the impressive array of steam-powered machinery, from pumping engines to printing presses. There are also some fine models of ships, particularly the 45-foot model of the naval cruiser *Antietam*. Frequent performances of films, puppetry, drama, dance, mime, and singing are presented in the **Discovery Theater** (☎ 202/357-1500 for details). Like the other Smithsonian museums, the Arts and Industries Building holds temporary exhibits and lectures, and has a well-stocked gift boutique.

B'nai B'rith Klutznick Museum

1640 Rhode Island Ave. NW, Washington, DC 20036. ☎ 202/857-6583. Open Sun–Fri 10am–5pm. Closed: Sat; Jewish and state holidays. Admission free. Metro: Farragut North.

This is the world headquarters of the B'nai B'rith (Sons of the Covenant), an international organization existing for the purpose of "uniting Jews in their highest interests and those of humanity." Judaica of all kinds is the theme of the museum. Frequent temporary exhibitions are held on various aspects of Jewish life and history. There is also a permanent exhibition of more than 400 objects: ancient Jewish pottery and coins, ritual implements, regalia, silverware, and much more. The museum store sells Jewish-American craftwork. Behind the museum is the Harold and Sylvia Greenberg Sculpture Garden.

Bureau of Engraving and Printing

Wallenburg Place, 15th and C St. SW, Washington, DC 20228. ☎ 202/447-9709 or 9976. Open Mon–Fri 9am–2pm. Closed: Sat–Sun; Christmas; New Year's Day. Admission free. Metro: Smithsonian. Tourmobile: Washington Mall.

The average life of a dollar bill is only 18 months, so the presses at the Bureau of Engraving and Printing, the U.S. government's security printer, stay busy replenishing the supply of banknotes. The world's largest establishment of its kind, it employs 3,500 people and operates 24 hours a day, using state-of-the-art technology. The bureau also prints Treasury Bonds, postage stamps, White House invitations, government certificates, and other official documents. Coins are produced not here but at the Mint, whose works are in Philadelphia, Denver, and San Francisco.

The self-guided tour of the building takes you along glassed-in galleries overlooking rooms where stamps and banknotes roll off huge presses and where bills are stacked ready for circulation. "This stack contains

"$6,400,000 in $20 bills," a recorded voice tantalizingly announces.

Free samples are not available. But in the souvenir store you can buy a small bag containing the shreddings from $150 worth of bills.

★ Capital Children's Museum

800 3rd St. NE, Washington, DC 20002. ☎ 202/543-8600. Open daily 10am–5pm. Closed major holidays. Admission free. Metro: Union Station.

One of the world's top kid-magnets, and good for them, too. If your child is itching to design computer graphics, write with a quill pen, run a printing press, or design a radio or television program, he or she can do it here, and much else besides. The Animation Lab reveals some of the secrets of creating cartoon characters. In the museum's computer section, each child sits in front of a screen with a computer keyboard and, under the guidance of instructors, can learn how to make pictures on the screen using different colors and shapes. There is also a talking computer. "My name is Wisecracker," it intones in an eerie, science-fiction voice, "come talk to me." It will then repeat whatever you type into it, even gibberish. The museum always provides free craft activities and, on many weekends, puppet shows and other special events.

★★ The Capitol

East end of Mall on Capitol Hill. ☎ 202/225-6827. Open June–Labor Day 9am–8pm; rest of year 9am–4:30pm. Closed some major holidays. Admission free. Metro: Capitol South or Union Station.

> **Emily was staring. 'The Capitol,' she said with reverence. Behind them Union Station, and its triumphal arches, behind them the central figures of Freedom and Imagination. The Capitol faced east. The dome was a massive bubble swimming in a golden heat haze.**
> —*Faith Baldwin,* **Washington, USA,** *1942*

The Capitol, seat of the Congress, was appropriately made the center of L'Enfant's plan of Washington, with all the streets numbered or lettered outward from it. Unlike the **White House,** it is unashamedly grand, standing on the hill that L'Enfant once described as "a pedestal waiting for a superstructure," its vast white dome surmounted by a figure representing Liberty. Its grandeur does not intimidate but rather encourages the visitor to enter and admire the place where the supreme

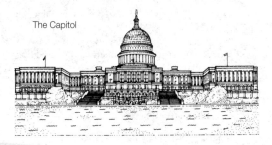

The Capitol

lawmaking body of the richest nation on earth meets, deliberates, and decides.

Even with increased precautions against terrorist attacks, how many other legislative buildings in the world are so freely accessible? To view a session of the House of Representatives or the Senate, U.S. citizens need a pass from their representative in Congress; overseas visitors require their passports or other identification (Congress is usually in session Jan–Oct, with occasional recesses).

The Capitol evolved piecemeal over many years. It was begun in 1793 to a design by the amateur architect Dr. William Thornton, one of a series of nine architects who shaped the building. By 1800 it was sufficiently far advanced for the House and Senate to move there from Philadelphia. The Supreme Court and the Library of Congress also used the building in the early days. In 1814 British forces set fire to the Capitol, and, although saved from total destruction by a heavy rainfall, it needed extensive rebuilding. By 1819 it was once again ready for occupation. Since then frequent modifications have been made. In the 1860s the old copper-covered wooden dome was replaced by the present cast-iron one, and in 1962 the east side was extended by 32 feet.

The point of departure for tours is the huge rotunda beneath the dome. A white marble disc in the center of the floor marks the spot where many presidents have lain in state. Among the works of art in the rotunda are statues of American statesmen, and 8 large paintings depicting scenes from American history. The four by John Trumbull of events from the revolutionary period are particularly interesting, as the artist was present on each occasion. The center of the dome also has a remarkable painting, *The Glorification of the Spirit of George Washington* by the Italian artist Constantino Brumidi, an immigrant who worked for 25 years on the Capitol's interior.

To the south of the rotunda is the Statuary Hall, filled with statues commemorating worthy citizens of various states. This room, formerly the House chamber, has a remarkable acoustic property called a parabolic reflection, which enabled John Quincy Adams (later president) to eavesdrop on members of the opposition. A brass disc marks the spot where Adams sat, and where he died. Stand here on the Whispering Spot and listen while the guide speaks very quietly from the other side of the room—you will be surprised at how clearly the voice carries.

Ascend to the next floor by one of the building's four grand staircases, and enter the visitors' galleries of both the Senate (in the north wing) and the House of Representatives (in the south wing). The Senate chamber seems surprisingly small, but there are only 100 senators—two for each state, irrespective of size. It is restrained in decor except for the huge tasseled canopy over the chair of the Speaker (who is always the U.S. vice-president). The much larger House chamber has some interesting decorative features including a frieze of medallions depicting great lawgivers of history from Moses to Thomas Jefferson. It is here that the president addresses the joint session of Congress. There is a fixed number of 435 representatives; each represents a given number of people within a given area rather than a state. The 2 houses are equal in legislative power.

The Senate offices are in 3 buildings north of the Capitol: the Russell Building, in use since 1909, the Dirksen Building, completed in 1958, and the Hart Building, occupied in 1982. These are connected to the Capitol by a special subway train, which the public can use. The representatives have their offices in the Cannon, Longworth, and Rayburn buildings to the south (dating from 1908, 1933, and 1965, respectively), which are connected to the Capitol by pedestrian tunnels. A special book-conveyor tunnel links the Capitol with the **Library of Congress.**

One last thing, if you visit the Senate cafeteria, try a bowl of the famous Senate bean soup—it has become a Capitol institution.

The Capitol is surrounded by a fine park, superbly laid out by the landscape architect Frederick Law Olmsted in 1872. To the west the land drops away in terraces to a pool overlooked by the dramatic bronze monuments to General (and later President) Ulysses S. Grant, showing a Civil War battle with the intrepid Grant surveying the scene from his horse. Note also, at the foot of the slope, just to the northwest of the Capitol building, the arched entrance to the Grotto, once a source of water for thirsty travelers, now used to provide municipal water. In the section of the park north of Constitution Avenue is an attractively terraced area with a large fountain; immediately west of this is a monolith commemorating Senator Robert A. Taft of Ohio and designed by Douglas W. Orr in 1959. It houses 27 bells, which chime every 15 minutes. Politicians and the public enjoy the Capitol park for its serenity and charm.

Chesapeake and Ohio Canal

Begins in Georgetown s of M St. ☎ 301/739-4200 (for information on canal near metropolitan D.C.) or 301/299-3613 (for information on upper canal). Two canal boats, *Georgetown* and *Canal Clipper,* operate mid-Apr–mid-Oct. ☎ 202/472-4376 (information and reservations).

The C&O Canal was originally intended to connect the Potomac with the Ohio River. Construction began in 1828 but ceased in 1850 once the canal had reached Cumberland, Maryland, a distance of 184 miles. Most of its length runs parallel to the Potomac. Although never a great financial success, it did carry goods such as grain, timber, and coal before commercial traffic stopped in 1924.

Today it is appreciated as one of the best-preserved old American canals. Now designated a National Historical Park, it has a new identity as a recreational facility, its paths used by walkers, joggers, cyclists, and bird-watchers.

At its Georgetown end, the canal is lined with picturesque houses, new condominiums, and chic restaurants. A short distance farther on, it enters more rural surroundings. Wildlife and history enthusiasts find much to engross them along the canal's banks.

The canal is ideal for an afternoon excursion or a week-long hike, and there are "hiker-biker" overnight campgrounds roughly every 5 miles, as well as 3 drive-in campgrounds. The Great Falls Tavern (☎ 301/299-3613; open 9am–5pm; closed holidays) houses a museum and a visitors center. Other visitors centers on the canal are located in Georgetown between Thomas Jefferson Street and 30th Street NW, and at the terminal in Cumberland, Maryland. They provide useful information about conducted walks and evening programs.

Chinatown

H and I streets NW (between 5th and 7th streets).

Optimistic promoters of D.C.'s dwindling Chinatown recently installed a grandiose gateway over H Street, funded in part by the People's Republic of China. A million dollars' worth of fierce dragons and colorful tiles, it heralds the presence of a handful of restaurants purveying Hunan, Szechuan, and Cantonese cookery.

The continuing eastward redevelopment of Old Downtown, spurred by the opening of the new Convention Center, has gobbled at the edges of what was once a 10-square-block Chinese enclave. What remains is a short strip of H and I streets NW between 5th and 7th streets, with a declining number of dingy side-street shops on its perimeter. An estimated 500 Chinese still live in the neighborhood, less than 1% of the total residing in the metropolitan area.

Architect Alfred Liu, who designed the dragon arch as well as a pair of matching columns of white marble at the other end of the street, has been influential in the continuing renovation of the broader area, a mix of old Germanic-style row houses and new office buildings with Chinese motifs.

Church of the Epiphany

1317 G St. NW, Washington, DC 20005. ☎ 202/347-2635. Open 10am–2pm. Sun services 8am, 11am. Organ recitals: Tues 12:10pm except during Lent, when there are services daily at noon. Metro: Metro Center.

A century ago this lovely neo-Gothic Episcopal church was attended by Washington's upper crust. Today, as the **Old Downtown** area steadily revives, the church is once again coming into its own. It has a graceful, soothing interior, lit by rich stained-glass windows, and possesses a fine pipe organ.

Corcoran Gallery of Art

17th St. and New York Ave. NW, Washington, DC 20006. ☎ 202/638-3211. Open Tues–Sun 10am–4:30pm; Thurs until 9pm. Closed: Mon; Christmas; New Year's Day; Thanksgiving afternoon. Donation suggested. Metro: Farragut West.

Recently made famous—or infamous—by the nationally-publicized Robert Mapplethorpe censorship flap, the Corcoran, which is not part of the Smithsonian empire, is one of the major galleries in the United States. Founded by the banker W. W. Corcoran in 1859, it was formerly housed in what is now the **Renwick Gallery** and later moved to its present building, an imposing edifice designed by Ernest Flagg in the palatial, classical style of the Beaux Arts school.

The collection divides into European and American sections. The former, enriched by the acquisition of the W. A. Clark collection in 1928, includes Renaissance works by Titian and others, 17thC Dutch and Flemish masters, British works of art by, among others, Gainsborough, Turner, and Raeburn, and French paintings up to the impressionists, including a particularly rich collection of Corots. There are also Greek and Egyptian figurines, Beauvais and Gobelins tapestries, majolica ware, stained glass from Soissons Cathedral, and an entire room of articles of the Louis XVI period, complete with Marie Antoinette's harpsichord, brought from the Hotel de la Tremoille in Paris.

The American collection is one of the nation's finest and reveals the extraordinary richness and diversity of American art. To view these works is to catch a glimmer of the soul of America. The collection embraces the stiff, amateurish portraiture of early colonial days, the romanticized Western scenes of Albert Bierstadt, the strange visionary works of Elihu Vedder, and the tranquil landscapes of the so-called Luminous School of 19thC artists. All the great names of American art are here: Winslow Homer, Mary Cassatt, John Singer Sargent. A surprising inclusion is Samuel F. B. Morse, inventor of the Morse code as well as a talented painter. His Old House of Representatives, an atmospheric painting of the chamber lit by candlelight, hangs in the main hallway. Contemporary American artists are well represented: They include Louise Nevelson, Joseph Cornell, Jules Olitski, and Helen Frankenthaler, among others. Temporary exhibitions are also held here.

The Corcoran is the only accredited art school in Washington, offering both full-time courses and classes for students at any level. Evening recitals are given, generally on Friday, in its acoustically fine auditorium. A courtyard cafe has recently been added, and the Sunday gospel brunch is as fine a time as you're likely to have in D.C.

Custis-Lee Mansion (See Arlington House)

Daughters of the American Revolution (DAR)

1776 D St. NW, Washington, DC 20006. ☎ 202/628-1776. Open Mon–Fri 8:30am–4pm; Sun 1–5pm. Closed Sat. Tours Mon–Fri 10am–3pm; Sun 1–5pm. Admission free. Metro: Farragut West or Farragut North.

The DAR is an organization of women whose direct ancestors helped in the struggle for American independence. The address and telephone number of its headquarters, which covers an entire city block, both contain the date 1776, the year of the Declaration of

Independence. Three connecting buildings occupy the site: the Administration Building; the Memorial Continental Hall, an imposing Beaux Arts edifice built in the early 1900s; and Constitution Hall, a 1920s' neoclassical building by John Russell Pope, which is used for conferences, concerts, and other cultural events.

The museum has 33 period rooms, representing various states of the Union and furnished in different styles. Their contents reflect the craftsmanship and decorative arts of America before the Industrial Revolution. They include a Californian adobe parlor of 1860, a 1775 Massachusetts bedroom, and a kitchen from an Oklahoma farmhouse complete with an assortment of 19thC kitchenware. A popular series of rooms, especially with children, is the New Hampshire attic with its marvelous collection of toys, dolls, and games.

The museum gallery contains permanent and changing exhibits from the museum's extensive decorative arts collection. The superb genealogical library is open to the public for a small fee.

Department of the Interior Museum
18th and C St. NW, Washington, DC 20240. ☎ 202/208-4743. Open Mon–Fri 8am–4pm. Closed: Sat–Sun; holidays. Admission free. Adults must present identification, such as a driver's license. Metro: Farragut West or Foggy Bottom.

The agencies that come under the umbrella of this department and are represented in its museum include the National Park Service, U.S. Fish and Wildlife Service, Bureau of Reclamation, Geological Survey, Bureau of Mines, Office of Surface Mining, Bureau of Land Management, Bureau of Indian Affairs, and Territorial and International Affairs Office.

The museum building itself has a historic resonance that sets it apart from the rather dull government edifices that surround it. Created in 1930, it contains displays of 1930s' craftsmanship, including unusual brass detailing, documents and pictures illustrating the opening of the West, and mineral samples from different parts of the country. One of the most interesting sections deals with Native Americans, through a diorama of a Navajo settlement, baskets and pottery of Indian tribes of the American Southwest, and other Indian artifacts. The museum shop sells attractive, if expensive, Indian craftwork. The department also has a comprehensive library (open Mon–Fri 7:45am–5pm). The National Park Service office provides useful leaflets about its facilities.

Dolls' House and Toy Museum

5236 44th St. NW (1 block w of Wisconsin Ave. between Jenifer and Harrison streets), Washington, DC 20015. ☎ 202/244-0024. Open Tues–Sat 10am–5pm; Sun noon–5pm. Closed: Mon; major holidays. $4 for adults, $2 children under 12, $3 seniors. Metro: Friendship Heights.

Flora Gill Jacobs, author of *A History of Dolls' Houses,* founded this entrancing museum in 1975, using her own extensive collection, only part of which is on display at any one time. The remainder is used for special and seasonal exhibitions. The emphasis is on dollhouses, but many antique toys are also represented. Most of the objects are Victorian.

The museum provides not only nostalgic interest but also a fascinating glimpse in miniature into social and architectural history. There is a terrace of typical Baltimore row houses in bright-red brick, a milliner's store complete with minute hats, a circus tent with clowns, acrobats and performing animals, and a family house where each room is perfect in every detail from the curtain tassels to a tiny pack of playing cards on a table. The museum shops sell books, toys, dollhouses, and related accessories.

Downtown (See Old Downtown)

★ Dumbarton Oaks

1703 32nd St. NW, Washington, DC 20007 (entrance to the collections on 32nd St., between R and S streets; garden entrance at 31st and R streets). ☎ 202/338-8278. Garden (weather permitting): Nov–Mar, daily 2–5pm; Apr–Oct, daily 2–6pm. Collections: Tues–Sun 2–5pm. Closed federal holidays and Dec 24. $3 adults, $2 children under 12 and senior citizens; collections free. Bus: Georgetown routes.

Washingtonians treasure their visits to the splendid garden at Dumbarton Oaks, undoubtedly one of the most memorable in the United States, built on a dramatically terraced slope and enriched by trellises, pergolas, pools, gazebos, and a profusion of statuary and ornament.

This remarkable institution is the result of the vision of Ambassador and Mrs. Robert Woods Bliss, who bought the house in 1920, remodeled it to contain their art collection and created a deliciously romantic garden. In 1944 the name of Dumbarton Oaks flashed briefly across the news headlines of the world when its Music Room was used as the setting for the conference that gave birth to the United Nations.

The recently renovated museum, now a branch of Harvard University, has 2 main collections: one of Byzantine art, the other of pre-Columbian art. Each collection is linked with a research center and library. The pre-Columbian collection is housed in a newly built postclassical pavilion, ingeniously designed by Philip Johnson, and consisting of a cluster of 8 small circular rooms. Stand and talk near the center of any of the rooms and observe the curious reverberating sound effect. There are also other works of art that are not part of the main collections—for example, El Greco's *The Visitation,* which hangs in the Music Room. The room is still used for concerts: Call for the schedule.

The house also has a landscape garden department, which runs a research program and a library. Although the Dumbarton Oaks libraries are restricted to scholars, the public can view displays in the rare-book room.

Executive Office Building

17th St. and Pennsylvania Ave. NW, Washington, DC 20503. Closed to public. Metro: Farragut West.

A vast, hulking, ornate building, this tourist-confusing landmark lies just to the west of the White House. Designed by A. B. Mullet in French Second-Empire style and completed in 1888, its incongruity with the other federal buildings around it bothered Washingtonians for decades, and the building narrowly escaped demolition. Now, cleaned and restored, it houses White House staff and various government agencies. The public are not allowed inside, but they can admire the exuberance of its facades, which provides a refreshing change from the neoclassical mode so prevalent in Washington. The building is especially appealing when illuminated at night.

★ Federal Bureau of Investigation (FBI)

J. Edgar Hoover Building, 10th St. and Pennsylvania Ave. NW, Washington, DC 20535. ☎ 202/324-3447. Tours every 15–20 mins. Open Mon–Fri 8:45am–4:15pm. Closed: Sat–Sun; holidays. Admission free. Metro: Metro Center or Federal Triangle.

When the FBI building was opened, a *Washington Post* writer remarked that it would make a perfect stage set for a dramatization of George Orwell's *1984.* Since 1975 the national crime-fighting force of the United States has occupied a forbidding, buff-colored concrete building occupying an entire city block. It was named after the formidable J. Edgar Hoover, who became head of the FBI in 1924 and ran it with an iron hand until he retired in 1972 at the age of 77.

Despite its austere building, the FBI does an excellent job in projecting to visitors its image of "Fidelity,

Bravery, Integrity." And the FBI tour is one of the most popular in the city. Friendly (for the FBI), uniformed young guides usher you through a startling series of exhibits, such as an arsenal of criminal weapons, a rogues' gallery of famous villains, including Al Capone, John Dillinger, and Bonnie & Clyde as well as a current list of America's 10 Most Wanted fugitives with their photographs (one visitor recognized his next-door neighbor). Some frightening statistics are given: a murder occurs in the United States every 23 minutes, a rape every 6 minutes, a burglary every 8 seconds. The reassurance offered is that wherever you are in the country an FBI agent can be on the spot within an hour.

The bureau deals with a variety of offenses including interstate flight, espionage, obscene telephone calls, and certain types of fraud, as well as matters such as requests for political asylum. It will also help local police forces investigate such crimes as kidnapping, rape, and murder. The FBI's resources include highly sophisticated laboratories (seen on the tour) where anything from blood to paint samples can be analyzed. The tour ends in the firing range, with an impressive display of sharp-shooting by an FBI agent.

Folger Shakespeare Library

201 E Capitol St. SE, Washington, DC 20003. ☎ 202/544-7077 (library), 202/546-4000 (theater box office). Open Mon–Sat 10am–4pm. Closed federal holidays. Admission free. Metro: Capitol South or Union Station.

Like so many other great American institutions of learning and culture, this one is the creation of a businessman with a dream: the late Henry Clay Folger, oil tycoon and Shakespearean scholar.

Its vast library of Shakespearean and Renaissance works is open to scholars only, but there is an exhibition gallery in the style of an Elizabethan great hall where many of Folger's treasures are displayed in rotation—books, manuscripts, portraits, and relics.

The library's Globe Theater, a faithful replica of the Shakespearean playhouse, occasionally stages plays by the Bard as well as by contemporary dramatists. The Folger is also a center for poetry readings, concerts, and lectures. The shop sells everything from busts of the Bard and Shakespearean slogan T-shirts (the most popular being that "let's kill all the lawyers" line) to books on the Renaissance. Note the simple elegance of the 1930s' exterior, with its series of reliefs of scenes from the plays.

Ford's Theatre

511 10th St. NW, Washington, DC 20004. For information ☎ 202/426-6924; tickets ☎ 202/347-4833 or 800/448-9009. Museum open daily 9am–5pm. Closed Thanksgiving and Christmas. Admission free. Metro: Metro Center.

This is the theater where President Abraham Lincoln was assassinated on the night of April 14, 1865, while he sat watching the comedy, *Our American Cousin.* As the house exploded into laughter at the words "sockdologizing old mantrap," another explosion was heard from the box to the right of the stage, where Lincoln sat. John Wilkes Booth, noted actor and Confederate fanatic, had entered the box and shot Lincoln in the head. Booth jumped from the box, breaking a leg, and fled through a back door, escaping on horseback. Some days later the Cavalry caught up with him, and he was shot while attempting to resist arrest.

The attractive theater is now owned by the National Park Service. Restored in the 1960s to its original appearance by producing director Frankie Hewitt, who has made the theater her life's work, Ford's again functions as a vital theater as well as a somewhat macabre museum. During the day visitors can view the auditorium and the fateful box and hear a short lecture on the assassination. In the basement are 2 exhibitions. One, focusing on Lincoln's life and career, has memorabilia (including an eerie plaster death mask), documents, and a taped commentary. The other, relating to Booth and the other conspirators, includes the murder weapon, a small Derringer pistol. (See also Petersen House.)

Fort Lesley J. McNair

4th and P St. SW, Washington, DC 20319. ☎ 202/693-8214. Not open to public.

Founded in 1791, this is the oldest functioning military post in America. The fort now houses the prestigious National War College, the Industrial College of the Armed Forces, the Inter-American Defense College, and the headquarters of the U.S. Army Military District of Washington. On a peninsula between the Washington Channel and the Anacostia River, it contains some impressive buildings, notably the War College—a rather forbidding redbrick structure with a vast portico, incongruously overlooking a little golf course for military personnel. Although the public cannot enter the buildings, the fort is worth a detour to drive through.

Frederick Douglass House (Cedar Hill)

1411 W St. SE, Washington, DC 20020. ☎ 202/426-5960 (house), 202/426-5961 (group tour reservations). Open Apr–Labor Day 9am–5pm; rest of year 9am–4pm. Closed: Christmas; New Year's Day. Admission free. Tourmobile. Metro: Anacostia.

The whole house is redolent of the spirit of a very remarkable man: Frederick Douglass (1817–95) was the leading spokesman for Americans of African descent in their struggle for freedom and justice during the 19thC. He lectured and wrote books about his own early life under slavery, campaigned tirelessly for abolition, helped recruit blacks for the Union army during the Civil War, and finally settled down to a distinguished old age in Washington. He lived first in A Street, in a frame house that later for a time housed the National Museum of African Art, then he bought Cedar Hill, this elegant white house on a height overlooking the Anacostia River. All the furnishings, except for the curtains and wallpaper, are original. Douglass's library and other belongings are still in situ. On arrival you are directed to the visitors center at the foot of the hill where a film is shown about Douglass's life, and books on black liberation, including Douglass's own, are on sale.

Freer Gallery of Art

1200 Jefferson Dr. SW, Washington, DC 20560. ☎ 202/357-2700 or 2020. Open daily 10am–5:30pm. Closed Christmas. Admission free. Metro: Smithsonian.

Most noted for housing the world's most important collection of James McNeill Whistler's work, the recently-renovated Freer was founded by the connoisseur and railroad-car manufacturer, Charles Lang Freer, who in 1906 donated his collection of exquisite Oriental art and Whistler paintings to the nation. The building, opened in 1923, is a low, gray structure in the style of a Florentine palace, surrounding a tranquil little courtyard. The Freer also houses a superb collection of 19thC Oriental, and a fine collection of 19th- and early 20thC American art. A new exhibition gallery now connects the Freer with the adjacent **Arthur M. Sackler Gallery** of Asian art, and the museums share most of the same staff and facilities.

Georgetown

Her imagination in those early days fastened itself on certain of these Georgetown dwellings. As the first dying leaves of October swirled on the rusty

> brick sidewalks and streets and the
> lamplights flickered in the dusk, she
> walked down the hill from Rock Creek
> Park toward her own apartment,
> admiring those mansions and quaint old
> townhouses and the clapboards with
> coach lamps and gabled roofs and
> dormers and brightly colored doors
> which to her seemed touched, ever so
> fragilely, with age and influence.
>
> —*Willie Morris,* **The Last of the**
> **Southern Girls,** *1973*

Georgetown is one of those urban villages, like Montmartre in Paris, that are almost as famous as the cities to which they belong.

In fact Georgetown, which was founded in 1751 and named after George II of England, predates Washington. Like its Paris counterpart, Georgetown is elegant and gracious in parts, while fraying to brash commercialism in others, in this case along the main drags of Wisconsin Avenue and M Street NW.

The best approaches to Georgetown are over the P or Q Street bridges into the prettiest part of the area, whose tree-lined, brick-paved streets with rows of neat houses have more than an echo of Georgian London. Solidly residential, save for an occasional recherché little shop, these hushed streets seem to wait perpetually for the twilight hour when congresspeople, lawyers, heiresses, and ambassadors gather in softly lit rooms for predinner cocktails and the gossip of power. Number 1607 28th St. was once the home of Senator Edward Kennedy. His brother John lived at 3307 N St., farther up to the west, before he became president.

Walk uphill to the north and you will pass many large, gracious mansions. Most of these are private homes, but an exception is Dumbarton House (2715 Q St.; ☎ 202/337-2288. Donations welcomed. Open Mon–Sat 9am–12:30pm. Closed: Aug; Christmas–New Year; holidays), not to be confused with nearby Dumbarton Oaks, the museum and garden (see above). A fine early Federal house of about 1799, Dumbarton House is now headquarters of the Colonial Dames of America, who preserve it as a museum with 18th- and 19thC furnishings, domestic objects and memorabilia.

Farther uphill, with its entrance in R Street, is Oak Hill Cemetery, a serene place with a romantic atmosphere reminiscent of Pere Lachaise. Next to the cemetery is the quiet oasis of Montrose Park, on the west side of which is Lover's Lane, leading down to the even more secluded Dumbarton Oaks Park. Dumbarton Oaks estate, with its museum and glorious gardens, is immediately to the west of Montrose Park.

In the opposite direction is the southern part of Georgetown and the environs of the Chesapeake and Ohio Canal. One of the most interesting historical buildings in this area is the **Old Stone House** (3051 M St. NW; ☎ 202/426-6851. Open Wed–Sun 9:30am– 5pm. Closed some major holidays). Now supervised by the National Park Service, this is believed to be the only surviving pre-Revolutionary building in D.C. Once a cabinetmaker's home and workshop, it has 5 rooms furnished in typical 18thC manner and a spacious garden at the back. Tour guides wear period costume.

On leaving this cozy haven you enter the commercialized environs of M Street, a thoroughfare which, together with the intersecting Wisconsin Avenue, represents the bustling, pleasure-seeking side of Georgetown. These streets are lined with boutiques, bars, discos, cafes, and restaurants with French names. At 3222 M St., backing onto the canal, is Georgetown Park, which is not a park but a multilevel modern development with shops and restaurants surrounding a central skylit atrium. Its prolonged construction, involving the demolition of several elderly buildings, aroused much controversy, but there is no denying that it is stylish and lively.

To the west of Wisconsin Avenue are more quiet, residential streets, and on the western fringe of the

Old Stone House

district is the prestigious, Jesuit-run Georgetown University, the oldest Catholic university in the United States. The main building, Healy, with its soaring Victorian Gothic spires, is one of the landmarks of western Washington, especially beautiful when viewed from George Washington Parkway or the Kennedy Center.

Hillwood

4155 Linnean Ave. NW, Washington, DC 20008. ☎ 202/686-5807. Tours available Tues–Sat (reservations required). Children under 12 not admitted. $10 donation suggested. Metro: Van Ness, then walk 1 mile.

Hillwood is a dazzling museum that was once the home of a dazzling woman: Marjorie Merriweather Post's life was the stuff of which Hollywood movies are made. Daughter of Charles William Post, founder of the Post Cereal Company, she inherited a fortune, beauty, and a taste for high living and high art. One of her 4 husbands, Joseph E. Davies, was Ambassador to the Soviet Union from 1937 to 1938. During their stay in Moscow she laid the foundation for her great collection, which focused mainly on the art of Imperial Russia and that of 18thC France. She acquired Hillwood in 1955 and enlarged it so that her collection could be installed there. After her death in 1973 the house became a museum, as she had intended.

Tours of the house, lasting about 2 hours, are limited to 25 people at a time, so reserve well in advance. The tour begins at the visitors center, where a film is shown about the collection and its creator, then proceeds through the house itself. The rooms on show include the Pavillon, where Marjorie Post used to hold square dances and show movies to her dinner guests; the French Drawing Room, in Louis XVI–style, with Beauvais tapestries, a chair from the household of Marie Antoinette, and a charming portrait of the Empress Eugenie by Winterhalter; the Porcelain Room, containing dinner services used by Catherine the Great; and the Icon Room, which has a staggering display of icons, chalices, Fabergé jeweled Easter eggs and other treasures. The more domestic rooms remain redolent of the privileged life lived here. The collection contains a number of portraits of Marjorie Post herself, a striking woman even in old age.

The museum has 3 annexes. One is a copy of a Russian dacha or country house containing more Russian works of art. The second annex houses the paintings, sculptures, and furnishings collected at the turn of the century by C. W. Post. The third, added in 1983, contains American Indian artifacts formerly exhibited by Marjorie Post at Topridge, her camp in the Adirondacks. There are also a gift store and a greenhouse with plants for sale.

The 25 acres of beautifully landscaped grounds are a delight, embracing a French formal parterre, rose garden, Japanese garden, pet cemetery, and many meandering paths and secluded corners.

Hirshhorn Museum and Sculpture Garden

Independence Ave. and 7th St. SW, Washington, DC 20560. ☎ 202/357-2700. Open daily 10am–5:30pm; Sculpture Garden 7:30am–dusk. Closed Christmas. Admission free. Metro: L'Enfant Plaza.

This is one of the world's most exciting places in which to look at modern art. The collection, one of the largest ever assembled by a private individual, was a gift to the U.S. government from the late Joseph Hirshhorn, a Latvian immigrant who made a fortune in uranium. A ravenous and independent-minded collector, he ignored fashion and stuck to gut reaction. The result is a collection of rare breadth and impact.

The building housing the collection, opened to the public in 1974 under the umbrella of the Smithsonian Institution, is a daring piece of work: a great concrete drum (or donut) on 4 massive legs. Some said it spoiled the **Mall,** but as the Smithsonian's then secretary S. Dillon Ripley said, "If it were not controversial in almost every way it would hardly qualify as a place to house contemporary art. For it must somehow be symbolic of the material it is designed to encase."

A useful orientation film, 12 minutes in length, is shown continuously in a room on the lower level. Only about 900 out of the many thousands of works in the collection can be shown at any one time. These are displayed in the galleries on the 2nd and 3rd floors—paintings in the artificially-lit outer circle, sculptures in the inner circle looking onto the courtyard. The emphasis is on American and contemporary artists, including Milton Avery, Stuart Davis, Robert Henri, Edward Hopper, Sol Le Witt, Richard Estes, Frank Stella, Kenneth Nolan, and so on. Many are by immigrant artists such as Josef Albers, Willem de Kooning, and Max Weber. But European artists are not under-represented. They include Balthus, Francis Bacon, Jean Dubuffet, Georg Grosz, Ren, Magritte, and Joan Miro.

The outside of the building is windowless, save for a 70-foot balcony and window commanding a superb view to the north across the Mall. On the museum's plaza are some monumental works of sculpture, including a huge, brightly colored, angular metal creation by Mark di Sivero entitled Isis, 42 feet high and weighing 30 tons. The plaza's outdoor cafe is open in the summer.

Other works of sculpture, many of them figurative bronzes, are displayed in the delightful sunken Sculpture Garden, opposite the museum on the other side of Jefferson Drive. This quiet oasis, with its lawns, pool, and greenery, is a marvelous environment in which to contemplate such works as Rodin's *Burghers of Calais,* Matisse's series of Backs and a number of Henry Moore's Reclining Figures.

Historical Society of Washington, D.C. (Christian Heurich Memorial Mansion)

1307 New Hampshire Ave. NW, Washington, DC 20036. ☎ 202/785-2068. Open Wed, Fri–Sat noon–4pm. Closed: Mon–Tues, Thurs, Sun; holidays. $3 adults, $1.50 seniors, children under 12 free. Metro: Dupont Circle.

Of all the great Washington houses open to the public, this is one of the most opulent. Since 1956 this assertive 31-room Romanesque Revival manse has been the home of what was formerly known as the Columbia Historical Society, founded in 1894 to record, teach, and preserve the historical heritage of Washington, D.C. The society maintains an extensive library of Washingtonia, publishes a periodical, *Records of the Columbia Historical Society,* and holds lectures. Appropriately, the house it occupies is itself a historic monument, which the society has maintained while keeping the decor and furnishings as close to the original as possible.

The house was built in the 1890s by Christian Heurich, a German immigrant who made a fortune as a brewer. His home combined advanced technological features, such as a poured concrete shell for protection

Historical Society

against fire, with an almost regal lavishness of decoration, carried out by German-American builders and craftsmen. The 3 floors of rooms open to the public include the Dining Room, with its rich woodwork, and the Blue Parlor resplendent with elaborate plaster moldings, a delicately painted ceiling, and original family furnishings. An added attraction is the charming garden, which is entered from Sunderland Place and used as a park by local people.

Holocaust Museum
(See U.S. Holocaust Memorial Museum)

House of the Temple

1733 16th St. NW, Washington, DC 20009. ☎ 202/232-3579. Open Mon–Fri 8am–4pm. Tours 8am–2pm last 2hrs. Closed: Sat–Sun; holidays. Admission free. Metro: Dupont Circle.

One of the true wonders of Washington: Everyone wonders, "What is *that?*"

The richly symbolic world of Freemasonry is powerfully exemplified in this building, headquarters of the Supreme Council of the 33rd Degree of the Scottish Rite of Freemasonry for the Southern Jurisdiction of the United States (to abbreviate an even longer title). The building, designed by the brilliant neoclassical revivalist John Russell Pope, was based on the Mausoleum at Helicarnassus in Asia Minor, one of the Seven Wonders of the ancient world, and thus complements the George Washington Masonic Memorial, inspired by another of the Seven Wonders, the Pharos Lighthouse. Pope's building is the more distinguished of the two (in fact he received a medal for it): a great square stone structure, surrounded by 33 Ionic columns and rising to a pyramidal roof. The imposing bronze door is approached by a long flight of steps guarded by 2 sphinxes representing Wisdom and Power.

The interior is equally impressive, especially the main Temple Room, a soaring chamber decorated with immense lavishness; the windows, for example, are glazed not with glass but with alabaster. Various museum rooms contain Masonic memorabilia and a superb library of books on masonry and related subjects. More unexpected is one of the world's greatest collections of books on and by the Scottish poet (and Freemason) Robert Burns.

Islamic Center

2551 Massachusetts Ave. NW, Washington, DC 20008. ☎ 202/332-8343. Open 10am–5pm. Closed Fri to non-Muslims. Metro: Dupont Circle. Metrobus: Massachusetts Ave.

Amid the discreet opulence of Massachusetts Avenue with its many embassies and mansions, there stands a corner of the Middle East, marked by a slender minaret. This is the Islamic Center, comprising a mosque, library, study center, and bookstore, which was built between 1949 and 1953 on the initiative of the ambassadors from leading Muslim nations. The construction was overseen by the Egyptian Ministry of Works, and the designer was an Italian expert on Islamic architecture, Mario Rossi, who himself became a Muslim late in life. Every Muslim country contributed money and objects.

The magnificent mosque room boasts carpets from Iran, tiles from Turkey, and a superb brass chandelier from Egypt. When entering the mosque, visitors must remove their shoes, and women must dress so as to expose only their hands and faces. The staff of the center are friendly and pleased to inform visitors about their religion.

Iwo Jima Statue (See Marine Corps War Memorial)

★ Jefferson Memorial

Tidal Basin, W. Potomac Park. ☎ 202/426-6821. Open daily 8am–midnight. Closed Christmas. Admission free. Tourmobile. Metro: Smithsonian, then a 20-minute walk.

Famously surrounded by cherry trees, this attractive monument was a cause *célèbre* at the time it was built. When in the 1930s it was decided to erect a memorial to America's third president, the site chosen was a point on the Tidal Basin directly south of the White House, forming the lower point of a cross whose other points were marked by the Lincoln Memorial, the White House, and the Capitol. The architect was John Russell Pope, designer of the west wing of the **National Gallery of Art** and of the Masonic **House of the Temple.** His elegant design for a shallow-domed neoclassical rotunda immediately aroused opposition. The Commission of Fine Arts condemned both site and design,

Jefferson Memorial

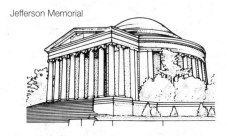

modernist architect Frank Lloyd Wright called it an "arrogant insult to the memory of Thomas Jefferson," and a group of female conservationists threatened to chain themselves to the cherry trees that stood in the way of construction.

But the project had the strong support of President Roosevelt, who admired Pope's building and wanted it in exactly that spot. If a tree was in the way, he said, "We will move the tree and the lady and the chains and transplant them to some other place." And so the building went ahead, although Pope did not live to see its completion in 1943.

The monument is a delight, with its ring of Ionic columns and its airy interior dominated by Rudolph Evans's vast bronze statue of Jefferson, that Renaissance man who, among other things, was architect, states-man, inventor, and botanist. Around the inner frieze are his words: "I have sworn upon the altar of God eternal hostility against every form of tyranny over the mind of man."

Works on Jefferson, postcards, and memorabilia are available at a small bookstall in the basement. On many summer evenings, military band concerts are given on the steps of this most serene monument.

Kenilworth Aquatic Garden

Kenilworth Ave. and Douglass St. NE, Washington, DC 20019. ☎ 202/426-6905. Open 7am–sunset. Admission free. Metro: Deanwood.

Washington's secret garden: Located on the edge of the Anacostia River opposite the National Arboretum, this too-often-overlooked and eerily beautiful nature re-serve consists of a series of ponds divided by paths. Water lilies, water hyacinths, lotuses, and a variety of other aquatic and waterside plants grow here in abundance, producing glorious blooms in spring, summer, and fall. It is best to visit the garden in the early morning, as many of the tropical flowers close during the day. The wildlife includes fish, turtles, frogs, muskrats, opossums, and raccoons.

★ Kennedy Center for the Performing Arts

New Hampshire Ave. and Rock Creek Pkwy., Washington, DC 20566. Tickets and information ☎ 202/467-4600 or 800/444-1324; tourist information ☎ 202/416-8300; restaurants ☎ 202/833-8870. Open daily 10am–midnight. Metro: Foggy Bottom.

The most surprising thing about this great cultural com-plex overlooking the Potomac is that it was not built many years earlier. Until it was opened in 1971,

Kennedy Center for the Performing Arts

Washington had no major center for the performing arts and was regarded as something of a backwater when it came to music, opera, and drama—an extraordinary state of affairs for a great world capital. To remedy the situation, a scheme for a national cultural center was initiated under Eisenhower in 1958 and received active support from John F. Kennedy. But, initially lacking congressional funding, the project progressed painfully slowly, until Kennedy's assassination in 1963, and the decision to turn the center into a memorial to him, finally spurred Congress into voting the money to finish it. The Kennedy family recently donated $1 million toward a monument in the center commemorating the handicapped.

The building was designed by the prominent architect Edward Durrell Stone and built on a grand scale. Two vast transverse halls connect with an even vaster Grand Foyer opening onto the river terrace and with access to the 3 main auditoriums: The Eisenhower Theater, the Opera House, and the Concert Hall. The American Film Institute Theater is on the ground floor, and the top floor has an intimate 500-seat auditorium called the Terrace Theater and a good library of the performing arts.

The National Symphony Orchestra, the Kennedy Center Orchestra, and the Washington Opera are based here. But the center is also host to many great companies and orchestras from all over the world. Materials, decorations, and fittings were donated by various countries: marble from Italy for the walls, chandeliers from Sweden and Austria, mirrors from Belgium, curtains from Japan, tapestries from France. The overall design of the building is a huge rectangle in plain white marble, surrounded on all sides by an immensely broad colonnade of slender metal pillars. It has the austere monumentality of a design by Albert Speer, but with a lightness of touch that saves it from being forbidding. From the roof terrace, there is a stunning view over the city and across the Potomac.

Some still scoff at the center and its design. Its furnishings and decorations undoubtedly do have a touch of department-store gaudiness; and the great rough-cast bronze head of Kennedy that dominates the Grand Foyer is not to everyone's taste. But these are minor quibbles. The Kennedy Center is a triumph, not least in the way that it has brought Washington into the major league of world cities in the fields of music, opera, and drama.

★ Korean War Veterans Memorial

Just across from the Lincoln Memorial (e of French Dr., between 21st and 23rd streets NW). Rangers on duty 8am–midnight daily. Admission free. Metro: Smithsonian.

This gets my vote as the most beautiful site to visit at night. Almost as much controversy raged over the design for this long overdue memorial, which opened in summer 1995, as over the nearby **Vietnam Veterans Memorial.** Finally, however, architect Kent Cooper's plan, revising the winning design of a team of architects from Pennsylvania State University, was accepted by the Commission of Fine Arts. Visitors walk between sculptor Frank Gaylord's row of soldiers, silhouetted against a 180-foot-long granite wall etched with a mural by Louis Nelson. The wall and sculptures flow into 2 semicircles of trees around a circular pool with an inscribed stone and an American flag.

Lady Bird Johnson Park and Lyndon Baines Johnson Memorial Grove

George Washington Memorial Pkwy. Open 8am–sunset.

Looking across the Potomac at Washington, sited on a long, narrow island running parallel to the Virginia shore of the river near Arlington Cemetery, this park was dedicated in 1968 to Mrs. Johnson, a lover of the countryside. Despite the noise from the hectic George Washington Memorial Parkway, which runs through the island, this is a refreshing place, which blazes every year with daffodils and flowering dogwood.

At the southern end of the park is a memorial grove named after Lyndon Baines Johnson. In the center is a monument to LBJ in the form of a pink granite monolith, large and rough-hewn like the man himself. There used to be a button you would push and Lady Bird's recorded voice would rhapsodize about the "big monument" across the river.

Lafayette Square

Pennsylvania Ave. and 16th St. NW. Metro: McPherson Square or Farragut West.

With the White House on its southern side, this square park is one of the focal points of Washington. The

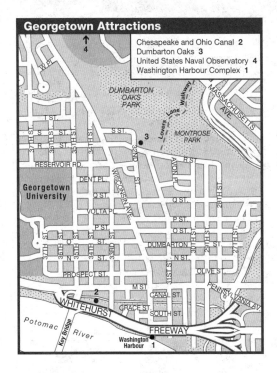

Georgetown Attractions

Chesapeake and Ohio Canal **2**
Dumbarton Oaks **3**
United States Naval Observatory **4**
Washington Harbour Complex **1**

equestrian statue in the center of the park is not of Lafayette but of Andrew Jackson, hero of the War of 1812 and later the first "log-cabin" president. Lafayette himself is portrayed in one of four statues, at the corners of the square, of foreigners who fought in the American Revolution. The others are Comte de Rochambeau, another Frenchman; Baron von Steuben, a Prussian; and Koscinszko, a Pole. The park is a pleasant, leafy oasis in the busy heart of the city, where office workers picnic, chess games are played, tent-dwelling demonstrators proclaim their various causes, and increasing numbers of homeless people simply exist.

This squirrel-ridden square was once the center of high social life in Washington (and was a gay meeting place at the turn of the century), but is no longer residential, and only its western side retains its facade more or less intact. This is thanks to President Kennedy, who prevented its demolition.

There's been some other, quite substantial, changes made to the park area, due to the security breaches of 1995—planes crashing into the White House, people taking shots at the house, more people than usual trying to climb over the fence. . . . The Secret Service decided enough is enough and decided to block the 2-block area of Pennsylvania Avenue in front of the White House to traffic. This threw the local traffic into a tizzy, but provided an unexpected bonus: The street in front of the White House serves as an extension of Lafayette Park, and people can bike and rollerblade in front of the White House.

The **Decatur House,** at the northwest corner of Lafayette Park, is open to the public. Its architect, Benjamin Latrobe, also designed St. John's Episcopal Church on the north side, which was completed in 1816 and is known as the "Church of the Presidents." Pew 54 has been reserved for worshipers from the White House since President Madison started the tradition. With its crisp, classical design, delicate wooden bell tower, and serene white interior, St. John's is one of the most pleasing churches in the city.

Another building worth noticing, although it is not open to the public, is Dolley Madison House at the corner of Madison Place and H Street. The widow of the president lived here from 1837 to 1849, a tireless socialite to the last.

★★ Library of Congress

10 1st St. SE, Washington, DC 20540. ☎ 202/707-5458. Open Mon–Fri 8:30am–9:30pm, Sat 8:30am–6pm. Call ahead for tour information. Closed: Sun; most major holidays. Admission free. Metro: Capitol South.

> **They crossed the green park to the new Library of Congress recently opened, glittering with mosaic, gorgeous with Pompeian red . . . hour after hour passed by, and still they had not half seen it all, the endless corridors, the wide, shallow-stepped staircases leading on and on to new wonders.**
>
> —*Frances Parkinson Keyes,*
> **Queen Anne's Lace, *1930***

This is indeed a library, probably the greatest library in the world, and, more than that, one of the most civilized institutions of learning ever created.

The wonderfully embellished building, which has recently been renovated, stands just to the east of the Capitol. A foretaste of the building itself is the superb Fountain of the Court of Neptune, which faces onto 1st Street below the entrance and is reminiscent of the Trevi Fountain in Rome.

But the fountain is overshadowed by the amazing Great Hall, a huge foyer with a great double marble staircase lit by a stained-glass skylight high above. There is a profusion of stone cherubs, garlands of fruit, bronze figures holding torches, balustrades, Corinthian columns, a floor inlaid with the signs of the zodiac, and acres of beautifully painted frescoes. The richness is breathtaking. But a closer examination of the frescoes will reveal that one series shows the colophons of the great printers of the past, and at the back of the hall a pair of glass display cases contain a Gutenberg Bible and a contemporary handwritten Mainz Bible.

The library was built when the collection of books became too large for the Capitol. It was designed by 2 mid-European architects, Smithmeyer and Pelz, who produced a richly eclectic mixture of styles. Much of the credit for the success of the main building, the Thomas Jefferson, goes to the army engineers who completed the job with military thoroughness. One officer, for example, was appointed to coordinate the color scheme, and the result is certainly pleasing. The building was finished in 1897, 24 years after the plans were originally chosen.

Even more impressive than the foyer is the Main Reading Room with its great soaring dome. The cupola is painted with a fresco of figures representing the nations and cultures that have most advanced the cause of learning. The figure for Germany is in fact a portrait of General Casey, the engineer who supervised the construction of the building (and also, incidentally, that of the Washington Monument).

The conducted tour starts with an introductory slide-and-sound presentation and takes in the most imposing parts of the building. Some of the less prominent areas are also worth seeing: for example, the Hispanic Division with its striking 1940s' murals by the Brazilian artist Candido Portinari.

The Library of Congress has two more recent buildings, which were necessitated by the continued growth of its collection. The John Adams Building to the east, dating from the 1930s, is a complete contrast, but a fine specimen of the architecture of its time, with rich Art Deco ornamentation. The James Madison Memorial Building to the south, completed in 1980, is the largest library building in the world, although its architecture is dramatic but sterile. The severity of the interior is relieved only by the James Madison Memorial Hall,

which is enlivened by a statue and exhibits. In all three
of the buildings, manuscripts, rare books, prints, drawings, and maps are exhibited in the hallways and on the
walls of many of the corridors.

The library was originally built for use only by the
Congress but has long since been open to the public.
Anyone above school age pursuing serious research may
use its vast facilities. It contains not only 20 million
books and pamphlets and more than 35 million manuscripts, but also nearly 4 million maps and atlases, 10
million prints and photographs, and copies of 1,200
different newspapers. Its music department has a vast
number of scores and a fine collection of musical
instruments. The Motion Picture, Broadcasting, and
Recorded Sound Division has, among other things,
more than 250,000 reels of motion pictures, which
researchers can arrange to view. An outpost of the
Performing Arts Library is situated on the roof terrace
of the Kennedy Center.

In the library's Coolidge Auditorium and the adjacent Whittall Pavilion, frequent concerts, poetry readings, lectures, and symposia are held. Once a month,
from May to October, folk music and dancing groups
from various traditions perform on the plaza in front of
the Jefferson Building.

Lillian and Albert Small Jewish Museum

701 3rd St. NW, Washington, DC 20001. ☎ 202/789-0900. Open
Sun–Thurs 10am–4pm. Closed: Aug; Jewish holidays. Admission free.
Metro: Judiciary Square.

The building housing this museum is the original Adas
Israel Synagogue, the first synagogue in Washington,
built in the 1870s and originally at 6th and G Street
NW. After the congregation moved away, the building
became a Christian church, then a grocery store. Saved
from demolition in the late 1960s, it was towed in a
precarious condition to its present site and lovingly restored. Apart from a small permanent exhibition on the
subject of the building itself, the museum mounts temporary exhibitions focusing on the life and history of
Washington's Jewish community.

★ Lincoln Memorial

Directly w of the Mall in Potomac Park (at 23rd St. NW, between
Constitution and Independence avenues). ☎ 202/426-6895. Park
staff on duty 8am–midnight daily. Admission free. Metro: Foggy Bottom
or Arlington Cemetery.

Everyone carries a pocket version of this one: It's the
grand structure on the flip side of the penny. On the

Lincoln Memorial

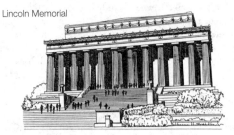

other side of the penny, of course, is Abraham Lincoln, 16th president of the United States and savior of the Union in the Civil War.

Lincoln has acquired a uniquely cherished place in the memory of the American people, and his memorial has become the most prestigious of the city's monuments. It is significant that it appears on both the penny and the $5 bill. It looks so harmonious where it stands at the west end of the Mall that it is surprising to learn of the controversy surrounding its planning.

A commission to plan the monument was set up 2 years after Lincoln's death in 1865, but it was many years before any agreement was reached on the design or position of the memorial. At that time the present site was an unattractive marsh at the edge of the Potomac, and Joseph ("Uncle Joe") Cannon, Speaker of the House of Representatives, declared that he would "never let a monument to Abraham Lincoln be erected in that God-damned swamp."

But the swamp was drained and became a worthy setting for the design by Henry Bacon that was finally chosen, a Parthenon-like structure surrounded by 36 Doric columns representing the 36 states that existed at the time of Lincoln's death. The design employs the same sleight-of-hand technique used by the ancient Greeks, whereby the walls and columns tilt slightly inward, the rows of columns bend outward and each one bulges a little around the waist. Without these tricks, the building would appear top-heavy and the rows of columns concave. The monument was completed in 1922.

Dramatically mirrored in the reflecting pool, it now forms a key element in the superb parkscape of the Mall. The seated statue of Lincoln inside, 19 feet high, was carved out of white marble by Daniel Chester French, who has captured powerfully the massive yet accessible personality of the man.

On the wall to the left is the Gettysburg Address, to the right is Lincoln's Second Inaugural Address, while behind the statue are the words: "In this temple as in the hearts of the people for whom he saved the Union the memory of Abraham Lincoln is enshrined forever."

The word "temple" is significant, for that is what this monument is. There was a time when visitors had to wear ties and speak in whispers in the presence of the statue. Now the atmosphere is less formal, but the mystique of the place is as powerful as ever. An intriguing sidelight is revealed while standing between the third and fourth columns to the left of the statue. The hair on the back of Lincoln's head appears to form the profile of Robert E. Lee, commanding general of the rebel army of the Confederacy.

At certain times of the year there are guided tours of the crypt below the monument, where the seepage of water from above has created curious formations of stalactites and stalagmites. Reservations can be made in advance by telephone, but these tours are so popular that there is often a waiting list of 2 months or more. Demonstrations and vigils are often held on the steps of this monument, the site of the 1963 March for Civil Rights.

Malcolm X Park (See Meridian Hill Park)

★★ **The Mall**
Metro: Smithsonian.

Call it the National Backyard: The Mall today is one of the finest town parkscapes in the world, but the effect was achieved with much toil and over a period of many years. Pierre L'Enfant saw its possibilities when he planned it in 1791, but the Mall remained more or less a visual mess until the early 1900s when Senator James McMillan, chairman of the Senate District Committee, launched a plan to landscape it in a way that incorporated many of L'Enfant's original proposals. Even then it took a long time to evolve to its present state.

Gradually the clutter disappeared. A railroad was removed, a canal along the north side was filled in (although a former lock-keeper's cottage still remains), and a number of unsightly shacks was demolished. The **Washington Monument** was finished in 1888, the **Lincoln Memorial** and the reflecting pool were added in the 1920s and the **Jefferson Memorial** in 1943.

In the 1960s and 1970s further improvements were made. The ugly temporary office buildings from the 2 world wars were removed, as well as the parking lots.

The Mall Attractions

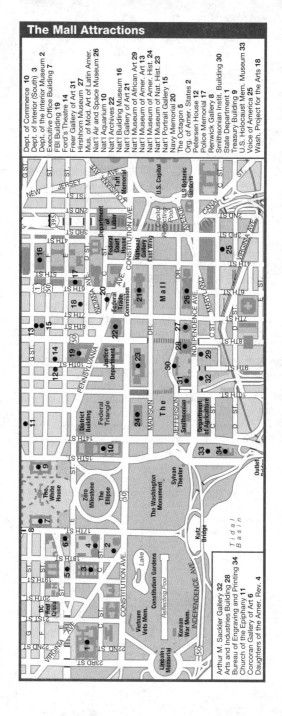

Dept. of Commerce **10**
Dept. of Interior (South) **3**
Dept. of the Interior Museum **2**
Executive Office Building **7**
FBI Building **19**
Ford's Theatre **14**
Freer Gallery of Art **31**
Hirshhorn Museum **27**
Mus. of Mod. Art of Latin Amer.
Nat'l Air and Space Museum **26**
Nat'l Aquarium **10**
Nat'l Archives **22**
Nat'l Building Museum **16**
Nat'l Gallery of Art **21**
Nat'l Museum of African Art **29**
Nat'l Museum of Amer. Art **13**
Nat'l Museum of Amer. Hist. **24**
Nat'l Museum of Nat. Hist. **23**
Nat'l Portrait Gallery **15**
Navy Memorial **20**
The Octagon **5**
Org. of Amer. States **2**
Petersen House **12**
Police Memorial **17**
Renwick Gallery **8**
Smithsonian Instit. Building **30**
State Department **1**
Treasury Building **9**
U.S. Holocaust Mem. Museum **33**
Voice of America **25**
Wash. Project for the Arts **18**

Arthur M. Sackler Gallery **32**
Arts and Industries Building **28**
Bureau of Engraving and Printing **34**
Church of the Epiphany **11**
Corcoran Gallery of Art **6**
Daughters of the Amer. Rev. **4**

In their place walkways and lawns were added. In 1976 Constitution Gardens was opened, with a lake and 50 acres of tree-shaded parkland. The gardens contain memorials to the dead of 2 wars: the cliff of black stone that is the **Vietnam Veterans Memorial** and, across the reflecting pool, the new **Korean War Veterans Memorial.**

Today the Mall forms a splendid, green triumphal way extending for some 2 miles from the **Capitol** in the east past the great buildings of the Smithsonian on either side, past the Washington Monument and on down to the Lincoln Memorial and the Watergate Steps by the Potomac. The west end of the Mall is known as West Potomac Park. There are playing fields here, where you can watch polo, rugby, soccer, and other sports (see "Staying Active").

One of the most beautiful features of the Mall is the Tidal Basin, overlooked by the Jefferson Memorial and surrounded by cherry trees given to Washington, D.C. by Japan in 1912, which make a dazzling array when in blossom. The occasion is celebrated by the Cherry Blossom Festival. Another splash of color is provided by the "floral libraries" to the east of the Tidal Basin, a series of flower beds planted with a variety of species. The Mall is the scene of a great number of other public events besides, including Washington's birthday celebration, the Festival of American Folk Life, concerts, and theatrical performances.

The Mall is much more than just a park: It is an arena, a forum, an outdoor room of vast proportions. To obtain the most dramatic vantage point, stand on the steps of the Lincoln Memorial and look past the Washington Monument toward the Capitol. Here the spirit of L'Enfant's vision is triumphantly realized.

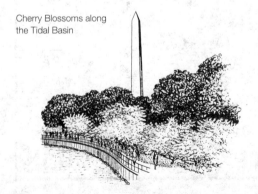

Cherry Blossoms along the Tidal Basin

Marine Corps War Memorial

Marine Corps War Memorial

Fort Myer Dr., Arlington, VA. Open daily Apr–Sept 8am–7pm, until 5pm the rest of the year. Metro: Arlington Cemetery.

In a commanding position just north of Arlington National Cemetery, this striking sculpture honors the men of the U.S. Marine Corps who have died for their country since 1775. It illustrates one of the most glorious moments in the history of the Marines: the capture of the Pacific island of Iwo Jima from the Japanese in 1945.

The monument is based on the famous photograph by Joe Rosenthal showing 6 men raising the U.S. flag on the island. It was designed by Horace W. Peaslee and sculpted by Felix de Weldon, who took 9 years to complete the job. Four times life-size, it is the largest sculpture ever cast in bronze. (There is a performance by the Marine Drum and Bugle Corps and Silent Drill Platoon mid-May–Labor Day every Tues at 7:30pm.)

A stone's throw to the south of the monument is the Netherlands Carillon, a tower with 49 bells presented to the United States by the Netherlands in thanksgiving for American aid in World War II. Free concerts are given there from April to September on Saturday, and on holidays. (Call ☎ 202/426-6700 for details.) And in early November, the annual Marine Corps Marathons, one of the largest in the country, attracting a field of more than 30,000 runners, many of them from various branches of the military, finishes its course here.

Meridian Hill Park

16th and Euclid St. NW, DC.

About 1 mile up 16th Street from the White House is an area, now called "the Gold Coast," that might have been one of the most fashionable in the city. That was the hope of a rich senator's widow named Mrs. John B. Henderson who lived here in a now demolished mansion in the early part of this century.

Her dream never came true, but the 12-acre park built by the government as a result of her agitation still remains. It is part French, part Italian in character, with a water cascade, a pond, terraces with balustrades, formal promenades, and statues of Dante, Joan of Arc, and President James Buchanan.

The park had become somewhat faded and melancholy, and in recent years acquired a dangerous reputation as a haunt of bums and drug addicts. But the Friends of Meridian Hill Park took it in hand, and restored it to a vestige of its former charm and beauty. Now there are lively soccer games on the long lawn, impromptu percussion conclaves on the park benches, and the cheering arrival of the "Dogs in the Hood" neighborhood dog-walking group every night, rain or shine, at 6pm. The D.C. government has tried, with limited success, to rename it Malcolm X Park, and many still refer to it as such, but the old name seems more appropriate, and has stuck.

Mormon Temple

9900 Stoneybrook Dr., Kensington, MD 20795. ☎ 301/587-0144. Temple closed to non-Mormons. Visitors center open daily 10am–9:30pm.

SURRENDER DOROTHY! Every day, thousands of commuters and tourists driving along the Capitol Beltway, see these words spray-painted in large letters across an overpass. The next thing they see is "the city of Oz"—what some irreverent residents have nicknamed this startling, almost shocking structure.

A soaring white edifice with 6 needle-sharp spires made of a gold and steel alloy, one of them surmounted by an 18-foot-high figure of the Angel Moroni covered in gold leaf, the Mormon Temple gives a first impression of a science-fiction illustrator's creation. In the sunlight, spires and angels gleam dazzlingly.

The temple, completed in 1971, is built of Alabama marble. Even the windows are marble, planed to a thickness of five-eighths of an inch so that they are translucent. Around the building, the 57 acres of grounds have won awards for their landscaping.

In the Mormon faith, or the Church of Jesus Christ of Latter-Day Saints, a temple, as distinct from a church, exists for marriage (for eternity) and for the baptism of ancestors by proxy. Only Mormons in good standing may enter the temple. Others, however, are given a cordial welcome at the visitors center. Here they can see a series of dramatic life-sized tableaux featuring the prophets Isaiah and Mormon, Christ and his Disciples, and Joseph Smith, the founder of the Church. Then, in a film, Mormons in different walks of life explain their beliefs.

Museum of Modern Art of Latin America

2018 18th St. NW (in the main building of the Organization of American States). ☎ 202/458-6016. Open Tues–Fri 10am–4pm. Admission free. Metro: Farragut West or Farragut North.

Devoted exclusively to the art of Latin America and the Caribbean, this museum houses both permanent and temporary exhibits by outstanding Hispanic and Caribbean artists, as well as a research library, an audio-visual program, and an outreach educational service offering films and slides. The garden is dotted with sculptures by Uruguayan artist Alfredo Halegua.

★★ National Air and Space Museum

6 Independence Ave. SW, Washington, DC 20560. ☎ 202/357-2700. Free highlight tours and for groups by arrangement. Open daily 10am–5:30pm; extended summer hours announced annually. Closed Christmas. Admission free. Metro: L'Enfant Plaza or Smithsonian.

It's the most popular museum in America, if not the world. And it would be hard to imagine a more compelling testament to man's age-old dream of flight than this dazzling museum with its unique array of flying machines, spacecraft, and exhibits relating to all aspects of air and space travel and technology.

The museum is housed in a crisp white building on the Mall, which opened in 1976, with 23 galleries, each devoted to a single subject or theme. All the aircraft are genuine, and most of the spacecraft, although occasionally a replica has been used where the craft was not brought back to earth.

From the Mall side, the first gallery is Milestones of Flight, containing such epoch-making craft as the Wright brothers' 1903 *Flyer,* Lindbergh's *Spirit of St Louis,* and the *Apollo 11* Command Module, all of which look impossibly fragile to have survived their legendary journeys. Room has recently been made for the *Voyager,* the lightweight plane that flew around the globe in 1986 without refueling. Galleries to the west contain other historic airplanes of various periods: gliders, passenger airliners, cargo carriers, and helicopters.

Turn left from the Mall entrance into the Space Hall, with examples of space boosters, guided missiles, and manned spacecraft. Exhibits here include the Skylab

Orbital workshop, America's first space station, which visitors can walk through. Other displays on this floor include Looking at Earth, Flight Testing, Stars, and Lunar Exploration Vehicles.

Also on the ground floor is the Langley Theater, which shows 5 Imax aviation- and space-related films daily. The films were produced using a large-format projection system and are shown on a screen the height of a 5-story building. So convincing is the illusion of reality in one film, *To Fly,* that you will literally want to hold on to your seat as you hurtle over a clifftop or swoop just above the surface of a river as it plunges into a waterfall—some people have actually become airsick from it, but you'll have to bring your own airsick bags. The Langley Theater is also used for free evening lectures.

Also well worth the small entrance charge is the Albert Einstein Planetarium on the 2nd floor, one of the most advanced planetariums in the world, which creates startling images of the sun, moon, planets, and stars by the use of a Zeiss model VI projector.

After visiting the planetarium, you can continue your imaginary space journey in the Exploring the Planets gallery, where the moving surface of Mars is visible through a porthole. To go back to the early days of flight, visit the Balloons and Airships gallery, which contains the original Zeppelin, and models of the ill-fated *Hindenburg* and the *Montgolfier* balloon. The 3rd floor of the building houses a library, offices, and a restaurant. Two new restaurants have been added in a glass annex east of the main structure.

If, having seen the museum, you are still eager to see more aircraft and spacecraft, take a trip out to the Paul E. Garber Facility (3904 Old Silver Hill Rd., Suitland, MD; ☎ 202/357-1400. Mon–Fri 10am; Sat–Sun 10am, 1pm; reservations must be made 2 weeks in advance). The facility is the storage, restoration, and preservation center of the museum, where you can see 90 aircraft as well as many spacecraft, engines, propellers, and other flight-related objects. Take a look also at the restoration workshop. Note, however, that this is a no-frills museum without heating or air-conditioning—it is strictly for the keenest air-and-space buffs.

National Aquarium

Department of Commerce Building, 14th St. and Constitution Ave., Washington, DC 20230. ☎ 202/482-2825. Open daily 9am–5pm. Closed Christmas. Shark feedings: Mon, Wed, Sat 2pm; piranha

feedings: Tues, Thurs, Sun 2pm. $2 adults, 50¢ children under 10.
Metro: Federal Triangle.

This is a strange (but almost poetically appropriate, if
you have a cynical cast of mind) place in which to find
an aquarium: tucked away in the basement of the Department of Commerce, one of the soberest government buildings in the Federal Triangle. It is in fact the
oldest aquarium in the country, dating from 1873, although it has only been at its present location since
1932. Originally run by the U.S. Fish and Wildlife
Service, it is now operated by a private nonprofit
group, the National Aquarium Society.

It has about 1,000 specimens representing 225 different species, half freshwater and half saltwater. There
is plenty to marvel at: the archer fish (*Toxotes jaculator*),
for instance, which shoots small jets of water to dis-
lodge insects from overhanging vegetation, or the blue
damselfish, a tiny, darting sapphire, as well as turtles,
sharks, horseshoe crabs, eels, and many other creatures
of the deep. There are also recordings of the sounds
made by marine animals.

On your way out, stop in the lobby to catch a glimpse
of a typical Federal Triangle interior with its neoclassical expanse of marble. And observe the meter that
continually records the growth of the U.S. population—
every 16 seconds it chalks up one more American.

National Arboretum

3501 New York Ave. NE, Washington, DC 20002. ☎ 202/245-2726.
Tours by reservation, for 10 or more. Open daily 8am–5pm. Closed
Christmas. Admission free. Metrobus from Stadium-Armory Metro
Station.

Another unfairly overlooked attraction, here is an
idyllic Arcadia incongruous among the bleak
postapocalyptic-looking surroundings of east Washington: The arboretum boasts an herb garden, a stunning bonsai collection, aquatic gardens, lakes, a nature
trail, and more than 400 acres of hilly countryside containing many varieties of trees, shrubs, and flowering
plants. The arboretum is particularly proud of its aza-
leas, a glorious riot of color in springtime. You can drive
around, and there is a designated picnic area. A visit to
this park is well worth the journey to the eastern fringes
of the city, but is awkward without a car.

★ National Archives and Records Administration

Constitution Ave. NW (between 7th and 9th streets), Washington, DC
20408. ☎ 202/501-5000. Exhibition hall: open Apr–Labor Day daily
10am–9pm; Sept–Mar daily 10am–5:30pm. Closed Christmas. Call for
research hours. Admission free. Metro: Archives.

"We hold these Truths to be self-evident, that all Men are created equal, that they are endowed by the Creator with certain unalienable Rights, that among these are Life, Liberty, and the Pursuit of Happiness. . . ." These words, which most American schoolchildren learn by heart, are part of the Declaration of Independence of 1776, written principally by Thomas Jefferson. The Declaration of Independence, the Constitution, and the Bill of Rights are known together as the Charters of Freedom, and the original documents are the most treasured possessions of the National Archives. They are displayed in a great domed, semicircular temple in which the public files reverently past a kind of altar where the charters are kept in helium-filled bronze cases that descend at night, or at times of emergency, into a bomb- and fire-proof vault. A new gallery staging temporary exhibits from the permanent collection circles around in back of the "shrine," as the guards call it, passing through the gift store (which sells facsimiles of the Declaration and charters, as well as pictures, books and postcards, and replicas of old-time political campaign memorabilia).

Also on display is one of 16 known copies of the Magna Carta, which inspired the drafting of the U.S. Constitution. This one is King John's 1297 version, on indefinite loan from a prominent Texan.

The Charters of Freedom are only a tiny part of the vast collection of U.S. government records housed in the archives, from Acts of Congress to applications for federal jobs. A selection of some of the more interesting documents is displayed in the corridors of the building, but access to the main files is reserved for serious researchers. But the public can hear the Watergate tapes: portions are played Monday to Friday from 10:15am. From the Pennsylvania Avenue entrance you will be directed to the appropriate room. Don't overlook the building itself. Designed by John Russell Pope, it is an imposing classical-style edifice approached by immense flights of steps.

National Building Museum (Old Pension Building)

F St. between 4th and 5th St. NW, Washington, DC 20001. ☎ 202/ 272-2448. Open Mon–Sat 10am–4pm; Sun noon–4pm. Closed: Thanksgiving; Christmas; New Year's Day. Admission free. Metro: Judiciary Square (F St. exit).

One of the most astonishing buildings in the city. Appropriately enough.

Based on the Palazzo Farnese in Rome and completed in 1885, the exterior is imposing in its own

Old Pension Building

right, with a one-quarter-mile-long encircling frieze in low relief of Civil War scenes, added in 1887. But the interior is yet more impressive—it's like being inside a wedding cake.

Once inside you are dwarfed by a vast courtyard divided by 8 columns the size of giant redwood trees. A fountain dominates the center, and around the sides several stories of arched galleries rise to a row of windows high above. This spectacular hall is used for grand festivities and has been the setting for several presidential inaugural balls, including President Reagan's second in January 1985. It would take the length of a waltz to dance once around the floor!

In 1926 the building ceased to house the Pension Bureau, and at one time it was threatened with demolition. It also served as the District Courthouse, where judges, jurors, bailiffs, cops, and criminals crisscrossed the grand expanse, while along the balconies overhead jurors awaited call-up. Now, securely protected as a National Historic Landmark, it houses the National Building Museum, a privately funded organization founded to commemorate and encourage the American building arts. The museum mounts temporary exhibitions on architectural and building themes. A museum store sells books and items of architectural interest, including toys (check out the Frank Lloyd Wright building blocks), jewelry, and other gifts.

This is one of the many Washington buildings reputed to be haunted; a number of strange apparitions have been seen, including a transparent horseman and malevolent skulls lurking around the pillars.

★★ National Gallery of Art

On the north side of the Mall (between 3rd and 7th streets NW), with entrances at 6th St. and Constitution Ave. or Madison Dr., also 4th and 7th streets between Madison Dr. and Constitution Ave., Washington, DC 20565. ☎ 202/737-4215. Open Mon–Sat 10am–5pm; Sun 11am–6pm. Closed Christmas and New Year's Day. Admission free. Metro: Archives or Judiciary Square.

This is a relative newcomer to the major league of art galleries, yet it is now ranked among the top dozen in the world. In its collection of paintings it outstrips most other galleries in North and Latin America, especially in the field of European Old Masters and impressionists.

The gallery owes its existence to the financier and statesman Andrew W. Mellon, who formed the nucleus of the collection, partly by buying from the Soviet government in the 1930s, when it was selling art treasures to pay for tractors and other necessities. Mellon bequeathed the collection to the nation and provided funds for the construction of the West Building. The daily running of the gallery is now funded by the federal government, but the acquisition of works of art is financed privately.

WEST BUILDING It is hard to believe that the massively neoclassical West Building, designed by the indefatigable John Russell Pope (National Archives, Jefferson Memorial, House of the Temple), was opened as recently as 1941. Unlike the Louvre and many other great galleries, it was purpose-built as a museum. It houses works of art from the 10thC up to the mid-20thC.

Tours of the West Building start in the great rotunda, which has a fountain to Mercury in the center and is encircled by massive pillars of green Tuscan marble. The works, divided by nationality and subdivided by time period, are arranged in the following 10 groups:

Florentine and Central Italian Art The range extends from the highly stylized paintings of the Byzantine period, with their deliberately stiff figures and lack of perspective, to the more naturalistic paintings of the Renaissance, when art had begun to free itself from religious constraints. The star item is the gallery's single Leonardo da Vinci, a small painting of ca. 1474 portraying the young Florentine noblewoman Ginevra de' Benci, so accurate in its detail that even the subspecies of tree in the background is identifiable: a kind of juniper, which is a pun on the subject's name. Its acquisition in 1967 helped to make this one of the most comprehensive collections of Italian medieval and Renaissance paintings in the world. Also remarkable is the ceremonial shield with Andrea del Castagno's painting *The Youthful David,* dating from about 1450 and very rare of its kind.

Venetian and North Italian Art The lavish art in this collection reflects the prosperity of the great maritime city of Venice in its heyday. Typical of this period is Giovanni Bellini's elaborate *Feast of the Gods,* reworked by his pupil, Titian. Other Titians, such as the arresting portrait of Doge Andrea Gritti, fill an entire room. Giorgione's peaceful *Adoration of the Shepherds* and Jacopo Sansovino's enchanting bronze figure of Venus Anadymone are also noteworthy.

Italian Art of the 17th–18th Centuries Visual drama and complexity of technique were the hallmarks of the Baroque era. One of the best examples is *The Lute Player,* painted by Orazio Gentileschi in about 1610, a masterly composition of abruptly contrasting light and shadow. By the 18thC view-painting had come into vogue to satisfy the demands of travelers who took the Grand Tour of Europe. Giovanni Paolo Panini's interiors of the Pantheon and of St. Peter's, Rome, are distinguished examples of this genre. There are also some Canalettos, including a typical example, *Venice, the Quay of the Piazzetta.*

Spanish Art During the 15th and 16th centuries, Spanish art was dominated by foreign immigrants such as El Greco, represented here by *Laocoön, Saint Martin and the Beggar,* and a cadaverous *St. Jerome.* But from the 17thC onward, Spain produced its own great artists: Zurbarán, Murillo, Velázquez, and Goya. All are included here. Note Velázquez's penetrating study for a portrait of Pope Innocent X—"All too true," said the Pontiff when he saw the finished work. Goya has a room to himself, whose highlights are his famous portrait of the beautiful Señora Sebasa Garcia and one of his paintings of the Duke of Wellington.

Flemish, German, and Dutch Art This is a particularly rich and extensive part of the collection. Here are encountered the austere, meticulous works of such early Flemish painters as Van Eyck and Rogier van der Weyden. Among the notable German works is a small Crucifixion by Matthias Grünewald, the only one of his paintings in the United States. This section also includes a great galaxy of Dutch artists of the 17thC. Among many fine Rembrandts, note particularly the *Self-Portrait,* with its troubled expression, painted when the artist was 53, after his fortunes had begun to decline. Rubens is here too: See, for example, his huge and dramatic *Daniel in the Lion's Den.* So too are Van Dyck, Vermeer, and other painters of the Dutch golden age. Look closely at the *Vase of Flowers* by Jan de Heem. Not only does it show an impossibility, since in nature none of the flowers depicted bloom concurrently, but it is full of symbolism: a butterfly at the top to indicate the spiritual life; moths, snails, and faded flowers at the bottom to stand for worldly decay.

French Art of the 17th, 18th, and Early 19th Centuries   The age of Louis XIII and XIV produced an art that looked toward classical and Renaissance models for inspiration. The masters of this era include Claude Lorrain (*Landscape with Merchants* and *The Judgment of Paris*) and Nicolas Poussin, with his serene colors and geometric harmony (*Holy Family on the Steps* is a fine example). In the late 17th- and early 18thC, French art became more light-hearted, developing into the delicate, sensual style known as rococo. The tone was set by Antoine Watteau whose work is here exemplified by his *Italian Comedians* and by *Ceres,* an oval panel with the 4 summer months of June, July, August, and September symbolized astrologically by a pair of twins, a crayfish, a lion, and the goddess Ceres herself representing Virgo. Paintings by Boucher (*Allegory of Painting*) and Fragonard (*A Young Girl Reading*) illustrate how this style was continued until well into the 18thC. Gradually, however, it gave way to the more severe, earnest neoclassical style. This section ends with the neoclassical masters, notably Ingres (*Portrait of Madame Moitessier*) and David (*Napoléon in His Study*).

British Art   Portraiture was one of the great fortes of British art in the 18thC and this collection contains some choice examples. The 2 supreme masters of the "Grand Manner," Gainsborough and Reynolds, are here. So are Romney, Hoppner, Raeburn, and Lawrence. There are works by both of the great early 19thC English landscape artists, Constable and Turner. Typical of Turner's genius is his *Keelmen Heaving Coals by Moonlight,* where the port of Newcastle is transformed into a glowing, dreamlike vision.

American Art   Portraiture, much influenced by English models, dominated American art in the 18th- and early 19thC. Benjamin West, one of the greatest American painters of this era, lived and worked in London, where he significantly influenced visiting compatriot artists. His masterly *Self-Portrait* hangs here, together with the works of other great portraitists such as Charles Wilson Peale and Edward Savage. Pride of place, however, goes to Gilbert Stuart, unofficial "court portraitist" of the young republic. The gallery possesses 41 Stuarts, including his famous set of the first 5 presidents. A total contrast is the large amount of naive or primitive art by untrained 19thC painters, much of it charming and fresh.

The late 19thC and early 20thC saw a notable flourishing of American art. The spirit of rural America at this time is vividly captured in the work of Winslow Homer. In his sea painting *Breezing Up,* you can almost feel the wind and the spray. One of the greatest American artists of all time, James McNeill Whistler, also has many paintings here, ranging from his exquisite portrait, *L'Andalouse, Mother-of-Pearl, and Silver,* to his typically hazy view of the Thames, *Chelsea Wharf, Grey and Silver.*

French Art of the 19th Century　Think of this period and you think automatically of the impressionists, who are here in full force: Renoir, Cézanne, Monet, Pissarro, Seurat—a feast of liberated light and color. Note the curiously untypical van Gogh, *Flowerbeds In Holland* (ca. 1883), a tranquil little scene quite unlike the feverish paintings of his later years. The Postimpressionists, such as Gauguin, are here too, as are the symbolists: See Puvis de Chavannes's matching pair *Le Travail* and *Le Repos.* These artists pave the way for the full impact of the 20thC art housed in the East Building of the gallery.

Lower-Level Galleries　In the mid-1980s a new set of galleries opened on the lower floor. There is a print gallery devoted to rotating exhibitions from the National's rich collection of prints and graphics. Another has exhibits of Chinese porcelain and small bronzes; yet another contains French furniture. Before leaving the West Building it is also worth taking a look at the large and well-stocked shop on the ground floor, which sells books, cards, and reproductions.

EAST BUILDING　Designed by I. M. Pei (who designed the controversial "pyramid" addition to the Louvre and the newly-opened Rock and Roll Hall of Fame Museum in Cleveland) and opened in 1978, the East Building looks like an iceberg with edges so sharp you could almost cut your fingers on them.

The East Building can be approached via an underground tunnel, which halfway along opens out into a spacious restaurant, fresh and airy with indoor plants and a huge window looking dramatically onto a falling wall of water. The passage continues with a moving sidewalk to the East Building. Alternatively, approaching from the outside, you will cross a plaza with a fountain and pass Knife Edge Mirror Two Piece, a great bronze sculpture by Henry Moore.

The East Building was endowed by Andrew Mellon, son of the Mellon responsible for the West Building. The new museum echoes the neoclassicism of Alexander Pope's Roman temple without imitating it, and the "father-and-son" facades face each other from a respectful remove, separated by a generation and a revolution in style. There are few triangular buildings in architectural history books.

The East Building cost $94.4 million, making it one of the country's priciest buildings. As the joke went, "With I. M., you Pei and Pei and Pei." Pei, who understood the competition in the neighborhood, himself said, "The buildiing has to be designed in such a way that young people will find it interesting to go there. Otherwise, the whole purpose is lost; they will spend 5 minutes there and then go to the Air and Space Museum to look at the moon rocket."

Inside, the iceberg impression continues, as if the ice had been hollowed out to create an immense space bathed in pale light.

It's an exciting building: Visitors walk under and around oversized abstract artworks. The Central Court is dominated by a vast, slowly rotating Alexander Calder mobile in red, blue, and black, while around the court are other impressive works such as Joan Miró's enormous tapestry *Woman*. Anthony Caro's steel *Ledge Piece* looms over the entrance to the south part of the building, which houses the library, the Center for Advanced Study in the Visual Arts, the graphics collection, and the administrative offices.

From the Central Court, there are stairs, escalators, and bridges, which lead up, down, and across to the various exhibition areas, as well as a secluded top-floor restaurant, and provide a constantly changing spectacle. Few works of art are permanently on view, and the building is primarily used for temporary exhibitions,

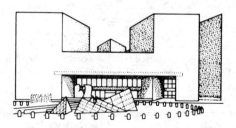

I. M. Pei's East Building of the National Gallery of Art

either on loan or from the gallery's own collection. The emphasis is not exclusively on contemporary art, and the temporary shows include work from many periods.

Free lectures (Sun afternoons) and film shows are held in the auditorium, often linked to exhibitions. These are among the best free events in the city. The museum will supply a program upon request.

A word of advice: Do not try to see all of the National Gallery in 1 visit, especially if you want to include both buildings. One of the richest collections in the world, it merits 2 or even 3 visits.

National Geographic Society Explorers Hall

17th and M St. NW, DC 20036. ☎ 202/857-7588. Open Mon–Sat 9am–5pm; Sun 10am–5pm. Closed Christmas. Admission free. Metro: Farragut North or Farragut West.

The National Geographic Society conveys the uniqueness and splendor of our planet through its monthly magazine and other publications. It does the same in the Explorers Hall in its headquarters.

The introductory video presentation about man's earliest ancestors is followed by a tour through simulated Neanderthal and Cro-Magnon caves, emerging by a pool over which is suspended a vast globe. Nearby stands a giant basalt head from Mexico. Mementoes of exploration include the binoculars carried by Admiral Byrd on his polar flights in 1926 and 1929, under the sponsorship of the society. Other displays include a specimen of the giant Goliath frog from Cameroon, a film of underwater exploration, a working model of the solar system, and many beautiful photographs of the natural and animal worlds.

A new interactive science center called "Geographica" incorporates an amphitheater simulating a space station, a planetarium, and touch screens chronicling undersea exploration. The displays employ computers and state-of-the-art electronics to mount their dazzling images, which include live feeds from a weather satellite and the formation of a nearly real tornado. Additional exhibits are planned. Related temporary exhibitions are also held, and a stall sells the society's familiar yellow-bordered publications and videotapes. This is a great place to take children, and an eye-opener for adults too.

★ National Museum of African Art

950 Independence Ave. SW, Washington, DC 20560. ☎ 202/357-2700. Open daily 10am–5:30pm. Admission free. Metro: Smithsonian.

Finding its old premises on Capitol Hill too cramped, this museum has moved to largely underground quarters in the new Quadrangle complex behind the Smithsonian Castle. The only museum in the United States devoted to the visual arts of sub-Saharan Africa, it has a collection of about 6,000 objects ranging from Benin bronze figures to vibrant woven textiles. Apart from a small number of objects on permanent display, the museum is devoted to temporary exhibitions, either of a thematic nature or dealing with particular regions or ethnic groups. The entrance to the museum is a striking pavilion with 6 shallow domes.

★ National Museum of American Art

8th and G St. NW, Washington, DC 20560. ☎ 202/357-2700. Open daily 10am–5:30pm. Closed Christmas. Admission free. Metro: Gallery Place.

A favorite museum of many residents, this is a Smithsonian museum with a personal feel. Here you can see such awe-inspiring works as James Hampton's visionary folk-art creation, *The Throne of the Third Heaven of the Nations' Millennium General Assembly,* consisting of 177 objects sheathed in glittering aluminum and gold foil (seen in the 1st-floor lobby).

There are some 32,000 works in this collection, illustrating the development of American painting, sculpture, and graphic art from the 18thC to the present day. A large and representative selection is on permanent display, and temporary exhibitions are also held. The museum is strong on the 19th- and early 20thC. Take a look at the works by Winslow Homer: limpid paintings bathed in a golden glow of fresh innocence that characterized the American world view during his creative life. Albert Bierstadt, although originally German, is American in another way, poignantly evoking the wild expanses of the West. Less typical are the works of Albert P. Ryder: eerie, dreamlike scenes reminiscent of the French symbolists.

Other great names of the period in this collection include George Catlin, Elihu Vedder, Thomas Moran, Frederic Church, Thomas Cole, James Whistler, Mary Cassatt, and the sculptor Hiram Powers. The modern period is also well represented by such artists as Franz Kline, Willem de Kooning, Robert Rauschenberg, Stuart Davis, and Edward Hopper.

The museum shop on the 1st floor sells books, catalogs, posters, and reproductions. The museum organizes periodic concerts, symposia, lectures, and other public programs.

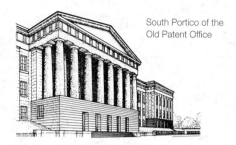

South Portico of the
Old Patent Office

The building, shared with the National Portrait
Gallery, is the Old Patent Office, a massive 19thC Greek
revival structure. The 2 museums also share a fine library and a good cafeteria, which in summer spills out
onto the attractive inner courtyard. A branch of the
museum is the smaller Renwick Gallery, near the White
House. It also administers the Barney Studio House,
built in 1902 on Sheridan Circle as artist Alice Pike
Barney's home, studio, and salon (open for guided tours
by appointment; ☎ 202/357-3111).

★★ National Museum of American History

Constitution Ave. and 13th St. NW, Washington, DC 20565. ☎ 202/
357-2700. Open daily 10am–5:30pm. Closed Christmas. Admission
free. Metro: Federal Triangle.

This museum will save archaeologists of the future a
great deal of work when they come to study the civili-
zation known as the United States of America.

It is as though someone had cut a trench through
the whole of the country's history and from it had taken
objects that reflect and have shaped the changing pat-
terns of life. In this immense collection, housed in an
austerely elegant 1960s building on the Mall, you can
learn how Americans of different eras worked, played,
tilled the soil, traveled, dressed, shopped, communi-
cated, entertained themselves, and coped with the
technical problems that confronted them.

Originally known as the National Museum of
History and Technology, the collection is very strong
on technological matters, and its scope extends beyond
America, as shown in the displays of Roman, Venetian,
and Islamic glass on the 3rd floor.

The 1st-floor lobby, which is entered from Constitution Avenue, is dominated by a Foucault pendulum,
a 240-pound brass bob suspended on a 70-foot wire,
which demonstrates the rotation of the earth. The
lobby area contains a bookstore, an auditorium, and a

complete country post-office-cum-general-store, where you can buy stamps, including special issues, and post a letter that will receive a "Smithsonian Station" postmark. On the same floor the electricity section has Edison's lightbulb; the motor vehicle room has the famous Model T Ford; and one of the jewels of the railroad collection is a majestic Pacific-type locomotive, which dates from 1926. Other displays are devoted to subjects as diverse as the physical sciences, medicine, folk art, typewriters, clocks, and farm machinery.

On the 2nd floor, which can be entered from the Mall, there is a souvenir store and a lobby dominated by the original "Star Spangled Banner." Concealed by a curtain, the much-restored flag is revealed briefly every hour on the half-hour. The galleries on this floor contain a more intimate kaleidoscope of American life: for example, a collection of first ladies' gowns, a display of the life of George Washington, a remarkable set of original interiors from different periods, and a permanent exhibition, After the Revolution: Everyday Life in America, 1780-1800, which illustrates the lives of 3 actual families.

The 3rd floor contains even more riches, among them displays of firearms, military history, photography, news reporting, money and medals, philately, and musical instruments; there is an auditorium where those instruments are played (Mon–Fri 11am). Other free demonstrations are given of spinning and weaving, printing and typefounding, and operating machine tools. In addition to the permanent displays, the museum also holds temporary exhibitions covering various aspects of American life and history.

★ National Museum of Natural History

10th St. and Constitution Ave. NW, Washington, DC 20565. ☎ 202/357-2700. Open daily 10am–5:30pm. Highlight tours at 10:30am and 1:30pm. Closed Christmas. Admission free. Metro: Smithsonian.

The great stuffed African bush elephant that stands in the huge central rotunda of this museum seems calculated, like the museum itself, to inspire the visitor with awe at the vast variety of life on our planet. There is plenty to marvel at here—most of all, the scope of the collection.

The natural history part of the museum traces life back to its earliest manifestations in the form of fossil ammonites 160 million years old. There are skeletons and models of prehistoric monsters and stuffed specimens of more recent origin: mammals, birds, sea life, and reptiles. A special section is devoted to bones, and another to the Dynamics of Evolution. The Insect Zoo houses live specimens.

Moving on to inorganic material, there are sections on the earth, moon and meteorites, minerals, and gems. The dazzling display of gems always draws a crowd; its primary attraction is the famous Hope Diamond, the largest blue diamond in the world. Other startling exhibits include the world's biggest star ruby and a topaz the size of a goose egg.

This museum also doubles as the Museum of Man, housing a vast range of anthropological material from many different periods and cultures: Stone Age North American ax heads, Inca artifacts, ancient Egyptian sarcophagi. There are also life-sized dioramas; the one in which an Indian on a pony chases an ostrich across the grasslands is particularly effective.

The museum's special facilities include a Naturalist Center (open Mon–Sat 10:30am–4pm; Sun noon–5pm) for the use of amateur researchers, with books, scientific instruments, and specimens that can be handled and examined. There is a Discovery Room (☎ 202/357-2747 for group reservations; open Mon–Thurs noon–2:30pm; Fri–Sun 10:30am–3:30pm), where children can handle a variety of objects from the world of nature. Youngsters also enjoy climbing on Uncle Beazley, a life-sized model of a triceratops dinosaur outside the Mall entrance.

The excellent museum shop sells books and museum-related objects. On the ground floor there is an auditorium for lectures and an area for temporary exhibitions. The self-serve cafeteria is a good place to grab a meal.

National Museum of Women in the Arts

1250 New York Ave. NW, Washington, DC 20005. ☎ 202/783-5000. Open Mon–Sat 10am–5pm; Sun noon–5pm. Closed New Year's Day. Suggested donation $3 adults, $2 children. Metro: Metro Center.

The newest of the cultural institutions in the rejuvenated Old Downtown district, this museum demonstrates the rich and long-neglected contribution women have made to the arts over the centuries. It is housed in a turn-of-the-century Renaissance Revival building, once a Masonic temple.

Wilhelmina Holladay founded the museum and, with her husband, assembled the permanent collection that is now at its heart. Painters and sculptors from a score of nations are represented, with works from the 16thC to the present. They include Georgia O'Keeffe, Helen Frankenthaler, Kathe Kollwitz, and Mary Cassatt, among the few women artists of the last 100 years to enjoy widespread recognition. Temporary exhibitions are frequently mounted, and the research center is a trove of information on the subject.

★ National Portrait Gallery

8th and F St. NW, Washington, DC 20560. ☎ 202/357-2700. Open daily 10am–5:30pm. Closed Christmas. Admission free. Metro: Gallery Place.

This gallery shares the splendid Old Patent Office building with the National Museum of American Art. Its collection consists of paintings, prints, drawings, photographs, and sculptures of "men and women who have made significant contributions to the history, development, and culture of the people of the United States." The presidents have a hall to themselves, with an anteroom devoted solely to George Washington. Most of the presidential portraits are predictably reverential, except for the most recent ones—Nixon, Ford, Carter, and Reagan—which are sharply penetrating. (We've seen schoolkids honk the nose on the bronze bust of Bill Clinton.) One 2nd-floor room is devoted to rotating exhibitions of *Time* magazine covers, based upon such themes as sports heroes, movie stars, or presidents.

The National Portrait Gallery has some 4,500 portraits in its collection. There is a museum store on the 1st floor, and the gallery shares a library and cafeteria with the National Museum of American Art.

National Shrine of the Immaculate Conception

Michigan Ave. and 4th St. NE, Washington, DC 20017. ☎ 202/526-8300. Open daily Apr–Oct 7am–7pm; Nov–Mar 7am–6pm. Metro: Brookland.

A glimpse of this building from the train is reminiscent of the view of the Sacre Coeur on leaving the Gare du Nord in Paris. There is the same dominating, hilltop position and the same echo of Byzantine splendor. Located next to Catholic University, the church was begun in 1914 and built in 2 stages: first the enormous crypt, completed in 1926; then the upper church, consecrated in 1959. Despite its imposing size, this is not a cathedral, nor does it serve a parish. It is primarily a shrine to the Virgin Mary in her capacity as Patroness of the United States, and it is filled with Marian imagery.

Descriptions of the church abound in superlatives. It is the biggest Catholic church in the Western hemisphere and possesses one of the largest church organs in the world. Its many splendid mosaics include the world's

National Shrine of the
Immaculate Conception

largest one of Christ (67 ft./20m high), and others re-
producing such works as Murillo's *Immaculate Conception* and Titian's *Assumption*. The whole interior, with
its magnificent soaring central dome, colored marble
pillars and domed baldachin over the altar, combines
richness, serenity, and dignity.

★ National Zoological Park

3000 Connecticut Ave. NW, Washington, DC 20008. ☎ 202/
673-4800. Open daily Apr 15–Oct 15 (weather permitting): grounds,
8am–8pm; animal buildings, 9am–4:30pm. Daily Oct 16–Apr 14:
grounds, 8am–6pm; animal buildings, 9am–4:30pm. Closed
Christmas. Admission free. Metro: Woodley Park-Zoo.

Before the National Zoo was established in 1889, the
Smithsonian Institution had only rudimentary facilities
for gifts of live animals. Early records indicate that
animals presented to the Smithsonian were sent to the
Philadelphia Zoo and to the U.S. Insane Asylum (now
St. Elizabeth's Hospital), where they were used as a
harmless diversion for patients.

By the late 1880s animals donated to the Smithsonian
formed a menagerie in the shadow of the Smithsonian
Castle. Finally in 1889 a proper home for the animals
was created when 163 acres of then-suburban northwest Washington were set aside for a National Zoological Park, to be run as part of the Smithsonian.

Conservation and preservation of endangered animals has been a central concept throughout the zoo's
history. The threatened extinction of the American bi-
son and the diminishing number of other native North
American species helped focus public interest and support for the founding of the zoo. Today the historic
commitment to the preservation of endangered species
persists.

The zoo is one of the finest in the world. Many of the exhibits have been skillfully laid out to resemble different types of habitats. Polar bears, for example, can be seen basking on simulated icebergs or watched through underwater windows as they swim in their pool. Some of the animals here, such as the rare Bongo antelope of central and western Africa, and the endangered Indian rhinoceros, are virtually impossible to see in the wild. Always popular is the giant panda Hsing-Hsing, presented to the zoo by the People's Republic of China in 1972. He is most active at feeding times (11am and 3pm). All the creatures that traditionally belong to zoos can also be found here: lions, tigers, giraffes, monkeys, exotic birds, and many more.

The zoo is continually being modernized and restructured, but the old Reptile House remains, its exterior reminiscent of a Byzantine cathedral. It contains a Herplab (open Tues–Sun noon–3pm, winter Fri–Sun noon–3pm), where children can explore the world of herpetology (the study of reptiles and amphibians). They will also enjoy the Zoolab (same opening times as Herplab) in the Education Building, where they can draw, read, or handle skulls, eggs, crocodile skins, and other animal materials. Films about animals and the workings of the zoo are shown in the Education Building on weekends and all week in the summer. The building contains a bookstore and gift store.

The zoo is mapped with a color-coded system of 6 different trails, named after types of animal. The zebra trail, for example, color-coded black, takes you past hoofed mammals as well as kangaroos and pandas. By following all 6 trails you will see the entire collection.

Navy Memorial

701 Pennsylvania Ave. NW, Washington, DC 20008. ☎ 202/737-2300 and 800/831-8892. Open Mon–Sat 9:30am–5pm, Sun noon–5pm. Closed Thanksgiving; Christmas; and New Year's Day. Admission free. Metro: Archives-Navy Memorial.

Built in 1987, this circular plaza so far contains 2 statues, commemorating *The Lone Sailor* and *The Homecoming*. They are standing on what is said to be the largest grid map of the world to be found anywhere. At the visitors center, you can type the name of a navy man into the computer and learn about his history and whereabouts. Navy bands present weekly alfresco concerts in summer.

Navy Yard

9th and M St. SE, Washington, DC 20024. ☎ 202/433-4882. U.S. Navy Memorial Museum open Mon–Fri 9am–4pm; Sat–Sun 10am–

5pm. Closed major holidays. U.S. Marine Corps Museum open Mon–Sat 10am–4pm. Closed: Sun; Christmas. Admission free. Metro: Navy Yard.

This yard, the oldest naval facility in the country, was opened in 1799. It no longer functions as a gun factory, which it did for a century, but is worth a visit, especially for children with nautical leanings. They can explore the dock area along the Anacostia River and climb on the old guns and other military objects exhibited in the grounds. There are 2 museums and an art gallery in the yard as well as the destroyer *John Barry,* which can be toured.

The U.S. Navy Memorial Museum, in Building 76, illustrates the history of the Navy from 1775 to the present. There are dioramas of battles, model ships, displays of weaponry and technology, flags, and uniforms. Children can sit behind guns and train them on imaginary targets, or enter a submarine room and operate a periscope. Nearby is the Navy Art Gallery, which contains naval art.

The U.S. Marine Corps Museum, in Building 58, is smaller but also interesting, explaining the history of the Corps with similar exhibits of weapons, uniforms, portraits, flags, and memorabilia. A series of dioramas re-creates great actions by the Corps. A popular event at the Navy Yard is the public presentation (June–Aug, Wed 8:45pm), which consists of a band concert and a historical review of the Navy with slides and films on a wide screen. Reserve ahead (☎ 202/433-2678).

The nearby Marine Corp Barracks (8th and I St. SE), the nation's oldest marine post, offers a spectacular sunset parade with marching band and precision drill teams (mid-May–mid-Sept, Fri 8:20pm). Make reservations at least 3 weeks in advance (☎ 202/433-4073).

The Octagon

1799 New York Ave. NW, Washington, DC 20006. ☎ 202/638-3105. Open Tues–Fri 10am–4pm; Sat–Sun noon–4pm. Closed: Mon; major holidays. $3 adults, $1.50 students and seniors, children under 5 free. Metro: Farragut West.

This is a house with a curious shape and a colorful history. Built between 1799 and 1801, it was designed by Dr. William Thornton, first architect of the Capitol. His design copes ingeniously with the awkward corner site, but the house is a heptagon, not an octagon, unless the bow at the front qualifies as an extra side.

The house was occupied by President Madison while the White House was under repair after being set on fire by the British in the War of 1812. It was here, in what is now called the Treaty Room, that Madison

The Octagon

signed the Treaty of Ghent, which ended the war. The dispatch box that contained it remains, as well as the table on which the signing is believed to have been done.

Owned by the American Architectural Foundation, a branch of the American Institute of Architects, the house has been well restored and furnished in the Federal style. Portraits include one of John Tayloe, the original owner, as well as those of Dolley Madison and Dr. and Mrs. Thornton. There is an interesting basement kitchen, complete with early-19thC implements, and on the 2nd floor are galleries for changing exhibitions relating to architecture. The new AIA headquarters next door also holds occasional exhibitions.

Old Downtown

The word "downtown" was once an inspiration for songwriters, before an epidemic of inner-city decay affected most of the northeastern United States, aggravated in many cities by the riots that swept the country in 1968. After years of blight the tide has turned and many inner cities, including Washington, are undergoing urban revival.

Symbolic of this renaissance is the Willard Hotel at the west end of Pennsylvania Avenue. An Edwardian byword for elegance and style, it was home to President Calvin Coolidge and provided guest accommodations to many foreign dignitaries, but was driven to closure by the 1968 riots. Now, however, its lavish renovation is one of the central elements in a huge scheme for the revitalization of the entire Downtown area, from the White House to Union Station and from Pennsylvania Avenue to M Street, a joint venture between the D.C. government and private enterprise.

Downtown Washington is now poised to become the city its founders promised through their planning 2 centuries ago. The biggest single development is the **Washington Convention Center,** occupying an entire block bounded by 9th, 11th, and H streets and New York Avenue. Opened at the beginning of 1983, it has acted as a catalyst, bringing other forms of new life to the area: hotels, restaurants, shops, places of entertainment. On the adjacent block, another huge complex, Techworld, incorporates a technological conference and exhibition center and 2 new hotels.

The rebirth of Old Downtown includes 7th Street, which bisects the area. Designated in the redevelopment plan as an "Arts Spine," it links the Old Patent Office (containing the **National Portrait Gallery** and **National Museum of American Art**) with the **National Gallery of Art** to the south. Smaller galleries are opening along this street.

The remainder of the area can be divided into 3 sections: Downtown, East Downtown, and Pennsylvania Avenue. The western part, concentrated around F and G streets between 9th and 15th streets, has a burgeoning new "Retail Core," dominated by the flagship store of Hecht's (see "Shopping").

A pedestrian mall stretches along G Street by the Martin Luther King Memorial Library. Although many new buildings are springing up, older ones of quality are not being neglected.

For example, **Ford's Theatre** at 511 10th St. was restored in the 1960s and functions once again as a stage as well as a museum. The graceful **Church of the Epiphany** at 1317 G St. has likewise been restored. The National Press Club at 14th and F streets has reopened its refurbished club to its members and for office suites. On the 3 lowest levels is a lively shopping arcade with restaurants. The old Masonic temple at New York Avenue and 13th Street has been transformed into the **National Museum of Women in the Arts,** which opened in 1987.

The area east of 7th Street similarly contains a mixture of fine buildings that are gradually coming into their own again as the surrounding areas are redeveloped. Judiciary Square, for example, is an attractive townscape, surrounded by municipal and federal buildings, with the splendid red brick **Old Pension Building** (now the National Building Museum) a contrast to the gray-stone government buildings. The axis of the square has been extended to the south with the creation of John Marshall Park leading down to Pennsylvania Avenue. Farther to the east, a new park and a cluster of office and hotel developments are gradually going up in the area along New Jersey Avenue.

Chinatown (roughly 5th to 7th streets at H and I streets) is a tiny enclave of Chinese restaurants and businesses. What remains of the once much larger neighborhood is now undergoing a needed facelift, and the new office buildings have Chinese motifs.

The south boundary of Downtown, Pennsylvania Avenue, is a noble thoroughfare connecting the White House with the Capitol. Like the Champs-Élysées in Paris, it seems expressly designed for parades and has often been used for this purpose. Unfortunately, however, the earlier decay of Downtown left it rather moth-eaten on the north side, in contrast to the somewhat monotonous neoclassicism of the Federal Triangle to the south. For years it was barren of restaurants and places to linger on a sunny day. As with the rest of Downtown, however, this has almost all changed.

Traveling east down the avenue from 15th Street you will pass Pershing Square, with its sunken park, pool, and outdoor cafe.

Facing the National Theater is Freedom Plaza, which has been lovingly and expensively restored to its Federal period elegance. (Notice the plan of Washington set into the paving of the plaza.) It has been unofficially taken over by skateboard rats, who execute their bruising stunts on its flat, treeless surface. The site of frequent free music festivals during the warm months, it has been nicknamed "the Griddle" by residents, because its shade-free expanses of granite could fry eggs in Washington's unforgiving summer glare.

A little farther east, on the south side, contrasting strikingly with the Federal Triangle buildings surrounding it, is the **Old Post Office,** a splendid piece of Victorian Romanesque, resembling a cross between Neuschwanstein Castle and the Palazzo Vecchio in Florence; its 315-foot clock tower is the third tallest structure in the city. A glass elevator will take you up to see the dramatic view of the city from the top of the tower. Saved from demolition by a vigorous conservationist campaign, this landmark building has been remodeled to serve 2 functions. The 7 upper floors house the National Endowment for the Arts and its twin the National Endowment for the Humanities. The focal point of the 3 lower floors, known as the Pavilion, is a dramatic skylit atrium; here there are shops, a food court

Old Post Office

with a profusion of fast-food restaurants, bars, cafes, and a stage for everything from ballet to jazz.

At the front of the building the cafes spill out onto Pennsylvania Avenue, adding a Parisian touch to the environment. The restoration of the Pavilion has given a tremendous boost to Downtown and the whole city.

Across the avenue, and a little farther east, is the **FBI Building.** The remainder of the avenue, on its Downtown side, is resplendent with new parks, plazas, and buildings, some of which mix luxury residences, corporate offices, and shops under one stately roof. See especially the monumental new Canadian Embassy at 501 Pennsylvania Ave., across from the National Gallery. Also, old buildings such as the twin-towered Apex Building are being restored. If all continues to go according to plan, Pennsylvania Avenue and all of Downtown, for too long prospering only in political promises, should emerge as L'Enfant himself envisaged.

Organization of American States
17th St. and Constitution Ave., Washington, DC 20006. ☎ 202/458-6016. Open Tues–Sat 10am–5pm. Admission free. Metro: Farragut West or Farragut North.

The striking Spanish-style headquarters of the Organization of American States, a coalition of the U.S. and Latin American and Caribbean countries, was designed by Albert Kelsy and Paul Cret and funded by Andrew Carnegie. Completed in 1912, it now also houses the Museum of Modern Art of Latin America, which opens onto the Aztec Gardens and reflecting pool.

The Pentagon
Department of Defense, Washington, DC 20301. ☎ 703/695-1776. Open Mon–Fri 9:30am–3:30pm. Closed: Sat–Sun; federal holidays. Admission free. Metro: Pentagon.

The Pentagon is one of the world's largest office build-ings, with 3 times the floor space of New York's Empire State Building. The architects who designed the head-quarters of the Department of Defense seem to have measured its dimensions by the fingers of 1 hand. It has 5 sides, 5 floors, and 5 concentric rings, and the center courtyard covers 5 acres. It was all built with incredible speed in 16 months and completed in 1943 to meet the sudden expansion of the armed forces caused by World War II.

Intended as a temporary solution, the Pentagon has instead become a permanent fixture, and its design is now recognized as brilliant. Although there are 17 miles of corridors and nearly 4 million square feet of office space, it takes no more than 7 minutes to walk from one side to the other—*if* you know the quickest route.

There are some surprising statistics: For example, 23,000 people work here, drinking 30,000 cups of cof-fee and making 200,000 telephone calls every day.

Guided tours of the building are very popular, so it is advisable to reserve in advance. Following a film presentation, the walking tour begins; it takes approxi-mately an hour and is conducted by a guide who walks backward so that he can keep an eye on his group. Ex-hibited in the corridors are examples of war art and photography, militaria such as army banners, and memo-rabilia of army, navy, and air force heroes. Recipients of the Medal of Honor are commemorated in the Hall of Heroes.

Petersen House

516 10th St. NW, Washington, DC 20004. ☎ 202/426-6830. Open daily 9am–5pm. Closed Thanksgiving and Christmas. Admission free. Metro: Metro Center.

After President Lincoln was shot in Ford's Theatre on April 14, 1865, he was carried across the street to a modest house built in 1849 by a German tailor named William Petersen, who ran it as a boarding house. The house, like the theater, is now owned by the National Park Service, and the ground floor is open to the pub-lic. The present furnishings are not original but are based on a study of contemporary inventories. Between visits to her husband's bedside, Mrs. Lincoln spent the an-guished night, consoled by her son and friends, in the front parlor. In the back parlor, Edwin M. Stanton, Secretary of War, at once launched an investigation into the shooting.

The room where Lincoln died, 9 hours after the shooting, is a small, low-ceilinged back bedroom. The only original object is one of the blood-stained pillows from his death bed, which is now reverentially glassed over.

The Phillips Collection

1600 21st St. NW, Washington, DC 20009. ☎ 202/387-0961. Open Tues–Sat 10am–5pm, Sun noon–7pm. Closed: Mon; New Year's Day; July 4; Thanksgiving; Christmas. Admission Sat–Sun, $6.50 adults, $3.25 seniors and students, free for children under 18; contribution suggested Tues–Fri. Metro: Dupont Circle.

Considered by many to be the loveliest museum in the world, this gallery bears the highly personal stamp of its founder, Duncan Phillips (1886–1966), a remarkably individual collector who refused to operate through dealers and followed only his personal judgment. The works he collected were "modern" in the broadest sense, including great innovative artists of the past as well as those of the 20thC. In 1921 he opened his collection to the public on 3 afternoons a week in the neo-Georgian house he had inherited off Massachusetts Avenue. This, the first permanent museum of modern art in the country, was such a popular success that Phillips and his wife, who was herself a painter, turned the whole house into a gallery and moved to another home.

In his book *A Collection in the Making*, Phillips described his type of gallery: "We plan to try the effect of domestic architecture, of rooms small or at least livable, and of such an intimate, attractive atmosphere as we associate with a beautiful home. To a place like that I believe people would be inclined to return once they have found it and to linger as long as they can for art's special study and its special sort of pleasure."

Although many extensions have been added to the house, including the highly modern new Goh addition that almost doubles the exhibit areas, it retains this intimate, private atmosphere.

In keeping with the eclectic scope of Phillips's taste, there are works here by artists as early as Giorgione and as avant-garde as Robert Cartwright. A highlight of the collection is Renoir's supremely joyful painting, *Luncheon of the Boating Party.*

Temporary exhibitions, concerts, and poetry readings are also held here. As Phillips intended, his gallery is a place where you will want to linger. There's a cafe and a gift shop on the premises.

Pierce Mill

Beach Dr. and Tilden St., Washington, DC 20008. ☎ 202/426-6908. Open Wed–Sun 8am–4:30pm. Closed: Mon–Tues; holidays. Grinding: Sat, Sun 1pm. Lectures: 2nd Sat of each month 11am. Admission free. Metro: Van Ness.

This simple stone building, nestling in a leafy dip in Rock Creek Park, is the only survivor of 8 water mills that operated on the creek during the 18th and 19thC. Completed in about 1829, Pierce Mill was technically advanced for its time, using conveyor belts and other labor-saving machinery. It ceased functioning in 1879 and is now run by the National Park Service. Milling has been revived, and visitors can buy corn, whole-wheat, rye, buckwheat, and oat flour in traditional cloth sacks from a miller in authentic dress. The millstones, chutes, and machinery are still here, and a friendly miller will always be happy to tell you about the mill's history. There are regular authentic craft demonstrations given by artisans in period costumes, and monthly lectures on the techniques and economics of 18thC milling.

Police Memorial

Judiciary Sq., between 4th, 5th, and E streets. NW. Metro: Judiciary Square (F St. exit).

Dedicated in 1991 to law enforcement personnel who lost their lives in the line of duty, this peaceful urban plaza is directly south of the National Building Museum. The low, concave marble wall encircling the memorial is engraved with the names of the fallen, and crowned at each entrance with recumbent, yet vigilant lions.

Potomac Park

South of Independence Ave., w of 14th St. NW, Washington, D.C. ☎ 202/426-6700.

This park is divided into 2 sections: West Potomac Park has the Lincoln Memorial and reflecting pool, playing fields and landscaped areas; and East Potomac Park, which extends in a long peninsula between the Potomac and the Washington Channel, has a golf course as well as facilities for swimming and tennis.

Hains Point, at the southern tip of the park, is a great place to take children. It has a playground, picnic tables, and a startling piece of outdoor sculpture entitled *The Awakening*—kids love to clamber all over this metal figure of a giant struggling up out of the earth from a horizontal position with only his head and part of his limbs visible.

Between the 2 parks is the Tidal Basin (where paddleboats can be rented in-season). It is overlooked by the Jefferson Memorial and ringed by cherry trees, which also extend down the side of East Potomac Park. Access to the latter is difficult unless you have a car or

Renwick Gallery

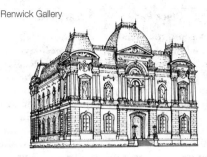

bicycle. From both parks there are splendid views across the Potomac.

Renwick Gallery

17th St. and Pennsylvania Ave. NW, Washington, DC 20560. ☎ 202/357-2700. Open daily 10am–5:30pm. Closed Christmas. Admission free. Metro: Farragut West.

Amid the bustle of Pennsylvania Avenue, this branch of the Smithsonian's National Museum of American Art comes as a delightful surprise. The building, originally constructed to house the Corcoran collection, is in the French Second Empire style with a high mansard roof and an ornate brick and sandstone facade. Named after the architect, James Renwick, it was saved from demolition in 1965 and beautifully renovated. Frequent temporary exhibitions are organized here, the emphasis being on American crafts and decorative arts.

A permanent display of painting and sculpture can be seen in the 2nd-floor Grand Salon and Octagon Room, both furnished in opulent Victorian style with velvet sofas. Luxuriously seated on one of these, you can admire works by such artists as G. F. Watts, Pierre Puvis de Chavannes, and Henry Brown Fuller.

Films, concerts, lectures, and craft demonstrations are held at both the Renwick and the National Museum of American Art (ask at either for the calendar of events).

Rock Creek Cemetery

Rock Creek Church Rd. and Webster St. NW, Washington, DC 20011. Information Office (☎ 202/829-0585) open Mon–Fri 8:30am–4:30pm; Sat 8:30am–1pm. Admission free. Metro: Fort Totten.

A tranquil place on rolling terrain, farther east than Rock Creek itself. St. Paul's Church, within its grounds, is the oldest in D.C. The cemetery contains some fine sepulchral art, notably the moody, shrouded figure by Augustus Saint-Gaudens called *The Peace of God,* or *Grief.*

★ Rock Creek Park

> **Washington weather, in the early fall, blew hot and cold. On the cool days people went horseback riding in Rock Creek Park and tired gentlemen, strangulating in red tape, took a new lend-lease on life. The multitudes . . . found that they could walk to work without frying. The crowded buses seemed less crowded, somehow, when there was more air to breathe. And in a mellow, more benevolent sunlight the working boys and girls of Mecca-on-the-Potomac went outside in the luncheon hour and ate their sandwiches under a pale blue sky.**
>
> **—*Faith Baldwin*, Washington, USA, *1942***

Washington's treasure, the local equivalent of Hampstead Heath or the Bois de Boulogne, this park consists of 1,754 acres of beautiful woodland. There are many different things to see and do: riding stables, tennis courts, a golf course, 30 picnic areas, playing fields, and an extensive system of routes for walking, jogging, riding, and cycling.

The **Carter-Barron Amphitheater** (16th St. and Colorado Ave. NW; ☎ 202/829-3200) is an impressive 4,000-seat outdoor theater that offers a variety of performing arts in an attractive rural setting during the summer months.

Other attractions of the park include **Pierce Mill**, and the Rock Creek Nature Center (5200 Glover Rd.; ☎ 202/426-6829, open Tues–Fri 9:30am–5pm; Sat–Sun noon–6pm; Dec–Apr Sat–Sun noon–5pm; closed Mon). Information on Rock Creek Park can be obtained from the park headquarters (☎ 202/426-6832), and a useful leaflet on the park is published by the National Park Service.

St. Matthew's Cathedral

1725 Rhode Island Ave. NW, Washington, DC 20005. ☎ 202/347-3215. Tours on Sun 2:30–4:30pm. Open daily 6:30am–6:30pm. Metro: Farragut North.

This is the Roman Catholic church that President Kennedy attended and where his funeral mass was held on November 25, 1963. In October 1979, during his American visit, Pope John Paul II celebrated the Eucharist here. Designed in the Renaissance style with a central dome, the cathedral has a remarkably rich interior, vibrant with Technicolor marble, mosaics, and murals.

Smithsonian Institution—Main Building

1000 Jefferson Dr. SW, Washington, DC 20560. ☎ 202/357-2700. Open daily 10am–5:30pm. Closed Christmas. Admission free. Metro: Smithsonian.

Popularly known as "the Castle," this is the headquarters of the Smithsonian Institution, the largest complex of museums and art galleries in the world. Its empire includes not only a dozen museums in Washington as well as the National Zoological Park, but other facilities elsewhere in the United States and abroad. It also conducts and sponsors research in science and the arts and issues a wide range of publications.

On the south side of the Mall stands a many-turreted, red sandstone building in a vaguely Romanesque style, which was built in 1849 to a design by James Renwick. An introductory slide presentation and talk, giving a bird's-eye view of all the Smithsonian museums in Washington, is held daily in the Great Hall on the 1st floor of the Castle (check at the information desk in the Great Hall or call ☎ 202/357-2700 in advance for the schedule).

This extraordinary institution owes its existence to the English scientist James Smithson, who died in 1829 and left a large fortune to the United States to found an institution in Washington bearing his name, "for the increase and diffusion of knowledge among men." Today, Smithson's tomb rests in a little room off the entrance lobby to the Castle, along with his portrait and a few mementoes. The Visitors' Information and Reception Center offers information on all parts of the Smithsonian.

Smithsonian Institution—Main Building

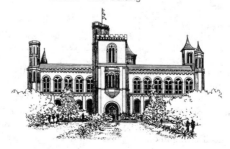

A museum complex is behind the Castle; known as the Quadrangle, the complex includes the **National Museum of African Art;** the **Arthur M. Sackler Gallery,** devoted to Asian and Near Eastern Art; and the **International Center,** which sponsors research, holds symposia, and mounts large exhibitions on themes that embrace many countries and cultures, especially those of the non-Western world. These 3 facilities, which opened in the summer of 1987, are located largely underground. At ground level is the Enid A. Haupt Garden, 4.2 acres beautifully planted and laid out in the manner of a Victorian garden and in keeping with the style of the Castle.

The Castle's main tower looks like a good home for owls, and that is exactly what it is. A colony was introduced there some years ago by Dr. Ripley, then Secretary of the Smithsonian.

State Department

Tour Office FMAS/GS, Room 7493, 2201 C St. NW, Washington, DC 20520. ☎ 202/647-3241. Tours by appointment only, 4–6 weeks in advance: Mon–Fri, tours at 9:30am, 10:30am, 3pm. Closed: Sat–Sun; holidays. Admission free. Metro: Foggy Bottom.

One of the less widely advertised attractions of Washington is the collection of art objects and furniture housed in the sumptuous reception rooms on the 8th floor of the State Department, the federal agency that handles foreign policy and relations. Most of the antique furnishings and decorative objects were given to the government in lieu of tax and are beautifully displayed in a series of interiors created in the 1960s in the gracious style of old American stately homes. One of the most attractive rooms is the John Quincy Adams State Drawing Room, with its portraits of Adams, Jefferson, Washington, Benjamin Franklin, and others. The room also contains the desk on which the Treaty of Paris, which ended the War of Independence, was signed.

★★ Supreme Court

1st and E. Capitol St. NE, Washington, DC 20543. ☎ 202/479-3000. Open Mon–Fri 9am–4:30pm. Closed: Sat–Sun; holidays. Admission free. Metro: Capitol South or Union Station.

Depending on your luck and timing, a visit to the Supreme Court, the highest court in the land, could be the most exciting—or most excruciatingly boring—federal tour in town. When the Court is in session (from the first Mon in Oct–May or June), you might find yourself sitting in on a key moment in history—maybe

Supreme Court

a crucial decision on abortion, free speech, or prayer in the schools.

More likely you'll just hear a bunch of attorneys orating ("the windy side of the law," as Shakespeare put it).

The function of the Supreme Court is to prevent infringements of the U.S. Constitution by reversing any unconstitutional laws or decisions that are referred to it. There are 9 members: a Chief Justice and 8 Associate Justices.

Visitors enter through the main entrance on 1st Street NE, beyond the white marble sculptures of *Contemplation of Justice* (left) and *Authority of Law* (right), and pass through airport-style security into a hushed, cathedral-like entrance hall. Straight ahead is the majestic Courtroom, with its heavy, burgundy-velvet draperies and marble pillars, and the Bench, where the 9 Justices hear about 120 of the more than 6,500 cases submitted to the Court each year.

When Court is in session, the public can see cases being argued Monday through Wednesday, 10am to 3pm (with a 1-hour lunch recess at noon). Oral arguments usually last about 1 hour. Call for the Court's tape-recorded schedule (☎ 202/479-3030) or check the *Washington Post*'s "Supreme Court Calendar" to find out what cases are on the docket, and arrive at least an hour early—the 150 first-come, first-served general public seats fill up fast. Before a session, 2 lines form on the plaza in front of the building, one for those who wish to hear an entire argument; the other is the "3-minute line" for those who just want a peek at the Court in session. Monday is the most popular day for observing, as the court's decisions are usually pronounced then. Visitors to either the morning or afternoon sessions must be prepared to arrive ahead of time and, if allowed to enter, to remain the entire session.

When Court isn't in session, there's a free lecture by curatorial staffers in the Courtroom every hour on the half hour, from 9:30am to 3:30pm, about Court procedure (including the ritual "conference handshakes") and the building's architecture. Copies of Court opinions are available from the Public Information Office (ground floor) about 30 minutes after they are announced from the bench.

The levels above the Courtroom are closed to the public (too bad—it would be fun to watch the jockier Justices and staffmembers play basketball in the 3rd-floor gym above the Courtroom). On the ground floor, you'll find a glass case with friendly portrait photographs of The Nine: Chief Justice William H. Rehnquist and Associate Justices Ruth Bader Ginsburg, David H. Souter, Antonin Scalia, John Paul Stevens, Sandra Day O'Connor, Anthony M. Kennedy, Clarence Thomas, and Stephen Breyer.

Skip the cafeteria and snack bar and proceed along the assembly of oil portraits and busts lining the corridor, past Philip Ratner's biblical-looking bronze of The Nine sitting at the wing-shaped 1972 Burger Bench, and the portrait of Oliver Wendell Holmes, Jr., who retired at 90, the oldest justice to have served on the Court. At the center of the ground floor is an imposing bronze sculpture of seated, robed John Marshall, known as the *Great Chief Justice*. There's also a handsome exhibit on the architecture and construction of the Supreme Court building, a faux-Greek temple finished in 1936, one of the last monumental buildings based on European classicisms to be built in D.C.

Kids will be drawn in by the scale models of the building and the interactive buttons here and there: Push a button to find who those people are up there in the West Pediment, above the words "Equal Justice Under Law" (one of them is Supreme Court designer Cass Gilbert, who put himself in there with 3 former Chief Justices, 3 classical Greek virtues, a former senator, and the pediment's sculptor). It's fun to look for the symbols hidden in the building's ornamentation: The Lamp of Learning (on elevator doors and in Courtroom friezes) represents the source of knowledge, wisdom, and truth; tortoises (found on supporting lamp standards) represent longevity and the slow, deliberate pace of justice; and the oak leaf and acorn (from the $6^{1}/_{2}$-ton west-front bronze doors, depicting historic scenes in the development of law) represents strength and longevity. (We learned all that in the gift shop.)

Speaking of which: Crime may not pay, but justice seems to do quite well, judging by the well-stocked Supreme Court gift shop, back on the ground floor. You can take home an 8x10 color glossy of your favorite Justice, settle those family disputes with a wooden gavel ($18.95–$23.95), or weigh the matter with "Corinthian-style" brass Scales of Justice ($54.95) or mini-Scales of Justice ($6.99).

Textile Museum

2320 S St. NW, Washington, DC 20008. ☎ 202/667-0441. Open Mon–Sat 10am–5pm; Sun 1–5pm. Closed holidays. Donation suggested. Metro: Dupont Circle.

Founded by George Hewitt Myers in 1925, this private nonprofit museum, occupying 2 handsome early-20thC brick houses in the Embassy Row area, contains more than 1,400 rugs and more than 12,000 other textile items, from Latin American ponchos to Indian shawls. All exhibitions are on a rotating basis, and average 6 to 7 per year. The museum shop offers some lovely textiles for sale, as well as books on the subject. The museum also has a library, and runs a program of lectures, demonstrations, and courses. The original large formal garden has benches where one may eat a picnic lunch.

Theodore Roosevelt Island and Memorial

George Washington Memorial Pkwy., Arlington, VA 22201. ☎ 703/285-2598. Tours by appointment a week in advance with a minimum of 10 people. Open daily 7am–sunset. Metro: Rosslyn.

Get a real Tom Sawyer/Huck Finn/Robinson Crusoe feeling on this "desert island" in the Potomac River. Visible from the outdoor terraces of the Kennedy Center, or from the restaurants and bars at Washington Harbour, the lushly vegetated 88-acre island is dedicated to Theodore Roosevelt, U.S. president from 1901 to 1909 and early champion of wildlife and nature conservation. The swamp, marsh, and forest contain a rich variety of native plants and provide a refuge for kingfishers, beavers, turtles, frogs, muskrats, squirrels, chipmunks, and many other fauna. The island boasts 2 miles of trails and an impressive memorial to Roosevelt: a 17-foot bronze statue at its heart.

Treasury Building

15th St. and Pennsylvania Ave. NW, Washington, DC 20220. ☎ 202/622-2000. Tours last for 90 mins, Sat only at 10am, 10:20am, 10:40am, 11:00am; reservations 1 week ahead. Must give social security or passport no. and bring document with photo ID. Admission free. Metro: McPherson Square or Metro Center.

Here it is: The Money Museum! The U.S. Treasury Department is a huge empire whose branches include the Internal Revenue Service, the Mint, the Bureau of Engraving and Printing, Customs; the Bureau of Alcohol, Tobacco and Firearms; and the Secret Service (surprisingly, those "heavies" protecting the president are Treasury men, not police or FBI). There was once a small museum in the basement of the impressive Greek Revival building, but it is now closed and much of the collection has been moved to the Bureau of Engraving and Printing.

Union Station

Massachusetts and Delaware Ave. NE. ☎ 202/371-9441 (general information) 202/484-7540 (Amtrak information). Open daily 24hrs. Shopping hours: Mon–Sat 10am–9pm; Sun noon–6pm. Admission free. Metro: Union Station.

Designed by Daniel H. Burnham, this station was completed in 1908 when rail journeys between big cities were rituals that began and ended in temples of awesome magnificence. This one has, as its main entrance, a portico based on the Arch of Constantine in Rome, surmounted by allegorical figures sculpted by Louis Saint-Gaudens (son of the more famous Augustus). The plaza in front is dominated by a great white-marble fountain, its focal point a 15-foot-high figure of Christopher Columbus standing in the prow of a ship.

By the 1970s, with the national decline in rail travel, the station had been allowed to deteriorate severely. An attempt to transform it into a National Visitor Center was a costly failure. Beset with crumbling walls and a leaking roof, it was closed while the authorities argued over its fate. Even the railroad tracks were moved to a new adjacent building. Happily, the decision was made to rehabilitate the building, a course that has saved many fine old edifices in the District.

After a reported expenditure of $100 million, at least $500,000 just for gold leaf, it reopened in 1988. Even a cursory look at the interior reveals that it has not merely reclaimed its past glory: It has surpassed it. The coffered, barrel-vaulted main concourse now soars above

Union Station

2 fountains and a round central cafe, and the space has been used for a presidential inaugural ball.

While the station continues to serve its original purpose, with Capitol Hill commuters and Amtrak passengers scurrying through, it also shelters more than 130 upscale shops, theaters, and a number of eating establishments that run from simple and fast to almost unimaginably grand. Union Station has been returned to the people; it's vibrant, exciting, and a superb foretaste of the capital for arriving travelers.

United States Botanic Garden

1st St. and Maryland Ave. SW, Washington, DC 20024. ☎ 202/ 225-8333. Open daily 9am–5pm. Admission free. Metro: Federal Center.

There is something irresistibly romantic about plant houses. In their steamy greenness it is easy to imagine once again playing a childhood game of jungle exploration where snakes and crocodiles lie hidden in the shadows. The central palm house in this building, complete with stream, lends itself to such flights of fancy. There are also sections for orchids, cycads, ferns, cacti, bromeliads, and other types of plants. And there are areas for temporary flower shows, notably the Easter Show (Palm Sun–Easter Sun), the Summer Terrace Display on the patio in front of the building (late May–Sept), the Chrysanthemum Show (mid-Nov–Thanksgiving), and the Poinsettia Show (mid-Dec through the Christmas holidays). The flower beds in the nearby parkland are spectacular, except in the dead of winter.

The building, just to the southwest of the Capitol, is in the grand manner of the great Victorian conservatories, but surprisingly it was built in the 1930s. The botanic garden also administers a public park on Independence Avenue opposite the rear entrance to the conservatory, which is used as a display garden for spring and summer flowering plants. The focal point of the park is the Bartholdi Fountain, named after its creator, the French sculptor Frederic Auguste Bartholdi, who also designed the Statue of Liberty.

★★ U.S. Holocaust Memorial Museum

100 Raoul Wallenberg Place SW (between 14th and 15th streets, sw of the Washington Monument). ☎ 202/488-0400. Open daily 10am–5:30pm. Closed Yom Kippur and Christmas. Admission free. Metro: Smithsonian.

You can be in "browser mode" for many museums, just skimming through and glimpsing only what interests you. Not so with the U.S. Holocaust Memorial

Museum. Be sure to set aside at least 3 hours for a visit here—and don't overschedule yourself afterwards. The emotional toll this museum takes cannot be overestimated.

Perhaps the most emotionally moving and physically taxing of Washington's museums, as well as the newest, the Holocaust Museum houses the world's most extensive collection of artifacts from the terrible years of the Holocaust. A boxcar that was used to transport prisoners to labor and death camps is on an upper floor. Thousands of photos, identity cards, and the scattered personal belongings—a torn book, a ragged doll—of those who were imprisoned and killed, fill the walls and display cases. The buildings themselves, designed by James Freed, are redolent of the terrible efficiency of fascist repression.

Situated symbolically close to the Mall, within view of the Washington Monument and Lincoln Memorial, the Holocaust Museum occupies a site between 14th Street and Raoul Wallenberg Place SW—a block of 15th Street renamed in honor of the Swedish diplomat who saved thousands of Hungarian Jews from the Nazis.

The newest Smithsonian museum opened in April 1993 after more than a decade of preparation. In 1979, President Jimmy Carter asked Holocaust survivor and author Elie Wiesel to rally support for the museum. Land was provided by the federal government, and the U.S. Holocaust Memorial Council began private fundraising efforts to pay for construction.

The living memory of the Holocaust is rapidly fading—and in danger of becoming increasingly distorted. From ingenious design and identification with the faces and identities of Holocaust victims and survivors, visitors to the museum actually experience the historical events from a personal perspective. Upon entering the Hall of Witness, the main entrance hall, visitors may take a passport-type booklet with the photo and description of a real Holocaust victim. As you make your way through the exhibits, the booklet gradually chronicles the changes in "your" life over the course of the war.

The overwhelming interest in the new museum has forced it to require all visitors to the permanent exhibition to have tickets. To get free tickets on the same day as your visit, line up before 9am at the 14th and C Street entrance. Tickets are good for admission at specific times; try to get an early one. You don't want to rush, and the crowds begin to clog and back up as people linger in the displays. Or you can buy advance tickets through the museum's ticket agent, Protix (out of area, 800/400-9373; in D.C., ☎ 703/218-6500; in MD, 410/481-6500) but be aware that there is a $2.75 service charge.

U.S. Naval Observatory

34th St. and Massachusetts Ave. NW, Washington, DC 20390.
☎ 202/653-1543 (tour information), 202/653-1541 (public affairs).
Tours on Mon only, at 8:30pm. Admission free.

When glancing at your watch, you probably forget that all measurement of time is ultimately determined by astronomical observations. The U.S. Naval Observatory is the source of all standard time used in the country. Special telescopes monitor the positions and movements of the heavenly bodies, while some 30 atomic clocks record an average time reading, accurate down to one trillionth of a second. In addition, the observatory has conventional telescopes for astronomical research. It also publishes the official almanacs for astronomers and navigators.

A visit to the observatory for one of the Monday night tours is a fascinating experience. The scientific complexities are well explained by the guides, and a slide show illustrates the work of the observatory. The 12-inch refracting telescope is available for celestial viewing.

As you walk up the driveway from the observatory gates, it is possible to see, behind a railing to the left, a spacious Victorian house that was for decades home to naval admirals. In 1975, it was designated the official residence of the U.S. vice president. (The Gores dress up every year in Halloween costumes and entertain trick-or-treaters at the residence.)

★★ Vietnam Veterans Memorial

Constitution Gardens, West end of Mall. Open daily 24 hours.
Admission free. Metro: Smithsonian.

Moving beyond words, this memorial, in Constitution Gardens to the west of the Lincoln Memorial, aroused much controversy when it was unveiled in 1982. Designed by Maya Ying Lin, it consists of a long tapering cliff of black polished stone set into a bank. It is inscribed with the names of all dead or missing combatants—more than 58,000—listed in order of their deaths from 1959 to 1975. There are alphabetical directories to help visitors find the names they seek. Many still-mourning survivors make paper rubbings of the names of friends and relatives; others leave flags, flowers, wreaths, and votive candles.

In answer to the original protests, a more traditional statuary group by Fredric Hall was positioned nearby in 1984. By then, however, opinion about the monument had shifted dramatically to its favor. It is a memorial of moving simplicity, testimony to a deeply traumatic episode in recent American history.

Voice of America

330 Independence Ave. SW, Washington, DC 20547 (entrance on C St. SW, between 3rd and 4th streets). ☎ 202/619-3919. Tours at 8:40am, 9:40am, 10:40am, 1:40pm, 2:40pm: groups of 25 people (reservations preferred). Open Mon–Fri 8:30am–5:30pm. Closed: Sat–Sun; holidays. Metro: Federal Center.

The Voice of America is a broadcasting division of the U. S. Information Agency. Its radio programs, designed to convey a positive image of the United States, are listened to by approximately 130 million people around the world, who receive a mixture of music, chat, and news. The station broadcasts 24 hours a day in English and more than 40 other languages. Visitors touring the building are shown staff at work and can hear a program being transmitted.

Washington Convention Center

900 9th St. NW, Washington, DC 20006. ☎ 202/789-1600, 202/371-4200 (events). Metro: Metro Center or Gallery Place-Chinatown.

Convention centers have become a popular way for cities to attract business and revenue. This one, opened at the beginning of 1983, boasts an impressive range of facilities for conferences and exhibitions: 378,000 square feet of exhibition space; 40 meeting rooms, capable of holding between 50 and 14,000 people; sophisticated security; closed-circuit television; and computerized air-conditioning and heating. Its Downtown location is convenient for access, and the center is part of the massive revival scheme for the area (see Old Downtown).

Washington Harbour Complex

K St., under Whitehurst Freeway, below Georgetown.

Designed by Arthur Cotton Moore and completed in 1986, this grandiose multilevel showpiece on a bank of the Potomac has never quite become the draw it was intended to be. Its dynamic postmodern architecture is worth seeing, however, and is especially dramatic at twilight, when the trees are strung with white lights. Amid the fountains, minipiazzas, restaurants, and boutiques are several startling statues.

★ Washington Monument

Center of the Mall, Constitution Ave. and 15th St. NW. ☎ 202/
426-6839. Open first Sun in Apr–Labor Day 8am–midnight; rest of year
9am–5pm. Admission free. Metro: Federal Triangle or Smithsonian.

The gleaming marble obelisk that rises from the center
of the Mall has become as much a symbol of Washington as the Eiffel Tower has of Paris. It is strong, simple,
majestic, and exquisitely proportioned. It positively sings
out across the skyline, sounding a clear note of classical
beauty that resonates powerfully with the rest of the
city. So perfect is it as a visual focal point of the capital
that it is impossible to imagine Washington without it.

When Pierre L'Enfant designed the city he intended
to position a monument to Washington occupying the
point at the intersection of the western axis of the Capitol and the southern axis of the White House. But the
ground there was too marshy, and another site had to
be chosen some 360 feet to the east and 120 feet to the
south. A stone marking the original site was placed there
in 1884 by Thomas Jefferson and replaced in 1889.

Although a monument to George Washington had
been mooted even before his death in 1799, it was not
until 1833 that a National Monument Society was set
up, largely by Washington's fellow Freemasons. A competition was held, and the winning design by Robert
Mills was for a great colonnaded circular mausoleum
with an obelisk projecting from the center. Gradually,
under financial pressure, the concept was whittled down
until only a simple obelisk remained.

The cornerstone was laid in 1848, but by 1865 only
about a quarter of the monument had been built, and
the Corps of Engineers of the U.S. Army took over the
construction, with the help of federal funds. The able
officer-in-charge, Lt. Col. Casey (who also built the
Library of Congress), reinforced the base, corrected a
tilt, and altered the proportions to conform to those of
the ancient obelisks. When Casey took over, a slightly
different marble was used, and it is evident how
the color changes about a quarter of the way up the
shaft. The monument was finally finished in 1885 and
opened to the public in 1888, equipped with a steam-
driven elevator that took about 10 minutes to reach the
summit.

Today you are whisked to the top in 70 seconds.
Despite the rather small windows, there is a magnificent view of the city in all directions, and from here
the full, formal grandeur of L'Enfant's town plan is
revealed. Come here on a summer night when all the

Washington Monument

monuments and the great public buildings are floodlit. (During the day you may have to line up for 40 minutes or so to get in.)

At 555 feet 5 inches, the monument was once the tallest building in the world. It has long since lost that title, but it remains an impressive tribute to the man who has been called "first in war, first in peace, and first in the hearts of his countrymen."

★ Washington National Cathedral

Massachusetts Ave. and Wisconsin Ave. NW, Washington, DC 20016. ☎ 202/537-6200. Open May 1–Labor Day, Mon–Fri 10am–9pm, Sat 10am–4:30pm, Sun 7:30am–4:30pm; the rest of the year Mon–Sat 10am–4:30pm, Sun 7:30am–4:30pm. Suggested donation $2 for adults, $1 for children under 12. Metro: Tenleytown.

Washington National Cathedral (officially the Cathedral Church of St. Peter and St. Paul and known also as the National Cathedral), seat of the Episcopal Bishop of Washington, is a glorious anachronism: A great medieval Gothic church built in the 20thC, it may be the last of its kind that will ever be constructed.

The foundation stone was laid in 1907, and the cathedral was completed 83 years later to the day, on September 29, 1990. The principal architect was Philip Hubert Frohman, who worked on the building from 1921 until his death in 1972.

Superbly located on Mount St. Alban in northwest D.C., the cathedral is laid out in the traditional form of a cross. At the intersection of nave, choir, and transept rises the Gloria in Excelsis Tower, 676 feet above sea level and having the unique feature of 2 sets of bells, one above the other. At the west end of the church are the 2 smaller towers of St. Peter and St. Paul.

The observation gallery below these twin towers affords a panoramic view of Washington and its environs, as well as some of the building's exterior stonework: pinnacles, gargoyles, and grotesques. Notice also from here the beautiful geometry of the flying buttresses. Not only for show, they structurally balance the outward thrust of the walls, so that no steel reinforcement was necessary anywhere in the building.

Stand in the vast interior where the nave meets the transepts, and the illusion of Chartres or Canterbury is powerful. Three superb rose windows blaze from west, north, and south, and the proportions of column, arch, clerestory, and soaring ribbed vaulting have an exhilarating harmony. The cathedral does have at least one advantage over its medieval counterparts: central heating under the marble floors, so there is no need to freeze while your spirit is nourished.

Other details also indicate that this is a 20thC cathedral: for example, the Space Window, halfway along the south side of the nave, commemorating man's journey into space. It depicts the spaceship's trajectory and contains a chunk of moon rock brought back from the flight and presented by the crew of *Apollo XI*. The next bay to the east houses the tomb of President Woodrow Wilson and has another striking window, depicting war and peace, by Ervin Bossanyi. (You may also find some impish details—see if you can find the gargoyle wearing a Walkman!) Notice the quality of fine detail throughout the building. Every boss and decorated column has been as lovingly carved as the great pulpit, made of French limestone from Caen, or the high altar with its assembly of prophets and saints.

Downstairs on the crypt floor is a visitors center, a shop selling books, souvenirs, and gifts, and 4 small chapels, including the Chapel of the Good Shepherd, which is open for private prayer 24 hours a day. Services in the cathedral are memorable for their music and choral singing; choirs from all across the country come here. There are Sunday afternoon organ recitals following evensong. The carillon in the main tower is played on Saturday, and a 10-bell peal is rung after the 11am service on Sunday.

In the extensive grounds of the cathedral you can linger in the Bishop's Garden, buy plants from the Greenhouse, or dried herbs, books, souvenirs, and a variety of gifts from the Herb Cottage.

Washington Post

1150 15th St. NW, Washington, DC 20007. ☎ 202/334-7969. Tours on Mon and Thurs by arrangement, but reserve well ahead; maximum group 25; 10am–3pm every hour. Admission free. Metro: McPherson Square or Farragut North.

The public can tour the offices of this famous newspaper, known worldwide for the journalistic investigation into the Watergate scandal that led to President Nixon's resignation in 1974. The conducted tour, which includes the newsroom (still recognizable as the scene of *All The President's Men* and other movies) and printing presses, gives a fascinating insight into the workings of a modern newspaper. Reserve in advance.

Washington Project for the Arts

400 7th St. NW in the Jenifer Bldg., entrance on D St. NW. ☎ 202/347-4813. Open Wed–Fri 11am–6pm; Sat–Sun 11am–5pm. Donation suggested. Metro: Gallery Place-Chinatown or Archives-Navy Memorial.

One of two "alternative" art spaces in Washington (the other is the even funkier District of Columbia Center for the Arts, or DCAC, in Adams Morgan), WPA is nationally known as an artist-directed, multidisciplinary nonprofit organization with programs spanning the visual, media, literary, and performing arts. Founded in 1975, WPA provides space and funding for progressive local, national, and international artists. The Book Works store is renowned for its beautiful limited-edition books, and a wide selection of international magazines.

Watergate Complex

Virginia and New Hampshire Ave. NW, Washington, DC 20037. Metro: Foggy Bottom.

One of the most iconic buildings in Washington, with its connotations of intrigue and scandal and presidential downfall, and Redford and Hoffman (oops, we meant Woodward and Bernstein), the Watergate is in reality just a big, boring shopping, residential, and office complex near the Kennedy Center.

In June 1972, 5 men working for the re-election of President Nixon were caught burgling the headquarters of the Democratic National Committee in the Watergate complex. Since then the name "Watergate" has been associated with the ensuing scandal that ultimately led to Nixon's resignation in 1974.

The sweeping curves of the building are striking. The 6th-floor offices, where the burglary took place, are no longer occupied by the Democratic National Committee. The Watergate Complex is not to be confused with the Watergate itself, which is a broad flight of steps leading down to the Potomac near the Lincoln Memorial.

★★ The White House

1600 Pennsylvania Ave. NW, Washington, DC 20500. ☎ 202/456-7041. Tues–Sat 10am–noon. Closed some days for official functions. Admission free. Metro: McPherson Square or Farragut West.

"It's very big, and it's very white," observed astute Brazilian actress Sonia Braga after a visit to the home of the president and first lady.

Theodore Roosevelt christened this mansion "The White House." It is the only residence of a head of state, anywhere in the world, that is open regularly to the public and free of charge, with more than 1.5 million visitors each year. That fact makes necessary a discussion of the practicalities of a visit.

Advance planning is rewarded. Residents of the United States can write to their senators or congresspersons to request passes for VIP tours, which are given at hours other than those listed above. Since the supply is very limited and demand is high, requests should be made 6 months or more in advance. Foreign citizens might be able to obtain passes at their consulates. All others must line up. And line up. No tickets are required for regularly scheduled tours from Labor Day to Memorial Day, when visitors simply join the line at the entrance on the east side of the White House. Even in bitterly cold, muggy, or rainy weather, lines are long, with a 2-hour wait far from unusual.

Once inside, the tour covers only 5 rooms, which do not include the Oval Office or the first family's living quarters. And finally, the building can be closed on short notice for occasions of state. For all these reasons, the elderly and parents with children or impatient teenagers in tow may wish to consider whether the time might be more comfortably and profitably spent at one of Washington's more accessible attractions.

The White House

All that said, the most striking thing about the president's official residence is that it is rather modest. It is elegant, distinguished but unostentatious, and all the better for that. For this we have to thank George Washington; he chose the site in 1791, and approved the simple dignity of the design by the Irish architect James Hoban. But Washington never lived here, and John Adams was the first to move into the house referred to as the "President's Mansion" or "President's Palace" in 1800, while it was still unfinished.

In 1814, during the War of 1812, the British burned the house, leaving only the shell. It was rebuilt, and the Virginia sandstone exterior walls were painted white to obliterate the fire marks. By the 1940s it was discovered to be so unsound that it had to be almost completely reconstructed around a new steel skeleton. During the rebuilding, from 1949 to 1952, President Truman and his family lived across the street in **Blair House** at 1651-3 Pennsylvania Avenue NW. The house you see today is therefore largely a skillful reproduction, altered and added to for more than a century.

A normal visit includes a tour of the 5 main public rooms of the house. There are many fine portraits, pieces of furniture and objets d'art, accumulated over the years as each president and his family added their own stamp to the presidential home. Here is the approximate order in which the rooms are viewed.

Entering via the east wing lobby, built in 1942 and hung with portraits of first ladies, you will first pass through the light Garden Room overlooking the Jacqueline Kennedy Garden, down a corridor (with more first ladies) flanked by rooms that can be glimpsed in passing. To the right is the cozy library, the room where the president traditionally gives his televised fireside broadcasts. On the other side are the Vermeil Room, with a Monet above the fireplace, the China Room, with a fine display of ceramics, and the oval Diplomatic Reception Room, with superb panoramic wallpaper and a carpet woven with the seals of the 50 states.

Up on the next floor is the largest room in the house, the East Room, used for dances, concerts, press conferences, and ceremonies of various kinds, none more awesome than the lying-in-state of 4 assassinated presidents. The portrait of George Washington by Gilbert Stuart was daringly saved by Dolley Madison when the house was under attack in 1814. This room was not always as elegant as it is now. When John Adams was president, his wife Abigail used it to dry laundry,

White House Floor Plan

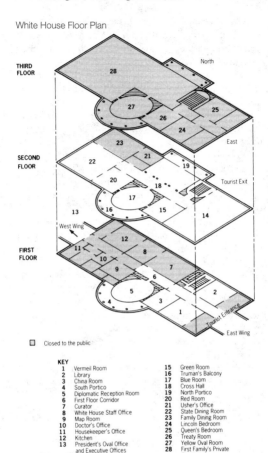

☐ Closed to the public

KEY

1	Vermeil Room	15	Green Room
2	Library	16	Truman's Balcony
3	China Room	17	Blue Room
4	South Portico	18	Cross Hall
5	Diplomatic Reception Room	19	North Portico
6	First Floor Corridor	20	Red Room
7	Curator	21	Usher's Office
8	White House Staff Office	22	State Dining Room
9	Map Room	23	Family Dining Room
10	Doctor's Office	24	Lincoln Bedroom
11	Housekeeper's Office	25	Queen's Bedroom
12	Kitchen	26	Treaty Room
13	President's Oval Office	27	Yellow Oval Room
	and Executive Offices	28	First Family's Private
14	East Room		Quarters

and, more than a century later, President Theodore Roosevelt's children roller-skated here in bad weather.

The next 3 rooms are designated by their colors: green, blue, and red. They face south over the garden and are filled with fine furniture and interesting portraits, such as that of the ornithological artist John James Audubon on the west wall of the Red Room. The last room to be visited is the State Dining Room, which is white with yellow curtains, and features a portrait of Abraham Lincoln over the fireplace. The inscription on the marble mantelpiece is from a letter by John Adams, written on his first night in the mansion to his wife Abigail, who was still in Massachusetts: "I pray heaven to bestow the best of blessings on this house and all that shall hereafter inhabit it. May none but honest and wise men ever rule under this roof." Here sometimes as many as 140 guests dine. Passing the long Cross Hall and Entrance Hall, hung with portraits of recent presidents, you emerge from the house on the north side under the great main portico.

Although Abigail Adams, first of the first ladies to attempt to make a home out of the White House, was most concerned simply to see the structure completed, other presidential wives have made the improvement of their executive residence a national priority. (It was not until 1902 that the first families could enjoy total privacy in their 3rd-floor quarters, although they continued to take their meals in the 2nd-floor dining room for another 60 years.) Mary Todd Lincoln spent compulsively (criminally, her critics said) on lavish French furnishings for the mansion while the nation was on the brink of the Civil War. A century later, Jacqueline Bouvier Kennedy spearheaded a worldwide campaign for private and public contributions to return to the White House those historically accurate and original furnishings that had been looted, loaned, or moved during 34 administrations.

This massive restoration has been carried on by successive first ladies, so that today the White House is a treasure trove of significant American furnishings and decorative objects, as well as the stately home of the nation's highest statesman.

Woodrow Wilson House

2340 S St. NW, Washington, DC 20008. ☎ 202/387-4062. Tours by arrangement (call 2 weeks ahead). Open Tues–Sun 10am–4pm. Closed major holidays. $5 adults, $4 seniors, $2.50 students, free for children under 7. Metro: Dupont Circle.

"An unpretentious, comfortable, dignified house, fitted to the needs of a gentleman's home" is how Mrs. Woodrow Wilson described the house that she and her husband settled into in 1921, following his retirement from the presidency. The handsome brick Georgian Revival house, designed in 1915, is preserved much as it was when the Wilsons lived there. This is the only presidential house preserved as a museum. Mementoes include the typewriter on which Wilson drafted the League of Nations proposal, the projector and screen that enabled him to enjoy silent movies at home, and numerous foreign gifts such as a large French tapestry, and a baseball given to Wilson by King George V.

Walks in Washington, D.C.

Washington stimulates and encourages the walker as many American cities do not. For all its leafy open spaces and broad boulevards, it is surprisingly compact. A single outing of a few square blocks can take in several museums and monuments or entire residential neighborhoods, with frequent opportunities to rest. Since no structure is permitted to be higher than the Capitol dome, streets are not thrown into shadow by intimidating ranks of faceless skyscrapers.

Public transportation is excellent, with bus stops and Metro stations readily available when a stroll starts to become a chore. Far from being regarded as eccentric, as it is in, say, Los Angeles, walking is a favored form of recreation here.

The possibilities are endless, but the following 3 very different walks take in parts of the city that are interesting, attractive, or both.

Walk 1: Getting to Know Central Washington

Allow 2–3hrs. Metro: Gallery Place-Chinatown.

This walk will introduce the visitor to 4 different aspects of the city: the **Old Downtown** area, the Federal Triangle, the environs of the **White House,** and finally the **Mall** and the **Washington Monument.**

Take the metro to ① **Gallery Place-Chinatown,** exiting at the intersection of 9th and G streets by the ② **Old Patent Office Building,** which now houses the **National Museum of American Art** and the **National Portrait Gallery.** Walk west along the pedestrian mall past the ③ **Martin Luther King Memorial Library** at 901 G St. NW. This is D.C.'s main public library, with a comprehensive collection of books, including a section on Washington, which visitors can use for reference purposes (☎ 202/727-1111).

Turn left down 10th Street past ④ **Ford's Theatre** at no. 511, the scene of Lincoln's assassination. Across the road at no. 516 is the ⑤ **Petersen House,** where he died. At E Street turn east past the colossal, forbidding, Cyclopean facade of the ⑥ **J. Edgar Hoover Building,** headquarters of the FBI, then go down 9th Street, leading into Pennsylvania Avenue. Across the avenue and slightly to the left you will see the ⑦ **National Archives** building. Directly across from the archives is the ⑧ **Navy Memorial** at Market Square.

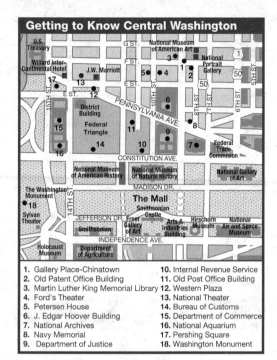

Getting to Know Central Washington

1. Gallery Place-Chinatown
2. Old Patent Office Building
3. Martin Luther King Memorial Library
4. Ford's Theater
5. Petersen House
6. J. Edgar Hoover Building
7. National Archives
8. Navy Memorial
9. Department of Justice
10. Internal Revenue Service
11. Old Post Office Building
12. Western Plaza
13. National Theater
14. Bureau of Customs
15. Department of Commerce
16. National Aquarium
17. Pershing Square
18. Washington Monument

Now cross the avenue into what is known as the "Federal Triangle." This massive government building project dates from the years 1928 to 1938 when the triangle bounded by Pennsylvania Avenue, Constitution Avenue, and 15th Street was filled with a series of matching federal buildings in a style reminiscent of the Italian Renaissance, with red-tiled roofs and imposing colonnades and porticoes.

After you've seen the ⑨ **Department of Justice** and the ⑩ **Internal Revenue Service,** the ⑪ **Old Post Office Building** is a welcome change of style, blending Neuschwanstein Castle with the Palazzo Vecchio, its massive clock tower vying with the Washington Monument for height. Pause inside, in one of the most staggering interiors in the city—a huge, glass-covered atrium, with shops, food-court cafes, and a performance stage—for coffee or a meal at a variety of prices and with a variety of ethnic origins. Take an elevator to the top of the tower for a superb view.

Continue up Pennsylvania Avenue to 13th Street, and cross over to ⑫ **Western Plaza,** opposite the ⑬ **National Theater.** Set into the white paving of the plaza is a map of central Washington laid out in black stone, with the floor plan of the White House and Capitol in brass. There are also plaques inscribed with memorable quotations about the capital, such as Henry Adams's back-handed compliment: "One of these days this will be a very great city if nothing happens to it."

If you look southeast from here, you can see another great chunk of the Federal Triangle, occupied by the ⑭ **Bureau of Customs.** Immediately to the south, across the road is the smaller but still imposing District Building, headquarters of the D.C. administration. Just to the west of this is the ⑮ **Department of Commerce,** which also houses the small but interesting ⑯ **National Aquarium.** Immediately west of the plaza is ⑰ **Pershing Square,** a pleasant little oasis of greenery with an open-air cafe by a pool, which in winter becomes a cute little ice-skating rink. Continue west, passing on your right the railings of the White House garden with a good view of the house itself.

Turn south, cross the Ellipse and head for the ⑱ **Washington Monument** in the center of the Mall. Take the elevator to the top of the monument (waits of half an hour are common during high season, but there are benches and plenty of people-watching to pass the time) and complete your introduction to Washington with a superb panorama of the city.

Walk 2: Monuments, Mansions & Embassies

Allow 1–2hrs. Metro: Farragut North, Farragut West, Dupont Circle.

This walk takes you through what was once an enclave of the very rich: the financiers, railroad kings, food manufacturers, and coal magnates who descended on Washington as it grew in importance, vying with one another in the magnificence of the houses they built. After the stock market crash of 1929, many of these stately mansions were sold for use as embassies, clubs, or institutions, while others were divided into apartments. The neighborhood gradually became the city's bohemian center, first attracting the beatniks in the fifties, then the hippies in the sixties. In the seventies it became the home to D.C.'s burgeoning gay population. The neighborhood is still strongly residential, with some charming streets.

From ① **Farragut North** or **Farragut West Metro,** walk northward up Connecticut Avenue to the intersection with M Street and Rhode Island Avenue, which is marked by a statue of the poet Longfellow. Turn right up Rhode Island Avenue, past the Roman

Catholic ② **St. Matthew's Cathedral** and the ③ **B'nai B'rith Klutznick Museum** and on up to Scott Circle.

A few paces back west, down N Street, you can take a tea or coffee break in the rustic English atmosphere of the ④ **Tabard Inn** at no. 1739. Then you could detour a few steps westward on N Street and down 17th to M Street to the ⑤ **National Geographic Building** and its high-tech Explorers Hall.

Scott Circle itself is named after the Mexican War General, Winfield Scott, who sits astride a horse in the center. After the statue was completed it was felt to be indecorous that the general should be riding a mare, so the sculptor obediently added male parts to the animal. On the west side of the Circle is a monument to the 19thC statesman Daniel Webster, while on the east is one to Samuel Hahnemann, the founder of homeopathy, whose principle, "Similia similibus curentur" ("like is cured by like"), is inscribed on the monument.

Now turn and walk northwest up Massachusetts Avenue, known as "Embassy Row." The ⑥ **Australian Embassy** is the first, a rather unmemorable modern building on the north side, by the Circle. Next to it is the ⑦ **Embassy of the Philippines.** A little farther down, on the opposite side, are those of ⑧ **Peru,** ⑨ **Trinidad and Tobago,** and ⑩ **Chile.** The Chilean Embassy at no. 1732 is a rather austere redbrick building by the architect Glenn Brown. A little farther on is the former ⑪ **Canadian Embassy** at no. 1746, the work of a prestigious architect of French origin, Jules Henri de Sibour. Completed in 1906, it was built in the fashionable Beaux Arts style for the coal magnate and financier Clarence Moore, who died in the Titanic disaster after only 6 years of residence. On the other side, at no. 1785, is another handsome ⑫ **Beaux Arts building,** now occupied by the National Trust for Historic Preservation. If you keep heading north, you'll come to the ⑬ **Indian Embassy** (no. 2107), guarded by a pair of carved elephants; the modernistic glass cube (shades of Brasilia) which houses the ⑭ **Brazilian Embassy** (no. 3006); and the ⑮ **British Embassy** (no. 3100).)

A few steps on is ⑯ **Dupont Circle.** Of the elegant mansions that once ringed the Circle, only two remain: 1801 Massachusetts Ave., now the Sulgrave Club, and 15 Dupont Circle, which houses the Washington Club. Both date from the turn of the century. The Women's National Democratic Club occupies

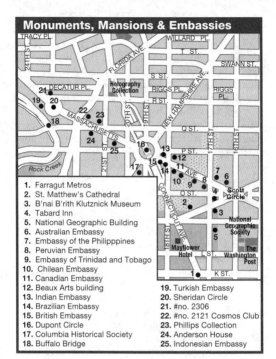

Monuments, Mansions & Embassies

1. Farragut Metros
2. St. Matthew's Cathedral
3. B'nai B'rith Klutznick Museum
4. Tabard Inn
5. National Geographic Building
6. Australian Embassy
7. Embassy of the Philipppines
8. Peruvian Embassy
9. Embassy of Trinidad and Tobago
10. Chilean Embassy
11. Canadian Embassy
12. Beaux Arts building
13. Indian Embassy
14. Brazilian Embassy
15. British Embassy
16. Dupont Circle
17. Columbia Historical Society
18. Buffalo Bridge
19. Turkish Embassy
20. Sheridan Circle
21. #no. 2306
22. #no. 2121 Cosmos Club
23. Phillips Collection
24. Anderson House
25. Indonesian Embassy

another lovely old building to the northeast, at no. 1526 New Hampshire Ave. The center of Dupont Circle is marked by a graceful white fountain commemorating Rear Admiral Samuel Francis Dupont (1803–65), with a bowl supported by 4 allegorical figures suggestive of the sea and navigation. In the surrounding little park are chess tables, used on fine days. Four descending staircases lead into the **Dupont Underground,** a former underground trolley tunnel beneath the Circle that now houses sub shops, pizza joints, delis, coffee bars and even a minimassage stand. It's also a good alternative to crossing the Circle during busy traffic.

Now follow New Hampshire Avenue down to no. 1307, currently the headquarters of the ⑰ **Columbia Historical Society,** with a delightful garden, entered from Sunderland Place.

From here go north up 20th Street and turn left down P Street. Near the bridge to **Georgetown** is a large and brooding bronze statue of the Ukrainian poet Tara Shevchenko.

Walk up 23rd Street, along the edge of Rock Creek, to the dramatic ⑱ **Buffalo Bridge,** so called because of the 4 great buffaloes that guard the corners. Designed by Glenn Brown, architect of the Chilean

Embassy, it was built between 1912 and 1915. Turn around to view the ornate bulk of the ⑲ **Turkish Embassy** at no. 1606 23rd St., designed in the early 20thC by George Oakley Totten for Edward H. Everett, who made his fortune from metal bottle tops.

⑳ **Sheridan Circle,** dominated by the equestrian statue of the Civil War hero, General Philip Sheridan, has more gracious houses, most of them now belonging to embassies, including those of Korea, Egypt, Greece, and Ireland. Facing the Circle, at ㉑ **no. 2306** Massachusetts Ave., is the former home and studio of the early 20thC artist Alice Pike Barney. The house, which contains her works and those of contemporaries, can be toured by reservation through the National Museum of American Art on Wednesday, Thursday, and 2 Sundays a month (☎ 202/357-3111). It is closed from July to September.

Walk around the Circle, then proceed southeast down Massachusetts Avenue. This stretch of the avenue has many remarkable mansions, each with its own story to tell. For example, ㉒ **no. 2121** was built in the style of the Petit Trianon for the railroad magnate Richard Townsend, whose wife insisted, for superstitious reasons, that the building should incorporate an existing house. Sadly, this did not prevent Mr. Townsend from dying of a riding injury soon after the house was completed. The building now houses the exclusive Cosmos Club.

Just around the corner at no. 1600 21st St. is the mansion housing the ㉓ **Phillips Collection,** austere outside but delightfully intimate inside. It adjoins a more contemporary addition. Across the road, at no. 2118 Massachusetts Ave., is the imposing and patrician facade of the ㉔ **Anderson House,** headquarters of the elite Society of the Cincinnati. The house is open to the public, providing an opportunity to inspect the even more lavish interior.

A little farther down at no. 2020 is the ㉕ **Indonesian Embassy,** a building of well-fed appearance, bulging out at the corners. Like the Townsend house, its story is marked by tragedy. It was built just after the turn of the century by Thomas F. Walsh, a wealthy Irishman who had struck gold in Colorado. His son and grandson were both killed in automobile accidents, and he died a sad recluse in 1910.

Continue down the avenue to return to the neighborhood of Dupont Circle, where there is a Metro station. Before leaving the area, go northwest from the

Circle along Connecticut Avenue, and have a snack or meal at one of the many lively cafes and restaurants, like the **Childe Harold** (1610 20th St. NW, between Q and R streets) or **Kramerbooks & Afterwords** (1517 Connecticut Ave. NW), a delightful bookstore-cum-cafe, and a true D.C. must-do.

Walk 3: Capitol Hill

Allow 2–3hrs. Metro: Union Station, Eastern Market.

This route includes not only the **Capitol** itself and the imposing buildings surrounding it, but also the charming and less well-known area to the east.

As on the other walks, you will pass some striking outdoor sculptures, such as the figures on the facade of ① **Union Station,** where the walk begins, and the Columbus fountain in the station plaza. The station's magnificent interior, its central concourse lined with stylish boutiques, cafes, and movie theaters, should not be missed.

From the station, walk down Louisiana Avenue to the intersection of North Capitol Street. Turn south toward the Capitol, passing through a park with an elegant fountain (which is turned off in cold months). From here, either continue down to the Capitol and return to the route after your visit, or turn up Constitution Avenue, where you will pass 2 of the ② **Senate office buildings.** At the northwest corner of 2nd Street NE stands the ③ **Sewall-Belmont House** at no. 144 Constitution Ave. A well-proportioned, red-brick townhouse built in 1800, it has been pleasingly restored.

From here continue along 2nd Street past the rear of the ④ **Supreme Court,** as far as the intersection with E. Capitol Street. Ahead is the ⑤ **Library of Congress** on the southwest corner and the ⑥ **Folger Shakespeare Library** on the southeast corner. There's a delightfully puckish statue of Puck out front, and the friezes on the Folger's exterior depict scenes from Shakespeare. Inside is a full-sized replica of the Globe Theatre.

Go down E. Capitol Street toward **Lincoln Park,** past many attractive 19thC houses in a great variety of styles. The park contains the ⑦ **Emancipation Monument,** showing Abraham Lincoln bidding a slave rise to freedom, and a memorial to the black educator ⑧ **Mary McLeod Bethune** (1875–1955).

Return southwest along N. Carolina Avenue and turn south down 7th Street. Here, in the first block to

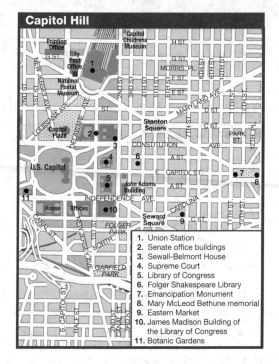

the right, is the redbrick building housing ⑨ **Eastern Market,** one of the few genuine farmers markets left in the city, where anything, from a side of Virginia ham, to a piece of ripe Stilton cheese, to fresh inexpensive seafood, may be bought. There is also a potters' studio upstairs in the market and, at the north end, an auditorium where art exhibitions and dance performances are held. The market (open Tues–Thurs 7am–6pm; Fri–Sat 6am–7pm) is liveliest on Saturday mornings. Nearby are boutiques, shops, and small restaurants. The Metro is at the intersection of 7th Street and Pennsylvania Avenue SE, but you could head back toward the Capitol along Pennsylvania Avenue SE, and lunch at the Hunan Dynasty, Greek Taverna, or one of several pubs, such as the Tune Inn. You will pass the ultramodern ⑩ **James Madison Building** of the Library of Congress and the **House of Representatives' Office Buildings** on Independence Avenue SE, on your way to the enormous greenhouse of the ⑪ **Botanic Gardens** and the southeast end of the Mall.

STAYING ACTIVE

ALTHOUGH D.C. IS CONSIDERED A CEREBRAL CITY—
with paper-pushing, red-tape relays, and power-talking the main forms of exercise—there are plenty of ways to stay active and fit.

Happily, the city enjoys a long playing season, thanks to the usually mild climate: Even in midwinter, cold spells are interrupted by occasional warm days that let everyone outside to play. For the latest in weather information call 202/936-1212. Call the National Capital Parks at 202/619-PARK for a daily recreation bulletin.

Spectator Sports

Come football season, the only game in town is the (controversially named) **Washington Redskins,** who play their home games at Robert F. Kennedy Memorial Stadium, 2001 East Capitol St. SE (☎ 202/547-9077). All games are technically sold out through the millennium, which means you can't just stroll up to the box office and buy a ticket. Still, there are ways of seeing a Skins game: Check the classified ads in the Friday *Washington Post* and Thursday *City Paper* for listings of season ticket holders looking to sell or swap seats for specific games.

If you do manage to score Skins seats, we strongly advise you to take the Metro. Parking at RFK Stadium is very limited, not to mention expensive.

The nearest professional baseball team is the **Baltimore Orioles,** and many Washingtonians are as devoted to them as they are to their own Redskins. The O's play at the glorious new Camden Yards state-of-the-art stadium, at Eutaw and Camden streets near Baltimore's fun, touristy Inner Harbor development of shops and restaurants. It's just a 1-hour trip from downtown Washington. For ticket information, call 410/547-6234.

It's somewhat easier to get tickets to D.C.'s NBA entry, the **Washington Bullets,** who make their home at the USAir Arena in Landover, Maryland (25 minutes from downtown via New York Ave. to Route 50, to the Capitol Beltway [I-95] south, to Exit 15A or 17A). The season runs from November through April, and into May if they make the playoffs. For ticket information, call 410/350-3400. College basketball teams stir up a lot of excitement, too. Since the **Georgetown Hoyas** took it all in 1987, they've been packing crowds into USAir Arena (☎ 301/350-3400).

Hockey fans have the **Washington Capitals** of the NHL, who play 40 home games from October through early April. Their home rink is the USAir Arena in Landover, Maryland (☎ 301/350-3400).

Two major **tennis tournaments** visit the area each year. In June, the men's tour comes to town for the Sovran Bank Classic at the Washington Tennis Center (16th and Kennedy St. NW; ☎ 202/429-0690). The women's Virginia Slims Tournament arrives in February at the Patriot Center at George Mason University (4400 University Drive, Fairfax, VA; ☎ 202/432-7328).

Polo is played every Sunday afternoon from May to October on the Lincoln Mall Field, southeast of the Lincoln Memorial, and the public is invited to attend, free of charge. Call the National Capitol Polo Club of Washington (☎ 301/972-7288). Tournaments are held in September and October.

Participant Sports
Beaches & Swimming

The nearest good beach is about an hour from downtown D.C., at **Sandy Point State Park,** the last exit off Route 50 before the Chesapeake Bay Bridge. The beach is wide and pleasant, but the sand is a bit gritty and oddly orange, and although you have quite a spectacular view of the Bay Bridge, it just doesn't feel like the real thing. Good for a quick day-trip, though.

Beach-bound Washingtonians head for the Delaware Shore, 3 hours away, especially to **Rehoboth Beach** (charming, aesthetically stuck in the 1950s, large gay and lesbian population sharing the beach and boardwalk with vacationing families); **Lewes** (quiet, secluded), and **Dewey Beach** (loud, rowdy, think *Animal House* at the beach). Baltimoreans head to the 10-mile strip of ocean-and-bayfront boardwalk known as **Ocean City,**

Maryland. The wise traveler will avoid driving on Friday and Sunday nights; the rush-hour traffic is worse than sand in your shorts.

If you don't feel like the drive but are desperate for a dip, several public pools are open year-round, including the **Capitol East Natatorium** (635 N. Carolina Ave. SE; ☎ 202/724-4495), **Woodrow Wilson High School** (Brandywine Street and Fort Drive NW; ☎ 202/282-2216) and the **Marie Reed Community Learning Center** (Kalorama Road and Champlain Street NW; ☎ 202/673-7771). In summer months, the **Georgetown Pool** is very pleasant and quite social (34th and Q St. NW; ☎ 202/282-2366).

For more information about D.C. public pools, call or visit the D.C. **Department of Recreation** (3149 16th St. NW; ☎ 202/673-7660) for a free Recreation Guide Book, which lists municipal facilities, including pools and tennis courts.

If you really want to make a splash, there's a giant wave pool and water theme park called **Adventure World** (Largo, Md., 3 miles e of Beltway exit 15A; ☎ 301/249-1500) open during the summer only. **Cameron Run State Park** in Alexandria, Virginia (☎ 703/960-0767), has water slides and a kid's water playground.

Biking

One of the best ways to see the city is by bike. The terrain is bicycle-friendly—lots of green stretches, especially along the Mall and in Rock Creek Park, and just hilly enough to keep things interesting.

You can rent bikes at **Big Wheel Bikes** (315 7th St. SE; ☎ 202/543-1600), **Fletcher's Boat House** (4940 Canal Rd. NW; ☎ 202/244-0461), and **Thompson Boat Center** (Virginia Ave. and Rock Creek Pkwy. NW; ☎ 202/333-4861).

Helpful area bicycling groups include the **Washington Area Bicyclist Association** (1015 31st St. NW; ☎ 202/944-8567) and the **Potomac Pedalers Touring Club** (P.O. Box 23601, L'Enfant Plaza Station, Washington D.C. 20026; ☎ 202/363-TOUR). Reliable, free bike maps are available from the **Metropolitan Washington Council of Governments** (☎ 202/962-3200) and the **Department of Public Works** (☎ 202/727-5090). A particularly good book is *Touring the Washington D.C. Area by Bicycle,* which presents 31 routes in D.C., Maryland, and Virginia.

One more thing: Please wear a helmet.

Boating

Whether you plan to rent a dinghy for a 3-hour tour, or charter a large boat for several days, there are plenty of opportunities for getting out on the water near Washington.

For a spin on the Potomac, you can rent boats, canoes, or Sunfish from **Buzzard Point Marina** (at the end of Half St. SW; ☎ 202/488-8400), **Thompson Boat Center** (Virginia Ave. at Rock Creek Pkwy. NW; ☎ 202/333-4861), **Fletcher's Boat House** (4940 Canal Rd. NW; ☎ 202/244-0461), and **Swain's Boat House** (10700 Swain Lock Rd., Potomac, MD; ☎ 301/299-9006), 10 miles from downtown D.C. At the **Tidal Basin Boathouse** (☎ 202/484-0206) near the Jefferson Memorial, you can rent 2-person paddleboats and 4-person boats for $7 to $14 an hour.

In nearby Annapolis, on the splendid Chesapeake Bay, there are a multitude of boat rental services, including the **Annapolis Sailing School** (601 6th St.; ☎ 410/261-1947) and the **Bay Yacht Agency** (321 First St.; ☎ 410/269-6772), which charters larger crafts. Annapolis hosts the famous **Chesapeake Bay Yachting Week** over Labor Day weekend, but there are races all year, including the **President's Cup Regatta** (with hydroplane, rowing, and canoe races) in early June.

Golf

Washington is big on golf; must be all those attorneys and politicians. The best courses in the area are membership clubs—including posh and exclusive places like Burning Tree, Congressional Country Club, and Chevy Chase Country Club—and the only way to play is either through a cooperative arrangement with your own club, or as the guest of a member.

But there are plenty of handsome and accessible courses in the area available to residents and visitors. Take a swing at one of these:

East Potomac Park Golf Course (900 Ohio Drive SW; ☎ 202/544-7660) in East Potomac Park, offers a fine view of the monuments as you play; it's on a spit of land jutting into the Potomac River. The facility includes an 18-hole championship par 72 course, and an easier 18-hole course, a driving range, and miniature golf. Tee times are first come, first served.

Greendale Golf Course (6700 Telegraph Rd., Alexandria, VA; ☎ 703/971-6170) is a pleasant par 70 course with tree-lined fairways.

Needwood Golf Course (6724 Needwood Road, Rockville, MD; ☎ 301/948-1075) is a fairly easy par 71 course.

Paint Branch Golf Course (4690 University Blvd., College Park, MD; ☎ 301/935-0330) is a 9-hole executive golf course open year-round.

Penderbrook Club (3700 Golf Trail Lane, Fairfax, VA; ☎ 703/385-3700) is an 18-hole, par 71 course carved out of the woods and surrounded by a golfing community.

Rocky Gorge Golf Fairway (8445 Old Columbia Rd., Laurel, MD; ☎ 301/725-0888) is the area's first all-weather golf driving range, complete with heaters for winter practice.

Health Clubs

You'll get a lot of exercise just walking around the city, but if you want a more rounded workout, check out one of the many sports clubs.

You're likely to spot George Stephanopoulous on the Stairmaster at **Washington Sports Club** (1835 Connecticut Ave. NW, ☎ 202/332-0100; also at 20th and M St. NW, ☎ 202/785-4900), both locations known for their fabulous clientele. Serious muscleheads head for Adams Morgan's **Muscle Beach** (2007 18th St. NW; ☎ 202/328-5201). The posh **National Capitol YMCA** (1711 Rhode Island Ave. NW; ☎ 202/862-9622) offers a pool, racquetball and handball courts, free weights, Nautilus, the works; and there's an equally swell YWCA branch downtown (9th and G St. NW; ☎ 202/638-2100). And there's a **Bally's Holiday Fitness Center,** too (2000 L St. NW; ☎ 202/331-7788).

The hotel health clubs are always a clean, dependable, and convenient alternative. The **Watergate Health Club** (2650 Virginia Ave. NW; ☎ 202/298-4460) has a swimming pool, gymnasium, fencing, sauna, massage, and exercise classes, and offers outside membership with flexible short-term arrangements. The **ANA Hotel** (formerly the Westin), recently was named "Best Hotel Fitness Center in the World," and indeed, it is so cushy and comfy, it seems almost a shame to sweat in it, although it has everything you need to get your heart rate going, including celebrities. This is where Arnold Schwarzenegger, Jean-Claude Van Damme, and John Kennedy, Jr. work out when they're in town. Other good hotel facilities include the **Washington Hilton** (1919 Connecticut Ave. NW; ☎ 202/483-3000),

Sheraton Washington Park (2660 Woodley Road NW; ☎ 202/328-2902), and the **Omni Shoreham** (2500 Calvert St. NW; ☎ 202/234-0700), all of which have sunny outdoor pools, available to visitors.

A few hotels offer luxurious weekend spa packages, providing unlimited access to high-tech fitness equipment, swimming, massage, sauna, and steam room, enhanced by gourmet low-calorie, low-fat spa cuisine. Try the **Four Seasons Hotel** (☎ 202/342-0444), the **Grand Hyatt** (☎ 202/582-1234), the **Washington Hilton** (☎ 202/483-3999), or the **Ritz-Carlton** in Pentagon City, Virginia (☎ 703/415-5000).

Hiking

Behind the scenes, the area is threaded with hiking trails, many right near downtown. The C&O Canal National Historical Park, for instance, has 184 miles of uninterrupted paths along the Potomac River, running from Georgetown to Cumberland, Maryland, and the trails along the Potomac near Great Falls, Virginia, 15 miles upriver from Washington, are justifiably famous.

Call the **National Park Service** (☎ 202/485-9666) for maps and information about area hiking trails. The **Rock Creek Nature Center,** in the heart of Rock Creek Park, offers lots of outdoor activities, including year-round hikes and nature walks guided by U.S. park rangers. For information on Sierra Club outings in the D.C. area, call **Dial-A-Hike** at 202/547-2326.

Horseback Riding

Horse country is right nearby, centered in Middleburg, Virginia, and lots of Washingtonians enjoy spending a day at the races. Point-to-Point races are held every weekend from February through April in different locations in hunt country. Contact the **Virginia Point-to-Point Council** (☎ 703/439-3669) for dates and locations. The Smithsonian Resident Associates Program offers an annual **Hunt Country Stable Tour,** visiting the stables of the "Rich and Famous." Call 202/357-3030.

But you can also get on your mustang, Sally, and ride right in the city: The **Rock Creek Park Horse Center** (Military and Glover Rd. NW; ☎ 202/362-0117) offers year-round trail riding through Rock Creek Park, lessons, and boarding. **Meadowbrook Stables** at Rock Creek Recreation Center offers full riding and horse-care facilities; call 301/585-6096.

Jogging

You could think of the National Mall as the country's most expensive and beautiful running track. The miles of gravel path give good traction, with frequent water fountains and plenty to look at, including the hundreds of government workers who run at lunchtime, rain or shine, back and forth over the bridges between D.C. and Virginia. The 15-mile length of Rock Creek Park is a busy paved trail, shared by runners, walkers, bikers, and in-line skaters; there's also an 18-station Parcourse exercise circuit along the trail near the Omni Shoreham hotel, where you can do push-ups, sit-ups and stretching exercises over a 1^1/$_2$-mile stretch. On weekends, the National Park Service closes off the north-south Beach Drive to traffic, creating a particularly bucolic running route alongside the creek, with gentle hills and thick forest. Another favorite city-exodus-run is the C&O Canal Towpath, which can be picked up off of Pennsylvania Avenue, just behind the Four Seasons hotel. Take it as far as you can.

There are lots of races in the area, the biggest of which is the annual **Marine Corps Marathon,** usually held in early November. The 26.8-mile (43km) course begins at the Pentagon and winds through Arlington, Virginia, into Georgetown and downtown Washington, passing most of the major monuments, and ending at the Iwo Jima Memorial. Preregistration is necessary; call 703/640-2741.

Shorter annual races, from 3Ks to 10Ks, include the **Cherry Blossom,** the **Bonne Bell Women's 10K,** the **Race for the Cure,** and the particularly picturesque **George Washington Parkway race.** Check the Friday weekend section of the *Washington Post.*

Skating & Skiing

When the ice is thick enough (call the U.S. Park Police at 202/426-6841 for an ice report), skating is permitted on the C&O Canal or the reflecting pools in front of the Lincoln Memorial and the west steps of the Capitol Building.

But it's safer to slide over to one of the public outdoor rinks. The **National Sculpture Garden Ice Rink** (Constitution Ave. between 7th and 9th St. NW; ☎ 202/371-5342) always attracts a fun crowd, gliding to funky music. There are 2 smaller rinks, as well: **Liberty Plaza** (17th and G St. NW; no phone) and **Pershing Park** (Pennsylvania Ave. between 14th and

15th St. NW; ☎ 202/737-6938). Inexpensive skate rentals are available. The Olympic-sized indoor rink at **Fort Dupont** (37th and Ely Place SE; ☎ 202/581-0199) is open September through April.

Skiers have to get out of town, but the snowy hills aren't too far away. Here are a few favorite locations:

The Homestead Ski Area (Hot Springs, VA; ☎ 703/839-5079)

Snowshoe Mountain Resort (Snowshoe, WV; ☎ 304/572-1000)

Wintergreen (Wintergreen, VA; ☎ 804/325-2200)

Wisp Ski Area (Oakland, MD; ☎ 301/387-5581)

Tennis

Around here, a lot of official business is transacted, or at least sparked, over the tennis net. There are many free year-round outdoor courts run by D.C. and the surrounding county and suburban governments. There are large indoor tennis facilities available year-round at **Hains Point** (1090 Ohio Drive, East Potomac Park, SW; ☎ 202/554-5962) and **Washington Tennis Center** (in Rock Creek Park, 16th and Kennedy St. NW; ☎ 202/722-5949). Reservations are necessary.

Courts are also available (on a first-come, first-served basis, of course) at several public parks. Call the D.C. **Recreation Department** (☎ 202/673-7660) or the **Washington Area Tennis Foundation** (☎ 202/291-9888).

The **Washington Hilton & Towers** (☎ 202/483-3000) has 3 outdoor courts that nonguests can rent by the hour.

SHOPPING

by Elise Hartman Ford

Washington's shopping scene is getting grander and more diverse all the time, the better to suit a clientele that ranges from ambassadors to aging baby boomers, college students, and suburbanites. The thing is, it's spread out. Instead of one single shopping district, the city has many.

If you're on Capitol Hill, Union Station is the best place, really the only place, to go. The turn-of-the-century Beaux Arts building has been magnificently restored to house not just train tracks but stores selling everything from political memorabilia to museum-quality, handcrafted jewelry. The arcade bustles with the activity of travelers wending their way trainward, lobbyists and hill staffers heading to the Metro or to lunch (Union Station has several good restaurants, as well as a food court), and throngs of shoppers and tourists.

If you want a business-day rush, mix with the suits on Connecticut Avenue NW, from K Street to Dupont Circle. Weekends, the avenue is fairly tame, but weekdays, shoppers and office workers jostle for sidewalk space past a stretch of stores that includes Burberry's and Victoria's Secret. Some of the best shopping—mainly upscale, and up-upscale—is found in a residential part of town along upper Wisconsin Avenue, where D.C. meets Maryland. Some of the best small malls and best department stores are here.

Shopping Districts & Streets

Adams Morgan

This is a lively part of town that spills over with the sounds, sights, and smells of different cultures. Defined by 18th Street and Columbia Road NW, Adams

Morgan is a neighborhood of ethnic eateries interspersed with the odd secondhand bookshop and eclectic collectibles store. The truth is, there are more nightclubs and bistros than actual stores; still it's fun to walk here, looking for them. Parking is impossible. Closest Metro: Dupont Circle; exit at Q Street NW and walk up Connecticut Avenue NW to Columbia Road NW.

Connecticut Avenue/Dupont Circle

Running from the mini–Wall Street that is K Street north to S Street, Connecticut Avenue NW is a main thoroughfare, where you'll find traditional clothing at Brooks Brothers, Talbots, and Burberry's, casual duds at the Gap and Liz Claiborne, discount items at Filene's Basement and Hit or Miss, and haute couture at Rizik's. The closer you get to Dupont Circle, the fewer business-types you see. People are younger, mellower, and have more pierced body parts. This pedestrian-friendly section of the avenue is studded with coffee bars and neighborhood restaurants, as well as art galleries, book and record shops, vintage-clothing stores, and boutiques of interest to gays and lesbians. Metro: Farragut North, at one end, Dupont Circle at the other, both stops on the Red Line.

Downtown

Between 12th and 14th streets NW lies a stretch of Pennsylvania Avenue that anchors a number of shops. On the White House side, within the Willard Inter-Continental hotel's courtyard, are 3 tony shops: Chanel, Harriet Kassman, Jackie Chalkley. Down 1 block are the Shops at National Place, a 4-level mall whose 80-some stores include Curious Kids and The Sharper Image. This is the section of Washington where beloved, family-owned department stores like Garfinckel's, Raleigh's, and Woodward & Lothrop used to be located. Now, it's up to Hecht's, at 12th and G streets, to carry the department store flag downtown. Metro: Metro Center, Red Line.

Meanwhile, back on Pennsylvania Avenue at 11th Street, the Pavilion at the Old Post Office is worth a visit, if only so you can admire its architecture or travel to the top of the 315-foot-high clocktower to view the city. The Pavilion's 3 lower levels contain 30 or so touristy shops and kiosks selling mostly souvenirs, novelty items, and food. Metro: Federal Triangle, (Blue/Orange).

Georgetown

Georgetown used to be more fun, when Hare Krishnas hung out on its corners and the streets were less, well, tourist-ridden. These days, Georgetown is a great place to shop—it's got so many good stores—but you may come away with a headache. Streets, sidewalks, and shops are crowded a lot of the time. Weekends, especially, bring out partiers of every persuasion, mainly intent on drinking. Visit Georgetown on a weekday morning, if you can. The heart of the shopping district beats at the intersection of Wisconsin Avenue and M Street NW, with shops fanning out like a compass: the Original Levis, Laura Ashley, the sophisticated Georgetown Park mall. New stores are opening all the time—a huge Barnes and Noble bookstore and Eddie Bauer are among the latest—while Washington legends, like Britches and Commander Salamander, rock on. If you need your hair done, Georgetown's salons are the best, and one of the larger ones can usually accommodate a last-minute appointment. Park on a side street—it's pretty easy to find a spot most mornings—so you can admire the handsome 18thC townhouses and cobblestone streets for which the neighborhood is famous. Weeknights are another good time to visit, for dinner and strolling afterwards. Afternoons, early evenings, and weekends, traffic is heavy and parking can be tough. Consider taking a bus or taxi—the closest Metro stop is at Foggy Bottom, a good 20- to 30-minute walk away. If you drive, you'll find parking lots expensive and parking tickets more so, so be careful where you plant your car.

Old Town Alexandria

If you've done Georgetown, or even if you haven't, Old Town is a nice place to visit. The drive alone is worth the trip. From Memorial Bridge, near the Lincoln Memorial, follow the George Washington Parkway alongside the Potomac River (the same route that takes you to National Airport) about 14 miles, where the parkway becomes Washington Street. Look for King Street and a parking spot and then walk. Shops run the length of King Street, from the waterfront up to Washington Street, and continue south on King Street to the Masonic Temple. Old Town isn't as hip or cosmopolitan as Georgetown, but it's cleaner, and less crowded, and just as quaint in parts, and the sidewalks are wider and the people more civil. It's also the best place to search for antiques. The area fills all sorts of shopping needs, from crafts at the Torpedo Factory Art Center, to specialty items like Mexican wedding dresses at Gossypia. Metro: King Street, Yellow Line; this puts you at the far end and a long walk from the action, so think about taking a taxi up King Street.

Upper Wisconsin Avenue Northwest

In a residential section of town known as Friendship Heights on the D.C. side and Chevy Chase on the Maryland side, lies a quarter-mile shopping district that extends from Saks Fifth Avenue at one end to Roche Bobois at the other. In between lie the Lord & Taylor, Neiman-Marcus, and Hecht Company department stores; a bevy of top shops, such as Tiffany's and Gianni Versace; 2 malls, the Mazza Gallerie and its younger, more chichi sister, the Chevy Chase Pavilion, whose offerings range from Country Road Australia to Hold Everything; and several stand-alone standards, such as Banana Republic. The street is too wide and traffic always too snarled to make this a strolling kind of shopping district. People head for particular stores and leave. Drive here if you want; the malls offer 2 hours of free parking. Or Metro it; the strip is right on the Red Line of the subway, with the Friendship Heights exits leading directly into each of the malls and into Hecht's.

Farmers & Flea Markets

Alexandria Farmers Market, 301 King St., at Market Square (in front of the city hall), Alexandria, VA.

The oldest continually operating farmers market in the country (since 1752), this market offers the usual assortment of locally grown fruits and vegetables, along with delectable baked goods, cut flowers, and plants. Saturday mornings, 5am to 10am, year-round.

D.C. Open-Air Farmers Market, Oklahoma Ave. and Benning Rd. NE (at RFK Stadium parking lot no. 6). Metro: Stadium/Armory, (Blue/Orange).

Fresh vegetables, seafood, hams, and arts and crafts. Thursday and Saturday 7am to 5pm year-round; Tuesday, 7am to 5pm June to September.

Eastern Market, 7th St. SE, between North Carolina Ave. and C St. Metro: Eastern Market, (Blue/Orange).

This is the one everyone knows about, even if they've never been here. Located on Capitol Hill, Eastern Market is an inside/outside bazaar of stalls, where greengrocers, butchers, bakers, farmers, artists, craftspeople, florists, and other merchants vend their wares daily (except Mon), but especially on weekends. Saturday morning is the best time to go. On Sundays the food stalls become a flea market.

Georgetown Flea Market, in a parking lot bordering Wisconsin Ave., between S and T streets NW.

Grab a coffee at Starbucks across the lane and get ready to barter. The Georgetown Flea Market is an institution frequented by all types of Washingtonians looking for a good deal, and often getting it, on antiques, painted furniture, vintage clothing, and decorative garden urns. Nearly 100 vendors. Open Sundays, March through December.

Montgomery County Farm Woman's Cooperative Market, 7155 Wisconsin Ave., Bethesda MD. Metro: Bethesda, Red.

The same vendors set up inside every Saturday, year-round from 7am to about 3:30pm, to sell preserves, homegrown veggies, cut flowers, slabs of bacon and sausages, and mouthwatering pies, cookies, and breads. Outside, on Saturdays and Wednesdays, are flea market vendors selling everything from rugs to tablecloths, furniture, and sunglasses.

Museum Shops

The gift stores in the Smithsonian's 16 museums are terrific places to shop. Wares are related to the focus of the individual museums. The largest Smithsonian store is in the National Museum of American History. The mart in the Smithsonian's Arts and Industries Building is nearly as extensive, since it sells all of the items offered in the museum catalogs. Smithsonian's museum-shop buyers travel the world for unusual items, many of which are made exclusively for the shops.

The Smithsonian doesn't corner the market on museum merchandise, however. The Corcoran Gallery of Art, the Phillips Collection, the National Building Museum—in fact just about all of Washington's museums have small shops with an array of interesting and beautiful objects. You shouldn't overlook shops at historic sites, either; the Washington National Cathedral (Wisconsin Ave. and Massachusetts Ave. NW), for example, has three. The main shop in the crypt of the Gothic cathedral sells books, stained glass, and tapes. The Herb Cottage is a delightful oasis, selling dried herbs and garden gifts. The Greenhouse shop is one of the best and certainly most charming places in town to buy flowering plants and live herbs.

Here's a list of museum stores:

Art and Industries Building

The Corcoran Gallery of Art

Department of the Interior Museum

Dolls' House and Toy Museum

National Building Museum

National Gallery of Art

National Museum of American Art

National Museum of American History

National Museum of Natural History

The Phillips Collection

Textile Museum

Washington National Cathedral

Shopping A to Z

Antiques

While you're not going to find many bargains, you can find a host of beautiful and rare examples of decorative furniture, silver, jewelry, art, and fabrics, from Amish quilts to Chinese silks. Antique shops dot the greater Washington landscape, with the richest concentrations found in Old Town Alexandria, Capitol Hill, Georgetown, Adams Morgan, and Kensington, Maryland.

Adam A. Weschler & Son
905 E St. NW. ☎ 202/628-1281. Metro: Metro Center (Red).
Regular Tuesday consignment/estate auctions, with seasonal Friday auctions of special fine objects.

Antique Row
Howard and Connecticut avenues, Kensington, MD.
A few miles north of the city is not far to go for a good deal or true bonanza at more than 40 antiques and collectibles shops. The stores line Howard Avenue and offer every sort of item, art to old prints, in a mix of styles, periods, and prices.

Antiques-on-the-Hill
701 North Carolina Ave., SE. ☎ 202/543-1819. Metro: Eastern Market (Blue/Orange).
This Capitol Hill institution since the 1960s sells silver, furniture, glassware, jewelry, porcelain, and lamps.

The Brass Knob Architectural Antiques
2311 18th St. NW. ☎ 202/332-3370. Metro: Dupont Circle (Red).
When early homes and office buildings are demolished in the name of progress, these savvy salvage merchants spirit away the salable treasures, from chandeliers to wrought-iron fencing.

Cherishables
1608 20th St. NW. ☎ 202/785-4087. Metro: Dupont Circle (Red).
An adorable shop specializing in 18th- and 19thC American furniture, folk art, quilts, and decorative accessories. Furniture is displayed in roomlike settings. A well-known spot for Christmas ornaments as well.

Georgetown Flea Market
On Wisconsin Ave., between S and T streets NW. Open Sun, Mar–Dec.
A 2-acre open-air delight for browsers and bargainers, with some real finds.

The Iron Gate
1007 King St., Alexandria, VA. ☎ 703/549-7429.
A little less expensive than some of its neighbors, this shop sells country pieces that seem to fit with any style of decorating.

James Wilhoit Antiques
150 N. St. Asaph St., Alexandria, VA. ☎ 703/683-6595.
American furniture and decorative arts from 1780 to 1840 are the main draw. Very high-quality pieces in a good-sized shop. Wilhoit will hunt down items for you.

Marston Luce
1314 21st St. NW. ☎ 202/775-9460. Metro: Dupont Circle (Red).
Fine 18th- and 19thC French, and some American, furniture, paintings, lamps, and garden items.

Millenium
1528 U St. NW. ☎ 202/483-1218. Metro: U Street/Cardozo (Green/Yellow).
Antique shopping for the TV generation, where anything before 1990 is considered collectible. Funky wares run from Heywood-Wakefield blond-wood beauties to used drinking glasses.

Old Print Gallery
1220 31st St. NW. ☎ 202/965-1818. Metro: Foggy Bottom (Blue/Orange), with a 20-minute walk.
Original American and European prints from the 18th and 19th centuries, including British political cartoons, maps, and historical documents.

Retrospective

2324 18th St. NW. ☎ 202/483-8112. Metro: Woodley Park/Zoo (Red).

Chic boutique full of well-designed relics of the pre-historic pre-1960s.

Silverman Galleries, Inc.

110 N. St. Asaph St., Alexandria, VA. ☎ 703/836-5363.

Known for its estate jewelry, especially diamonds. Also sells 18th- and 19thC paintings, silver, and furnishings. You're going to spend a lot of money here.

Sumpter Priddy III Antiques

1201 King St., Alexandria, VA. ☎ 703/299-0800.

Specializes in Southern furniture and decorative arts, especially from Virginia and North and South Carolina. Priddy sells to museums and historic sites; colleagues consider him very well informed.

Susquehanna Antiques

3216 O St. NW. ☎ 202/333-1511.

Specializes in Americana, with a focus on pre-1840 American and European furniture and paintings.

Art Galleries

Art galleries abound in Washington, but are especially prolific in 2 sections of the city: Dupont Circle and the downtown area of D and 7th streets NW. Here's a selection from these 2 neighborhoods.

DUPONT CIRCLE   Metro: Dupont Circle (Red):

Addison/Ripley Gallery, Ltd., 9 Hillyer Court NW. ☎ 202/328-2332.

Contemporary works by Americans, some but not all locals. Edith Kuhnle, Richard Hunt, and Wols Kahn are a few represented.

Anton Gallery. 2108 R St. NW. ☎ 202/328-0828.

Contemporary American paintings, photography, ceramics, prints, wood sculpture, metal sculpture, everything. All of the artists live locally but hail from around the world, Japan to Chile, New Zealand to California.

Fonda del Sol Visual Arts and Media Center. 2112 R St. NW. ☎ 202/483-2777.

A lively gallery in a picturesque townhouse, showcasing the art and cultures of Latin American, Native American, Caribbean, and African-American artists.

H. H. Leonards' Mansion on O Street. 2020 O St. NW. ☎ 202/659-8787.

Not an art gallery in the usual sense. Three 5-story Victorian townhouses are joined together and are decorated throughout with more than 5,000 antiques and artworks, in styles ranging from Art Deco to avant garde, and everything's for sale, even the beds on which owner H. and son Z. sleep. This is Leonards' home, a special events spot, and a luxurious B&B to boot. (Christie Brinkley, Alec Baldwin, and Kim Bassinger are among her clients.) H. tells you to help yourself to champagne or coffee in the English kitchen and then wander around on your own, which you could do for hours. Parking is such a problem that neighbors are trying to shut her down.

Osuna. 1914 16th St. NW. ☎ 202/296-1963.

Around since 1979, this gallery features Old Masters paintings, Italian (early 17thC artist Guido Reni is one example) and Baroque paintings in particular.

Very Special Arts Gallery. 1300 Connecticut Ave. NW. ☎ 202/628-0800.

Represents about 800 American artists with disabilities. Astounding works that include folk art, paintings, and sculptures.

SEVENTH STREET ARTS CORRIDOR   Metro: Archives/Navy Memorial, Yellow/Green or Gallery Place, Red/Yellow/Green:

406 Group, 406 7th St. NW, between D and E streets. Several first-rate art galleries, some interlopers from Dupont Circle, occupy this historic building, with its 13-foot-high ceilings and spacious rooms. They include:

David Adamson Gallery. ☎ 202/628-0257.

The largest gallery space in D.C. has 2 levels of works by contemporary artists, including those of locals Kevin MacDonald and rising star Renee Stout, and prints and drawings by David Hockney.

Baumgartner Gallery. ☎ 202/232-6320.

National and international artists are shown, including painters Ross Bleckner and Peter Halley. Gets a lot of good press, although other galleries are showing works every bit as impressive, or more so.

Touchstone Gallery. ☎ 202/347-2787.

An artist-run co-op of 15 artists who take turns showing their work.

Zenith Gallery. 413 7th St. NW. ☎ 202/783-2963.

This established gallery, across the street from the 406 Group, shows diverse works of contemporary artists, most American, about half of whom are local. You can get a good deal here, paying anywhere from $50 to $50,000 for a piece. Annual humor shows, annual neon exhibits, realism, abstract expressionism, landscapes.

Mickelson Gallery. 709 G St. NW. ☎ 202/628-1734.
Around the corner from the 7th Street gang, is one of
the oldest D.C. galleries, approaching 40 years, with a
framing business going back 80 years. Shows contemporary artists and is the sole rep for M. C. Escher and
George Bellows.

Beauty

With a few exceptions, the best salons are in Georgetown and cater to both men and women. If you don't
want to take a chance, these are the places to go.
Expect to spend a little money.

Bogart

1063 Wisconsin Ave. NW. ☎ 202/333-6550.
Favored by certain local TV news anchors. Facials cost
$50; haircuts average $45 for women, $35 for men.

Elizabeth Arden

5225 Wisconsin Ave. NW. ☎ 202/362-9890. Metro: Friendship
Heights (Red).
Does it all. Facials cost $65; haircuts average $65 for
women, $30 for men.

Georgette Klinger Skin Care Salon

Chevy Chase Pavilion. ☎ 202/686-8880. Metro: Friendship Heights
(Red).
Where the pampered of Washington get even more so.
Facials are $72, and include a complimentary makeup
treatment; haircuts average $60 for women, $45 for men.

Ilo Day Spa

1637 Wisconsin Ave. NW. ☎ 202/342-0350.
This large and trendy operation may not be as gracious
as other top salons, but neither is it as intimidating.
Facials cost $70; haircuts start at $60 for women, $40
for men.

IPSA for Hair

1629 Wisconsin Ave. NW. ☎ 202/338-4100.
This salon was voted favorite hairstyling salon in a local
count, but it only does hair. Provides valet parking for
$2. Haircuts average $55 for women, $35 for men.

Jacques Dessange/Elodie

5410 Wisconsin Ave., Chevy Chase, MD. ☎ 301/913-9373.
Metro: Friendship Heights (Red).
Staff is friendly but styling is inconsistent. Facials are
$47; haircuts average $50 for women, $30 for men.

Okyo

2903 M St. NW. ☎ 202/342-2675.
Owner Bernard Portelli used to color Catherine
Deneuve's hair in France, which means he's so booked

that he isn't taking any new clients. They only do hair here, at surprisingly reasonable rates: cuts start at $40 for women, $25 for men.

Saks Fifth Avenue
5555 Wisconsin Ave., Chevy Chase, MD. ☎ 301/657-9000.
Metro: Friendship Heights (Red).

Caters to an older clientele. Facials cost $50; haircuts average $30 for women and men, without a blow-dry.

3303 Inc.
3303 M St. NW. ☎ 202/965-4000.

Facials cost $75; haircuts start at $55 for women, $40 for men. You have to know what you want, but these stylists can do it.

Ury & Associates
3109 M St. NW. ☎ 202/342-0944.

Lots of model-types come here, where they get rapt attention from Ury. Facials cost $55; haircuts start at $55 for women, $35 for men.

Books

Washingtonians are readers, so bookstores pop up throughout the city. An increasingly competitive market means that it's not just Crown Books who offers discounts. Here are some favorite bookstores in each of the general, old and used, and special-interest categories.

General

Barnes and Noble
3040 M St. NW. ☎ 202/965-9880. Metro: Foggy Bottom
(Blue/Orange).

Three-level store, often the scene of author appearances, readings, and other events. Barnes and Noble discounts 10% on all hardcovers, 30% on *New York Times* hardcover bestsellers, 20% on *New York Times* paperback bestsellers.

B. Dalton
Union Station. ☎ 202/289-1750. Call for other locations.
Metro: Union Station (Red).

Your average all-round bookstore, heavy on the bestsellers. Sells magazines, too.

Borders Books and Music
1800 L St. NW. ☎ 202/466-4999. Call for other locations.
Metro: Farragut North (Red).

An overwhelming array of books, records, videos, and magazines. Most hardcovers are 10% off, *New York*

Times and the *Washington Post* hardcover bestsellers are 30% off. People like to hang here, hovering over the magazines, or sipping espresso in the cafe as they read their books. The store often hosts performances by local musicians.

Bridge Street Books

2814 Pennsylvania Ave. NW. ☎ 202/965-5200. Metro: Foggy Bottom (Blue/Orange).

A small, serious shop with a good selection of current fiction, literary criticism, and publications you won't fine elsewhere. Bestsellers and discounted books are not its raison d'etre.

Chapters Literary Bookshop

1512 K St. NW. ☎ 202/347-5495. Metro: McPherson Square (Blue/Orange) or Farragut North (Red).

Strong in new and backlist fiction. Always hosting author readings. No discounts. Tea always available. Friday afternoons they break out the sherry and cookies.

Crown Books

2020 K St. NW. ☎ 202/659-2030. Call for other locations. Metro: Foggy Bottom (Blue/Orange).

The best discounts but not the best selection: 10% off all paperbacks, 20% off all hardcovers, 40% off hardcover bestsellers, and 25% off paperback bestsellers.

Kramerbooks & Afterwords

1517 Connecticut Ave. NW. ☎ 202/387-1400. Metro: Dupont Circle (Red).

The first bookstore/cafe in the area, has launched countless romances. It's jammed and often noisy, offers live music Wednesday through Saturday evenings, and is open all night on weekends. Paperback fiction takes up most of its inventory, but the store carries a little of everything. No discounts.

Olsson's Books and Records

1307 19th St. NW. ☎ 202/785-1133. Call for other locations. Metro: Dupont Circle (Red).

Great selection, with helpful staff who know what they're talking about and will order books they don't have in stock. Twenty-five percent off *Washington Post* bestsellers, 20% off certain hardcover books, and 10% off paperbacks that are promoted as "good reads" by store staff.

Politics and Prose Bookstore

5015 Connecticut Ave. NW. ☎ 202/364-1919. Metro: The closest is Van Ness-UDC, on the Red line, but you'll have to walk about a half-mile from there.

This 2-story shop is in a residential part of town. A devoted neighborhood clientele helped move the inventory, book by book, across the street to larger quarters in 1990 (it's expanded again since then). Vast offerings in fiction and nonfiction alike, with the largest psychology section in the city (possibly on the East Coast). Warm, knowledgeable staff. Downstairs is a cozy coffeehouse frequented by book-lovers of all description: professorial types to moms lingering over cappuccinos. No discounts.

SuperCrown Books

11 Dupont Circle. ☎ 202/319-1374. Metro: Dupont Circle (Red).

Same discounts as regular Crown (see above), but wider selection.

Trover Shop

227 Pennsylvania Ave. SE. ☎ 202/543-8006. Call for other locations. Metro: Capitol South (Blue/Orange).

The only general bookstore on Capitol Hill, Trover's strengths are its political selections and its magazines. The store discounts 20% on *Washington Post* hardcover fiction and nonfiction bestsellers, computer books and cookbooks, and nonreference books costing more than $25.

Waldenbooks

Georgetown Park. ☎ 202/333-8033. Call for other locations. Metro: Foggy Bottom (Blue/Orange), with a 20-minute walk.

Another chain, general selection bookstore.

Old & Used Books

Booked Up

1204 31st St. NW. ☎ 202/965-3244.

An antiquarian bookstore in Georgetown where you can stumble upon some true collectors' items.

Idle Time Books

2410 18th St. NW. ☎ 202/232-4774. Metro: Woodley Park/Zoo (Red).

A dusty, 2-story treasure trove of used books in Adams Morgan.

Second Story Books

2000 P St. NW. ☎ 202/659-8884. Call for other locations. Metro: Dupont Circle (Red).

If it's old, out of print, custom-bound, or a small-press publication, this is where to find it. They specialize in used CDs and vinyl, and an amazing collection of antique French and American advertising posters.

Special-Interest Books

American History Museum Bookstore
National Museum of American History Giftshop, Constitution Ave. between 12th and 14th streets NW. ☎ 202/357-1784. Metro: Federal Triangle or Smithsonian (Blue/Orange).

A wonderful selection of books on American history and culture, including some for children.

American Institute of Architects Bookstore
1735 New York Ave. NW. ☎ 202/626-7475. Metro: Farragut West (Blue/Orange).

Books and gifts related to architecture.

Backstage
2101 P St. NW. ☎ 202/775-1488. Metro: Dupont Circle (Red).

Headquarters for Washington's theatrical community, which buys its books, scripts, trades, and sheet music here.

Cheshire Cat Children's Bookstore
5512 Connecticut Ave. NW. ☎ 202/244-3956.

Owners are extremely knowledgeable about children's literature, classics to current market. They are also big promoters of local talent. Frequent author visits.

Franz Bader Bookstore
1911 I St. NW. ☎ 202/337-5440. Metro: Farragut West (Blue/Orange).

Books on art, art history, architecture, and photography.

Lambda Rising
1625 Connecticut Ave. NW. ☎ 202/462-6969. Metro: Dupont Circle, Red.

It was a big deal when this gay and lesbian bookstore opened with a plate-glass window revealing its interior to passersby. Now it's an unofficial headquarters for the gay/lesbian/bi community.

Mystery Books
1715 Connecticut Ave. NW. ☎ 202/483-1600. Metro: Dupont Circle (Red).

The name of the store should give you a clue. Here's where to find out whodunnit. More paperbacks than hardcovers.

Travel Books & Language Center
4931 Cordell Ave., Bethesda, MD. ☎ 301/951-8533. Metro: Bethesda (Red).

A 20-minute ride on the Metro from downtown takes you to the heart of Bethesda and this bookstore, which has the best-in-the-area assortment of guidebooks and maps covering the entire world, as well as language dictionaries and learning tapes, travel diaries, memoirs, and novels famous for their evocation of particular places.

Yes! Bookshop

1035 31st St. NW. ☎ 202/338-6969.

The largest New Age/alternative bookstore in the country, and it's in cynical old D.C. Go figure. Holistic medicine, meditation, yoga, music, and other essentials for enlightenment.

Cameras & Photographic Equipment

Photography is a big business in this image-conscious tourist town. A wide range of services and supplies, from inexpensive point-and-shoot cameras to deluxe German and Japanese equipment, is available at competitive prices. Some shops offer repair services and have multilingual staff.

Baker's Photo Supply

4433 Wisconsin Ave. NW. ☎ 202/362-9100. Metro: Tenleytown (Red).

Hasselblad, Nikon, Graflex, Beseler, and other less expensive equipment. Also a repair service.

Congressional Photo

209 Pennsylvania Ave. SE. ☎ 202/543-3206. Metro: Capitol South (Blue/Orange).

The professionals' choice for custom finishing. Full camera repair service and budget processing are available.

Penn Camera Exchange

915 E St. NW. ☎ 202/347-5777. Call for other locations. Metro: Gallery Place (Red/Yellow/Green) or Metro Center, (Red/Yellow/Blue).

Across the street from the FBI Building, Penn Camera does a brisk trade with professionals and concerned amateurs. Its specialty is quality equipment and processing—not cheap, but worth it.

Ritz Camera Centers

1740 Pennsylvania Ave. NW. ☎ 202/466-3470. Call for other locations—there are many throughout the area. Metro: Farragut West (Blue/Orange).

For your average photographer. Sells camera equipment and develops film; 1-hour processing.

Crafts

The American Hand

2906 M St. NW. ☎ 202/965-3273. Metro: Foggy Bottom (Blue/Orange).

Primarily contemporary American ceramics, glass, and jewelry, and some international design items for the home and office. Prices range from $10 for a candle or mug to the tens of thousands for fine art pieces. Some articles are from the Museum of Modern Art collection.

Appalachian Spring

Union Station, 50 Massachusetts Ave. NE. ☎ 202/682-0505. Call for other locations. Metro: Union Station (Red).

Quintessential Americana: handmade pottery, woodwork, glasswork, quilts, children's items, jewelry.

Indian Craft Shop

Department of the Interior, 1800 C St. NW. ☎ 202/208-4056. Weekday hours only. Metro: Farragut West or Foggy Bottom (Blue/Orange).

Has represented authentic Native American artisans since 1938. Sells handwoven rugs and handcrafted baskets, jewelry, figurines, and other items.

The Phoenix

1514 Wisconsin Ave. NW. ☎ 202/338-4404.

Around since 1955, the Phoenix still sells those embroidered Mexican peasant blouses popular in hippie days, as well as Mexican folk and fine art; hand-crafted, sterling silver jewelry from Mexico and all over the world; clothing in natural fibers from Mexican and American designers; collectors' quality masks; and decorative doodads in tin, brass, copper, and wood.

Torpedo Factory Art Center

105 N. Union St. ☎ 703/838-4565.

This 3-story, converted munitions factory houses more than 83 working studios and the works of about 160 artists, who tend to their crafts before your eyes, pausing to explain their techniques, if you inquire, or sell their pieces, if you desire. Paintings, sculpture, ceramics, glasswork, textiles—all forms.

Crystal/Silver/China

Neiman-Marcus and Tiffany's sell many of these items, so you may want to visit these stores. First, though, consider these 2 Washington landmarks.

Little Caledonia

1419 Wisconsin Ave. NW. ☎ 202/333-4700.

Anyone who ever visits this 60-some-year-old shop once makes it a point to return. Behind an unassuming facade lies a meandering collection of small rooms crammed with precious housewares, fabrics, furniture, stationery, and gifts to please even your toughest customer. French and other china, a little crystal, but no silver. All types shop here: the young and the very old, sophisticates, ingenues, and hardboiled bargain hunters.

Martin's
1304 Wisconsin Ave. NW. ☎ 202/338-6144.

If you want something in the finest crystal, silver, china, or porcelain, you should come directly here. Waterford, Lalique, Baccarat, Herend, Christofle, Buccellati, and Rosenthal are the names on the shelves.

Department Stores

The excesses of the 1980s radically changed the face of American retailing: Many old-line local and national favorites disappeared. Specialty stores have captured portions of department store markets—children's clothing is one example. Washington still mourns the loss of hometown institutions like Garfinckel's and Woodward and Lothrop's, even as it celebrates the arrival of upscale East and West Coast retailers, and the diversity they bring with them.

Bloomingdale's
White Flint Mall, Kensington, MD. ☎ 301/984-4600. Call for other locations. Metro: White Flint (Red).

This outpost of the famous New York–based chain features trendsetting fashions for men, women, and children, as well as shoes, accessories, household goods, furnishings, and cosmetics. Don't look for the same variety and selection found in New York's Bloomingdale's stores, however; the Washington versions seem restrained by comparison.

Hecht's
Metro Center, 1201 G St. NW. ☎ 202/628-6661. Call for other locations. Metro: Metro Center (Red/Yellow/Blue).

Everything from mattresses to electronics, children's underwear to luggage, can be bought in this midpriced emporium.

Lord & Taylor
5255 Western Ave. NW. ☎ 202/362-9600. Call for other locations. Metro: Friendship Heights (Red).

Another lesser version of a New York chain. Its women's clothing and accessories department are probably its strong suit; go elsewhere for gadgets and gifts.

Macy's
Fashion Center at Pentagon City, 1000 S. Hayes St., Arlington, VA. ☎ 703/418-4488. Call for other locations. Metro: Pentagon City (Blue/Orange).

This Macy's (though nowhere near the same size as its New York cousin), hopes to fulfill the same omnipotent role for Washington customers. Mid- to upscale merchandise and prices.

Neiman-Marcus

Mazza Gallerie, 5300 Wisconsin Ave. NW. ☎ 202/966-9700. Call for other locations. Metro: Friendship Heights (Red).

The legendary Texas institution's catalogs and "his-and-hers" Christmas gifts are exercises in conspicuous consumption. Look for remarkably good bargains at their "Last Call" half-yearly sales. Otherwise, this store is pretty pricey. No furniture or home furnishings, except for exquisite china and crystal.

Nordstrom's

Fashion Center at Pentagon City. 1400 S. Hayes St., Arlington, VA. ☎ 703/415-1121. Call for other locations. Metro: Pentagon City (Blue/Orange).

This Seattle-based retailer's reputation for exceptional service is well-deserved—a call to the main information number confirms this. In keeping with the store's beginnings as a shoe store, this location has 3 entire departments devoted to women's shoes (designer, dressy, and just plain fun); if you can't find your size or color, they'll order it.

Saks Fifth Avenue

5555 Wisconsin Ave., Chevy Chase, MD. ☎ 301/657-9000. Metro: Friendship Heights (Red).

If you can make it past the cosmetics counters without getting spritzed by the makeup-masked young women aiming perfume bottles at you, you've accomplished something—unless, of course, you enjoy that sort of thing. On other levels you'll find designer and tailored men's and women's clothing, and some for children.

Good Food to Go

Demanding jobs and hectic schedules leave Washingtonians less and less time to prepare their own meals. Or so they say. At any rate, a number of fine-food shops and bakeries are happy to come to the rescue. Even the busiest bureaucrat can find the time to pop into one of these gourmet grocers for a moveable feast.

For additional shops, see "Farmers & Flea Markets"

Dean & Deluca

3276 M St. NW. ☎ 202/342-2500. Metro: Foggy Bottom (Blue/Orange).

The New York–famous store has set down roots in Washington, too, in a historic Georgetown building that was once an open-air market. Though closed-in now, an airy feeling continues because of the scale of the room, its high ceiling, and the windows on all sides. You'll pay top prices, but for some it's worth it, for the charcuterie, produce, prepared foods, such as sandwiches and cold pasta salads, and hot ticket desserts, like crème brûlée and tiramisu. Also on sale are housewares. On site is an espresso bar/cafe.

Lawson's Gourmet

1350 Connecticut Ave. NW. ☎ 202/775-0400. Call for other locations. Metro: Dupont Circle (Red).

At this subway-situated Lawson's, with its cluster of outside tables and chairs, you're at a real Washington crossroads, watching the comings and goings of sharply dressed lawyers, bohemian artistes, and panhandling unfortunates. You can buy elaborate sandwiches made to order and very nice desserts, wines, breads, and salads.

Marvelous Market

1514 Connecticut Ave. NW. ☎ 202/986-2222. Call for other locations. Metro: Dupont Circle (Red).

First there were the breads: sourdough, baguettes, olive, rosemary, croissants, scones. Now, there are things to spread on the bread, like smoked salmon mousse and tapenade; pastries to die for, from gingerbread to flourless chocolate cake; and prepared foods, such as empanadas and pasta salads. The breakfast spread on Sunday mornings is sinful; and individual items, like the croissants, are tastier and less expensive here than at other bakeries.

Reeves Bakery

1305 G St. NW. ☎ 202/628-6350. Metro: Metro Center (Red/Yellow/Blue).

Razed to the ground in 1988 to make way for yet another office building, this dieter's nightmare took more than 3 years to find a new home 2 blocks away. Meanwhile, fans pined for the famous strawberry pie, the pineapple dream cake, the blueberry doughnuts, and chicken salad sandwiches at the counter. The offerings here are 1950s' style, not gourmet or elegant in the least.

Sutton Place Gourmet

3201 New Mexico Ave. NW. ☎ 202/363-5800. Call for other locations.

In 1980, Sutton Place was the first, full-scale, one-stop fancy-food store to open in the Washington area, and residents took to it immediately. Now there are nine.

Shoppers can be obnoxious—everyone who comes here is "Somebody," or thinks they are. It's an expensive store, but reliable: the best meats, raspberries when no one else has them, a zillion types of cheeses, ingredients for recipes in *Gourmet* magazine.

Uptown Bakers

3313 Connecticut Ave. NW. ☎ 202/362-6262. Metro: Cleveland Park.

If you're visiting the zoo and need a sweets fix, walk down the street to this bakery for a muffin, sweet tart, or a delicious "Vicki" bun, a cinnamon roll named for the long-gone worker who invented it. Coffee, sandwiches, and a wide range of breads also available.

Jewelry

Luxurious, close-carpeted boutiques, brightly lit middle-price shops, and bustling department stores feature a variety of precious and semiprecious jewelry, from heirloom to souvenir quality. Prices range accordingly.

C de Carat

Mayflower Hotel, 1127 Connecticut Ave. NW. ☎ 202/887-5888. Metro: Farragut North (Red).

The district's only authorized Cartier dealer is also known for its Italian designer jewelry: Antonini, Cassis; Lagos sterling silver and 18-karat gold jewelry; and Breitling watches. Amiable staff.

Charles Schwartz & Son

Willard Inter-Continental Hotel, 1401 Pennsylvania Ave. NW. ☎ 202/363-5432. Metro: Metro Center (Red/Yellow/Blue). (Also at the Mazza Gallerie, Metro: Friendship Heights, Red.)

In business since 1888, Charles Schwartz specializes in diamonds and in sapphires, rubies, and emeralds; also repairs watches and jewelry. This jewelers is one of the few distributors of Baccarat jewelry. Staff are extremely professional.

Galt & Brothers

607 15th St. NW. ☎ 202/347-1034.

In existence since 1802, Galt's is the capital's oldest business and America's oldest jewelers. The shop sells and repairs high quality jewelry, diamonds, and all manner of colored gems. Gifts of crystal, silver, and china are also sold.

Tiffany and Company

5500 Wisconsin Ave., Chevy Chase, MD. ☎ 301/657-8777. Call for other locations. Metro: Friendship Heights (Red).

Known for exquisite diamond and other jewelry that runs in the hundreds of thousands of dollars category, but what you may not know is that the store carries less expensive items as well—candlesticks at $35 a piece, for example. And if you've ever seen the movie *Breakfast at Tiffany's,* you know the jewelers performs engraving, too. Other items include tabletop gifts and fancy glitz: china, crystal, flatware, and bridal registry service.

Tiny Jewel Box
1147 Connecticut Ave. NW. ☎ 202/393-2747. Metro: Farragut North (Red).

The first place Washingtonians think to go for estate and antique jewelry.

Malls

Chevy Chase Pavilion
5345 Wisconsin Ave. NW. ☎ 202/686-5335. Metro: Friendship Heights (Red).

A manageable-sized mall with about 50 stores and restaurants, anchored by an Embassy Suites hotel. This is a pretty mall, whose 3 levels wind round a skylit atrium. Giant palm trees, arrangements of fresh flowers, and seasonal events, such as a ballet performance by a visiting Russian troop at Christmastime, add panache. Stores include the outrageously priced Oilily for children's and women's clothing, Laura Ashley, a shop selling National Cathedral knickknacks, and a Joan and David Shoe Store. A small food court, the Cheesecake Factory, and the California Pizza Kitchen are among the eating options.

Fashion Center at Pentagon City
1400 S. Hayes St., Arlington, VA. ☎ 703/415-2400. Metro: Pentagon City (Blue/Orange).

Nordstrom's and Macy's are the biggest attractions in this block-long, 5-story, elegant shoppers' paradise that also houses a Ritz-Carlton hotel, office suites, multiplex theaters, and a sprawling food court. Villeroy and Boch, Crate & Barrel, and Eddie Bauer are among the nearly 150 shops.

Georgetown Park
3222 M St. NW. ☎ 202/342-8180. Metro: Foggy Bottom (Blue/Orange), then a 20-minute walk.

This is a mall-deluxe, where you'll see beautiful people shopping for beautiful things, paying stunning prices at stores with European names: Christian Bernard, Arpelli's (leather goods), and Tartine et Chocolat (children's clothes from Paris). The diplomatic set and well-heeled foreign travelers favor these stores so you're bound to hear a number of languages, especially French and Italian. Wander here, then set off for the streets of Georgetown for more shopping.

Mazza Gallerie

5100 Wisconsin Ave. NW. ☎ 202/966-6114. Metro: Friendship Heights (Red).

Despite the presence of Neiman-Marcus, this mall is less luxurious than it used to be, thanks to the additions of discount/low-priced stores Filene's Basement and Paul Harris—and maybe because McDonald's is the mall's only restaurant at the moment. But the Mazza remains an attractive shopping center, with its skylit atrium and stores like Ann Taylor and Benetton's. Theaters on the lower level; access to Chevy Chase Pavilion, the subway, and to the Hecht's department store, via the Metro tunnel.

The Pavilion at the Old Post Office

1100 Pennsylvania Ave. NW. ☎ 202/289-4224. Metro: Federal Triangle (Blue/Orange).

Mainly a tourist trap holding souvenir shops and a food court. Noontime concerts are a draw, as is the view of the city from the building's clock tower, 315 feet up.

Potomac Mills

30 miles s on I-95, accessible by car only. ☎ 703/490-5948.

When you are stuck in the traffic that always clogs this section of I-95, you may wonder if a trip to Potomac Mills is worth it. Believe it or not, this place attracts more visitors than any other in the Washington area, and twice as many as the next top draw, the Smithsonian's National Air and Space Museum. It's the largest indoor outlet mall around, and its shops include New York's Barney's, DKNY, Nordstrom's, and IKEA.

The Shops at National Place

1331 Pennsylvania Ave. NW. ☎ 202/783-9090. Metro: Metro Center (Red/Blue/Orange).

You enter the complex either through the J.W. Marriott Hotel or at F Street, between 13th and 14th streets. More than 80 specialty shops are represented, including Papillon and Cignal, for men, and Casual Corner, Express, and Victoria's Secret, for women.

Tyson's Corner, Tyson's I

9160 Chain Bridge Rd., McLean, VA ☎ 703/893-9400. Metro: West Falls Church, take shuttle.

Tyson's Corner II, The Galleria
2001 International Drive, McLean, VA ☎ 703/827-7700. Metro: West Falls Church, take shuttle.

Facing each other across Chain Bridge Road, these 2 gigantic malls could lead to shopper's overload. Tyson's I, the first and less expensive, has Nord-strom's, Bloomingdale's, and J.C. Penney's, and specialty stores, such as Abercrombie & Fitch and Armani's Exchange. The Galleria has Macy's, Saks Fifth Avenue, and more than 100 upscale boutiques.

Union Station
50 Massachusetts Ave. NE. ☎ 202/371-9441. Metro: Union Station (Red).

After the National Air and Space Museum, this is the next most popular stop for D.C. visitors. The architecture is magnificent. Its more than 120 shops include the Nature Company, Brookstone, and the Limited; among the places to eat are America, B. Smith, and an international food court. There's also a 9-screen movie theater complex.

White Flint Mall
11301 Rockville Pike, Kensington, MD. ☎ 301/468-5777. Metro: White Flint, take shuttle.

Another Bloomingdale's, another long trip in the car or on the Metro, but once you're there, you can shop, take in a movie, or dine cheaply or well. Notable stores include Lord & Taylor, a huge Borders Books, Ann Taylor, and the Corcoran Gallery of Art shop.

Men's Clothes & Shoes

It's true that the Washington "look" often leans toward traditional, conservative fashions, but the possibilities for trying on hipper gear do exist. (Neiman-Marcus and Saks Fifth Avenue, in particular, sell top-drawer men's designer fashions. See listings under "Department Stores.") Here's where you can find both styles for men in the area.

Banana Republic
Wisconsin Ave. and M St. ☎ 202/333-2554. Call for other locations. Metro: Foggy Bottom (Blue/Orange), with a 20-minute walk.

All Banana Republic labels: casual to dressy: wool gabardine and wool crepe pants, khakis, shorts, vests, and jackets. Mid to high prices.

Beau Monde
International Square, 1814 K St. NW. ☎ 202/466-7070. Metro: Farragut West (Blue/Orange).

This boutique sells all Italian-made clothes, some double-breasted traditional suits, but mostly avant-garde.

Britches of Georgetown
1219 Connecticut Ave. NW. ☎ 202/347-8994. Call for other locations. Metro: Farragut North (Red).

Washington's own trendy clothiers offers trim tailoring in tuxedos, tweed jackets, traditional suits and casual wear, shoes, and accessories. Ask about **Britches Great Outdoors** store locations, as well; this line sells a preppier look.

Brooks Brothers
1840 L St. NW. ☎ 202/659-4650. Call for other locations. Metro: Farragut West (Blue/Orange) or Farragut North (Red).

This is where to go for the K Street/Capitol Hill pinstriped power look, from boxer shorts to wingtips. Brooks also sells the fine line of Peal's English shoes.

Burberry's
1155 Connecticut Ave. NW. ☎ 202/463-3000. Metro: Farragut North (Red).

Here you find those plaid-lined trenchcoats, of course, along with classic English clothing, well-tailored but conservative, men's and women's.

Church's English Shoes
1742 L St. NW. ☎ 202/296-3366. Metro: Farragut North (Red).

Church's sells superior, bench-made English shoes—expensive, but they're almost always running a sale.

Gianfranco Ferre
5301 Wisconsin Ave. NW. ☎ 202/244-6633. Metro: Friendship Heights (Red).

Shop here for the sleek and sexy European look: interesting suits and some casual wear.

Giotto
Georgetown Park. ☎ 202/338-6223. Metro: Foggy Bottom (Blue/Orange), with a 20-minute walk.

Italian designer sports and dress wear: Missoni, Red Star, Millibar.

Niccolo
Georgetown Park. ☎ 202/338-3638. Metro: Foggy Bottom (Blue/Orange), with a 20-minute walk.

Italian designers Serre, Venturi, and Verri evening and sports clothes; some women's clothes.

The Polo Store/Ralph Lauren
Georgetown Park. ☎ 202/965-0904. Metro: Foggy Bottom (Blue/Orange), with a 20-minute walk.

A good mix of sportswear and dress wear, covering shirts, ties, dress pants, shoes, and toiletries, with career and casual clothes for women. Prices range from $40 for a pair of shorts to $1,250 for a sport jacket.

Urban Outfitters
3111 M St. NW. ☎ 202/342-1012. Metro: Foggy Bottom (Blue/Orange), with a 20-minute walk.

For the unisex, ugly-is-in look. Salespeople wear suitably disgusted expressions.

Miscellaneous

Al's Magic Shop
1012 Vermont Ave. NW. ☎ 202/789-2800. Metro: McPherson Square (Blue/Orange).

A first-rate novelty shop, presided over by prestidigitator and local character Al Cohen, who is only too happy to demonstrate the latest magic trick or practical joke.

Animation Sensations
1083 Thomas Jefferson St. NW. ☎ 202/965-0199. Metro: Foggy Bottom (Blue/Orange), with a 20-minute walk.

Original cartoon art, in the form of sketches, paintings, and "cels," from Disney to Hanna-Barbera, to the Power Rangers.

Beadazzled
1522 Connecticut Ave. NW. ☎ 202/265-BEAD. Call for other locations. Metro: Dupont Circle (Red).

The friendly staff helps you assemble your own affordable jewelry from an eye-boggling array of beads and artifacts.

Capitol Coin and Stamp Co. Inc.
1701 L St. NW. ☎ 202/296-0400. Metro: Farragut North (Red).

A museum of political memorabilia—pins, posters, banners—and all of it for sale. Also a fine resource for the endangered species of coin and stamp collectors.

Chocolate Moose
1800 M St. NW. ☎ 202/463-0992. Metro: Farragut North (Red).

Here's where to go when you need a surprising and unexpected gift. Wacky cards; a range of useful, funny, and lovely presents; candies; eccentric clothing; and jewelry.

Ginza
1721 Connecticut Ave. NW. ☎ 202/331-7991. Metro: Dupont Circle (Red).

Everything Japanese, from incense and kimonos, to futons, to Zen rock gardens.

Map Store

1636 I St. NW. ☎ 202/628-2608. Metro: Farragut West (Blue/Orange).

Going somewhere? Or just daydreaming about leaving? This fascinating boutique is always packed with map and globe fetishists. A good spot for D.C. souvenirs.

Political Americana

Union Station. ☎ 202/547-1685. Call for other locations. Metro: Union Station (Red).

This is another great place to pick up souvenirs from a visit to D.C. The store sells political novelty items, books, bumper stickers, old campaign buttons, and historical memorabilia.

Pharmacies

The wise traveler always carries a signed prescription form for any necessary medication. Luggage can be lost, medicines can be spilled or spoiled, and a trip to a private physician or clinic can cost precious time and money for a replacement prescription.

CVS Drugstores

7 Dupont Circle NW. ☎ 202/785-1466. Call for other locations— there are many. Metro: Dupont Circle (Red).

This CVS and the one at Thomas Circle are open 24 hours, carrying everything you might need in the way of medicines and the little necessities.

Foggy Bottom Apothecary

1118 22nd St. NW. ☎ 202/296-9314. Metro: Foggy Bottom (Blue/Orange).

A reliable choice for unusual prescriptions.

Morgan Pharmacy

3001 P St. NW. ☎ 202/337-4100.

A drugstore cut from the old mold, providing caring service to regulars and travelers. This well-stocked pharmacy offers free delivery, an excellent selection of cosmetics and perfumes, and a fax service.

Records

Borders Books and Music

1800 L St. NW. ☎ 202/466-4999. Call for other locations. Metro: Farragut North (Red).

Besides being a fab bookstore, Borders happens to offer the best prices in town for CDs and tapes, and a wide range of music.

HMV

1229 Wisconsin Ave. NW. ☎ 202/333-9292. Metro: Foggy Bottom (Blue/Orange), with a 20-minute walk .

This London-based record and tape store is fun to visit, with its cunning clientele, party atmosphere, and headphones at the ready for easy listening. But you can get a better deal almost anywhere else.

Olsson's Books & Records

1239 Wisconsin Ave. NW. ☎ 202/338-6712. Call for other locations. Metro: Foggy Bottom (Blue/Orange), with a 20-minute walk.

Two doors up from HMV is Olsson's, which started selling books and records 20 years ago. The store offers a good selection; staff graciously help you find what you're looking for. Background music is as apt to be classical as current. Prices are pretty good.

Tower Records

2000 Pennsylvania Ave. NW. ☎ 202/331-2400. Metro: Foggy Bottom (Blue/Orange).

When you need a record at midnight on Christmas Eve, you go to Tower. The large, funky store, across the street from George Washington University, has a wide choice of records, cassettes, and compact discs in every category—but the prices are high.

12" Dance Records

2010 P St. NW, 2nd floor. ☎ 202/659-2010. Metro: Dupont Circle (Red).

Disco lives. If you ever moved to it on a dance floor, Wresch Dawidjian and his staff of DJs have got it here, or they can get it. There's always a DJ mixing it up live in the store, and they pump the beats out into the street.

Sports & Camping

Eddie Bauer

3040 M St. NW. ☎ 202/342-2121. Call for other locations. Metro: Foggy Bottom (Blue/Orange), with a 20-minute walk.

Mostly sweaters and other clothes to keep you warm in the great outdoors, plus luggage, backpacks, knives, and watches.

Fleet Feet

1840 Columbia Rd. NW. ☎ 202/387-3888. Metro: Woodley Park/Zoo (Red).

Everything for the runner, and the running-savvy staff knows where the trails are. A citywide running group meets here on Saturday mornings.

Hudson Trail Outfitters
4530 Wisconsin Ave. NW. ☎ 202/363-9810. Call for other locations.
Metro: Tenleytown (Red).

Specializes in outdoor recreational equipment: for backpacking, flyfishing, kayaking, canoeing, and mountain biking.

Wine & Spirits
The following liquor stores are among the best in the city for choice and value.

Calvert Woodley Liquors
4339 Connecticut Ave. NW. ☎ 202/966-4400. Metro: Van Ness/
UDC (Red).

A large store with friendly staff and nice selections. Good cheeses and other foods also sold.

Central Liquor
726 9th St. NW. ☎ 202/737-2800. Metro: Metro Center
(Red/Blue/Orange).

Like a clearinghouse for liquor: its great volume of business allows the store to offer the best prices in town on wines and liquor.

Eagle Wine & Liquor
3345 M St. NW. ☎ 202/333-5500. Metro: Rosslyn (Blue/Orange)
and right at Key Bridge.

A longtime Georgetown establishment, residents come for the discounts and for assistance from the well-informed staff.

MacArthur Liquor
4877 MacArthur Blvd. NW. ☎ 202/338-1433. Metro: None.

Always busy, because the staff is so knowledgeable and enthusiastic, and because the shop has such an extensive selection of excellent wines, both imported and domestic. Reasonable rates, too.

Women's Clothes & Shoes
If Washington women don't dress well, it isn't for lack of stores. The following boutiques run the gamut in styles, from baggy grunge, to crisply tailored, to ultra-feminine, to fantastically sexy.

Ann Taylor
Union Station. ☎ 202/371-8010. Call for other locations.
Metro: Union Station (Red).

Specializes in American-look, chic clothing, Joan and David and other footwear, and accessories.

Betsy Fisher
1224 Connecticut Ave. NW. ☎ 202/785-1975. Metro: Dupont
Circle (Red).

A walk past the store is all it takes to know that this shop is a tad different. Its windowfront and racks hold the whimsically feminine fashions, including hats, of new American designers. Dresses start at about $100; a good suit runs in the $200 to $400 range.

Chanel Boutique
1455 Pennsylvania Ave. NW, in the courtyard of the Willard Inter-Continental Hotel. ☎ 202/638-5055. Metro: Metro Center (Red/Blue/Orange).

A modest selection of Chanel's signature designs, accessories, and jewelry, at immodest prices.

The Coach Store
1214 Wisconsin Ave. NW. ☎ 202/342-1772. Call for other locations. Metro: Foggy Bottom (Blue/Orange), with a 20-minute walk.

Fine leather handbags, belts, and other goods.

Commander Salamander
1420 Wisconsin Ave. NW. ☎ 202/337-2265. Metro: Foggy Bottom (Blue/Orange), with a 20-minute walk.

Too cool. Little bit of everything: Jean Paul Gaultier and Oldham creations; Betsey Johnson dresses for no more than $130; and handmade jackets with Axl jewelry sewn on, for more than $1,000. Loud music, young crowd, funky.

Gianfranco Ferre
5301 Wisconsin Ave., Chevy Chase, MD. ☎ 202/244-6633. Metro: Friendship Heights (Red).

A shop for men and women, its women's fashions are brighter, but also carry a distinctly European feel.

Gianni Versace
5454 Wisconsin Ave., Chevy Chase, MD. ☎ 301/907-9400. Metro: Friendship Heights (Red).

Outré fashions for men and women.

Harriet Kassman
4400 Jenifer St. NW. ☎ 202/363-1870. Metro: Friendship Heights (Red).

Where haute Washington ladies of a certain age have always shopped, and where their granddaughters cut their teeth on couture.

Jackie Chalkley
5301 Wisconsin Ave. NW. ☎ 202/537-6100. Call for other locations. Metro: Friendship Heights (Red).

A contemporary boutique specializing in handmade clothes that can go from a day at the office to an evening event. Doesn't do much sporty wear. Clothes generally are loose-fitting, not tailored, and are sophisticated, one-of-a-kind pieces. Also jewelry, handmade knits, and crafts. You pay a pretty price.

Joan and David Shoe Store
Chevy Chase Pavilion, ☎ 202/686-6920. Metro: Friendship Heights (Red).

A full selection of finely crafted shoes, from sandals to boots. Made to last, but rather expensive.

Laura Ashley
3213 M St. NW. ☎ 202/338-5481. Call for other locations. Metro: Foggy Bottom (Blue/Orange), with a 20-minute walk.

The too-precious, small-flowered dresses, blouses, slacks, sweaters, and other clothes, and home furnishings in English country fashion, for women and children.

Micmac Bis
5301 Wisconsin Ave. NW. ☎ 202/686-9840. Metro: Friendship Heights (Red).

French owners, so this cute store's kicky, colorful clothes are often, though not always, from France. Designers represented include Issey Miyake.

Neiman-Marcus
Mazza Gallerie, 5300 Wisconsin Ave. NW. ☎ 202/966-9700. Call for other locations. Metro: Friendship Heights (Red).

The legendary Texas institution's catalogs and "his-and-hers" Christmas gifts are exercises in conspicuous consumption. Look for remarkably good bargains at their "Last Call" half-yearly sales. Otherwise, this store is pretty pricey. No furniture or home furnishings, except for exquisite china and crystal.

Pirjo
1044 Wisconsin Ave. NW. ☎ 202/337-1390. Metro: Foggy Bottom (Blue/Orange), with a 20-minute walk.

The funky, baggy and pretty creations of designers like the Finnish Marimekko and others: Bettina, Flax, VIP. Casual to dressy. Also elegant jewelry.

Polo/Ralph Lauren Shop
Georgetown Park. ☎ 202/965-0904. Metro: Foggy Bottom (Blue/Orange), with a 20-minute walk.

Career and casual clothes for women, along with menswear.

Rizik's
1100 Connecticut Ave. NW. ☎ 202/223-4050. Metro: Farragut North (Red).

High fashion in the downtown: Clothing works of arts by Caroline Herrara, Armani, Oscar de la Renta, and their ilk.

Saks Fifth Avenue

5555 Wisconsin Ave., Chevy Chase, MD. ☎ 301/657-9000.
Metro: Friendship Heights (Red).

If you can make it past the cosmetics counters without getting spritzed by the makeup-masked young women aiming perfume bottles at you, you've accomplished something—unless, of course, you enjoy that sort of thing. On other levels you'll find designer and tailored men's and women's clothing, and some for children.

Saks-Jandel

5510 Wisconsin Ave., Chevy Chase, MD. ☎ 301/652-2250.
Metro: Friendship Heights (Red).

Elegant afternoon and evening wear. Major European and American designers Chanel, Valentino, Christian Dior, Yves Saint-Laurent rive gauche, Isaac Mizrahi (this was the site of the designer's promo for his movie, *Unzipped*), John Galliano, Prada, and many others. Saks-Jandel has an international clientele.

Secondhand Rose

1516 Wisconsin Ave. NW, upstairs. ☎ 202/337-3378. Metro: Foggy
Bottom (Blue/Orange), with a 20-minute walk.

As it sounds, this is a consignment shop for women's clothes and you can often pick up contemporary fashions and accessories in fine shape.

Talbots

1227 Connecticut Ave. NW. ☎ 202/887-6973. Call for other
locations. Metro: Farragut North (Red).

Career and casual clothes with a decidedly conservative bent, and accessories to go with them.

Toast & Strawberries

1608 Connecticut Ave. NW. ☎ 202/234-2424.

Clothes from around the world and from local designers, too. Many in the collection are one-of-a-kind; some are casual, some ethnic, all are fun to wear. The shop also sells some accessories.

Victoria's Secret

The Shops at National Place. ☎ 202/347-3535. Call for other
locations. Metro: Metro Center (Red/Blue/Orange).

Washington women really like the chain's feminine, sexy array of lingerie, so you'll find you're never too far from one of the shops.

THE ARTS

**What is capital life after all? Small talk
and lots to eat, an infinite series of teas
and dinners. Art? There is none.**

—*Alice Pike Barney
(painter and society hostess), 1902*

WASHINGTON IS WELL KNOWN AS THE SCENE OF
political theater—there's always a backroom
power-play or dramatic hearing going on somewhere.
Happily for us, Washington has been steadily evolving
into a cultural capital, as well.

From grand operas at the Kennedy Center to poetry readings at the Library of Congress, from the treasures in its 27 museums to alfresco Shakespeare on the
Mall, Washington today provides a menu that is rich
enough to satisfy the most voracious cultural appetite.

There was a time, however, when the capital's cultural diet was as meager and monotonous as its cuisine,
and the only art that flourished was the art of politics.
While the city was going through the long, slow process of transforming itself from a glorified shantytown
into an effective capital, its inhabitants had little time
or inclination for cultural refinements.

The opening of the National Theater in 1835 at
least brought regular theatrical performances. Ford's
Theatre was open until Lincoln's assassination in 1865,
after which it was closed for about a century. Still, the
theatrical bill of fare was hardly impressive, and the
musical fare even less so, although by the 1850s certain
federal buildings were being used after office hours for
concerts. Until recently, however, facilities for large-
scale musical performances were very limited.

Lovers of painting and sculpture were less deprived.
In 1869 the Corcoran Gallery opened, and numerous
other galleries followed, making Washington one of the

richest cities in the world for the visual arts. Yet it was a long time before Washington had anything approaching an artists' colony, and it was left to Henry Adams and a tiny handful of other writers to carry the torch for literature in the U.S. capital.

The fact is that for the first century and a half of its existence, Washington lacked the kind of social and urban fabric that makes for a thriving cultural life. In Paris and Vienna there were cafes where artists, writers, and composers could gather and exchange ideas in a heady atmosphere, fueled by the feverish energy of a great metropolis with centuries of cultural history behind it. Washington had no such milieu. Its steak-and-potatoes eating houses were no substitute for the cafes of Montmartre or the Ringstrasse.

Washingtonians eager for cultural nourishment were acutely aware of these deficiencies. The words quoted at the start of this section are those of the painter and society hostess Alice Pike Barney, whose Studio House on Sheridan Circle was, in the early years of the 20thC, one of the few centers of real cultural exchange in the city. Until she moved to Los Angeles in 1924, the house was the scene of continuous artistic activity. She herself not only painted but also taught art, wrote and produced plays, and promoted the cultural life of the city as a whole. In 1917 she was instrumental in creating the Sylvan Theater in the Washington Monument grounds, the first federally supported outdoor theater in the United States.

Apart from valiant efforts by individuals such as Mrs. Barney, Washington remained culturally malnourished until long after World War II—one of the reasons why foreign embassy staffs had to be compensated for a posting here. The world's great orchestras and opera and ballet companies were reluctant to include Washington on their tours, mainly because the facilities for performances were so poor. The only large auditorium suitable for musical events was the Constitution Hall of the Daughters of the American Revolution. Otherwise, performances had to be held in museums, galleries, libraries, and churches around the city (where fortunately many continue to be held, frequently free of charge).

Clearly such a situation could not be allowed to continue, as President Eisenhower realized when in 1955 he appointed a commission to examine the feasibility of building a new auditorium in the capital. Three years later he signed the legislation for the creation of a National Cultural Center, which, after a further 13 years and much heroic battling on the part of its supporters, finally opened as the Kennedy Center in 1971. Now at last Washington had, under one roof, an opera house, a concert hall, and a theater, all of them large, and all with the finest acoustics and facilities.

The Kennedy Center has moved Washington into the major league of world cities for the performing arts, and today it features very firmly on the itinerary of the great touring companies and orchestras. Its opening was therefore a major turning point. But it is not the only factor in the city's cultural strides. Before the appearance of the Kennedy Center, Arena Stage was already winning a reputation as one of the most vital and innovative theaters in the country, drawing audiences with its imaginative productions ranging from Chekhov to Tom Stoppard. At the Folger Shakespeare Library, the plays of the Bard and of some of his most ultramodern successors were, until 1992, regularly staged in a replica of the Globe Theatre. The Folger Players moved to the much larger Shakespeare Theater in order to accommodate the enthusiastic audiences they have attracted. A host of small experimental theaters, such as the Woolly Mammoth Theatre Company, Studio Theatre, and Source Theatre Company, offer a consistently exciting range of drama. Washington's small theaters have not been smothered by the Kennedy Center, but have benefited from the heightened cultural atmosphere that it has created.

Much the same is true in the field of music. Opera thrives at the Kennedy Center and in many smaller venues. In addition to the National Symphony Orchestra, numerous other orchestras, large and small, perform regularly in Washington and its environs. In fact, Washington today is possibly the richest city in the world for chamber music. Gone is the climate of musical philistinism in which President Grant could say proudly: "I know two tunes; one of them is Yankee Doodle and the other isn't."

Eclectic music is happening here, too. Bluegrass and swing music have inexplicably strong roots in the D.C. area, which has also sprouted several enduring homegrown pop music genres, from go-go to "harDCore punk" to the jangly postadolescent "Arlington Sound" of alternative pop made in basements and garages.

The same healthy balance of great and small can be seen in the visual arts. Washington has not only the great galleries around the Mall but also a host of small private galleries, many of which can be found near

Dupont Circle, in Georgetown, and in the Old Downtown area, where the work of African-American artists is much in evidence.

One outstanding—and very attractive—feature of Washington's cultural life is that so much of it is available for free. It would be possible to go to an exhibition, concert, lecture, or poetry reading every day without paying a cent. It is no wonder that other American cities have grown envious of the capital, and little wonder that diplomats no longer find Washington, D.C. a hardship post.

What's Doing, Getting Tickets, Etc.

The best places to find schedules of upcoming performances are the Friday "Weekend" section of the *Washington Post* and the weekly listings in *City Paper*, the free alternative weekly. *Washingtonian*, the glossy monthly city magazine, also features a good, extensive advance listing of performing events. For theatrical performances, you can call the **Cultural Alliance** (☎ 202/638-2406) or the **League of Washington Theatres** (☎ 202/638-4270).

Now that voicemail is an accepted fact of modern life, most performance venues have self-serve recorded hot-lines offering updated schedules, prices, and credit card sales. Of course, you can walk up to the box office before a performance in most instances, but reserved tickets make everyone's life easier.

Tickets for most musical events and theatrical performances can be purchased at the box office or through computerized ticket agencies. The most comprehensive is **Ticketmaster** (1101 17th St. and other locations; ☎ 202/432-7328), which sells advanced-reservation, full-price seats to performing arts, sports, and special events. Credit cards are accepted. Some theaters offer discounts to students, the elderly, the disabled and/or enlisted military personnel.

Check out the half-price ticket booth **TICKETplace,** D.C.'s equivalent of Manhattan's Times Square TKTS kiosk. TICKETplace (George Washington University, Lisner Auditorium, 730 21st St. NW; ☎ 202/842-5387; Metro: Farragut West, Blue/Orange) can tell you what's onstage all over town, and offers advance tickets and half-price day-of-show tickets.

Cinema

The powerhouse Cineplex Odeon chain has the local big-screen scene pretty well sewn up, having recently snapped up most of the town's best theaters and multiplexes.

Washingtonians will go see just about anything if it's shown in 70 millimeter on the grand screen at the **Cineplex Odeon Uptown** (3426 Connecticut Ave. NW; ☎ 202/966-5400. Metro: Red to Cleveland Park). The Uptown seats more than 1,000, and there's even a balcony. Woody Allen has called the **CO Avalon** (5612 Connecticut Ave. NW; ☎ 202/966-2600) his favorite movie house (in Washington, anyway). You're likely to catch foreign, independent, and gay-themed films at the 5-screen **CO Dupont Five** (1350 19th St. NW; ☎ 202/872-9555. Metro: Dupont Circle, Red) and the tiny, eccentrically-shaped 3-screen **CO Janus** (1660 Connecticut Ave. NW; ☎ 202/265-9545. Metro: Dupont Circle, Red).

Another major player in the multiplex arena is the **AMC Union Station Nine** (50 Massachusetts Ave. NE; ☎ 202/842-3751. Metro: Union Station, Red), offering the latest movies in 9 screening rooms, within the boisterous, bustling Union Station complex, which features Metro access and free parking. Credit cards are accepted.

First-run attractions generally change on Friday; the Friday "Weekend" section of the *Washington Post* and the free *City Paper* (distributed Thurs) carry synopses of all movies currently playing, with their locations. Most theaters have multiple showings; many offer screenings at reduced prices.

Thankfully, a few independent repertory houses remain, including the **American Film Institute Theater** (in the Kennedy Center, New Hampshire Ave. and Rock Creek Pkwy. NW; ☎ 202/254-3600. Metro: Foggy Bottom, Blue/Orange), which regularly presents classic movies for courteous, knowledgeable audiences in a well-designed auditorium. These people come to *worship* the movies, and are rewarded with good prints and creative double and triple bills. The theater is programmed by the national nonprofit organization, formed to preserve the best in American film.

Georgetown has an estimable pair of busy repertory houses: **The Biograph** (2819 M St. NW; ☎ 202/333-2696. Metro: Foggy Bottom, Blue/Orange) is a small, family-run repertory house that pays for its ambitious roster of arty, foreign, and obscure films by screening lunch-hour adult movies. The box office for **The Key** (1222 Wisconsin Ave. NW, Georgetown; ☎ 202/333-5100) is smack on the sidewalk of the busy Wisconsin Avenue main drag, and there is no lobby to speak of, but the lively mix of art movies, foreign-language imports, and American classics attracts cineasts to 5 cozy screening rooms.

Other moviegoing venues in D.C. range from the sublime to the ridiculous. On the highbrow side, in the elegant, intimate **Mary Pickford Theater** at the Library of Congress (1st St. and Independence Ave. SE; ☎ 202/707-5677. Metro: Capitol South, Blue/Orange; Union Station, Red), you can enjoy free showings of historic, sometimes forgotten, American movies from the library's extensive cinema archive. Reservations are required. The **Smithsonian**'s Hirshhorn Museum (☎ 202/357-2700) often shows art films and documentaries about modern art; the Museum of American History screens classic films, usually with a guest speaker.

Perhaps the ideal environment for viewing any Swayze, Stallone, or Bruce Willis epic is the **Bethesda Theater Cafe** (7719 Wisconsin Ave. NW, Bethesda, MD; ☎ 301/656-3337. Metro: Bethesda, Red), because at this homey, half-price rep house, you can eat pizza and drink beer or wine and talk during the movie, just like in your own living room.

The **Washington Psychotronic Film Society** really separates the cineasts from the sissies. There's a determinedly cultish feeling to the weekly Tuesday night screenings at the funky Grand Poobah bar (2001 U St. NW; ☎ 202/588-5709) which always begin with cartoons, shorts, and trailers, leading up to the main-course movie: Will it be kung-fu/beach-party double-feature? A seminal ultraviolent influence on the young, impressionable Quentin Tarantino? An entire evening of old toy and cereal commercials? Food is available and moviegoers are invited to bring their own snacks. Even if you can't make it to a movie, you owe it to yourself to call the constantly updated, always demented Psychotronic Hot Line at ☎ 202/736-1732, which as a bonus often tips you off to the worst/best drek on TV that night (without it we would have missed the night Tori Spelling and George Stephanopoulos were on Leno's "Tonight Show" together).

Concerts

Classical Music

Because the Kennedy Center is the home of the **National Symphony Orchestra**, it tends to overshadow the local classical music scene. But magnificent music can be heard every day throughout this city, in churches, museums, art galleries, libraries, historic homes, and national parks. Many free concerts are scheduled every week; check the *Washington Post* or the *City Paper* for details.

The 2,300-seat **Concert Hall** at the **John F. Kennedy Center for the Performing Arts** (New Hampshire Ave. and Rock Creek Pkwy. ☎ 202/416-8000. Metro: Foggy Bottom, Blue/Orange) is just one of the center's 3 auditoria. The National Symphony Orchestra's season runs from October to April, under new conductor Leonard Slatkin, who recently replaced cellist Mstislav Rostropovich. The NSO gives free outdoor concerts on Memorial Day, the Fourth of July, and Labor Day. The Kennedy center Orchestra accompanies ballets, operas, etc. Upstairs, down the hall from the Center's impressive Performing Arts Library, the more intimate **Terrace Theater** is an acoustically friendly site for recitals and chamber music.

Other major venues include the **Wolf Trap Farm Park** (1624 Trap Rd., Vienna, VA; ☎ 703/255-1800), a national performing arts center set amid almost 120 acres of gently rolling Virginia farmland. The permanent stage of the Filene Center is surrounded by grassy terraces. It's a summer ritual to spread a blanket, open a picnic basket (some of them get quite elaborate, with crystal, candlesticks, and the works) and listen to programs ranging from the New York City opera to acoustic folkie Shawn Colvin. Many Sunday afternoon concerts are free. The outdoor season runs from May to September. One of the best things about winter is the busy schedule of (mostly folk, acoustic, and jazz) performances in The Barns, Wolf Trap's handsomely converted, acoustically perfect, former stables.

The soaring sounds of choirs, resonant pipe organ, and chamber ensembles are an aural match for the magnificent Gothic ecclesiastical architecture of **Washington National Cathedral** (Massachusetts Ave. and Wisconsin Ave. NW; ☎ 202/537-6207). The cathedral schedules regular choral and organ recitals after Sunday evensong, and carillon performances on Saturday afternoons.

George Washington University's **Lisner Auditorium** (21st and H St. NW; ☎ 202/822-4757. Metro: Foggy Bottom, Blue/Orange), a comfortable, acoustically pleasing, 1,500-seat auditorium, is the site of frequent classical concerts and lectures. Also check the newspaper for concerts at other area uni-versities, including the Catholic University of America, Georgetown University, and American University.

The 4,000-seat auditorium in the handsome Beaux-Arts–styled **DAR Constitution Hall** (18th and D St. NW; ☎ 202/638-2661. Metro: Farragut West or Farragut North. draws enthusiastic crowds for classical concerts and other music events, especially R&B concerts.

There's a collection of fine period instruments, including several Stradivarius violins, at the **Library of Congress** (1st St. and Independence Ave. SE; ☎ 202/707-5677. Metro: Capitol South, Blue/Orange), and they must be exercised regularly to keep them fit—one reason for the regular concerts held in the library's Coolidge Auditorium.

The city's plentiful museums and galleries provide handsome settings for fine music. The **National Gallery of Art** (6th St. and Constitution Ave. NW., ☎ 202/737-4215. Metro: Archives-Navy Memorial, Red, Green/Yellow) offers free concerts on Sundays at 7pm amid the palm fronds and ornate Beaux Arts surroundings of the East Garden Court. The Sunday chamber music concerts at the **Phillips Collection** (1600 21st St. NW; ☎ 202/387-2151. Metro: Dupont Circle, Red), are a local favorite. Concerts are held in the Music Room of what was once a private home. The museum also has a superb collection of impressionist art.

A near neighbor to The White House, the **Corcoran Gallery of Art** (17th St. and New York Ave. NW; ☎ 202/638-3211. Metro: Farragut West, Blue/Orange) stages frequent free classical concerts, usually on Friday (phone for the weekly program). There is also a program, "Contemporary Music Forum," at 8pm on the 3rd Monday of every month from September to May. At the **National Building Museum** (F St. between 4th and 5th streets NW; ☎ 202/272-2448. Metro: Judiciary Square (F St. exit), there are free musical performances each Friday at noon, in the breathtaking 4-story-high central court, which looks like the inside of a wedding cake.

The Smithsonian's Division of Performing Arts offers frequent concerts in the various **Smithsonian Museums.** Call 202/357-1300 for recorded information or consult the "Smithsonian Bulletin" page in the *Washington Post* on the last Sunday of each month.

Smaller recital venues include **Anderson House,** home of the Society of the Cincinnati (2118 Massachusetts Ave. NW; ☎ 202/785-0540. Metro: Dupont Circle), a historic Palladian townhouse, full of eye-inspiring art and furnishings. Free organ recitals are given every Friday at noon, except during Lent, at **Church of the Epiphany** (1317 G St. NW; ☎ 202/347-2635. Metro: Metro Center) in the heart of downtown Washington.

Opera queens (of all persuasions) are kept content by the **Washington Opera** (Kennedy Center, New Hampshire Ave. and Rock Creek Pkwy. NW; ☎ 202/254-3600. Metro: Foggy Bottom, Blue/Orange), a nationally well-regarded company. But its all-too-brief fall-to-winter season is very quickly oversubscribed—it's the cultural equivalent of hard-to-get Redskins football tickets.

On the lighter side, the **Summer Opera Theatre Company,** based at the Catholic University's Hartke Theatre (☎ 202/526-1669) mounts a serious summer season. And the **Washington Savoyards** present yearly productions of Gilbert & Sullivan operettas (venues vary; call 202/965-7678). You've heard of dinner theater, but are you ready for dinner opera? The Italian restaurant **Papa Razzi** (1066 Wisconsin Ave., ☎ 202/298-8000. Metro: Foggy Bottom or Rosslyn), reserves Monday nights for lovers of singing and spaghetti, with aspiring aria-lists tackling "opera's greatest hits" at tableside. Better than it sounds, it's a delightfully unstuffy way to learn to love opera. Pass the breadsticks.

Dance

As with music, the D.C. dance scene is monopolized by the **Kennedy Center** (New Hampshire Ave. and Rock Creek Pkwy. NW; ☎ 202/254-3600. Metro: Foggy Bottom, Blue/Orange), which draws the biggest names in the dance world; distinguished visiting companies such as New York City Ballet, American Ballet Theater, Joffrey Ballet, Dance Theatre of Harlem, and the innovative Mark Morris and Twyla Tharp troupes keep it moving in the 2,300-seat Opera House.

The home team is the **Washington Ballet** (21st and H St. NW; ☎ 202/822-4757. Metro: Foggy Bottom, Blue/Orange), a company with a wide repertoire, from classical to very modern, which has given the dance world such names as ABT ballerina Amanda McKerrow, and the late choreographer Choo San Goh.

In addition to being the only downtown space that consistently showcases cutting-edge performance art and music, the downtown experimental studio/theater **Dance Place** (3225 8th St. NE; ☎ 202/269-1600. Metro: Brookland/CUA, Red) offers ongoing modern dance classes and provides a home base for such nationally known choreographers as Liz Lerman and Dance Exchange (known for her innovative movement works involving senior citizens and very young children), Wendy Woodson & Present Company, Douglas Dunn Dancers, Toe Jam, and Jelly.

If you want to do it yourself, good places to start are the **Joy of Motion Dance Center** (1643 Connecticut Ave. NW; ☎ 202/387-0911) and **Synergy Dance Center** (4321 Wisconsin Ave. NW; ☎ 202/363-4664).

Theater

Arena Stage, 6th St. and Maine Ave. SW. ☎ 202/488-3300. Metro: Waterfront (Blue/Orange).

The city's first professional repertory theater, Arena is now such an established part of the cultural scene that it is hard to remember when Zelda and Tom Fichandler risked everything on pioneering the concept of theater-in-the-round in the city's Waterfront district. Forty-two years later, they have passed the baton to younger producers and directors, and take pride in the number of actors (James Earl Jones, Robert Prosky) they have graduated to Broadway, Hollywood, and TV. Their permanent headquarters includes the 800-seat Arena Stage, the 500-seat Kreeger Theater, and the 180-seat Old Vat Room cabaret.

Church Street Theater, 1742 Church St. NW. ☎ 202/265-3748. Metro: Dupont Circle (Red).

Former home to the New Playwright's Theatre, this lovely redbrick building on a quiet Dupont Circle side street is now a for-rent playhouse, which provides a temporary home to such nomadic local troupes as the acclaimed gay-and-lesbian Freedom Stage.

Elizabethan Theatre, The Folger Shakespeare Library, 201 E. Capitol St. SE. ☎ 202/547-7070. Metro: Capitol South (Blue/Orange).

A faithful, 243-seat replica of Shakespeare's Globe Theatre, this was often the only stage on which the Bard's plays could be seen in Washington. While the Shakespeare Theatre, formerly the resident company here, has decamped to new purpose-built quarters at the Lansburgh Building (see the Shakespeare Theatre), one or two intimate productions of Elizabethan drama are mounted each season.

Ford's Theatre, 511 10th St. NW. ☎ 202/347-4833. Metro: Metro Center (Red, Blue/Orange).

In the daytime, busloads of schoolchildren dutifully file through this theater, maintained by the National Park Service, to see where President Lincoln was shot, and view such artifacts as the creepy death mask in the basement museum. But at night this antebellum jewel of a theater stages anything from new musicals to political satire and period revivals. Aside from updating sound and lighting of course, producing artistic director Frankie Hewitt has kept the place looking much the same as it did in Lincoln's day, but theatergoers bless her for replacing the severe old straight-backed chairs with new semi-cushioned seats.

GALA Hispanic Theatre, 1625 Park Road, NW. ☎ 202/234-7174.

Based in the primarily Hispanic Mount Pleasant neighborhood, the 15-year-old, nationally-noted GALA (Grupo de Actores Latino Americanos) presents classic and contemporary works by Latin American or Spanish playwrights in both Spanish and English.

Kennedy Center Eisenhower Theater, Terrace Theater and Theater Lab, New Hampshire Ave. and Rock Creek Pkwy. ☎ 202/416-8000. Metro: Foggy Bottom (Blue/Orange).

This national performing arts center manages to attract at least one Broadway blockbuster a season, usually into the 2,300-seat Opera House. Serious plays and comedies are customarily booked into the 1,100-seat Eisenhower Theater. The upstairs Terrace Theater, a gift from the people of Japan, is a beautifully intimate 513-seat house in soothing lavender and rosewood tones, best suited for the occasional 1-person show or small play. The "franchise" comedy whodunit *Shear Madness* has monopolized the experimental Theater Lab for 10 years now, making it the longest running show in Washington history, but the space still provides a home for great kid's-theater during the day. Watch for frequent free festivals and performance showcases, such as the annual American College Theater Festival each spring, and the Kennedy Center Open House in late summer.

Lincoln Theater, 1215 U St. NW. ☎ 202/328-6000. Metro: U Street/Cardozo (Green/Yellow).

Situated in the middle of what was once the burnt-out U Street "riot corridor," this historic theater, a former mainstay of the black vaudeville circuit, recently rose from the ashes. The theater is right across the street from a Metro station and hosts big name jazz and R&B concerts as well as plays, gospel musicals, and comedies, usually focused toward black audiences.

The National Theatre, 1321 E St. NW. ☎ 202/628-6161. Metro: Federal Triangle (Blue/Orange), Metro Center (Red, Blue/Orange).

Another Washington landmark, established in 1835, this downtown stage received a multimillion-dollar facelift in the 1980s, but its then-trendy aqua-and-peach look is due for another makeover. Booked by that Broadway powerhouse, the Shubert Organization, the 1,672-seat theater schedules touring Broadway musicals, but has lately remained dark in between long stretches of *Cats* visits. Free programs in the Helen Hayes Lounge include theater-themed movies, mad magicians, Shakespearean soliloquists, and other eclectic fare that draws faithful local audiences.

Olney Theatre, 2001 Route 109, Olney, MD. ☎ 301/924-4485.

One of the area's old-timers, the Olney is also known as the State Summer Theater of Maryland, but it has undergone an ambitious weatherizing program in recent years, and now presents plays year-round. Half the fun of going is the semirural drive out to the rustic 713-seat theater (try and arrive early enough to have dinner at the earthy Olney Ale House across the street). The Olney's actors and visiting stars live next door, in a (reputedly haunted) big old farmhouse.

The Shakespeare Theatre, 450 7th St. NW, in the Lansburgh Building. ☎ 202/393-2700. Metro: Archives-Navy Memorial (Green/Yellow), Gallery Place-Chinatown (Red).

Michael Kahn, the talented artistic director of this internationally-respected Shakespearean company, has taken to augmenting his permanent ensemble with such carefully chosen Broadway or Hollywood stars as Stacey Keach, Kelly McGillis, and Pat Carroll (who cross-dressed to play Falstaff, to great acclaim) as "resident actor" each season. These visiting luminaries somehow gratefully accept minimal salaries and rigorous rehearsals to play unexpected roles with surprising and audience-pleasing results. The plays of the eponymous Shakespeare, naturally, take pride of place, but the works of other classic dramatists such as Molière are also presented in this new 447-seat theater. The troupe's annual "Free for All" Shakespeare-in-the-park offerings, usually one of Shakespeare's comedies, are a highlight of summer in the city.

Signature Theatre Company, 3806 S. Four Mile Run Drive, Arlington, VA. ☎ 703/820-9771.

Just outside the city, this frisky young Arlington company has made its mark with its annual lovingly staged productions of Sondheim musicals, its marketing savvy, and its eagerness to shock and shake up its mostly suburban audiences with such Jesse Helms-bait creations as Brad Frasier's frank *Poor Super Man*.

Source Theatre Company, 1835 14th St. NW. ☎ 202/462-1073.

The anchor stage in the once-dangerous 14th Street "arts corridor," the Source is one of the Capitol's prime showcases for all sorts of experimental plays, revivals, and performance art. The theater's annual summer Washington Theatre Festival presents scores of new plays in locations all around the city, and has given many performers a first shot at the stage. The theater offers valet parking, and there are a handful of cool cafes nearby. You should still watch your step in this neighborhood.

Studio Theatre, 1333 P St. NW. ☎ 202/332-3300. Metro: Dupont Circle (Red).

Visionary artistic director Joy Zinoman transformed a former auto-repair shop into 2 state-of-the-art stages, the handsome Mainstage, which houses solid local productions of recent off-Broadway plays, and the still-industrial looking 2nd-story Second Stage, which gives young, adventurous directors and new plays a first chance to work without fear of criticism.

Warner Theatre, 1299 Pennsylvania Ave. NW. ☎ 202/628-1818. Metro: Metro Center (Red or Blue/Orange).

This former vaudeville palace was recently restored to rococo glory, and its gilt balconies and *Hello, Dolly!* staircase in the lobby is a great place for posing with a cocktail at intermission. The Warner competes with the Kennedy Center and the National Theatre for the fewer and fewer touring productions on the road, so it's sadly dark lots of the time, but brightens up for short-term runs by acts like David Copperfield and Penn & Teller.

Washington Stage Guild, Carroll Hall, 924 G St. NW. ☎ 202/529-2084. Metro: Metro Center (Red).

Specializing in Shaw and contemporary European playwrights, this highly regarded small theater works out of a converted church—the late Helen Hayes performed in plays here when she was a schoolgirl parishioner.

Woolly Mammoth Theater Company, 1401 Church St. NW. ☎ 202/393-3939. Metro: Dupont Circle (Red).

Notorious and naughty playwrights like Nicky Silver, Harry Kondoleon, and Wally Shawn fit right in at the Woolly Mammoth, Washington's answer to off-Broadway's avant-garde. The Woollies have an outstanding ensemble of area actors, and usually choose plays about angst, alienation, and our desperate need to connect in modern times. Most plays have a "pay-what-you-can night," and there are usually half-price "stampede seats" sold at the door an hour before curtain.

Jazz

This city loves its jazz: It even named a beautiful bridge and a lively school for the performing arts after jazz great and D.C. native Duke Ellington. And several jazz greats still call it home, including nonpareil singer/pianist Shirley Horn, saxman Ron Holloway, and guitarist Buck Hill.

Jazz venues include **Blues Alley** (1073 Wisconsin Ave. NW, just s of M St. in Georgetown; ☎ 202/337-4141), which books internationally known jazz and cabaret performers in an informal (which is *not* the same as inexpensive) and intimate atmosphere. How intimate? Blues Alley was a favorite of the late singer Phyllis Hyman, who was known to nibble from the plates of audience members—the club even named a dish after her. Restaurant seating with dinner is available, as well as a sandwich menu for midnight shows. Well worth the substantial cover and minimum. Another hot spot on the upscale side of jazz is the **Nest Lounge** (1401 Pennsylvania Ave. NW; ☎ 202/628-9100), the penthouse cabaret at the posh Willard Inter-Continental hotel.

The newest jewel in the jazz scene is **Bar Nun** (1326 U St. NW; ☎ 202/332-0533), a velvet-draped, Greenwich Village–style jazz club in the groovy U-Street zone.

Former D.C. schoolteacher Roberta Flack was discovered killing them softly with her song at the well-worn, welcoming Capitol Hill location of **Mr. Henry's** (601 Pennsylvania Ave. SE; ☎ 202/546-8412. Metro: Capitol South; Blue/Orange). This decade's best-kept vocal secret is singer Julia Nixon, a weekly fixture at the Adams Morgan location of this friendly neighborhood saloon (1836 Columbia Rd. NW; ☎ 202/797-8882), which managed to squeeze a stage and a room-length bar into cozy quarters. The entertainment menu is varied, but weekends are reserved for jazz.

One of the last original blocks left untouched by D.C. developers shelters **One Step Down** (2517

Pennsylvania Ave. NW; ☎ 202/331-8863. Metro: Foggy Bottom, Blue/Orange), an authentic basement jazz bar that hosts some of the area's most talented musicians. There are 3 sets a night, and jam sessions Saturday and Sunday afternoons.

And **City Blues** (2651 Connecticut Ave. NW; ☎ 202/232-2300. Metro: Woodley Park/Zoo, Red), virtually across the street from the Sheraton Washington and Omni Shoreham hotels, is a townhouse restaurant that offers jazz and blues with its menus. If you don't feel like dinner, you can listen from the bar instead.

Who says the suburbs don't swing? Takoma Park, the D.C. suburb that once declared itself a nuclear-free zone, where natural-food stores and other icons of the sixties positively flourish, also possesses a fine jazz club in **Takoma Station Tavern** (6914 4th St. NW; ☎ 202/829-1999. Metro: Takoma Park, Red). At the **Basin Street Lounge** (219 King St., Alexandria, VA; ☎ 703/549-1411), the brick arcades, lush foliage, and French-inspired menu at the downstairs 219 Restaurant all whisper New Orleans, but the star attraction of the casual upstairs lounge is jazz, not Dixieland.

Pop/Rock/Funk/Techno/Rave

D.C.'s not just a one-industry town: Somehow it has developed a reputation for several musical genres. Alienated teens and 20-somethings know D.C. as one of the world capitals of hardcore punk (some even spelled the genre harDCore for awhile), with the best-known and most influential proponent, the ultraidealistic Fugazi, based across the Key Bridge in Arlington, Virginia. Must be something in that Arlington water: A loose network of fresh-faced suburban kids and their indie pop bands (Tsunami, Air Miami, Edsel, Velocity Girl, and others), are busy making peppy 7-inch singles in basements and bedrooms. The energetic, cowbell-driven, percussion-based, neo-big-band music known as go-go still thrives in its birthplace, the black dancehalls of D.C. And Baltimore has found itself on the Generation-X map as an East Coast center for rave and techno events.

The big acts—Rolling Stones, Springsteen, Pink Floyd, Madonna—play the sports arenas when they're in town. If it's summer, you'll see them at **RFK Stadium,** and year-round at the indoor **USAir Arena** (call Ticketmaster for concert schedules and ticket information 202/432-7328). Also in summer, you can catch middle-to-big name bands at **Merriweather Post Pavilion** (Rt. 29, Columbia Pike, Columbia, MD; ☎ 410/730-2424), which offers a choice of sheltered reserved seats and general admission, picnic-style lawn seating.

For 15 years, the once cutting-edge **9:30 Club** (815 V St. NW; ☎ 202/393-0930. Metro: Gallery Place-Chinatown, Red) was *the* best place in the city to catch up-and-coming (and already arrived) bands. It still is, but the dark, dank club, which once seemed thrillingly seedy and dangerous is now a piece of mainstream local tradition. The 9:30 Club is owned and booked by Seth Hurwitz, whose IMP Productions presents most of the big concerts in town, so 9:30 gets first pick of nationally known bands who want to play small clubs.

Competition for the 9:30 Club recently arrived in the newest addition and brightest hope, the **Capitol Ballroom/Half Street Club** (1015 Half St. SE; recorded concertline ☎ 703/549-7625. Metro: Navy Yard, Green), which is booked by national competitor, the locally based Cellar Door booking agency. Set in the dicey southeast warehouse district (the club is just a block from a Metro station, and the Ballroom and its neighboring dance clubs team up to provide good security), it's a combination Manhattan-style standup rock venue and dance club, all inside a warehouse with an intriguingly eerie *Eraserhead*-industrial look.

Another new hot spot for live music is **Black Cat** (1831 14th St. NW; ☎ 202/667-7960), which rumbles and jangles 7 nights a week with clangorous alternative rock.

Billy Joel recorded his live album at Georgetown's roomy concert-hall/saloon the **Bayou** (3135 K St. NW; recorded concert listing ☎ 202/333-2897). And Hootie and the Blowfish were frequent visitors before they made it big; they were the perfect draw for the frat-boy crowd that hangs out there.

Local pop culture entrepreneur Joe Englert began his empire of theme-crazy nightclubs with **15 Minutes** (1030 15th St. NW; ☎ 202/408-1855. Metro: MacPherson Square, Blue/Orange), one of the friendliest spots in town for local and visiting bands. A business-crowd cafeteria by day, this eclectic joint is a Ray Bradbury-esque carnival by night, hosting bands, and broadcasting national trivia game linkups on its big screens.

It's dark, impossibly narrow, tiny (no more than 50 patrons, decrees the fire marshall), but that hasn't stopped the strange little **Roratonga Rodeo** (1127 Wilson Blvd., Arlington, VA; ☎ 703/525-8646. Metro: Clarendon or Courthouse Square, Blue/Orange) from attracting the best in local and regional bands. The most reliable part of the menu is the 56 brands of beer, including some excellent local microbrews.

The **Roxy** (1214 18th St. NW; ☎ 202/296-9292. Cover. Metro: Dupont Circle, Red) splits its time between pleasing reggae fans with an impressive roster of visiting live acts, and the techno-rave-gothic crowd, with local star DJ Mohawk Adam Lief spinning on alternating nights.

Perhaps because of the boisterous appreciation of its fans and followers, punk music is not always welcome in mainstream clubs, but moshers have found a home at **Asylum In Exile** (1210 U St. NW; ☎ 202/319-9353. Metro: U Street/Cardozo, Green/Yellow).

Lectures & Literary Events

Washington loves to hear itself talk, but occasionally lets someone else gets a chance to slip a word in edgewise.

Actually, Washingtonians are avid listeners (when they're not talking, that is), and there's usually a feast of lectures and discussions on a bewildering range of topics, on any day or night of the week.

Subjects can range from astronomy at the National Air and Space Museum to Zoroastrianism at a New Age bookstore. For information on lectures and literary happenings, check the *Washington Post*'s Friday Weekend section, the *City Paper,* or the Smithsonian Resident Associates program (☎ 202/357-3030), which publishes a bulletin of scheduled events.

Bookstores are doing big business in town, and as the bookstores keep getting bigger, readings and author appearances are on the rise. Numerous lectures and readings are given by touring authors and members of the city's burgeoning community of writers, poets, and playwrights. The *Washington Post* publishes a "Literary Calendar" on the last Sunday of each month in its *Book World* literary supplement, but it is also worth contacting the Writers' Center (☎ 301/654-8664) and the Library of Congress Poetry Office (☎ 202/707-5394).

D.C. AFTER DARK

QUICK—MAKE A LIST OF THE FIRST 5 ADJECTIVES that come to mind when you think of Washington, D.C.

Don't stop to think—Go!

Time's up. Let's see what you came up with: "Workaholic." Yup. "Conservative." Right. "Pretentious." Check. "Hypocritical." Uh-huh. "Tourist Trap. . . ."

Hey, wait a minute—you left out "Fun!"

OK, OK, we grant you that fun is not a top priority around here, but if you know where to look, you'll find it. That's where we come in.

Welcome to a city with a split personality.

On the one hand, D.C.'s still a very conservative, serious-minded city that works hard, and goes to bed early.

On the other hand there's a new, young Washington that shows up after dark, when the federal buildings empty out, the beltways drain the town of nonresidents, and the lights go up on the monuments.

Because of the constantly changing populations—students, tourists, international employees, gays and lesbians, immigrants, and more—nightlife is constantly changing, with clubs and restaurants here one season, gone the next. Something's lost—jazz is an endangered species, and the urban cowboy craze is steppin' out—but something's gained. Ambient, techno, and rave music and their attendant fashions and followers are making a colorful mark, and swing music is heating up. And certain things remain perennially big here: For some reason, Washington has long been a stronghold of bluegrass, roots-rock, and Irish folk, as well as the thriving homegrown punk, alternative and go-go/hip-hop sounds.

Most of the after-dark action is centralized in a handful of neighborhoods. In recent years, the spotlight has shifted away from Georgetown to Adams Morgan, a gumbo of Third World, Hispanic, and Asian restaurants and international and avant-garde clubs. It's still the most exciting and ever-changing neighborhood. Pockets of after-hours life persist in and around the waterfront district, and a meet market of dance clubs and bars catering to young white- and baby-blue-collar professionals has its nexus at 21st and M in the business district.

Even many locals have bought into the media image of D.C. as Danger City. Don't believe the hype, and don't let it make you miss out on the silly side of this most serious-minded city. Sure, you need to keep your wits about you and watch where and when you're going out, but the same goes for any major town. Just play it safe and call a cab or hop aboard a nearby Metro.

So welcome to our workaholic, conservative, pretentious, hypocritical, tourist trap city.

And have fun.

Bars & Clubs

The stylish trio of **Fifth Column** (915 F St. NW; ☎ 202/396-3632), **Club Zei** (415 Zei Alley NW; ☎ 202/842-2445), and **Spy Club** (808 15th St. NW; ☎ 202/289-1779) are all New York–style dance clubs catering to the young, the restless, and the slickly styled, with a distinctly Euro-flavor.

The black-owned-and-operated megaclub the **Ritz** (919 E St. NW; ☎ 202/638-2582; Red Line Metro to Metro Center or Gallery Place) is one of the city's biggest and busiest nightspots, with 5 separate areas showcasing live and recorded hip-hop, reggae, jazz, funk, and soul.

On the far side of things, something strange is always going on at **Planet Fred** (1221 Connecticut Ave. NW; ☎ 202/331-FRED), which is usually the site of nightly *Animal House* dance bacchanals, but has also been the scene of men's underwear parties and an indescribable weekly event called Drag Freak Bingo. **Club Heaven** (2327 18th St. NW; ☎ 202/667-HELL) is a tiny upstairs dance bar famous for its always-packed Thursday night "Eighties Party"—doorman Neil is likely to greet you wearing a halo and horns. When you're done dancing in Heaven, you can go to Hell—the Boschian basement bar, that is. Another place to bug out is the, um, atmospheric, **Insect Club** (625 E St. NW; ☎ 202/347-8884; Red Line Metro to

Gallery Place or Judiciary Square), a multilevel ant farm of a nightclub.

When the moon rises and the weekend comes, Mr. Day's Sports Bar undergoes a strange transformation into **Back Alley** (1111 rear 19th St. NW; ☎ 202/296-7625), mutating from a place where clean-cut college kids dance to Top 40 to a leather and Gothic dance club—this is the true D.C. underground. The fevered brainchild of underground impresario "Big Al" Jiricowicz, **Chief Ike's Mambo Room** (1725 Columbia Road NW; ☎ 202/797-4637) is a low-rent but highly entertaining bar complex in multi-culti Adams Morgan. The downstairs offers live blues bands; upstairs you can play pool or dance as local star DJ Stella Neptune spins in the miniclubs called Chaos and Pandemonium.

The **Crow Bar** (1006 20th St. NW; ☎ 202/223-2972) is a self-styled biker bar that takes its theme to the extreme, with black leather, chrome, POW/MIA flags, tattoos, long hair, and a Pabst-Jack-and-Jose-drinking crowd whose Harleys clog traffic outside. On Thursday nights, perennial mayoral candidate/performance artist Russell Hirshon is guest bartender, and he'll gladly update you on the state of the city.

When we're in a strange mood, we drop in on **Grand Poobah** (2001 U St. NW; ☎ 202/588-5709), a sweetly strange spot that welcomes anyone and anything that wanders up the stairs. Perched atop a barbecued-ribs joint, it offers grand views of very urban 14th Street. The closed-captioned TV adds a surreal touch to lurid old movies or the Monday night "Melrose Place" party, which draws a flock of the faithful. It's mostly a bar, but you can get food, including Pop Tarts (they won't heat them up for you) or your own individual can of Cheez-Whiz and crackers. The club plays host to the monthly screenings of Washington's Psychotronic Film Society, and you're invited to bring your own popcorn.

Pool players cue up at the roomy, underground **Buffalo Billiards** (1333 New Hampshire Ave. NW; ☎ 202/331-7665); the kitschy-cool **Bedrock Billiards** (1841 Columbia Road NW; ☎ 202/667-7665); and equally funky **Atomic Billiards** (3427 Connecticut Ave. NW; ☎ 202/363-7665). **Babes** (4600 Wisconsin Ave. NW; ☎ 202/966-0082) and **Georgetown Billiards** (3251 Prospect St. NW; ☎ 202/965-POOL) drop the ironic trappings; they're no-frills pool halls for straight shooters.

There are plenty of options when you're in the mood for plain old beer and burgers, starting with the genuinely friendly **Acme Bar & Grill** (1207 19th St. NW; ☎ 202/833-2263). The **Bottom Line** (1716 I St. NW; ☎ 202/298-8488) is a business district bar with a neighborhood feel. **Brickskeller** (1523 22nd St. NW, ☎ 202/293-1885), is Valhalla for beer lovers, with more than 500 brews on the menu. For some reason, this cozy basement pub decided it would be a good idea to specialize in buffalo burgers. I guess you have to try them once. **Bullfeathers** (401 South St. SE; ☎ 202/543-5005) is a comfy neighborhood saloon packed with Capitol Hill staffers. Buy someone a drink and you just may pick up a State secret, if nothing else. We'll see whether **Slick Willie's** (319 Pennsylvania Ave. SE; ☎ 202/544-6600) has to change its name after '96, but for now it's a nice, nonpartisan saloon.

Caution: You're nearing the perpetual frat party of the Singles Zone, which has its epicenter at 21st and M Street NW. The long-running meet market **Rumours** (corner of 19th and M St. NW; ☎ 202/466-7378) beats at the heart of it all, with a continuous flow of shiny happy-hour people. Other places to find Mr. or Ms. Right (or Right Now) include **Madhatter** (1831 M St. NW; ☎ 202/833-1495), and **Sign of the Whale** (1825 M St. NW; ☎ 202/785-1110). A younger crowd gravitates toward the cavernous dance club the **Cellar** (2100 M St. NW; ☎ 202/457-8180), which serves as sort of a training bar for the former.

Older and more upscale singles looking to pair up head for the **River Club** (3223 K St. NW; ☎ 202/965-3229). Deco-ed out like an ocean liner, this supper club is a virtual "Love Boat," with schmooze director Tommy Curtis, the Dolly Levi of the over-30 set, as your cruise director. Permission to come aboard?

Let's take a walk on the mild side: Famous for the "yard" of beer, the **Tiber Creek Pub** (15 E St. NW; ☎ 202/638-0900), provides first-class comfort for its clientele of congressional staffers, with tuxedoed waiters and bartenders, and a 1947 Packard parked out front for effect. Tonier still is **F. Scott's** (1232 36th St. NW; ☎ 202/965-1789), for the lost generation of the nineties. The 18thC townhouse near the Georgetown University campus that houses this chic cafe is also home to 1789, an elegant restaurant, and the casual, collegiate Tombs bar, populated by burger-loving Catholic University students.

The happy hour scene reaches its apex on Friday nights. The most phenomenal gathering is at the **Ha'Penny Lion** (1101 L St. NW; ☎ 202/296-8075). A business lunchroom by day, it turns into a wall of hungry, horny human flesh at 5pm on Friday, as the post-college TGIFers are packed into a little pen of outdoor tables. At least there's air out there, so the mingled fumes of Polo and Charlie are survivable. At the same time, kitty-corner from the Ha'Penny Lion, a comparable crowd of dressed-up young blacks and Latinos fill up the **Ascot** (1708 L St. NW; ☎ 202/296-7640). Happy Hour is a synonym for free snacks, and some of the best in town are found at **Ciao Baby** (1736 L St. NW; ☎ 202/331-1500), where the dressy crowd mingles over spicy appetizers and music in a Tuscan atmosphere.

Hotel bars are one of the few truly dependable things in modern nightlife. The essential hotel bar is the **Fairfax Bar** at the Ritz-Carlton hotel (2100 Massachusetts Ave. NW; ☎ 202/293-2100). Attracting the rich and powerful, it's the real deal, with gleaming wood-paneled walls, comfortable leather chairs, and superb, unobtrusive service. Light meals are available, and a magnificent tea is served from 3pm to 5pm. Jackets required after 5pm.

Other exemplars include **Allegro Lounge** at the Sheraton Carlton (16th and K St. NW; ☎ 202/638-2626); the airy and elegant **Garden Terrace** at the Four Seasons (2800 Pennsylvania Ave. NW; ☎ 202/342-0444); **Jockey Club** at the Ritz-Carlton hotel (see above); the **Retreat** at the Madison Hotel (15th and M St. NW; ☎ 202/862-1600), which is a good spot for spotting international VIPs, who are often housed here during state visits; **Round Robin Bar** and the **Nest Lounge** in the Willard Inter-Continental hotel (1401 Pennsylvania Ave. NW; ☎ 202/628-9100), one of the city's most historic bars, and its most intime cabaret; **Sky Terrace** at the Washington hotel (15th and Pennsylvania Ave. NW; ☎ 202/638-5900); the **Spy's Eye Bar** at the Hyatt Regency (400 New Jersey Ave. NW; ☎ 202/737-1234); **Tabard Inn** (1739 N St. NW; ☎ 202/833-2668); **Town & Country Lounge** at the Mayflower Hotel (1127 Connecticut Ave. NW; ☎ 202/347-3000); and 2 merrie olde English pubs, the **Union Jack** at the Canterbury Hotel (1733 N St. NW; ☎ 202/393-3000), and the **Rose Crown Pub** at the Grand Hotel (2350 M St. NW; ☎ 202/955-4488).

Grand Slam at the Grand Hyatt Washington hotel (1000 H St. NW; ☎ 202/582-1234) is easily the best sports bar in town, with 2 huge TV screens, free popcorn, video games, foosball, pool, darts, and lots of sports memorabilia.

There's no more civilized spot in the cosmopolitan Dupont Circle area than **Kramerbooks and Afterwords Cafe** (1517 Connecticut Ave. NW; ☎ 202/387-1462), one of the original bookstore-cum-cafes, and a genuine Washington landmark. Pick up an overseas magazine, a paperback classic, or the latest bestseller, then enjoy a coffee, a drink, or a light meal. Maybe you'll meet someone who can read!

The **Pop Stop** (1513 17th St. NW; ☎ 202/ 328-0880), in the très gay 17th Street strip, is where you'll find everyone checking out everyone else over lattés and the like. The scoping and staring spills right out onto the streets, where the curb-squatters do everything but hold up cards with rating numbers as you pass by.

If you can't sleep or you're planning to be up all night, you'll find good company at **SOHO Tea & Coffee** (2150 P St. NW; ☎ 202/463-7646), which features frighteningly enormous bowls of coffee or tea (50 loose-leaf varieties and counting), and night creatures playing games and tapping at laptops at the welded aluminum tables (which are available for sale if you really become attached).

Step into the after-"Twilight Zone," a pocket of strangeness in a city that prides itself on keeping up appearances (and dares to define normality for the rest of the country). Lit like a bordello and painted red from top to bottom, **Madam's Organ** (2003 18th St. NW; ☎ 202/667-5370) may just be the strangest place in town, but some of the city's most loveable characters call it home. On Tuesday nights, homeless guy Richard LeKook wanders in, sits down at the piano and plays an hour or two of lovely arpeggios, which he tape-records for his own archives.

D.C.'s not usually ahead of the pack, trendwise, but the Adams Morgan world music listening post called **Kala Kala** (2439 18th St. NW; ☎ 202/232-5433) was one of the country's first successful nonsmoking nightspots. **Manute Bol's Spotlight** (1211 U St. NW; ☎ 202/265-5833) is part-owned by the 7-foot-2-inch basketball player. If he's there, you can't miss him. If you like to drink with comrades, **State of the Union** (1357 U St. NW, ☎ 202/588-8810) is the ticket: The music is up-to-the-minute (and into the future) acid jazz, reggae, and ambient. The ambiance is pure Cold War, with authentic Commie posters and an impressive collection of vodkas and caviar.

No one does bars like the Irish, and D.C. has at least 4 Celtic classics. Just down the street from Union Station in Capitol Hill, the cavernous **Dubliner** (520 N. Capitol St. NW; ☎ 202/737-3773) and its cozier next-door-neighbor **Irish Times** (14 F St. NW; ☎ 202/543-5433) are hearty pubs offering live American and Irish folk music and American versions of Irish food favorites (and brews). Also doing their bit to keep the cheerful drinker stereotype alive are the roomy **Ireland's Four Provinces** (3412 Connecticut Ave. NW; ☎ 202/244-0960) and, across the street, the neighborhood pub **Nanny O'Briens** (3319 Connecticut Ave. NW; ☎ 202/686-9189). Standing room only on St. Patrick's Day, of course.

The college crowd doesn't really ask much of its favorite hangouts—they just want a place that lets them unwind, be as loud and late as they want, and eat and drink (and inevitably puke) junk food and beer on the cheap. The Georgetown University gang has the saloon-choked streets of Georgetown to choose from, but they remain loyal to the **Tombs** (1226 36th St. NW; ☎ 202/337-6668), which is so close to campus it might as well offer night courses with its burgers and beers. George Washington University students favor **G.G. Flipps** (915 21st St. NW), which masquerades as a mild-mannered Kusam Indian restaurant by day; its aroma is a heady mix of pungent cumin and years of spilled beer. The Catholic University kids keep the faith at **Colonel Brooks Tavern** (901 Monroe St. NE; ☎ 202/529-4002). **Jenkins Hill and Underground** (319 Pennsylvania Ave. SE; ☎ 202/544-4066) used to be known as President Nixon's favorite bar, now it's packed on weekends with interns letting it all loose and dancing on the tables to Motown on Saturday nights.

Even with all of the shifting trends and international flavors swirling around them, neighborhood dives remain happily oblivious and unchanged, and cherished by connoisseurs. Some neighborhood favorites: In Adams Morgan it's **Millie & Al's** (2440 18th St. NW; ☎ 202/387-8131) for the pizza, pitchers, and softball team spirit; and the 1-room, defiantly nondescript **Dan's Cafe** (2315 18th St. NW; ☎ 202/265-9241), which always looks like it's closed. Below Dupont Circle, there's **Mr. Eagan's** (1343 Connecticut Ave. NW;

☎ 202/331-9768). At the center of the très gay 17th Street neighborhood, **Fox & Hounds** (1537 17th St. NW; ☎ 202/232-6307), is a neutral hangout zone where everyone feels comfortable, no matter who they choose to cruise.

In Georgetown, try **Garrett's** (3003 M St. NW; ☎ 202/333-1003). **The Grog & Tankard** (2408 Wisconsin Ave. NW; ☎ 202/333-3114) is a dependable tavern (with a very young clientele) that always has a full roster of local bands, unplugged and otherwise, with a special affinity for Grateful Dead–inspired groups. Capitol Hill has **Hawk & Dove** (329 Pennsylvania Ave. SE; ☎ 202/543-3300), a venerable Capitol Hill hangout and hideout, encrusted with stuffed and mounted animals, old shotguns, and a hunting-lodge look. And year in, year out, the **Tune Inn** (33½ Pennsylvania Ave. SE; ☎ 202/543-2725) wins honors as "Best Dive." History has been made here, as decades of preppy Hillites have passed through, loving without irony the cranky waitresses, cheap beer, good greasy burgers, and the stuffed deer behinds over the bathroom doors.

Dancing

Black owned and operated, the **Ritz** (919 E St. NW; ☎ 202/638-2582) packs 5 dance floors into a 4-story building, mixing live music and DJs, reggae, R&B, funk, hip-hop and go-go, and whatever's new. If you came to dance, the megadisco **Tracks** (1111 1st St. SE; ☎ 202/488-3320) is really the only game in town. It's in a dicey neighborhood, but safely accessible by Metro. It recently began sharing security costs with the hip clubs sprouting up around it. In good weather, you dance on the outdoor dance floor and even play volleyball.

Those in search of cutting-edge dance sounds go to the new **Capitol Ballroom/Half Street Club** (1015 Half St. SE; ☎ 703/549-7625, the number for the Virginia-based booking and ticket office), where eerie ambient and techno tones pulse from an awesome sound system within a converted warehouse that looks like the setting for David Lynch's midnight movie classic *Eraserhead*. The revered Temple of Boom for the coolest kids, and also the best multiracial mix, is at the **Chamber of Sound** (925 5th St. NW; ☎ 202/898-0761), started by DJ team Dario Garioni and Palash Ahmed. After all the office workers have cleared out of the K Street business zone, the line starts to form at **Bravo Bravo** (1001 Connecticut Ave. NW; ☎ 202/223-5330), a roomy basement club with a boxing ring–like raised dance floor and a frisky young crowd.

If familiar music is what moves you, go play in **The Cellar** (2100 M St. NW; ☎ 202/457-8180), an enormous underground rec room that advertises itself as playing "music you know," and packs in an 18-and-over crowd on the weekends. For an older more upscale crowd, spin backwards in time at **Deja Vu** (2119 M St. NW; ☎ 202/452-1966), where downtown professionals in their 30s and 40s dance to sounds of the 1960s and 1970s; it's adjacent to LuLu's New Orleans Cafe, which mixes up some mean and mellow Southern drinks. And now that the 1980s are already nostalgia, ascend to **Club Heaven** (2327 18th St. NW; ☎ 202/667-HELL). On Wednesday nights, everyone heads up the skinny stairs to the long-running weekly eighties party with host Neil, who is likely to greet you with tinsel halo *and* devil's horns, and DJs Jim and Jon, who look like escapees from a vintage Duran Duran video. And if you don't want to dance, you can go to Hell. The downstairs bar, that is.

The terminally stylish gravitate toward **Fifth Column** (915 F St. NW; ☎ 202/393-3632), a former bank. The club sports a different name, style, sound, and group of dancers every night of the week, although you can always be sure of a mix of stylish Euro-kids and punks. If you want to stay up past everyone's bedtime, Tuesday is Cocktail Lounge Night, candlelit, with Basia and Gypsy Kings on the stereo, and a very grown-up, international cafe society crowd cuddling by candlelight.

Dancers used to find a home on every block in Georgetown. Today, **Paul Mall** (3225 M St. NW; ☎ 202/965-5353) is about the only reliable option. It might not look trendy—it doesn't even look open— but the management knows about bands. Just as much fun is the Karaoke session each Monday night.

For lots of room to cut loose and swing, try **Tornado Alley** (11319 Elkin St., Wheaton, Md.; ☎ 301/652-3383), a carpet warehouse transformed into a New Orleans–style roadhouse with a short but redolent Cajun menu.

Gay & Lesbian

It's one of the government's best-kept secrets: D.C. is a gay old town, with a gay/lesbian population estimated at more than 200,000. You'll see your more stylized-looking gay people around pockets like Dupont Circle Capitol Hill, and Logan Circle, which, as in many cities, were gentrified by gays and lesbians. But most of the gay population is so well integrated (perhaps because so many work for the government), that the uninitiated might never realize.

Gay visitors might want to plan their visit to coincide with Gay and Lesbian Pride Day Festival, which occurs in June; usually on Father's Day (just a coincidence). Orient yourself with a copy of the *City Paper,* (free alternative weekly newspaper, available from street-corner boxes and at bookstores and record shops), The *Washington Blade* (the well-regarded free gay weekly), *Metro Weekly* (a sassy, free, gay arts-and-entertainment magazine and bar guide with good maps and updates on events at bars and clubs), or *Scene* magazine (a free weekly alternative-oriented entertainment guide). Aside from being good full-service bookstores, the gay-and-lesbian **Lambda Rising** (1625 Connecticut Ave. NW; ☎ 202/462-6969) and the lesbian-centric **Lammas Bookstore** (1426 21st St. NW; ☎ 202/775-8218) serve as unofficial town centers.

The latest fashionable queer strip, the Chelsea or West Hollywood of D.C., is 17th Street, just west of Dupont Circle. There you'll find **Annie's Paramount Steak House** (1609 17th St. NW; ☎ 202/232-0395), a carnivore's dream (not much here for vegetarians, unless you enjoy iceberg lettuce). Next door and down a flight of stairs is **Trumpets** (17th and Q streets NW; ☎ 202/232-4141), an industrial-chic restaurant/club presided over by David Hagedorn, one of Washington's more innovative and publicity-savvy chefs. After dinner, plan to mingle with lots of guys (and gals on Wednesday nights—an interesting crowd of guys goes to women's night) in the adjoining video bar. Just a block down the street is **J.R.'s** (1519 17th St. NW; ☎ 202/328-0090), a long, narrow room that's always packed with hunky men engaged in boisterous pursuit of conversation and whatever.

Over on Connecticut Avenue, north of Dupont Circle, is the newcomer **The Circle** (1629 Connecticut Ave. NW; ☎ 202/462-5575)—three, three, three bars in one. Below sidewalk level it's the **Underground,** a dance/show bar; at street level is the **Tavern,** with regulars holding up the mahogany bar in the storefront window; and the uppermost level offers the **Terrace,** featuring an outdoor balcony with a stunning view of Connecticut Avenue.

West of Dupont, on P Street, is a cluster of legendary local gay nightspots. **Badlands** (1413 22nd St. NW;

☎ 202/296-0505) is the hot dance spot on Fridays, with a recently renovated video room, and a Magritte-influenced Karaoke room, where flocks of Marines (and those who just have the look) try their hand at singing off-key. Other P Street havens include **Mr. P's** (2147 P St. NW; ☎ 202/293-1064), the **Fraternity House** (2122 P St. NW; ☎ 202/223-4917), and the some-what risky-feeling the **Fireplace** (22nd & P Streets NW; ☎ 202/293-1293), which has developed a repu-tation as a place to meet, ahem, working men and pickpockets. The new kid on the block, **Escandalo!** (2122 P St. NW; ☎ 202/822-8909), is adjacent to Lone Star West, a good Tex-Mex restaurant, swiveling to salsa sounds. The Sunday drag brunch is a must—the "girls" wake up, put on their make up, and serve you with a song and a (somewhat scary) smile.

For women who love women, there are 2 bars geared exclusively to a lesbian crowd: The **Hung Jury** (1819 H St. NW; ☎ 202/279-3212), where men are usually allowed in only with a female escort, and **Phase One** (525 8th St. SE; ☎ 202/544-6831). Trumpets and the Circle also draw a sizable lesbian following (see above).

For those who are into the manly, leather scene—and we're not talking upholstery here—there's the **Green Lantern** (1335 Green Court, behind the park-ing lot at 1335 L St. NW; ☎ 202/638-5133). Down-stairs is okay. Upstairs is better. You'll see. A cab ride away, sits the **DC Eagle** (639 New York Ave. NW; ☎ 202/347-6025), the city's oldest leather bar.

And speaking of leather, let's talk boots and chaps: Capitol Hill boasts one of the finest queer country-western clubs you're likely to find on the East Coast: **Remington's** (639 Pennsylvania Ave. NW; ☎ 202/543-3113) is pure cowboy class, featuring several spa-cious rooms, an ample dance floor for two-steppin', and a kick-back lounge with overstuffed couches and chairs—perfect for resting sore saddles. Also on Capitol Hill is **Bachelor's Mill** (1104 8th St. SE; ☎ 202/544-1931), catering to a predominantly black gay clientele.

By far, the biggest boom area has been southeast, home for a decade to the behemoth gay-owned and operated **Tracks** megadisco (1111 1st St. NW; ☎ 202/488-3320), which is open to anyone with an open mind. And there must be a lot of open-minded people in town, because Tracks is always packed. Visit Tracks on Satur-day night: The music is hot, the light show dazzling, the crowd, often drop dead (there are lots of shirtless men showing muscles you didn't know existed).

Even the fringe has its fringe, and over on U Street, a short walk from the 17th Street Strip is **Bent** (1344 U St. NW; ☎ 202/986-6364), a willfully freaky queer bar that plays an appealing combo of seventies disco and eighties funk. Those seeking quieter gay-friendly establishments ought to consider the nearby **Grand Poobah** (2001 14th St. NW; 588-5709), or the librarylike **Larry's Lounge** (1836 18th St. NW; ☎ 202/483-0097).

Comedy, Cabarets & Revues

You've just got to laugh at a town that takes itself so seriously. A number of topical comedy and improv troupes and satirists have found a home here. If he's in town, nationally known PBS star political satirist Mark Russell often appears at Ford's Theatre. Long-running musical satirist Mrs. Foggybottom & Friends, addresses issues of the day, and is as popular with locals as with visitors in the jewel-like **Marquee Cabaret** (Omni Shoreham, 2500 Calvert St. NW; ☎ 202/234-0700).

The mainstream leader of the pack is the Capitol Steps, most of whom did, and some of whom still do, work on Capitol Hill. They present their wry insiders' view every Friday and Saturday night at **Chelsea's** (1055 Thomas Jefferson St. NW; ☎ 202/298-8222). No relation to the president's daughter. On the more irreverent side, there's **Gross National Product** (☎ 202/488-3300), who take bipartisan pokes at the passing political parade. GNP also operates a riotous weekly excursion called Scandal Tours that stops at all the red-hot sites (the Tidal Basin, Gary Hart's old townhouse, et al.) and features some terrific impersonators on board—check the *Post* "Weekend" section for times. A handful of other improv troupes, including Comedy Sportz and Dropping the Cow, in the style of "Second City" and "Saturday Night Live." perform at a variety of venues around town; check the *Post*.

The big names in comedy make 'em laugh at the **Improv** (1140 Connecticut Ave. NW; ☎ 202/296-7008), the local outpost of the quality comedy chain. The underground venue is a large cabaret room with good sightlines and sound, and a decent saloon menu. Located upstairs from the Fanatics Sports Bar, **Comedy Cafe** (1520 K St. NW; ☎ 202/638-JOKE) is a small but hip showcase for nationally known names like Judy Tenuta and Emo Phillips.

XXX

**Scandalous, shocking, cheeky, impudent
are words that will be used to describe
this uncensored account of the hidden
side of our glamorous, riotous capital
city.**

—*from* **Washington Confidential: The
Lowdown on the Big Town,** *1951*

Sex and scandal are words that have long been synonymous with Washington, D.C.

And we're just talking about the politicians.

In reality, the city of Washington has taken great pains to keep it clean for the tourists. The police and neighborhood associations have been busy chasing the prostitutes from neighborhood to neighborhood—soon the poor girls will be hawking their wares on the bridges between Virginia and Maryland. Likewise, the rise of gleaming, sterile office buildings has squeezed and shrunk the city's once-thriving porno district, which has all but slunk out of town. Tatters remains on 7th Street NW, just around the corner from hipper clubs, offering 25¢ peep booths. This sort of thing is almost obsolete anyway, because you can rent flicks from nearly any neighborhood video shop.

A handful of strip clubs have managed to hang on by their painted fingernails—there's got to be somewhere for congressmen to get caught. Be prepared for a stiff cover charge, and an even stiffer drink tab. But then, you're paying for the, um, ambiance.

The pick of the litter is **Good Guys** (2311 Wisconsin Ave. NW; ☎ 202/333-0128), a 3-ring circus (there are 3 continuously active dance floors) with tremendously acrobatic performers swinging it to loud rock and roll; nearby is **J.P.'s** (2412 Wisconsin Ave. NW; ☎ 202/333-7625), which offers more of the same sort of dancing-for-dollars but on 1 stage (but 2 floor-to-ceiling poles). **Archibald's** (1520 K St. NW; ☎ 202/737-2662) is substantially more subdued—the dancers sit around watching their friends between shifts, and pick their own tunes from the jukebox. **Camelot** (1823 M St. NW; ☎ 202/887-5966), **Joanna's 1819 Club** (1819 M St. NW; ☎ 202/296-2191), and the **Royal Palace** (1805 Connecticut Ave. NW; ☎ 202/462-2623) serve up expensive distractions to a lunchtime crowd of hungry businessmen.

There are fewer options for women to get a gander at the guys. The **Hangar Club** (☎ 301//449-6970) in suburban Oxon Hill, Maryland, hosts "bachelorette parties," with a squad of Chippendale-style studs, and now and then a club will advertise a special "Ladies Only" night with visiting male dancers, allowing the men in to meet the warmed-up gals only after showtime.

By comparison, gay men have it good. Even visitors from jaded cities like New York and L.A. are shocked—shocked!—by what the dancers get away with in the stripper bars in the southeast quadrant of the city. Though all these joints are close—a sort of open-air sex mall—it's still a good idea to catch a cab between venues, especially if you've had a few drinks.

At the **Edge/Wet** (56 L St. SE), a combination funky dance bar (complete with an outdoor deck) and erotic stripper bar, dancers first take showers and then stride around a bartop in athletic socks. Wet is rivaled only by **Secrets** (1345 Half St. SE), which, while it doesn't possess onstage showers, has plenty of socks on display. Secrets is attached to Ziegfeld's, Washington's premiere drag club, where the Friday night drag show, headlined by Ella Fitzgerald and her Illusionists, is legendary.

The southeast area also features an all-male adult movie house: the **Follies** (24 O St. SE) and **La Cage** (18 O St. SE), yet another stripper bar. Fun and games of a more hands-on sort can be found at the downtown **Crew Club** (1321 14th St. NW), billing itself as "your other gym and more," which claims in its ads to be "naturalist friendly." A bathhouse by any other name, but the owner swears no sexual activity goes on.

Only in Washington

SAFE WALKS   Your best bet for a safe, but still interesting nighttime walk is probably the National Mall; well-lit, spacious and pleasant, with good views of the Capitol building, monuments and museums, all glowing like familiar giant night-lights. It's still a good idea not to walk alone. You might also head for the commercial main drags of **Dupont Circle** (Connecticut Ave. NW between N and S streets) and **Adams Morgan** (18th St. NW between Columbia and Kalorama roads). Both are colorful, trendy, and well-populated until the early hours.

NIGHT VISION   Oddly, the best views of Washington at night are across the river in Arlington. If you can get yourself invited up by a resident of the Propect House apartment building, you've got it made (bring your camera!). Otherwise, anywhere in the vicinity of the Gannett/USA Today Towers or the Iwo Jima Memorial will give you a postcard-quality view.

Within the city, the best view in town is said to be from Senator Bob Dole's Capitol office, taking in a sweeping view of the Mall from the Washington Monument to the Lincoln Memorial. If you can't get past Dole's administrative aides, though, settle for the famous rooftop view at the **Washington's Sky Terrace** (15th St. and Pennsylvania Ave. NW; ☎ 202/638-5900).

NIGHT FLAVOR   It's late, but you can still get a true taste of D.C., and a splash of local color on the side at **Ben's Chili Bowl** (1213 U St. NW; ☎ 202/667-0909). Other options: Take your pick of more than a dozen open-late restaurants in **Chinatown** (H St. NW between 6th and 7th streets), or cruise into the 24-hour **American City Diner** (5532 Connecticut Ave. NW; ☎ 202/244-1949), a spiffy recreation of a *Grease*-y 1950s' diner. A visit to **Dolce Finale** (2653 Connecticut Ave. NW; ☎ 202/667-5350) is the end to a perfect evening—it's an all-dessert restaurant!

ALL-NIGHTY THEN   If you're in search of fellow insomniacs and/or midnight snacks, head for **Au Pied de Cochon** (1335 Wisconsin Ave. NW; ☎ 202/333-5440), a round-the-clock bistro where you can balance the guilt of their perfect French fries with the relative healthfulness of a salade Nicoise. At **SOHO Coffee and Tea** (2150 P St. NW; ☎ 202/463-7646), you're likely to find someone who wants to play games (board games, computer games, or any other sort of game you're in the mood for at that hour), and at **Kramerbooks & Afterwords** (1517 Connecticut Ave. NW; ☎ 202/387-1400), you can browse the books (and the bookworms) till it's time for brunch.

EXCURSIONS

Not far from downtown Washington is a region full of natural beauty and historic interest. This section describes some of the areas that can be toured on a a day's excursion from the capital. Some of them can be visited on organized bus tours, although a car offers greater flexibility.

Many Civil War battlefields lie within reach of the capital. **Fredericksburg,** 50 miles from Washington, has no fewer than 4, a fact that is commemorated by its Battlefield Park Museum. Two more battles took place at **Manassas,** some 25 miles west of Washington, where the battlefield is now a park with a historical museum.

Another Civil War site is **Harpers Ferry** in West Virginia, about 50 miles northwest of the capital, a charming town that was the scene of much action, including John Brown's raid in 1859. The fort where he was captured is now a museum. Not far away is the **Antietam Battlefield,** also known as Sharpsburg. But the most famous of all Civil War battlefields is **Gettysburg** in Pennsylvania, which is about 80 miles to the north. The vast battle site, with its numerous relics and markers, is best toured with a guide.

Virginia

To the southwest of Washington lies Virginia, a state that is very conscious of its historic importance, not least as a provider of presidents. Thomas Jefferson lived at **Monticello,** the beautiful hilltop house—now a museum—he designed himself, just over 100 miles from Washington. The splendid university in nearby **Charlottesville** was also designed by Jefferson.

The state's prosperity owes a great deal to the tobacco leaf, and many picturesque old plantation houses, a number of them along the James River between

Monticello

Richmond, the state capital, and **Williamsburg,** are open to the public.

Virginia's great scenic boast is the spectacular **Shenandoah National Park,** which follows the crest of the Blue Ridge Mountains for 85 miles. Its Skyline Drive affords impressive panoramas and good hiking trails.

Alexandria

6 miles (10km) s of Washington. Population: 111,000. By car, on George Washington Pkwy. or Rte. 1. By Metro, to King St. or Braddock Rd. (it's still quite a hike to the main drag on the waterfront). By bus, on Metrobus network; or tour with Gray Line (☎ 202/289-1995), which also includes Mount Vernon.

Biking is the preferred way—it's fun, scenic, and you work up a guilt-free appetite for lunch and a schooner of beer at the Fish Market restaurant in Old Town. Just join the well-marked bicycle trail on the Mount Vernon Bike Trail anywhere in D.C. along the Potomac. The trail passes by National Airport. At the halfway point, there's a sweet spot where you can stand beneath the end of the runway, and watch the planes zooming overhead—so close it feels as if you could touch them.

Today Alexandria is part of the Washington metropolitan area, and a fashionable residential enclave for city professionals, but Alexandria is still very much a town in its own right, with an old-world Virginian atmosphere entirely different from that of D.C.

The spirit of the Confederacy lives on in the old houses, the mellow, tree-lined streets, and the soft lilt of the local accent. But Alexandria also has its chic, modern side. In and around its main artery, **King Street,** are many chic shops, art galleries, and a proportionally richer selection of good restaurants than in the capital.

Allow an entire day to appreciate Alexandria to the fullest. A good place to start is the **Ramsay House Visitors Center** (221 King St.; ☎ 703/838-4200).

This small 18thC clapboard house, the oldest surviving Alexandria property, was the home of William Ramsay, a Scottish merchant who was one of the founders of the town and its first postmaster. Here you can obtain brochures, tourist advice, and a free parking pass.

Now walk along to Alexandria's **Heritage Museum,** which is housed in the **Lyceum** (201 S. Washington St.; ☎ 703/838-4994; open Mon–Sat 10am–5pm, Sun 1–5pm; closed major holidays), an imposing Greek Revival building dating from 1839. Also in the Lyceum is a cultural center, with a museum of decorative arts and artifacts, which stages free concerts.

By now you can hardly have avoided an awareness of Alexandria's strong sense of history. The town is named, not after Alexander the Great, but after a Scotsman named John Alexander who settled here in 1669. As Alexandria developed into an important port for tobacco and other goods, the Caledonian connection continued. A Scotsman, John Carlyle, built the grand stone building called **Carlyle House** (121 N. Fairfax St.; ☎ 703/549-2997; open Tues–Sat 10am–4:30pm, Sun noon–4:30pm; closed major holidays). Take a guided tour of the interior, which has been restored to as near to its original state as possible.

Another reminder of the city's Scottish founders is the **Old Presbyterian Meeting House** (321 S. Fairfax St.; ☎ 703/549-6670), a dignified, redbrick building.

A link also exists with the town's Egyptian namesake, in the form of the **George Washington National Masonic Memorial** on Old Shuter's Hill (King St. and Callahan Dr.; ☎ 703/683-2007; open 9am–5pm; closed some major holidays). This 333-foot-high edifice, built in the 1920s, is based on the Pharos Lighthouse at Alexandria in Egypt, one of the Seven Wonders of the World. It contains a replica of the lodge room of Alexandria Lodge no. 22, of which Washington was Worshipful Master. Various memorabilia of Washington, the man and the Mason, are displayed both here and in the **George Washington Museum,** located on a higher floor. The observation floor at the top of the tower has a fine view. Children are always intrigued by the mechanical parade perpetually filing past a model of the Taj Mahal in one of the **Shrine Rooms** on the 1st floor.

Although Washington's main home was at Mount Vernon, he kept a house in Alexandria, where he was a leading citizen. A pew was reserved for him at **Christ**

Church (Cameron and North Washington St.; ☎ 703/549-1450).

Other prominent Alexandrians included General "Light Horse" Harry Lee, a hero of the Revolutionary War, and his son Robert E. Lee, the famous Confederate general in the Civil War. The Lee family is associated especially with 2 houses in Alexandria. The **Lee-Fendall House** (614 Oronoco St., on the corner of N. Washington St.; ☎ 703/548-1789; open Tues–Sat 10am–3:45pm, Sun noon–3:45pm), was built by Harry Lee's relative, Philip Richard Fendall. It was there that Harry Lee wrote the funeral oration for George Washington, containing the famous words, "First in war, first in peace, and first in the hearts of his countrymen." Besides heirlooms and furnishings, the house has a fine collection of antique dollhouses. Across the road is Harry Lee's last residence, now known as the **Boyhood Home of Robert E. Lee** (607 Oronoco St.; ☎ 703/548-8454; open Mon–Sat 10am–3:30pm, Sun 1–1:30pm; both Lee Homes are occasionally closed to the public, so phone first). Beautifully furnished, the house contains many Lee portraits and memorabilia.

It is pleasant to stroll through the streets between the town center and the Potomac River, enjoying the architecture and browsing in the shops and galleries. On the south side of Prince Street near its eastern end stand 2 charming groups of houses, **Gentry Row** and **Captain's Row.** On the opposite side of Prince Street at no. 201 is the **Athenaeum** (☎ 703/548-0035), a Greek Revival building of about 1850, once a bank but now an art gallery showing temporary exhibitions.

Around the corner at 101 N. Union St. is the old **Torpedo Factory** (☎ 703/838-4565), imaginatively converted to a complex of artists' studios and crafts stores where you can buy handicrafts or simply watch the artists at work.

There is no shortage of traditional events. On the 1st Saturday in December, Alexandria celebrates its Scottish heritage in the **Annual Scottish Christmas Walk.** The town rings to the sound of bagpipes, and citizens in kilts greet each other in Gaelic. **Fort Ward** (4301 W. Braddock Rd.; ☎ 703/838-4848; park, daily 9am–sunset; museum, Tues–Sat 9am–5pm), a partially restored Civil War fort that is now a park and museum, sponsors "living history" activities at various times of the summer. A calendar of events is available from the visitors center.

Alexandria lies on the route to Mount Vernon, and the two can easily be combined in one excursion.

For a substantial meal in traditional surroundings, go to **Gadsby's Tavern** (138 N. Royal St.; ☎ 703/548-1288), a famous hostelry, once the haunt of many of the Founding Fathers. The older part of the tavern, next door to the restaurant at no. 134, is a museum (☎ 703/838-4242).

Mount Vernon & Environs

15 miles (24km) s of Washington. By car, George Washington Memorial Pkwy. By bus, tour with Gray Line (☎ 202/289-1995), which also includes Alexandria. By Tourmobile, from Washington Monument or Arlington Cemetery. By boat, Mar–late fall with Spirit Lines (Pier 4, 6th and Water St. SW; ☎ 202/554-8000). By bicycle, on the Mount Vernon Bike Trail along the Potomac.

"No estate in United America is more pleasantly situated than this," wrote George Washington to an English friend in 1793, describing his house and farm at Mount Vernon. Now owned and maintained by the Mount Vernon Ladies' Association, it is a popular place of pilgrimage, not only because of its link with America's great hero but because of its singular charm and beauty.

Washington acquired the property in 1754, following the death of his half-brother, and had the house enlarged and redecorated. After an eventful career in the Virginia militia, he settled down there in 1759 with his new wife Martha. Washington adored Mount Vernon and hoped to spend the rest of his life there as a hard-working farmer. But his plans were interrupted first by the War of Independence, in which he commanded the American forces, then by his 2 terms as president of the United States. Throughout the momentous events of his life he longed for the peace and solace of Mount Vernon. After his final retirement from politics, he enjoyed fewer than 3 years on his farm before his death in 1799.

It is clear why Washington loved Mount Vernon so much. The house (☎ 703/780-2000; open Apr–Aug daily 8am–5pm; Mar, Sept, and Oct daily 9am–4pm, Nov–Feb 9am–4pm; smoking, eating, and drinking are

Mount Vernon

forbidden throughout house and grounds) is a gracefully proportioned neo-Georgian style building with a facade that looks like stone but is in fact painted wood. Washington himself was the mastermind guiding the alterations to the house, whose many unusual features include twin open colonnades connecting with the dependencies on either side, and the spacious porch at the back known as the "piazza," 2 stories high and running the full length of the house. It is easy to picture George Washington on a summer evening, sitting with his friends and looking out across lawn and woodland to the broad sweep of the Potomac.

The restrained, unpretentious dignity of the architecture is in keeping with the character of Washington himself. The interior has been restored as closely as possible to the way it looked in his time. The grandest room in the house is the **Large Dining Room,** with its Hepplewhite and Sheraton furniture, delicate plaster moldings, and marble mantlepiece carved with agricultural motifs. Most evocative of Washington's spirit, however, is the **Study,** from which he administered his estate. Among the original items are his dressing table, chair, and secretary-desk.

The many outbuildings surrounding the house deserve a visit. The kitchen, smokehouse, coach-house, stable, and greenhouse have all been restored to their original state. A small museum contains portraits and memorabilia of George and Martha Washington. Their bodies lie in a brick tomb, ordered by Washington in his will, which stands in a secluded part of the grounds to the west of the house. About 50 yards to the southwest of this is an area where the slaves of Mount Vernon were buried. Washington came to oppose slavery and in his will provided for the freedom of his slaves.

The formal **Flower Garden** and **Kitchen Garden** are both delightful. A shop by the Flower Garden sells souvenirs and a variety of plants and seeds, many from the garden itself. Along the driveway leading to the house are elms, tulip poplars, and other trees planted by Washington himself—he was no armchair gardener. Just by the estate's main entrance are a gift store and the pleasant **Mount Vernon Inn** (☎ 703/780-0011).

A number of other places near Mount Vernon are well worth visiting.

Woodlawn Plantation (3 miles to the west via Rte. 235; ☎ 703/780-4000; open Mar–Dec daily 9:30am–4:30pm; Jan–Feb, Sat–Sun 9:30am–4:30pm; closed major holidays) was built in the early 1800s on land given by George Washington to his nephew, Lawrence Lewis, and foster daughter, Eleanor Parke Custis, when they married in 1799. The house, designed by the versatile Dr. William Thornton, first architect of the Capitol, breathes the atmosphere of gracious Southern living. Set in beautiful grounds, it is a center for courses in horticulture and landscape architecture.

In the grounds of Woodlawn is the crisply modern **Pope-Leighey House** (☎ 703/780-4000; Sun 9:30am–4:30pm and by appointment), built by Frank Lloyd Wright in 1940 and considered a pioneering design in small-scale domestic architecture. It was moved in its entirety from Falls Church, Virginia, when it stood in the way of highway construction.

Pohick Church (3 miles to the west via Rte. 1; ☎ 703/339-6572; open daily 9am–4pm) is a chaste, redbrick structure dating from 1774. Washington attended here regularly, sitting in pew no. 28. From Pohick Church continue for about 1 mile southwest on Route 1, then double back for 4 miles southeast down SR 242. This will bring you to **Gunston Hall** (☎ 703/550-9220; open daily 9:30am–5pm; closed New Year's Day, Thanksgiving, and Christmas), one of the most elegant colonial homes in Virginia, built by the Revolutionary statesman George Mason (1725–92). Inside, note particularly the **Chinese Chippendale** and **Palladian Rooms** with their fine wood carvings. The house is set on beautiful grounds, with a grand view across the Potomac.

Williamsburg

150 miles (241km) s of Washington. Population: 10,000. By car, Interstate highways 95, 295, and 64. By bus, Greyhound-Trailways (☎ 800/231-2222 or 804/229-1460).

Williamsburg offers the visitor a vivid illusion of stepping back into an 18thC American town. Capital of Virginia in colonial and Revolutionary times, it was superseded by Richmond, and for a century and a half remained in obscurity, until the 1920s when John D. Rockefeller provided money for its restoration and preservation. Run today by the nonprofit Colonial Williamsburg Foundation, it is both a working town and a living museum.

Before going into the center of Williamsburg, it is advisable to report to the **Information Center** (Colonial Williamsburg Foundation, P.O. Box C, Williamsburg, VA 23187; ☎ 804/229-1000 or 800/447-8679), on the outskirts to the north and, if you are driving, to leave your car. You can buy a ticket here for the historic area, which will also entitle you to use the buses that run throughout the day from the Information Center and around the historic area. A conducted walking tour can also be arranged. The Information Center has a modern cafeteria and restaurant and a large shop selling books, gifts, and souvenirs. Before leaving the center, try to see the 35-minute film *Williamsburg: The Story of a Patriot,* a semifictional re-creation of the town in the period leading up to independence.

The film is intended to prepare you for the bizarre moment when you step off the bus in the historic center of Williamsburg. In the tranquil, tree-lined streets with their replica 18thC houses, you will encounter men and women in colonial garb. In workshops, other people in period costume are busy working at traditional crafts. They include a printer, a papermaker, a cooper, a gunsmith, and a cabinet-maker, all dressed in stockings and breeches and all actually working here for a living, although they tend to spend as much time giving visitors impromptu lectures on their crafts as they do working at them. "This is how we do things in the 18thC," they explain patiently to their 20thC guests. Occasionally a horse-drawn carriage passes, driven by a coachman in livery and filled with 20thC time-travelers. A number of shops in Williamsburg sell items typical of 18thC Virginia, from hand-printed books to 3-cornered hats.

Williamsburg today is naturally only a partially accurate reflection of 18thC life; at that time the streets would have been unpaved and unlit and the sidewalks made of mud instead of neat brick. The town would have been noisy and smelly, in contrast to the beautifully maintained place it is today. So Williamsburg is certainly something of a charade, but one so brilliantly executed that the most skeptical visitor is almost bound to be charmed by it.

A ticket from the Information Center will admit you to most of the places of interest in the historic area. An exception is the **Governor's Palace** (Palace Green; open 9am–5pm), but a visit to this building is well worth the extra fee. The palace seen today is a skillful 1930s' replica of the original, which was destroyed by fire in 1781. Visitors pay an imaginary call on the governor's secretary and are taught to bow and curtsey in 18thC manner. The beautiful gardens have been meticulously reconstructed and make a delightful place to linger.

Another skillfully reconstructed building is the **Capitol** at the east end of Duke of Gloucester Street, where many of the principles of American democracy were worked out. At the opposite end of Duke of Gloucester Street stand the buildings of **William and Mary College,** the second oldest college in the United States, which still functions as a respected place of higher education.

Even food and drink have a colonial flavor in Williamsburg, as served in its taverns, such as **Chowning's** on Duke of Gloucester Street, on pewter plates by waiters in appropriate costumes.

The **Williamsburg Inn** (Francis St.; ☎ 804/229-1000) is one of several pleasant hotels and motels, offering modern comforts within a stone's throw of the 18thC charm of old Williamsburg. But accommodations fill up quickly, so reserve ahead.

If you're taking kids with you, stop at Universal's **Amusement Park** and associated **Water Park** across the street.

Maryland

Barely a 2- or 3-hour drive to the east of Washington via the Chesapeake Bay Bridge (avoid Fri and Sun eves in summer) is the eastern shore of the state of Maryland, which surrounds the capital on 3 sides. This is an area of quiet, rich countryside, wooded inlets, charming old-world towns, and an abundance of excellent seafood. The fine beaches of **Lewes, Rehoboth, Dewey,** and **Ocean City** (really a 10-mile honky-tonk boardwalk collection of hotels and condominiums) tend to be crowded on summer weekends, so reserve accommodations in advance.

More accessible from Washington are the parallel peninsulas of **Calvert** (south on Rte. 4) and **St. Mary's** (south on Rte. 5) counties. They jut into the Chesapeake to the southeast of Washington and are linked by a bridge at **Solomon's Island,** a waterman's village whose marinas are now full of yachts. While both counties are currently being developed, beautiful fields, woods, and coves remain, and in the deeply rural areas of St. Mary's county you might catch an occasional glimpse of the black-clad Amish in their horse-drawn buggies. At the southwest end of the peninsula, you can visit charming **St. Mary's College** (which has an art gallery in its modern, wooden Humanities Building), or the reconstructed colonial village of **St. Mary's City** on the St. Mary's River, and on summer weekends, attend an outdoor concert or play. Also, between June and October, visit magnificent **Sotterley Mansion** (☎ 301/373-2280), the oldest continuously working plantation in America, now a National Historic Trust, where the sheep graze on meadows rolling down to the Patuxent River.

An interesting 2-day excursion might begin by going down Routes 5 and 235 to Sotterley, continuing to St. Mary's City. Then loop back and over the bridge to **Solomon's Island** for a late lunch at one of several good restaurants overlooking the water. This can be followed by a visit to the fine **Marine Museum,** which brings maritime history alive with old wooden boats, a lighthouse to climb, and plenty of hands-on exhibits of maritime and environmental interest. Afterwards, charter a boat to tour the river or chase the bluefish, enjoy delicious seafood, and stay at the new Holiday or Comfort Inns at Solomon's Island. Otherwise, drive north on Routes 2 and 4 through Prince Frederick, and veer off on Route 2 to **Annapolis** and **Baltimore.**

Annapolis

33 miles (53km) e of Washington. Population: 31,700. By car, from Solomon's Island, Rte. 2; from Washington, Rte. 50. For bus schedule, call Greyhound-Trailways, ☎ 800/231-2222.

Annapolis, capital of Maryland, is one of those places where you can still catch a glimpse of the gracious, old-world face of America. On the Severn River close to where it meets Chesapeake Bay, the town's thriving economy is based on the sea and history. The sea brought Annapolis early prosperity as a trading port; today it retains a maritime image through its great Naval Academy and justified fame as a sailing and fishing center. Many Washingtonians keep their weekend yachts here in the numerous marinas of Spa and Back creeks. If you want to go out into the bay, sail- and motorboats of various sizes can be chartered; or take a 40-minute narrated tour on the steamer *The Harbor Queen.*

Few towns in the United States have so proud and well-presented a heritage. Originally settled in 1649 by Puritans from Virginia, Annapolis was first laid out as a planned unit in 1694 when Washington, D.C. was still a swamp. In the same year it became the capital of Maryland, and for a short period (Nov 1783–Aug 1784) it was actually the capital of the United States.

Today it is a charming town with quiet, brick-paved, tree-lined streets, much fine architecture, and an active community of contemporary artists. The best way to explore the small historic center is on foot; you may wish to follow one of the self-guided audiocassette walking tours provided by the **Historic Annapolis**

Walk with Walter Cronkite (77 Main St., Annapolis; ☎ 410/268-5576) or by **Three Centuries Tours** (48 Maryland Ave., Annapolis; ☎ 410/263-5401), with guides in 18thC costume. The most significant old buildings are marked with plaques, color-coded according to period: terra-cotta for pre-Revolutionary; blue for Federal (from the Revolution to about 1820); green for Greek Revival (1820–40); mauve for Victorian (after 1840). Annapolis brick is a beautiful soft red, and in the older buildings the mortar is made out of burned and crushed oyster shells.

Sights & Places of Interest

Banneker-Douglas Museum. 84 Franklin St. ☎ 410/974-2893. Open Tues–Fri 10am–2pm; Sat noon–4pm. Closed Sun.

A handsome Victorian-Gothic structure, formerly the Old Mount Moriah African Methodist Church, the museum offers exhibitions of Afro-American art and history.

Chase-Lloyd House. 22 Maryland Ave. ☎ 410/263-2723. Open Tues–Sat 2–4pm. Closed Sun; Mon.

In this fine 18thC building, across the road from the Hammond Harwood House and possessing a similar doorway, Mary Lloyd married Francis Scott Key, author of "The Star Spangled Banner." It is now a ladies' retirement home.

City Dock.

This is an attractive harbor, busy with pleasure craft and fishing boats and lined with historic buildings.

Middletown Tavern. ☎ 410/263-3323.

Established at no. 2 Market Place in 1750 and still going strong. Washington, Jefferson, and Franklin were among its patrons. You can dine or lunch here on such traditional fare as oysters or Maryland crab. Note also the 19thC Market House, which contains food stores.

Hammond Harwood House. Maryland Ave. and King George St. ☎ 410/269-1714. Open Mon–Sat 10am–4pm, Sun noon–4pm. Closed New Year's Day, Thanksgiving Day, and Christmas Day.

This graceful Georgian house, now a museum, was designed by William Buckland, architect of Gunston Hall in Virginia and many other fine houses. It has a particularly elegant doorway with egg-and-dart moldings, Ionic columns, and a fan window. The house is filled with 18thC furniture and objets d'art. The gift store is closed on Sunday and Monday.

Helen Avalyne Tawes Garden. Taylor Ave. at Rowe Blvd. ☎ 410/974-3717. Open Mon–Fri 7:30am–3pm. Picnics allowed (no fires). Gift store open Mon–Fri 11am–3pm.

This garden, featuring native plants, was designed to represent Maryland's coastal, mountain-foot, and mountain environments.

Maryland Federation of the Arts Gallery on the Circle. 18 State Circle. ☎ 410/268-4566. Open Tues–Sun 11am–5pm.

This nonprofit gallery offers changing exhibitions of local and regional fine arts and crafts.

Maryland Hall for the Creative Arts (Anne Arundel Community Center). 801 Chase St. ☎ 410/263-5544. Open Mon–Fri 8am–10pm; Sat 10am–5pm. Closed Sun except for special events.

You can see—and hear—artists at work in this old brick school, now home to the Annapolis Symphony Orchestra, the Ballet Theater, and the Annapolis Chorale. There are 3 exhibition spaces, an 855-seat auditorium, and various classrooms for the visual and performing arts. Some arts and crafts are offered for sale.

Maryland State Archives/Hall of Records. 350 Rowe Blvd. ☎ 410/974-3914. Open Mon–Sat 8:30am–4:30pm. Closed Sat noon–1pm; Sun.

Documents, maps, photographs, genealogical information, and official Maryland records, as well as changing exhibitions of regional interest, serve as a reminder that Annapolis is the capital of Maryland.

Maryland State House. State Circle. ☎ 410/269-3400. Open 9am–5pm. Closed New Year's Day, Thanksgiving, and Christmas.

This beautiful building is the oldest state capitol remaining in continuous use in the country. Its dome, which dominates the town center, was built entirely without nails, using only wooden pegs. The building contains many portraits of men prominent in the history of Maryland, from the first Lord Baltimore onward. You can view the present House of Delegates and Senate chambers and also the Old Senate chamber, now a museum and preserved exactly as it was in 1783 when George Washington stood here to resign his commission as commander-in-chief of the Continental Army. A painting in the room portrays the event.

Old Treasury Building. Grounds of Maryland State House.

This small brick building is believed to be the oldest public building in Maryland. It was here that the country's first paper money, in the form of Bills of Credit, was kept. Restored in 1950, it now houses the tour offices of Historic Annapolis, Inc. Exhibits relevant to the town's history are on display.

Quiet Waters Park. Hillsmere Drive at Forest Drive. ☎ 410/222-1777. Open daily 7am–dusk; winter 7am–8pm for skating.

Hiking and bicycling trails, playgrounds, boat dock, picnic pavilions, and ice-skating in winter can give the tourist a pleasant break from museuming.

St. John's College. 60 College Ave. ☎ 410/263-2371.

One of the first private schools in the United States, St. John's opened in 1696 as King William's School, with many historic buildings on campus. In the grounds is the so-called **Liberty Tree,** under which many ceremonies have been held. In the mid-19thC some rowdy youths tried to blow the tree up with gunpowder. In doing so they unwittingly saved the tree by killing all the vermin in it. The **Mitchell Art Gallery** on campus shows traditional and contemporary work from national, international, and museum collections (☎ 410/626-2556; open Sept–May, Tues–Sun noon–5pm, Fri 7–8pm; closed Mon; see local papers for summer schedule).

Shiplap House. 18 Pinkney St. ☎ 410/626-1033. Open daily 10am–4pm.

This 1715 tavern has exhibitions on taverns and archaeology, an herb garden, and a gift store.

United States Naval Academy. Ricketts Hall. ☎ 410/263-6933. Open Mar–Nov daily 9am–5pm, Dec–Feb daily 9am–4pm.

Founded in 1845, the U.S. Naval Academy was designated a National Historic Site in 1963. It has beautiful grounds and some fine buildings, notably **Bancroft Hall,** a dormitory for 4,400 midshipmen, and the **Chapel** with its crypt containing the remains of the naval hero John Paul Jones. Model ships, paintings, nautical relics, and other items of naval history are on display in the museum, in **Preble Hall.** The guided tours start from the **Visitor Information Center** in Ricketts Hall (☎ 410/263-6933; open 9am–4pm; closed some major holidays), reached via Gate 1 at the foot of King George Street.

William Paca House. 186 Prince George St. ☎ 410/263-5553. Tour includes garden; open Mar–Dec, Mon–Sat 10am–4pm, Sun and holidays noon–4pm; Jan–Feb, Fri–Sat only, 10am–4pm.

Built in 1765 by William Paca, who signed the Declaration of Independence and was 3 times governor of Maryland, this mansion is now beautifully restored. The delightful garden (open year-round Mon–Sat 10am–4pm, May–Oct Sun noon–5pm), entered from 1 Martin St., also deserves a visit.

Annapolis has hotels to suit most tastes, from the large and modern **Holiday Inn** (Route U.S. 50 going west; ☎ 410/224-3150) to **Gibson's Lodgings** (110 Prince George St.; ☎ 410/268-5555), a charming old-world guest house. The town also boasts numerous good restaurants, especially around the harbor area, where the specialties are seafood and other traditional Maryland fare. For something a little more

European, try **Cafe Normande** (195 Main St.; ☎ 410/263-3382), which is excellent for a coffee and croissant or a full meal. Ten minutes from State Circle and worth the drive is **Northwoods** (609 Melvin Ave.; ☎ 410/268-2609), with fine continental cuisine. Reservations suggested.

Baltimore

35 miles (56km) ne of Washington. By car, from Annapolis, follow signs for Rtes. 2 and 3; from Washington, Interstate 95. By train, frequent departures from Union Station. By bus, consult Greyhound-Trailways.

Baltimore. Setting of *Avalon* and *Diner*. Sigh. But also the setting of *Polyester* and *Homicide: A Life on the Street*. Eeew.

A visit here is a must. More fun than Washington, Baltimore is a real city, with ethnic and neighborhood flavor, a living waterfront, industry, eccentricity, and vitality.

Edgar Allan Poe, H. L. Mencken, Babe Ruth, Bromo-Seltzer, General Motors, and Bethlehem Steel are all names associated with Baltimore, Maryland, second largest port on the East Coast and a proud city whose history dates back to 1729. Although a working city, it possesses a strong sense of culture and a fine architectural heritage. Baltimore has had its ups and downs, but at present is very much enjoying an "up" phase, thanks in large measure to William Donald Schaefer, who became mayor in 1970 and implemented a program of development that has turned Baltimore into one of America's liveliest and best-run cities. Schaefer is now governor, and Kurtis Schmoke, Baltimore's first black mayor, is further improving the city.

Epitomizing this transformation is the **Inner Harbor,** until the early 1970s a sad area of rotting buildings, ramshackle piers, and rubbish tips, but now the site of one of the most stylish and imaginative urban developments in the world, an object lesson in combining modernity with grace, beauty, and the human touch. One of its features is a smart shopping and restaurant complex called **Harbor Place,** comprising 2 separate pavilions. Sitting here on a fine day under the awning of an open-air cafe, sipping a cool drink while sailboats whip across the sparkling water, you will feel that Baltimore can match anything that Europe's most elite watering-holes can offer. (See Elisabeth Stevens's *Guide to Baltimore's Inner Harbor*.)

The Inner Harbor is dominated by the tall, pentagonal **World Trade Center** (401 E. Pratt St.; ☎ 410/837-4515), designed by I. M. Pei. Travel up to the

27th-floor **Top of the World** (open Mon–Sat 10am–5pm, Sun 11am–5pm), for a superb panorama over the city. There is also a boutique and exhibits on Baltimore's history. There is another dramatic view from the 178-foot **Washington Monument** (Mount Vernon Place; 410/396-0929; open Wed–Sun 10am–4pm).

The **National Aquarium in Baltimore** (Inner Harbor; ☎ 410/576-3800; open Jul–Aug, Sun–Thurs 9am–6pm, Fri–Sat 9am–8pm; Mar–Jun and Sept–Oct, Sat–Thurs 9am–5pm, Fri 9am–8pm; Nov–Feb Sat–Thurs 10am–5pm, Fri 10am–8pm) must be one of the most imaginative aquariums in the world. Youngsters will love the Children's Cove, where they can pick up fearsome-looking but harmless horseshoe crabs. At the top of the building, you walk through a re-creation of a tropical Amazon rain forest, with no glass between you and the iguanas and brightly colored birds. A Marine Mammal Pavilion opened in 1990, with dolphin performances, cafeteria, and gift store.

Another remarkable new museum on the Inner Harbor is the **Maryland Science Center and Planetarium** (☎ 410/685-5225; open Mon–Fri 10am–5pm, Sat–Sun 10am–6pm; extended hours in summer). In this huge scientific adventure playground, you can watch a show in the planetarium, work on a computer, experiment with illusion-creating devices that tease your perception of reality, and learn about the ecology of the Chesapeake Bay.

Three ships in the harbor can be visited. Moored on the north side is the graceful sailing ship, the *U.S. Frigate Constellation,* launched in 1797 and the oldest American warship afloat (open mid-May–mid-Oct 10am–6pm; rest of year Mon–Sat 10am–4pm, Sun 10am–5pm). Not far away, in the **Baltimore Maritime Museum** (☎ 410/396-3453; Mon–Fri 10am–5pm, Sat–Sun 10am–7pm), 2 more ships are open to the public, the U.S. submarine *Torsk* and *Lightship Chesapeake.*

As a change from sightseeing you can rent a paddleboat, or on certain days watch an open-air show at the northwest corner of the harbor. You can also shop in the stylish new **Pratt Street Pavilion,** offering a wide variety of merchandise and a cafe or two. A complementary building, the **Light Street Pavilion,** is devoted to a mouth-watering variety of food stores and restaurants. You can eat anything here from a sandwich to a high-class meal. Try the friendly, dependable **American Cafe** or **City Lights Restaurant.** Both have good food and open-air terraces commanding fine views of the harbor.

After lunch you could take a boat out to **Fort McHenry** on the end of a peninsula in the bay (boats leave every 30 mins, 10:30am–5pm, depending on weather and season). This fort successfully warded off a British attack during the War of 1812 and inspired Francis Scott Key to write "The Star Spangled Banner," now the U.S. national anthem. The fort is also accessible by land.

From the harbor a pedestrian walkway passes a fountain; it is possible to walk behind the falling water and on to the award-winning **Convention Center** and the new Hyatt Regency Hotel. The city center to the north has been revitalized with new plazas, walkways, and shopping areas. But the city also has some fine townscapes of an earlier period, notably the magnificent **Mount Vernon Place,** with its parks, statues, and fountains, dominated by the Washington Monument and surrounded by such fine buildings as the **Peabody Institute of Music.** Unlike Washington, Baltimore has many skyscrapers, some charmingly whimsical, such as the **Bromo-Seltzer Tower,** based on the Palazzo Vecchio in Florence.

Nicknamed the "All-American City," Baltimoreans are all-American. Baltimoreans are as devoted to their baseball Orioles as Washingtonians are to their football Redskins, and they've shown their love by building a gorgeous, state-of-the-art stadium called **Oriole Park at Camden Yards** (west of Inner Harbor at Eutaw and Camden streets; ☎ 410/685-9800; tours hourly Mon–Fri 11am–2pm, Sat 10am–2pm, Sun 12:30pm and 2pm). Gorgeous new vintage-style but state-of-the-art baseball stadium

If you're looking for Eccentric Baltimore, **Johns Hopkins University,** is responsible for more sex changes than anywhere else in the world. "Charm City" has also been called "the hairdo capital of the world," and is home of John Waters, the king of bad taste, director of cult flicks *Pink Flamingos, Polyester,* and *Serial Mom.* The neighborhood to find students, artists, bohemians, and just outright nutty people is Fells Point (Broadway at Eastern Ave.). Pick up a copy of the free alternative weekly, the *Baltimore City Paper,* to find out what's happening in town. Strangely, Baltimore is a crucial nexus on the North American rave scene.

Sights of historical interest include the 215-foot-high **Shot Tower** (801 E. Fayette St.; open 10am–4pm);

the **Star Spangled Banner Flag House** (844 E. Pratt St.; ☎ 410/837-1793; open Apr–Oct, Tues–Sun 10am–4pm; Nov–Mar, Mon–Sat 10am–3:15pm), where the famous flag was sewn by Mary Pickersgill; **Babe Ruth House** (216 Emory St.; ☎ 410/727-1539; Apr–Oct, daily 10am–5pm, until 7pm on Orioles home-game days; Nov–Mar daily 10am–4pm), birthplace of the great baseball player; and the recently renovated **Edgar Allan Poe House** (203 Amity St.; ☎ 410/396-7932; open Wed–Sat noon–3:45pm).

Baltimore has 2 very fine art galleries. The **Baltimore Museum of Art** (Art Museum Dr. and 32nd St.; ☎ 410/396-7100; open Wed–Fri 10am–4pm, weekends 11am–6pm; closed Mon), includes a particularly good impressionist collection. **Walters Art Gallery** (Charles and Centre streets; ☎ 410/547-9000; open Tues–Sun 11am–5pm) exhibits works from ancient Egyptian times to the early 20thC. A nice feature of the Walters is that relevant books are placed in certain galleries so that you can read up on the background of the objects on display. The Hackerman House, formerly the Thomas-Jencks-Gladding House, on Mount Vernon Place has recently opened to house the Walters's Asian art collection.

The **Maryland Historical Society** (201 W. Monument St.; ☎ 410/685-3750; open Tues–Fri 10am–4pm, Sat 9am–4:30pm, Sun 1–5pm; closed Sun in summer) contains the original manuscript of "The Star Spangled Banner," as well as paintings, prints, decorative arts, and genealogical and marine collections.

For children, Baltimore has many attractions in addition to the aquarium and all the ships in the harbor. The **Baltimore Zoo** (Druid Hill Park; ☎ 410/396-7102; open 10am–4:15pm; closed Christmas), houses more than 1,000 species of animals and includes a children's zoo with farm animals and playground equipment. Youngsters also love the **B&O Railroad Museum** (Pratt and Poppleton St.; ☎ 410/752-2490; open Tues–Sun 10am–4pm; closed Mon), with its superb collection of old locomotives and rolling stock.

An attractive aspect of Baltimore is the high number of ethnic traditions—black, Hispanic, Polish, German, Greek, Irish, and many more—vibrantly represented in the city. The ongoing round of festivals and celebrations organized by several of these communities helps create the colorful and very human city that is Baltimore today. Call 410/837-INFO for details of events and to order a free information pack.

THE BASICS

Before You Go
Tourist Offices

For information on the District of Columbia, call or contact the following organizations:

Washington, D.C. Convention and Visitors Association, ☎ 202/789-7000 (sightseeing, hotel, restaurant, convention information; visitor's guide/map and calendar of events). This is the best office to contact for sightseeing information.

American Express Travel Service, 1150 Connecticut Ave. NW); ☎ 202/457-1300.

D.C. Committee to Promote Washington, ☎ 202/724-4091. Tourist brochures galore.

U.S. Government Printing Office (write Superintendent of Documents, U.S. Government Printing Office, Washington, DC 20402); ☎ 202/512-1800. Pamphlets and publications.

United States Travel and Tourism Administration (write c/o Department of Commerce, Room 1860, 14th and Constitution Ave. NW, Washington, DC 20230); ☎ 202/482-4003. Tourist literature.

Washington, D.C. Accommodations, ☎ 202/289-2220 and 800/544-2220. Advises on and arranges hotel reservations.

White House Visitor Information Center, ☎ 202/208-1631. White House tour info, maps to National Parks Services attractions and D.C. sights.

Travelers Aid Society, Central Office, 512 C St. NE, Union Station, ☎ 202/546-3120; National Airport, ☎ 703/684-3472; Dulles Airport, ☎ 703/661-8636). Provides emergency help and advice to visitors in need, or lacking accommodations.

Emergency Services

Police/fire/ambulance, ☎ 911

Medical referral service, ☎ 301/963-3100

Dental referral service, ☎ 202/547-7613

Hospitals with Emergency Departments

Ambulances called at 911 will carry the patient to the nearest municipal hospital. In Upper Northwest, you can also call the Chevy Chase Rescue Squad (301/652-1000). If you wish to go directly to a hospital, a list of the most important follows:

Upper Northwest or Northeast: Washington Hospital Center, 110 Irving St., between North Capitol Street and 9th Street NW (Trauma Unit), ☎ 202/877-6701; Children's Hospital, National Medical Center, 111 Michigan Ave. NW, ☎ 202/885-5000.

Northwest (Downtown): George Washington University Medical Center, 901 23rd St. NW, ☎ 202/994-1000.

Upper Northwest: Sibley Memorial Hospital, 5255 Loughboro Rd. NW, ☎ 202/537-4000.

Georgetown: Georgetown University Hospital, 3800 Reservoir Rd. NW, ☎ 202/687-2000.

For minor emergencies, treatment is available at clinics, listed in the Yellow Pages under Clinics.

Help Lines: 24-Hour Hot Lines

Suicide Prevention and Emergency Mental Health, ☎ 202/362-8100

Travelers Aid Society, ☎ 202/546-3120

Poison Control Center, 24-hour hot line, ☎ 202/625-3333

Automobile Accidents

Call the police immediately. If the car is rented, call the number in the rental agreement. Do not admit liability or incriminate yourself. Ask witnesses to stay and give statements. Exchange names, addresses, car details, insurance companies, and 3-digit insurance company codes. Remain at the scene of the accident to give your statement to the police.

Car Breakdowns

Call one of the following from nearest telephone:

Number indicated in car rental agreement

Local office of AAA (☎ 703/222-5000, if you are a member)

Nearest garage or towing service

Lost Passports
First, report the loss or theft to the police. Then, get in touch with your embassy, where you will be issued emergency travel documents.

Lost Travelers Checks
It is essential that you notify the police immediately. Then, follow the instructions provided with your travelers checks, or contact the nearest office of the issuing company. If you find yourself stranded with no money, you should contact either your consulate or American Express Travel Service.

Lost Property
Rail, ☎ 202/484-7540 (AMTRAK at Union Station)

Metro Subway, ☎ 202/962-1195

In the street, ☎ 202/727-4326 (Police Communications)

Money
ATMS
Banking hours vary widely, but are normally 9am to 3pm, Monday to Friday. A few banks are open on Saturday mornings. All close for legal holidays. Travelers checks can be cashed at all banks.

Automated Teller Machines (ATMs) are plentiful in the D.C. area. Before you arrive, it's a good idea to check if your home bank is compatible with any of the more popular D.C. ATM networks, including **Cirrus** (☎ 800/424-7787) and **Plus** (☎ 800/843-7587). Cash advances on credit cards can also be obtained at ATMs; be sure to obtain a PIN (Personal Identification Number) from your issuing bank or credit card company.

Getting Money from Home
American Express has a MoneyGram money transfer service that makes it possible to wire money worldwide in just minutes from any American Express Travel Service Office (☎ 800/543-4080). This service is available to all customers and is not limited to American Express Card members.

The traditional (and expensive) way of getting emergency funds from home is having it wired via Western Union (☎ 800/325-6000), which has many locations in the D.C. area. You or another party can phone in a credit card number, or your friend on the other end can take the cash to a Western Union office; the fee depends on how much is being sent: $29 for $250, $40 for $500, and so on. Money may be available within 15 minutes; you'll need ID to get your cash, of course.

Credit Cards

Credit cards are accepted nearly everywhere—particularly American Express, Diners Club, MasterCard, and Visa. While personal checks drawn on out-of-town banks are seldom accepted, many hotels will cash small amounts in conjunction with a credit card.

For Foreign Visitors
Tourist Information

Write to: **U.S. Travel and Tourism Administration,** c/o Department of Commerce, Room 1860, 14th Street and Constitution Avenue NW, Washington, DC 20230, or call 202/482-4003.

Visitors may also contact the **International Visitor Information Center,** (Reception Center, 733 15th St. NW, Suite 300), ☎ 202/783-6540 (comprehensive service for tourists, especially from abroad); and the **Meridian International Center,** 1630 Crescent Place NW, Washington, DC 20009, ☎ 202/ 667-6800 (tourist brochures in several languages).

Visitors from the United Kingdom can obtain much useful information from the **U.S. Travel and Tourism Administration,** P.O. Box 1EN, London W1A 1EN, ☎ 071/495-4466.

Documents

British citizens (except those from Northern Ireland), and citizens of New Zealand, Japan, and all Western European countries except Greece, no longer need a visa to visit the United States, provided that their stay will last for 90 days or less and is for vacation or business purposes.

If arriving by air or sea, the visitor must be traveling with an approved carrier (most are) and must have an onward or return ticket. (Open or standby tickets are acceptable.) If entering overland from Canada or Mexico, no visa is required. A valid passport is also essential.

British subjects will need to obtain a visa, as will any British citizen who wishes to stay more than 90 days for whatever reason, has a criminal record, has suffered from tuberculosis, is suffering from AIDS, is HIV-positive, or has previously been refused a visa. The U.S. embassy in London has a useful recorded message for all general visa inquiries (☎ 0891-200290).

Travel & Medical Insurance

Medical insurance is strongly recommended. U.K. travel agents have the necessary forms, and tour operators frequently include medical coverage in their packages. Baggage insurance is recommended in case of theft.

Money

The basic monetary unit is the dollar ($). It is divided into 100 cents (¢). Coins are: The penny, 1¢; nickel, 5¢; dime, 10¢; quarter, 25¢; and half dollar, 50¢. Bank notes (bills) in general circulation are in denominations of $1, $5, $10, $20, $50, and $100. A few $2 bills are in circulation. Any amount of money may be imported or exported, but when the total exceeds $10,000 you must register with the U.S. Customs Service.

Travelers Checks

Many travelers prefer to carry cash in small amounts and to use ATMs or travelers checks. Those issued by American Express, Bank of America, Barclays, Citibank, and Thomas Cook are widely recognized, and MasterCard and Visa have also introduced them. Make sure to note separately the serial numbers and the telephone number to call in case of loss. American Express provides extensive local refund facilities through their own offices or agents. Many shops accept dollar travelers checks denominated in U.S. dollars.

Most banks will cash foreign currency. There are exchange offices at all 3 airports and in some hotels, but rates are more favorable at banks. The main American Express office (1150 Connecticut Ave. NW; ☎ 202/457-1300) will change foreign currency.

Customs & Duties

Returning U.S. citizens present themselves and their luggage to a single officer for inspection. All others must first clear passport control, collect their baggage, and then move on to a customs official. Although the process has been streamlined, the combination of 3 jumbo jets disgorging at once and government concern over smuggling can slow things down to a crawl. It may take no more than 30 minutes from plane to street, but an hour or more is not unusual.

Nonresidents can bring in any items clearly intended for personal use, duty-free, with the exceptions noted below.

Tobacco goods: 200 cigarettes or 50 cigars or 4 pounds (1.8kg) of tobacco. An additional 100 cigars may be brought in under your gift exemption (see below).

Alcoholic drinks: Adults over 18 are allowed up to 1 quart (1 liter) of spirits.

Other goods: Nonresidents may also import up to $100 in gifts without tax or duty if remaining in the United States at least 72 hours. Returning residents are granted a duty-free allowance of $400 on goods brought back personally. Families traveling together can pool their allowances to cover joint purchases.

For more information on customs regulations, a brochure entitled *U.S. Customs Hints* can be obtained from U.S. embassies and consulates, or directly from the Department of the Treasury, U.S. Customs Service, Box 7407, Washington, D.C. 20044.

Mail

U.S. Postal Service branches are usually open Monday through Friday, 9am to 5pm, and on Saturday in some locations (call 202/682-9595 to locate the nearest branch). All branches close on legal holidays.

Postcards mailed to locations in the United States cost 20¢ and letters are 32¢ for the first ounce; 23¢ per each additional ounce. Up to 2 pounds of material can be sent Priority Mail (which takes 2–3 days to reach domestic locations) for $3. Sending a postcard overseas costs 40¢; letters are 50¢ for a half-ounce, 95¢ for an ounce, and 30¢ for each additional half ounce.

The United States is divided into postal zones identified with a 5- or 9-digit ZIP code; including this code with addresses is essential for prompt delivery. For information on postal services and rates, call the 24-hour Postal Answer Line at ☎ 202/526-3920.

If you want to get mail while traveling, you can have it sent to you care of General Delivery the Central Post Office (900 Brentwood Rd. NE, Washington, DC 20066), where it should be held until collected. The office is between 9th Street and New York Avenue NE, not the most easily reached or hospitable of locations. Make sure the envelope says "Please hold until arrival." Be sure to bring your ID to pick up mail.

American Express offices will also provide "Client Letter Service" for cardholders. Contact them in advance for details (☎ 800/528-4800).

When & Where to Go

Each season in Washington has its own individual appeal, but also its drawbacks.

Yes, spring bursts in a pink blizzard of cherry blossoms around the Tidal Basin and the Mall—but the blossoms bring swarms of tourists. Summer is slightly less crowded, thanks to the heat and humidity (mitigated slightly by arctic blasts of air-conditioning in every building). This is the season of special events: festivals, sporting contests, open-air concerts, and the 4th of July Independence Day celebrations.

During the fall, the crowds diminish still further, the weather is pleasantly cool, and the pace of the city's cultural life intensifies. I can't think of anything bad to say about fall, try as I may.

In winter the opportunities to enjoy theater, music, opera, and ballet are at their best. This is the quietest season for visitors, with correspondingly low hotel prices. However, the weather is unpredictable; the normal, relatively mild conditions are punctuated by occasional snowstorms (which throw this southern city into an almost laughable state of panic) and a few days of bitter cold.

Weather

For a local weather report, call 202/936-1212. You can obtain a weather report or fore-cast for anywhere in the world by calling 1-900-WEATHER, for a charge of 95¢ per minute.

Calendar of Events

See also the *Washington Post*'s Thursday "District Weekly Calendar," Friday "Weekend" guide and Sunday "Arts" sections. For information on events run by the Smithsonian Institution, or call 202/357-2020 or 3030.

January
1st Monday: *Opening of Congress.*

Early January: *Washington Antique Show* at Omni Shoreham hotel (☎ 202/234-0700).

3rd Monday: Celebration of *Martin Luther King, Jr.'s birthday* (☎ 202/789-7000).

Late January: Tours in Alexandria to celebrate *Robert E. Lee's birthday* (☎ 804/786-1919).

Late January: *Washington International Boat Show* at D.C. National Guard Armory (events info: ☎ 202/547-9077).

January or February every odd year: *Biennial exhibition of contemporary American art* at Corcoran Gallery.

February
Late January or early–mid-February: *Chinese New Year* celebrations in Chinatown (☎ 202/789-7000).

February 12: Celebration of *Abraham Lincoln's birthday* at Lincoln Memorial (☎ 202/426-6895).

Mid-February: *Ice Capades* family ice-skating show at USAir Arena (☎ 301/350-3400).

Mid–late February: *George Washington Birthday Events* with festivities at Washington Monument (☎ 202/426-6841), birth-night ball at Gadsby's Tavern and a parade in Alexandria (☎ 703/838-4200).

March
March 17: *St. Patrick's Day Parade,* downtown via Constitution Ave. (☎ 301/879-1717).

Late March: *Smithsonian Kite Festival* on the Mall (☎ 202/357-2700).

Late March: *U.S. Botanic Gardens Spring Flower Show* (☎ 202/225-8333).

Late March or early April: *Cherry Blossom Festival* (☎ 202/547-1500).

Late March or early April: *Easter Egg Roll* on the White House Lawn (☎ 202/208-1631).

Late March or early April: *Easter sunrise services* in Arlington National Cemetery and other locations (☎ 202/685-2892).

April
Early April: *Imagination Celebration* at Kennedy Center. Festival of youth-oriented performing arts events, many free (☎ 202/467-4600).

Early April: *Ringling Brothers/Barnum & Bailey Circus* at D.C. National Guard Armory (☎ 202/547-9077).

April 13: *Thomas Jefferson's birthday* celebrated at Jefferson Memorial (☎ 202/456-2200).

Mid-April: *American College Theater Festival* at the Kennedy Center (☎ 202/467-4600).

Mid-April: *White House Gardens.* For 2 days only, the gardens are open to the public for free tours between 2 and 5pm (☎ 202/456-2200).

April 20: *Duke Ellington Birthday Celebration,* with concerts and workshops to celebrate the music of the D.C. native (☎ 202/331-9404).

Late April: *Smithsonian Institution's Spring Celebration,* with clowns, mimes, and other attractions for children (☎ 202/357-2700).

Late April: *Historic Garden Week Tour,* Alexandria Tourist Council (☎ 804/644-7776).

Last Saturday in April: *Hunt Cup,* organized by the National Steeplechase Association, Elkton, Md. (☎ 410/392-0700).

Late April or early May: Public tours of embassies and Georgetown houses (☎ 202/338-1796) and gardens (☎ 202/333-6869).

Late April or early May: *Annapolis Spring Boat Show,* Annapolis Harbor (☎ 410/380-0445).

May

1st weekend in May: *Washington Cathedral Flower Mart and Fair* (☎ 202/537-6200).

1st weekend in May: *Asian Pacific American Heritage Festival* (☎ 703/354-50360).

Mid-May: Start of *U.S. Marine Corps Sunset Parades,* at 8th and I St. SW. (☎ 202/433-4011).

Mid-May: *Cherry Blossom Rugby Tournament,* the Mall (☎ 202 789-7038).

Mid-May: *Preakness Celebration,* Pimlico Racecourse, Baltimore, Md. (☎ 301/642-9400).

Last Monday in May: *Memorial Day* events include free National Symphony concert in Capitol grounds (☎ 202/619-7222); Memorial Day Jazz Festival in Old Town Alexandria (☎ 703/838-4200); wreath laid by president at Tomb of the Unknown Soldier (☎ 202/685-2851).

June

1st weekend in June: *Washington International Arts Fair* with exhibitions of contemporary work mounted in private galleries throughout the city.

Early June: *Dupont-Kalorama Museum Walk Day,* museums and galleries show off for free in this pretty neighborhood (☎ 202/667-0441).

Early June: *Gay and Lesbian Pride Festival,* with downtown parade and outdoor fair at Freedom Plaza (☎ 202/797-7000).

Mid-June: *Smithsonian Institution Children's Day* (☎ 202/357-2700).

Mid-June: *Smithsonian Boomerang Festival,* Washington Monument grounds (☎ 202/357-2700).

Late June and early July: *Smithsonian Festival of American Folklife,* on the Mall. A rich cross-section of America's cultural heritage on display, with different ethnicities and cultures highlighted each year, and all sorts of music, dancing, crafts, and food (☎ 202/357-2700).

July

July 4: *Independence Day* events include 4th of July parade, fireworks, and festivities on the Mall (☎ 202/789-7000); neighborhood parades in Palisades and Takoma Park; free National Symphony concert at the Capitol grounds (☎ 202/416-8100).

Early July: *Chesapeake Bay Yacht Racing Week,* Annapolis, Md.

Mid-July: *Legg Mason Tennis Classis,* Rock Creek Tennis Stadium, 16th and Kennedy St. NW (☎ 703/276-3030).

Late July: *Virginia Scottish Games,* one of America's largest Scottish festivals (☎ 703/838-4200).

Late July: *Hispanic Festival* on Washington Monument grounds (☎ 202/789-7000).

August

August: *U.S. Army Band* performs the 1812 Overture at Washington Monument (☎ 703/696-3399).

Mid-August–early September: Shakespeare Theatre presents *Free for All,* free Shakespeare production at Carter-Barron Amphitheatre in Rock Creek Park (☎ 202/628-5770).

Early August: *Redskins football* exhibition season begins (☎ 202/547-9077).

September

1st Monday in September: *Labor Day* events include free National Symphony concert in Capitol grounds (☎ 202/789-7038).

1st Monday in September: *International Children's Festival* in Wolf Trap Farm Park. Performances and workshops of all kinds (☎ 202/642-0862).

Early September: *Black Family Reunion,* a celebration of the black family, on the Mall (☎ 202/463-6680).

Early September: *Kennedy Center Open House,* weekend-long arts festival (☎ 800/444-1324).

Early September: *Maryland Seafood Festival,* 3-day event held at Sandy Point State Park (☎ 410/333-6611).

Early September: *National Frisbee Festival* on the Washington Monument grounds (☎ 301/645-5043).

Early September: *D.C. Blues Festival,* 3-day celebration of the blues at Carter-Barron Amphitheatre in Rock Creek Park (☎ 202/828-3028).

Mid-September: *Adams-Morgan Day,* biggest citywide festival, a pan-cultural celebration of arts, crafts, music, and food (☎ 202/332-3292).

Mid-September: *Constitution Day,* with band concert at National Archives (☎ 202/789-7038).

Late September: *Washington National Cathedral Open House,* including extensive tours of the cathedral, organ recitals, and activities for children, such as antique merry-go-round rides (☎ 202/537-6200).

October

1st Monday in October: *Opening of Supreme Court* (☎ 202/479-3000).

Early October: *U.S. Navy Band Birthday Concert,* DAR Constitution Hall (☎ 202/433-2525).

Mid-October: *White House Fall Gardens Tours* (☎ 202/456-2200).

Late October: *Washington International Horse Show,* Capital Centre (☎ 301/840-0281).

Late October: *Marine Corps Marathon* in which thousands of entrants race a 26.2-mile course, beginning at Iwo Jima statue (☎ 703/690-3431).

October 31: *Halloween Street Parade,* Georgetown; high-heel "drag" race, 17th and P St. NW.

November

Mayflower Hotel. Fashionable charity sale annually opens the Capital's holiday season (☎ 202/347-3000).

November 11: *Veterans Day ceremony,* Arlington National Cemetery (☎ 202/619-7222).

Late November–December: Numerous Christmas craft fairs at locations around the city.

December

Early–mid-December: *Nutcracker Suite* ballet at Kennedy Center (☎ 202/467-4600).

Mid-December: *Lighting of the national Christmas tree* by the president at the Ellipse (☎ 202/619-7222).

Mid-December–January 1: *Pageant of Peace* includes nightly festivities and choral performances on the Ellipse and the Mall (☎ 202/619-7222).

Late December: *Christmas candlelight tours* of the White House (☎ 202/456-2200).

Throughout December: *Candlelight tours and caroling* at many historic houses in the area.

Regular Summer Events

Saturdays and Sundays: Artists at work; mimes, musicians, and dancers perform along the Mall, near the National Gallery of Art.

Every other Sunday afternoon: Folk and pop music concerts on C&O Canal at 30th and Jefferson St. NW.

Mid-May–mid-August: Concerts and parades by Army (☎ 703/696-3399), Navy (☎ 202/433-2525), Air Force (☎ 202/767-5658), and Marine (☎ 202/433-4011) bands.

What to Pack

However warm it is in Washington, always carry something extra to put on indoors, as the almost universal air-conditioning can make buildings seem positively arctic. In winter the central heating can be equally extreme, so be prepared to peel off. Washington is both a formal and an informal city, but sightseers tend to dress casually. Few restaurants require ties during the day, but it is advisable for men to wear both tie and jacket for dinner at smarter places.

Ideas for Further Reading

Specialized guides include: *A Museum Guide to Washington, D.C.* by Betty Ross; *Literary Washington* by David Cutler; *Washington Adventures for Kids,* by Marti Weston and Flori DeCell; *Greater Washington Area Bicycle Atlas* by the Washington Area Bicyclist Association; and *Short Bike Rides In and Around Washington* by Michael Leccese.

General Tours

Sightseeing companies are numerous. One of them, **Tourmobile Sightseeing** (1000 Ohio Dr. SW; ☎ 202/554-7950) operates the Tourmobile, a popular shuttle bus service with running commentary that connects the major sights of Capitol Hill, the Mall, and Arlington National Cemetery. It operates continuously from mid-June to Labor Day (1st Mon in Sept) 9am to 6:30pm and the rest of the year 9:30am to 4:30pm.

After purchasing a daily ticket from the driver or at one of the Tourmobile booths, you can break your journey as often as you like without paying additional fares. Fares vary according to distance, and there are discounts for students, senior citizens, and children under 12. Fares for excursions to Mount Vernon, the Frederick

Douglass House, and Arlington National Cemetery are slightly higher.

A similar service is provided by **Old Town Trolley Tours** (Union Station; ☎ 202/682-0079), which can be joined at any of a dozen major hotels and sites. This company runs open-air, green-and-orange motorized replicas of electric streetcars, stopping at or near all major museums and monuments. Leave or reboard at will throughout the day at a single fare. Students and senior citizens receive discounts, and children under 12 ride free with adults. The trolleys follow a regular route at 30-minute intervals. They operate from Memorial Day (last Mon in May) to Labor Day 9am to 5pm, the rest of the year 9am to 4pm.

Other tour operators include:

All About Town Sightseeing, 519 6th St. NW; ☎ 202/393-3696

City Sights Tours, 2025 I St. NW; ☎ 202/785-4700

Gray Line, Union Station, Bus Level; ☎ 202/289-1995

For Travelers with Disabilities

Provisions for disabled travelers are better in Washington than in many other U.S. cities, since the federal government controls so many of the museums, monuments, and sightseeing attractions. Much of the terrain is flat, and curbs are well ramped, especially around such major sightseeing areas as the Capitol building and the Mall. Many of the higher-priced hotels have specially converted rooms, as do a number of suburban motels.

The Metro has superb facilities for those with impairments of sight, hearing, or mobility, including elevator access from the street entrances and between platforms. Wheelchair lifts on Metrobuses are not too reliable. When a wheelchair-lift van is required, contact **Murray's Non-Emergency Transportation Ser-vice** (3031 8th St. NE; ☎ 202/269-0865).

For further information, contact the nonprofit **Information Protection Advocacy for Handicapped Individuals (IPACHI)** (4455 Connecticut Ave. NW, Suite B-100, Washington, DC 20008; ☎ 202/966-8081; Metro: Van Ness/UDC, Red line) and ask for its *Access Washington* guide. You may also contact **Rehabilitation International USA** (1123 Broadway, New York, NY 10010; ☎ 212/420-1500).

Some of the following numbers might also prove useful:

Paralyzed Veterans of America Association,
☎ 202/872-1300

Easter Seal Society for Disabled Children and Adults, ☎ 202/232-2342

Travelers Aid Society, Central Office,
512 C St. NE; ☎ 202/546-3120

Car Rentals

Major car rental firms have offices in Union Station, the airports, downtown, and in the suburbs. Rates vary widely.

Major credit cards are usually required to rent a car. Minimum age requirements for drivers is often 25. Make sure you're covered against theft and collision. Some credit card companies automatically insure any car rented with the card; call and ask. Comprehensive insurance is compulsory in Virginia, Maryland, and Washington, D.C.; still, make sure you are covered against accidents involving uninsured drivers.

Some popular rental agencies:

Alamo, ☎ 800/327-9633

Avis, ☎ 800/331-1212

Budget, ☎ 800/527-0700

Dollar, ☎ 800/800-4000

Enterprise, ☎ 800/325-8007

Hertz, ☎ 800/654-3131

National, ☎ 800/227-7368

Rent-A-Wreck, ☎ 800/421-7253

Thrifty, ☎ 800/367-2277

Arriving by Plane

Three airports serve the Washington area. **Washington National Airport** (☎ 703/685-8000), the closest to the center of Washington (15–20 minutes), is restricted to domestic flights of less than 1,000 miles, and most planes fly only between 7am and 11pm. International flights and additional domestic routes are served by **Dulles Airport** (☎ 703/471-7838; 40 mins to the west), and **Baltimore-Washington Airport,** which lies between the 2 cities (45mins–1hr to the northeast). You can often find better fares departing the city if you're willing to use either of the latter two.

Air Canada, 1000 16th St. NW; ☎ 202/ 869-9000 or 800/766-3000

American, 1721 K St. NW; ☎ 800/ 433-7300

British Airways, 1830 K St. NW; ☎ 800/ 243-6822

Continental, Capitol Hilton hotel, 16th and K St. NW and Dulles Airport; ☎ 703/ 478-9700 or 800/231-0856

Delta, 1605 K St. NW; ☎ 301/468-2282 or 800/221-1212

Northwest, Capitol Hilton hotel; ☎ 202/ 737-7180

Pan Am, 1600 K St. NW; ☎ 800/221-1111

TWA, 1601 K St. NW; ☎ 202/737-7404 or 800/221-2000

United, Capitol Hilton and ANA hotel, 2401 M St. NW; ☎ 703/742-4600 or 800/241-6522

USAir, 1601 K St. NW, 1830 K St., 1001 G St. NW; ☎ 202/783-4500

Arriving by Train or Bus

Long-distance and commuter trains arrive at the beautifully restored **Union Station,** bordering Capitol Hill on the eastern edge of the central city area at Massachusetts Avenue and North Capitol Street. Many trains also stop at suburban stations, such as the Capitol Beltway and Alexandria.

Union Station is well served by bus routes, the Metro subway, cabs (Taxi Dispatch: ☎ 202/898-1221), and various tour bus and car rental companies with offices there.

A Travelers Aid center at the station provides tourist information and guidance on finding accommodations (☎ 202/546-3120).

Amtrak (the Federal rail system) handles passenger inquiries (1721 K St. NW; ☎ 202/484-7540, 800/ 872-7245, or 800/USA-RAIL).

The long-distance bus company, **Greyhound-Trailways,** serves Washington. The not-unpleasant (that's the best we can say for it) terminal is at 1005 1st St. NE (☎ 202/289-5154; ☎ 800/231-2222), a short walk from Union Station.

Arriving by Car

From New York, you can go via Baltimore and then take Interstate 95 or the Baltimore-Washington Parkway; or go south from Wilmington, Delaware, on U.S. 301, across the Chesapeake Bay and on to the capital via Annapolis. From the northwest you approach by Interstate 270, from the west by Interstate 66, and from the southwest by Interstate 95/395. The famous **Capitol Beltway** (Interstate 495) encircles the city at a radius of about 10 miles (16km) from the center.

Staying in Washington, D.C.
Getting Around

The city center is small enough to make walking a feasible way to get around. The excellent system of public transport is cheap and efficient. Washington's clean, quiet Metro subway system is an international model.

Between the Airport & the City

Washington National Airport is the closest to the District, just across the Potomac in Virginia and a 15-minute drive from downtown. The least expensive way to get downtown is by taking a courtesy bus from the airport terminal to the Metro on the Blue and Yellow line. From Baltimore-Washington and Dulles Airports, the taxi fare is expensive because of the distance (both about 45 minutes from downtown).

The **Washington Flyer** (☎ 703/685-1400) operates buses between the very centrally located airport terminal building at 1517 K St. NW and both Dulles and National airports. Fares to/from Dulles are $16 one way, $26 round-trip; to/from National, $8 one way, $14 round-trip. Children 6 and under ride free. There are departures in each direction about every 30 minutes. At the K Street terminal building you can board a free loop shuttle that goes to 8 Washington hotels—the Sheraton Washington, Omni Shoreham, Washington Hilton & Towers, Renaissance Mayflower, Renaissance Washington, Grand Hyatt Washington, J. W. Marriott, and Harrington. The Harrington alone requires an advance reservation, since it's not on the loop unless someone requests it.

The **Airport Connection II** (☎ 301/261-1091, 301/441-2345, or 800/284-6066) runs buses between the airport terminal building at 1517 K St. NW and Baltimore-Washington International Airport, with departures about every hour or two in each direction;

call for exact times. The fare is $14 one way, $25 round-trip, free for children 5 and under.

The **Super Shuttle** buses (☎ 800/809-7080) run every hour between 1517 K St. NW and Baltimore-Washington Airport.

By Metro

The Washington Metropolitan Area Transit Authority (WMATA) runs the superb Metro system. Opened in 1973 and still being extended, it has well-designed stations and sleek, quiet, comfortable trains. There are 5 Metro (subway) lines: Blue, running from Van Dorn Street in the south to Addison Road in the eastern (Maryland) suburbs; Orange, running roughly east and west; Red, forming a loop to the north with both ends extending into Maryland; Yellow, running from Mount Vernon Square-UDC via National Airport to Huntington station in Alexandria; and Green, between Anacostia and U Street-Cardoza. Trains run Monday to Friday from 5:30am to midnight, Saturday from 8am to midnight, and Sunday from 10am to midnight.

Unless you want to be branded a tourist, stand to the right on the long escalators (the Wheaton Metro station has the world's longest at 230 ft.), and leave the left lane free for those who want to walk.

Fares begin at $1.10 and rise as the distance increases; they're also higher during rush hours (6–9:30am and 3–6:30pm). Fare cards are obtained from a machine: Insert a 1- or 5-dollar bill and get change; in some stations you can also use a 10- or 20-dollar bill. You can put up to $45 on a card, making it valid for many journeys. Flash passes (available at banks and some grocery stores; call 202/637-7000) are good for 2 weeks or a month of unlimited travel—special 1-day passes are available for $5 per person.

When entering the station, insert your card in a slot at the turnstile. Retrieve it when it pops back out, and keep it at hand for the exit turnstile, which will either swallow it up (in the case of exact fare), deduct the fare and print out the value remaining in the card, or tell you to add additional change at the nearby AddFare machine.

You can change to, but not from, the buses without extra charge in D.C. Outside the city, there's a small extra charge. Pick up a free transfer ticket from a separate machine at your station of entry.

Detailed information on how to get to a specific address by metro or bus is available by calling the Metro

Information Center at 202/637-7000. Staffers can even tell you exactly how long your trip will take.

By Bus

The Metrobus system is efficient and comprehensive, but can be baffling in its size and complexity. It has about 400 city and suburban routes, some of which operate only in rush hours. Most routes run from about 5am to midnight, and a few continue until about 2am. There is 1 flat fare (regular fare is $1.10) for the city and another for suburban journeys; both are higher during rush hours. Exact fares are required.

Bus and subway maps are available at most Metro stations, WMATA headquarters at 600 5th St. NW (☎ 202/637-7000), and at Metro Center.

By Taxi

Most cabbies speak at least 2 languages (English is not always their first). They seem to enjoy listening to talk radio and eavesdropping on passengers, so quite a few of them have opinions about what's going on in Powertown.

Taxis can usually be hailed quite easily, except in bad weather or during rush hours. The rooftop lights on cabs have no significance—the cabs may be occupied or not, whether or not the lights are lit.

They can also be ordered by phone: try **Diamond Cab Company** (☎ 202/387-6200), **Yellow Cab** (☎ 202/544-1212), or **Capitol Cab** (☎ 202/546-2400).

Before entering a taxi, be sure to look for the driver's taxi license, which is required to be visibly posted. Don't get into an unauthorized taxi.

It's a particular oddity of Washington, and a headache to cabdrivers and visitors alike, that the city cabs have no meters; fares are based on a zone system. (This system was devised for the convenience of members of Congress, who made sure that the city center and the Capitol buildings be encompassed by 1 low-cost zone.)

When you take a cab from one point to another in the same zone, the fare is the same, no matter how many miles are traveled. Fortunately, most of the major sightseeing attractions are within Zone 1, and travel within 1 zone should cost around $3. Fares between other zones run from $3.20 to $10.80, the maximum fare for any ride within city limits. There is also a $1.25 charge for each additional passenger after the first, a $1 rush-hour surcharge between 4pm and 6:30pm on weekdays, and usually a $1 per bag luggage charge.

Travel into Maryland or Virginia costs $2 for the 1st half-mile and 70¢ for each additional half-mile, so it might be wise to take Metro as close to your destination as possible, and then hail a cab from the station.

Don't be startled if your cab suddenly swerves to pick up another passenger—they're allowed to pick up additional fares en route. Suburban cabs' metered rates are reasonable. You're expected to tip 15% of the fare. If you have a complaint, call or write the **D.C. Taxicab Commission** (☎ 202/767-8380; 2041 Martin Luther King, Jr. Ave. SE, Washington, D.C. 20020) or the office of the Mayor (☎ 202/727-2980).

By Car

With such good public transportation, the visitor to Washington scarcely needs a car. However, for trips outside the city a car is often indispensable. Maryland and Virginia tend to be strict about enforcing the maximum speed limit of 55 mph (90kmph) on freeways. In D.C. the limit is 25 mph (40kmph) unless otherwise indicated.

If you cannot avoid driving in the city, try to keep clear of rush hours (7–9:30am and 3–6:30pm), when congestion is heavy and changes in traffic regulations can be perplexing: Certain streets become one-way, and at many intersections left turns are forbidden. Unless otherwise indicated, you may turn right on red at a traffic light. Pedestrians have the right of way.

Parking downtown can be a severe problem, especially in Georgetown and Adams Morgan. D.C. is notorious in enforcing its parking laws, employing an enormous force of implacable ticket-givers, who are astonishing invulnerable to pleas and curses (it's illegal to curse or threaten them, by the way).

Some areas have meters, which operate from 9:30am to 6:30pm. Most have a 2-hour limit. In areas with resident-only parking, you may park for 2 hours, and in an unrestricted area for up to 72 hours. Visitors staying in a private house (but not a hotel) can obtain a free permit from the nearest police station, allowing 15-day parking, provided the car does not remain in one place for more than 72 hours.

You can expect to pay from $7 to $10 for garage parking.

By Foot

It's easy, it's good for you, and, you'd miss many of the city's charms if you drove all the time. Washington is a pleasant city to walk in, more suited to the pedestrian than many other American cities. It is little more than 10 miles (16km) across at its widest point, and the main tourist attractions are concentrated in a relatively small area.

The Mall, for example, home to the Smithsonian Institution complex of museums, can keep you engrossed for days. All within walking distance of one another are the National Air and Space Museum, National Museum of American History, National Museum of Natural History, Arts and Industries Building, Hirshhorn Museum and Sculpture Garden, the Museum of African Art, and the Sackler and Freer galleries of art. The East and West Buildings of the National Gallery are also on the Mall.

A Sense of Direction   Finding your way around Washington is a simple matter, once you get the hang of it, although it can be daunting at first. The city is laid out on a gridlike plan and divided into 4 quadrants, northwest, northeast, southwest, and southeast.

Downtown, lettered streets run east to west. Numbered streets run north to south. On lettered streets, the 1st 2 digits of the number indicate the nearest street; for example, 2112 R St. NW is between 21st and 22nd streets. On numbered streets, count the letters of the alphabet; no. 511 10th St. NW, for example, is between E and F streets. There are no J, X, Y, or Z streets, so K becomes the 10th letter, and so on.

Beyond the lettered streets, most street names still retain an alphabetical order, first with two-syllable names, then three. Meanwhile, avenues named after the 50 states cut diagonally across the regular street grid in various parts of town.

By Limousine

Admiral Limousine Service, Madison Hotel, 15th and M St. NW; ☎ 202/554-1000

Carey Limousine, 4530 Wisconsin Ave. NW; ☎ 202/362-7400

DRM Limousine & Tour Services, Union Station; ☎ 202/544-0437

Manhattan D.C. Executive Transportation, 2500 Calvert St. NW; ☎ 202/775-1888

By Boat

River cruises on the Potomac are operated by: **Potomac River Cruises,** Pier 4, 6th and Water St. SW, ☎ 202/554-8000; **Cruise Ship Dandy,** Old Town

Alexandria, ☎ 703/683-6076; and **Potomac River-boat Co.,** The Admiral Tilp, Old Town Alexandria, ☎ 703/548-9000.

By Bike & Canoe

One of the most pleasant ways to see Washington is by bicycle. For information contact the **Washington Area Bicyclist Association** (1819 H St. NW; ☎ 202/872-9830).

The following firms rent bicycles, and the last two also rent canoes in season:

Big Wheel Bikes, 315 7th St. SE, ☎ 202/543-1600; and 1034 33rd St. NW, ☎ 202/337-0254

Fletcher's Boat House, 4940 Canal Rd. NW; ☎ 202/244-0461

Thompson Boat Center, Rock Creek Pkwy. and Virginia Ave. NW; ☎ 202/333-4861

Publications

Washington's main newspaper, the renowned *Washington Post,* appears daily. The Sunday "Arts," Friday "Weekend," and Thursday "District Weekly" sections are all good sources of information on cultural events and entertainment.

Also try the newer daily, the *Washington Times;* the monthly magazine *Washingtonian;* the free weekly *City Paper;* the free neighborhood papers (the *Uptown Citizen, Georgetowner,* and *Northwest Current*); and the gay and lesbian weeklies the *Washington Blade* and *Metro Weekly.*

Newspapers and magazines from all over the world are sold at the News Room (on the corner of Connecticut Ave. and S St. NW).

Public Holidays

New Year's Day, January 1; Martin Luther King, Jr. Day, 3rd Monday in January; President's Day, mid-February; Memorial Day, end of May; Independence Day, July 4; Labor Day, 1st Monday in September; Columbus Day, 2nd Monday in October; Veterans Day, November 11; Thanksgiving, 4th Thursday in November; Christmas, December 25.

Rest Rooms

Washington has few public rest rooms, except for a few questionable ones in some parks. But there are plenty

of clean facilities available in public buildings—
museums, libraries, coffee bars, and restaurants—
so there will usually be one not far away.

Safety

Despite negative publicity, Washington is no more (and
unfortunately no less) dangerous than many other big
cities in the world. This means that precautions must
be taken, especially in any tourist area, where pickpockets and thieves are on the lookout for easy prey.
Walking alone after dark can be dangerous for men as
well as women, especially outside the main tourist
areas.

Apart from this, all the usual advice applies: Keep a
tight hold on cameras, handbags, and other valuables,
or lock them in your hotel safe. Carry the minimum
amount of cash. In a crowd of tourists or on a crowded
bus or subway, be alert for pickpockets. Keep your doors
locked when driving; many thefts occur at traffic lights.
When leaving your car, take your valuables with you or
least lock them in your trunk.

Shopping Hours

Big department stores generally open at 10am and close
between 6pm and 9pm, depending on the day of the
week and the season. Shopping hours vary widely. Many
shops, especially in smart areas such as Georgetown,
and in the suburban shopping malls, are open on Sunday. Some large food stores stay open until midnight; a
few are open 24 hours all week.

Smoking

Smoking is now banned in elevators, subways, buses,
some taxis, most public buildings, and offices. It may
look as though everyone in the city smokes, for all the
smokers are standing in front of their places of business,
getting their nicotine fix. Most restaurants are entirely
nonsmoking; a few cater to cigar smokers as a gimmick, but they, too, provide nonsmoking sections.

Taxes & Tipping

Sales tax in D.C. is 10%. There's a hotel tax of 13%, and
an additional $1.50 occupancy tax per room per night.

Service is not usually included on restaurant tabs
(except in the case of some restaurants, who will note
"gratuity included" on the bill for large parties). In hotels
and restaurants, it is customary to tip 15% to 20%. Taxi
tips should be 15%. Tips for airport, rail, and hotel

porters are at your discretion: 50¢ to $1 per bag, depending on distance and service, is a fair guideline. Bartenders seem much friendlier when they get 50¢ or $1 per drink.

Telephones

Public telephones are available and they'll cost 25¢ for a local call. The area code for D.C. is 202, but if you are dialing within the District, simply use the 7-digit number. To call suburban Northern Virginia, you must use area code 703 plus the 7-digit number; for Maryland, it's either 410 (Baltimore/Annapolis) or 301 (the rest of Maryland). For information, call 411, or the area code plus 555-1212.

Dial 0 to get an operator, who can assist you in placing a call. To obtain the toll-free numbers of many hotels, airlines, and other companies, call 800/555-1212.

In addition to coin-operated pay phones, you can pay for your calls with prepaid phone cards, which are similar to credit cards. They are widely available (at drugstores and post offices) in increments from $5 to $20 and can be "recharged" with funds from your credit cards. To place a call, just follow the instructions on the back of the card.

Useful Addresses & Phone Numbers

Emergency

Police/Fire/Ambulance, ☎ 911; TDD: ☎ 202/727-3323

Police (nonemergency), ☎ 202/727-1010

Help Lines

AIDS Information Line, ☎ 202/332-2437

Alcohol and Drug Hot Line, ☎ 202/783-1300

Department of Human Services Crisis Line, ☎ 202/561-7000

Gay and Lesbian Hot Line, ☎ 202/833-3234

Medical Referral (George Washington University Hospital), ☎ 202/994-4112

National Organization for Victim Assistance, ☎ 202/232-6682

Park Police, ☎ 202/619-7300

Poison Center, ☎ 202/625-3333

Rape Crisis Center, ☎ 202/333-7273

Travelers Aid Society, Central Office, 512 C St. NE, Union Station, **☎** 202/546-3120; National Airport, **☎** 703/684-3472; Dulles Airport, **☎** 703/661-8636

Telephone Services

Time, ☎ 202/844-1212

Weather, ☎ 202/936-1212

Postal Service Information, ☎ 202/682-9595

General Tourist Information, ☎ 202/737-8866

Metrobus/Metrorail Information, ☎ 202/637-7000 or 637-1328

Congresspersons/Senators Capitol switchboard, ☎ 202/224-3121

D.C. Department of Recreation (events/activities), ☎ 202/673-7671

Dial-a-Museum (Smithsonian activities), ☎ 202/357-2020

Dial-a-Phenomenon (what's up in the night sky), ☎ 202/357-2000

Main Post Office

900 Brentwood Rd. NE; **☎** 202/682-9595 (open 24 hours)

Embassies

Australia, 1601 Massachusetts Ave. NW; **☎** 202/797-3000

Canada, 501 Pennsylvania Ave. NW; **☎** 202/682-1740

Ireland, 2234 Massachusetts Ave. NW; **☎** 202/462-3939

Japan, 2520 Massachusetts Ave. NW; **☎** 202/234-2266

New Zealand, 37 Observatory Circle NW; **☎** 202/328-4800

South Africa, 3051 Massachusetts Ave. NW: **☎** 202/232-4400

United Kingdom, 3100 Massachusetts Ave. NW: **☎** 202/462-1340

Major Libraries

Folger Shakespeare Library, 201 E. Capitol St. SE; ☎ 202/544-4600

Library of Congress, 1st St., between E. Capitol St. and Independence Ave. SE; ☎ 202/707-5000

Martin Luther King Memorial Library, 901 G St. NW; ☎ 202/727-1111. Consult the phone directory for neighborhood branches.

Places of Worship

Check Saturday's *Washington Post* or *Washington Times* for hours of services and special occasions, and the Yellow Pages for neighborhood churches and synagogues.

Adas Israel Synagogue, Connecticut Ave. and Porter St. NW; ☎ 202/362-4433

Church of the Epiphany (Episcopal), 1317 G St. NW; ☎ 202/347-2635

Church of St. John the Baptist (Russian Orthodox), 4001 17th St. NW; ☎ 202/726-3000

First Baptist Church, 16th and O St. NW; ☎ 202/387-2206

First Church of Christ Scientist, 1770 Euclid St. NW; ☎ 202/347-6336

Franciscan Monastery (Roman Catholic), 1400 Quincy St. NE; ☎ 202/526-6800

Friends Meeting House (Quakers), 2111 Florida Ave. NW; ☎ 202/483-3310

Islamic Mosque and Cultural Center, 2551 Massachusetts Ave. NW; ☎ 202/332-8343)

Luther Place Memorial Church, 1226 Vermont Ave. at Thomas Circle; ☎ 202/667-1377

Metropolitan African Methodist Episcopal Church, 1518 M St. NW; ☎ 202/331-1426

Mormon Temple (Church of Jesus Christ of Latter Day Saints), 9900 Stoneybrook Dr., Kensington, MD. 20895; ☎ 301/587-0144

National Shrine of the Immaculate Conception (Roman Catholic), 4th St. and Michigan Ave. NE; ☎ 202/526-8300

New York Avenue Presbyterian Church, 1313 New York Ave. NW; ☎ 202/393-3700

Russian Orthodox Church of St. Nicholas, 3500 Massachusetts Ave. NW; ☎ 202/333-5060

St. John's Lafayette Square (Episcopal), 16th and H St. NW; ☎ 202/347-8766

St. Matthew's Cathedral (Roman Catholic), 1725 Rhode Island Ave. NW; ☎ 202/347-3215)

Saint Sophia's Cathedral (Greek Orthodox), 36th St. and Massachusetts Ave. NW; ☎ 202/333-4730

Washington Hebrew Congregation, Massachusetts Ave. and Macomb St. NW; ☎ 202/362-7100

Washington National Cathedral (Episcopal), Massachusetts and Wisconsin Ave. NW; ☎ 202/537-6200

PORTRAITS

The work is no different than that done
in Hartford, Connecticut, or Atlanta,
Georgia. Some of us will pass laws;
others will filibuster; and still others will
read Sandra Day O'Connor's mail. One
man in a small office might give a
squadron of jets to an Arab country, and
another man in a small office will send
missiles to Israel. . . . Some people
might be assigned to following Soviet
diplomats all over town, and others could
be in charge of selling them wheat. . . .

People should stop thinking just because
we live in Washington we're different.

—*Art Buchwald*

The Political City

Now in the moments before the Senate
was about to begin the chamber re-
sembled a sort of tan, marble-paneled
fishbowl in which pageboys in their
white shirts and black pants darted about
like minnows distributing bills and copies
of the legislative calendar to all the desks,
whisking off stray specks of dust, shoving
the spittoons carefully out of sight,
checking the snuff boxes to make sure
they were full, joking and calling to one
another across the big brown room.

—*Allen Drury,* Advise and
Consent *(1959)*

Politics is Washington's raison d'être. To understand the city one should know something of the complex web of power that underlies it.

By looking at a map, it becomes apparent that the streets of Washington converge on 2 points: the White House and the Capitol. Between them, like a rope in a tug-of-war contest, stretches Pennsylvania Avenue. Since the United States came into existence, power has alternated between the two, depending on the relative force and prestige of the president and Congress.

The day-to-day business of the country's domestic and foreign affairs is controlled by the president. He does so with the aid of a cabinet, made up of the appointed heads of the various executive departments, and an Executive Office consisting of a large number of aides, special advisers, and advisory councils, also not elected. There is a great deal of coming and going between the White House and the neighboring Executive Office Building, which is used by many of the president's advisory staff.

The president can initiate bills in Congress and veto legislation coming from Congress; but Congress can vote to override a presidential veto. Furthermore it can (and frequently does) block legislation emanating from the White House. There is a passage in Gore Vidal's novel *Washington, D.C.* in which a senator expresses the way in which Congress jealously guards the right to curb excessive presidential power:

"You see, I think our kind of government is the best ever devised. At least originally. So whenever a president draws too much power to himself, the Congress must stop him by restoring the balance. Let him reach too far and . . . we shall. . . .' The Senator's other hand, rigid as a knife, made as if to chop the tyrant's hand from its wrist."

It was in this way that Congress blocked Kennedy's Civil Rights legislation in the 1960s, and it was Kennedy's successor Johnson, the wily catcher of congressional votes, who was able to push the legislation through.

Behind the Congress on Capitol Hill sits the gleaming marble palace of the Supreme Court, representing the third branch of government: the Judiciary. The Court, which upholds the U.S. Constitution, has on occasion opposed both president and Congress. Some of its decisions have had epoch-making consequences, such as its famous 1954 ruling that racial segregation in the public schools was unconstitutional.

These 3 institutions are the most conspicuous pinnacles of the citadel of federal power, but a glance at the map of Washington reveals the extent of the government's presence. Central Washington is dominated by the vast departments and agencies, such as the State Department, the Treasury, the Department of Commerce, the Internal Revenue Service, the National Aeronautics and Space Administration, the Department of Justice and its offshoot, and the Federal Bureau of Investigation. Across the Potomac in Virginia is the Pentagon, housing the Department of Defense, and the Langley headquarters of the Central Intelligence Agency, which, unlike the FBI, is not open to the public.

These and the other government organizations employ more than 360,000 civilians in Washington alone—a far cry from the 130 clerks who made up the total federal workforce in 1800 when the government first moved here. In 1991 the total workforce in the metropolitan area was 2.25 million. While the federal workforce comprises 16.7% of this total, many of the rest work for enterprises that do business with the government.

Washington is continually besieged by lobbyists representing special-interest groups seeking to make the government receptive to their needs. They may be companies angling for contracts, farmers' representatives seeking bigger subsidies, environmental groups agitating for stricter pollution controls, or foreign governments looking for financial aid. These groups generally employ professional lobbyists—often lawyers and public relations people, a number of them former civil servants—who frequently earn large sums of money for pleading their clients' causes over lunch or cocktails or at lavish receptions.

Another important element in Washington political life is the media: Syndicated columnists, investigative journalists, and television interviewers from around the nation and the world both reflect and monitor current events in the political sphere. The media can also influence events directly and crucially—an obvious instance was the *Washington Post*'s investigations into the Watergate scandal, which led to President Nixon's resignation. The *Washington Post* is the largest private enterprise in the city.

Social life too has its part to play in the political drama. Power and prestige go hand in hand, and Washington's social world acts as a barometer of status. Washingtonians covet invitations to White House receptions, embassy functions, and private parties in the fashionable suburbs. At these events alliances are forged, deals made, gossip exchanged, and reputations enhanced or diminished.

Much of America resents the size of the federal government and the growing dominance of Washington. Every so often a president, capitalizing on this resentment, sets out to reduce the federal bureaucracy, but invariably with little result. The great engine of government that drives the city continues to grow in size and power, and the lure of Washington grows ever stronger.

A Brief History

Until a decade or so ago, our nation's capital was a Cinderella among American cities, scorned by her wicked big sisters (New York, Chicago, and Los Angeles) as a provincial backwater, a "company town" dominated by the federal government and lacking in culture, refinement, and most of the good things in life.

Now the tables have turned; Washington has become one of the most desirable U.S. cities in which to live, and a top tourist destination.

It has taken surprisingly long for the city to achieve this transformation. The reasons lie in the multiple conflicts, anomalies, and paradoxes that have marked its history from the beginning.

The choice of site for the capital was the outcome of a deal between the northeastern and southeastern states. In the War of Independence, the North, which had incurred bigger debts than the South, asked Congress to bail out the Union. Secretary of State Thomas Jefferson, a Southerner, struck a bargain with his Northern rival Alexander Hamilton, Secretary of the Treasury, whereby the South would yield in the matter of the debts if the North would agree to a new national capital being located in the South. In due course President George Washington himself chose the site, a diamond of territory 10 square miles (26km²) in area, taken from Virginia and Maryland. Subsequently the area west of the Potomac seceded back to Virginia, spoiling the symmetry of the diamond.

The president appointed 3 commissioners to administer this territory and to oversee the creation of the city within it. They decided to name the city Washington, after him. To lay out the city, the president chose a brilliant, irascible Frenchman, Pierre *continues*

Chronology of U.S. Presidents & First Ladies

Some presidents are known for their good deeds, some for their mistakes, and others only for their ability to win.

Presidents	Years in Office	Party	First Ladies
George Washington	1789–97	None	Martha Dandridge Custis Washington
John Adams	1797–1801	Federalist	Abigail Smith Adams
Thomas Jefferson	1801–9	Democratic-Republican	Martha Wayles Skelton Jefferson
James Madison	1809–17	Democratic-Republican	Dolley Payne Todd Madison
James Monroe	1817–25	Democratic-Republican	Elizabeth Kortright Monroe
John Quincy Adams	1825–9	Democratic-Republican	Louisa Catherine Johnson Adams
Andrew Jackson	1829–37	Democrat	Rachel Donelson Jackson
Martin Van Buren	1837–41	Democrat	Hannah Hoes Van Buren
William H. Harrison	1841	Whig	Anna Tuthill Symmes Harrison
John Tyler	1841–5	Whig	Letitia Christian Tyler, Julia Gardiner Tyler
James K. Polk	1845–9	Democrat	Sarah Childress Polk
Zachary Taylor	1849–50	Whig	Margaret Mackall Smith Taylor
Millard Fillmore	1850–3	Whig	Abigail Powers Fillmore

Chronology of U.S. Presidents & First Ladies, continued

Presidents	Years in Office	Party	First Ladies
Franklin Pierce	1853–7	Democrat	Jane Means Appleton Pierce
James Buchanan	1857–61	Democrat	Harriet Lane Johnston (niece)
Abraham Lincoln	1861–5	Republican	Mary Todd Lincoln
Andrew Johnson	1865–9	National Union	Eliza McCardle Johnson
Ulysses S. Grant	1869–77	Republican	Julia Dent Grant
Rutherford B. Hayes	1877–81	Republican	Lucy Ware Webb Hayes
James A. Garfield	1881	Republican	Lucretia Rudolph Garfield
Chester A. Arthur	1881–5	Republican	Ellen Lewis Herndon Arthur
Grover Cleveland	1885–9	Democrat	Frances Folsom Cleveland
Benjamin Harrison	1889–93	Republican	Caroline Lavinia Scott Harrison
Grover Cleveland	1893–7	Democrat	Frances Folsom Cleveland
William McKinley	1897–1901	Republican	Ida Saxton McKinley
Theodore Roosevelt	1901–9	Republican	Edith Kermit Carow Roosevelt
William H. Taft	1909–13	Republican	Helen Herron Taft
Woodrow Wilson	1913–21	Democrat	Ellen Louise Axson Wilson, Edith Boling Galt Wilson

Warren G. Harding	1921–3	Republican	Florence Kling Harding
Calvin Coolidge	1923–9	Republican	Grace Anna Goodhue Coolidge
Herbert C. Hoover	1929–33	Republican	Lou Henry Hoover
Franklin D. Roosevelt	1933–45	Democrat	Anna Eleanor Roosevelt
Harry S. Truman	1945–53	Democrat	Elizabeth Virginia Wallace Truman
Dwight D. Eisenhower	1953–61	Republican	Mamie Geneva Doud Eisenhower
John F. Kennedy	1961–3	Democrat	Jacqueline Bouvier Kennedy Onassis
Lyndon B. Johnson	1963–9	Democrat	Claudia Alta Taylor (Lady Bird) Johnson
Richard M. Nixon	1969–74	Republican	Patricia Ryan Nixon
Gerald R. Ford	1974–7	Republican	Elizabeth Bloomer Ford
James E. Carter, Jr.	1977–81	Democrat	Rosalyn Smith Carter
Ronald W. Reagan	1981–89	Republican	Nancy Davis Reagan
George H. W. Bush	1989–92	Republican	Barbara Pierce Bush
William Clinton	1992–	Democrat	Hillary Rodham Clinton

Charles L'Enfant, an army engineer who had fought for the Americans in the War of Independence. Inspired by the best examples of European town planning, L'Enfant designed a city that he considered worthy of the new nation's lofty ideals: Triumphal avenues radiated out from the president's mansion and the Capitol on its hilltop, with broad streets in a grid pattern, circles, squares, generous parks, and imposing vistas. He drew the plan on a grand scale, foreseeing that as the United States grew in prosperity it would be able to flesh out his scheme and eventually achieve a most impressive capital. As L'Enfant put it in a letter to Washington:

"It will be obvious that the plan should be drawn on such a scale as to leave room for the aggrandizement and embellishment which the increase of the wealth of the nation will permit it to pursue at any period however remote."

L'Enfant's plan was astonishingly bold for its time. He insisted, for example, on very wide streets. At that time 50 feet would have been more than generous, but L'Enfant wanted 90 to 130 feet for ordinary thoroughfares and 180 to 400 feet for the grander ones. The capital of the United States deserved no less.

Unfortunately, L'Enfant's vision was not matched by the commissioners', nor by the local landowners', and there were bitter quarrels over the implementation of his plan.

Daniel Carroll, nephew of one of the commissioners, built a farmhouse on a site earmarked to become what is now Garfield Park to the southeast of the Capitol. After writing twice to Carroll and receiving no reply, L'Enfant had the building dismantled and moved away. In the ensuing outcry, L'Enfant prevailed, but in the end opposition to him became so fierce that Washington felt obliged to dismiss him a year after his appointment. It was the first of many setbacks suffered by the city as a result of pettiness and lack of imagination.

L'Enfant's basic scheme, however, was retained, and the construction of the city limped along. By 1800 it was sufficiently far advanced for Congress to move there, but for decades Washington remained a sorry sight. The Capitol and the White House stood out amid the chaos of sporadic housing development, farmyards, and areas of swamp. The city had no proper sidewalks, street lighting, or sanitation.

To add insult to injury, the District of Columbia was made a politically neutral federal district—residents did not have the right to vote in congressional or presidential elections (the idea was to protect the government from local interference).

Belonging to no state, the District was given short shrift by Congress, which was preoccupied with other matters.

The miserliness with which the city was (and arguably, still is) treated was astounding. Oil lamps were installed in the vicinity of the Capitol and the White House, but not enough money was allocated for oil, so the lamps became mere ornaments. Meanwhile planning control was lax. Not until 1820 did the government order farmers to stop fencing in and planting areas that had been designated as streets. Periodically, congressmen would agitate for the removal of the nation's capital to a more westerly (and hence central) location, but nothing came of it.

The city languished without proper amenities until the 1870s, when a dynamic city administrator named Alexander ("Boss") Shepherd forced through a vast scheme of public works without worrying about where the money would come from. Sidewalks were laid, sewers and street lights installed, and thousands of trees planted.

Although he bankrupted the city, posterity should be grateful to Shepherd. The response of Congress, however, was to dissolve the city council and take over the government of the District through congressional committees, thus leaving the citizens with neither federal nor local representation—an extraordinary state of affairs for the capital of a great democracy.

During the late 19th and early 20th centuries the situation improved, partly owing to a steady influx of wealthy people who colonized areas such as what is now Cleveland Park in the northwest. The city gained some fine buildings, including the Library of Congress and Union Station, and in the same period the Mall was laid out more or less in its present form. With World War I, the New Deal, and World War II, the ranks of Washington's bureaucracy swelled, but as late as 1960 it still felt like a company town.

In that year, African-Americans became the majority in this formerly and famously segregated city (vividly symbolized in 1939 when opera star Marian Anderson sang to a crowd of 75,000 on the steps of the Lincoln Memorial after being barred from performing at Constitution Hall, and again in 1963 when a quarter of a million Americans of all races gathered on the

National Mall to hear Martin Luther King, Jr.'s "I Have A Dream" speech after the March on Washington). And another turning point was achieved with the election of John F. Kennedy as president. Kennedy appointed his own adviser on Washington, preserved threatened historic houses, had a new code for public buildings drawn up, approved the plan for the Metro, and presided over the rebuilding of the old slum area in the southwest. As Kennedy put it, "The Nation's capital should represent the finest living environment in which America can plan and build."

Washington always finds new ways to remain in the public eye: The city is still recovering from the destructive 1968 riots that followed the assassination of Martin Luther King, Jr., and was forever changed by the notoriety of the 1973/74 Watergate break-ins and the resignation of disgraced President Richard Nixon. The 1976 Bicentennial celebration brought visitors in record numbers to the capital city. Presidents and their administrations, particularly Kennedy, Reagan, and Clinton, left their mark on the tone and lifestyle of the city.

And the local government has occasionally provided drama on a national scale, as when longtime Mayor Marion S. Barry was arrested in 1990 in an FBI sting that caught him on camera using crack at the downtown Washington Vista hotel. After a brief honeymoon with the administration of Mayor Sharon Pratt Kelly, the city re-elected Barry as mayor in 1994—one of the most unbelievable comebacks in political history. The man who has been called "Mayor for Life" remains in office until 1998.

As a city, Washington, D.C. has undergone rapid and accelerating change. Today it has its own elected mayor and city council, drawn largely from the African-American areas, and D.C. residents can at last vote in presidential elections, although they still have only "shadow" representation in Congress. After the "white flight" of the 1970s, which caused a decrease in urban population and a swelling of the Maryland and Vir-ginia suburbs, the 1980s saw the revitalization and gentrification of many formerly rundown neighborhoods. And continuing waves of immigrants poured into neighborhoods; Latinos and Eritreans to Adams Morgan and Mount Pleasant, and Vietnamese and Koreans to Arlington. The whole city has been infused with new flavor and vitality.

The John F. Kennedy Center for the Performing Arts, opened in 1971, has helped to fuel a cultural boom in the city. The Smithsonian Institution has expanded its already vast museum facilities. The building of the Metro system, which is being extended to the far suburbs, has linked ethnically and culturally disparate areas of the region. It has also triggered the dramatic growth of suburban business centers such as Bethesda, Rosslyn, and Crystal City, where large corporations have rushed to set up their headquarters, bringing affluent and discriminating new customers to the area's restaurants and nightspots, which have consequently blossomed.

Splendid new luxury hotels, office buildings, and shopping malls are mushrooming, new monuments and museums—including the powerful memorials to Vietnam and Korean War veterans and the unutterably moving Holocaust Museum—have arisen on the National Mall, while historic buildings such as the Old Post Office and the Pension Building have been restored to their former glory. At the same time a strict ban on high-rise buildings has kept the District's delicate skyline intact.

However, not all the news is good, as D.C. made headlines in the early 1990s as the "murder capital" of the country, due largely to the omnipresence of crack cocaine and turf wars among dealers in some of the city's more desperate and desolate areas.

Large areas of deprivation and poverty remain in the predominantly African-American sectors in the northeast and southeast, and there are jarring contrasts between rich and poor neighborhoods, one of the contradictions the capital has yet to overcome. The District of Columbia runs a $700 million budget deficit relative to that of the federal government. Due to the recent revocation of the Washington Home Rule Charter, the embattled, all-but-powerless mayor and city council have neither the funds nor the prestige to make it work. Mayor Barry and his administration have to answer to a congressionally-appointed financial control board until the city is back in the black. And these paper-pushing power mongers on Capitol Hill—the majority of whom were imported from other cities, and many of whom leave at the end of the day for homes in the affluent suburbs of nearby Virginia and Maryland—have little vested interest in shoring up the city, outside of the fairly well-defined and pristinely maintained tourist track visited by their constituents, of course.

One of America's most-visited cities, Washington is also one of the most European of U.S. cities: Its scale is human; its streets invite you to stroll rather than rush;

and unfolding vistas of townscape and a mixture of grandeur and intimacy have a distinctly European feel. Washington has been appropriately dubbed "Paris on the Potomac."

Pierre L'Enfant, whose grave is in Arlington Cemetery, would be pleased if he could see his city now, for Washington is on its way to becoming the gracious capital that he wanted it to be—even if it has taken 2 centuries. For today's visitor, Washington is a rich feast.

Landmarks in Washington, D.C.'s History

1608: English adventurer Captain John Smith explored the Potomac. His enthusiastic descriptions of the area encouraged settlement.

1634: Colonization of Maryland was begun.

1749: The town of Alexandria was created on the Virginia shore of the Potomac.

1751: Georgetown was founded.

1775–83: The American Revolutionary War (the War of American Independence).

1789: George Washington became the first president of the United States. Georgetown University was founded.

1790: A Southern location was agreed upon for the new federal capital, and Congress asked President Washington to choose a site on the Potomac River.

1791: Pierre Charles L'Enfant began planning the city.

1792: L'Enfant was dismissed. Work on the White House, then called the President's House, began.

1793: Work began on the construction of the Capitol.

1800: The government moved to Washington from Philadelphia. President John Adams took up residence in the unfinished White House.

1801: Thomas Jefferson became the first president to be inaugurated in the new capital.

1802: A local government, consisting of a mayor and an elected council, was established.

1814: British forces raided Washington, burning the White House, the Capitol, and other public buildings. President James Madison moved temporarily to the Octagon. Congress was housed in a brick building while the original Capitol was restored.

1820: Washington residents were given the right to elect the city's mayor.

1835: The U.S. came into possession of the fortune bequeathed by James Smithson, which led ultimately to the creation of the Smithsonian Institution.

1846: The portion of the District of Columbia southwest of the Potomac seceded back to Virginia, reducing the District to approximately 69 square miles (179km²) instead of its original 100 square miles (259km²).

1848: Work began on the construction of the Washington Monument on the Mall.

1861–65: American Civil War. Washington found itself the focal point of the war effort.

1863: President Lincoln signed the Emancipation Proclamation.

1864: Arlington National Cemetery was established.

1865: President Lincoln was assassinated during a performance at Ford's Theatre.

1867: African-Americans voted for the first time in local elections.

1868: President Andrew Johnson was impeached by the House of Representatives, but was narrowly acquitted by the Senate.

1871: Congress established a new form of city administration under a governor appointed by the president.

1871–74: A public works program under Alexander ("Boss") Shepherd turned Washington for the first time into a city with proper urban amenities.

1878: Government of D.C. by commissioners appointed by the president was re-established, leaving residents with no say in the running of the city or the nation.

1884: The Washington Monument was completed.

1896: For the first time an automobile was driven down Pennsylvania Avenue.

1902: A large-scale program of city beautification was implemented.

1910: Height restrictions were imposed on buildings in the city.

1917: The United States entered World War I. In a few months the population of Washington increased by about 50%.

1921: The first bathing beauty contest in America was held beside the Tidal Basin. Miss Washington, D.C. was elected Miss America in Atlantic City.

1924: Washington Senators baseball team defeated the New York Giants to win the World Series.

1929: Beginning of the Great Depression.

1931: Hunger March on Washington.

1932: Washington invaded by Bonus Marchers, veterans seeking immediate payment of their war bonuses. The U.S. Army dispersed the marchers.

1933: Election of Franklin D. Roosevelt as president. Roosevelt introduced the New Deal, and the country began to recover from the depression. The population of the city swelled as federal jobs multiplied and people were drawn to Washington by New Deal activity and lobbying.

1941: The United States entered World War II, following the Japanese attack on Pearl Harbor. War activity swelled Washington's population further.

1943: The Pentagon was completed.

1950–60: The African-American population of Washington rose from 35% to 54%, especially due to migration from Southern states.

1954: Washington became the first major American city to introduce racial integration in schools.

1964: Washingtonians were, for the first time since 1800, able to vote in a presidential election.

1968: The assassination of Martin Luther King Jr. sparked violent riots, blighting some areas of the city, especially Old Downtown, and U Street NW, still referred to as "the riot corridor."

1971: Walter Fauntroy was elected D.C.'s first congressional representative in a century. The seat to this day carries no vote except in committee. The John F. Kennedy Center for the Performing Arts was opened, with an inaugural performance of Leonard Bernstein's "Mass."

1974: Resignation of President Richard Nixon, following the Watergate scandal.

1975: Washington regained an elected city council, and Walter Washington, an African-American, was elected the city's first mayor in more than a century.

1976: The first stretch of the Metro subway was opened. It will never make it to Georgetown.

1980: Building of the Convention Center was begun, a key element in the continuing revitalization of Old Downtown.

1979–1991: "Bitch set me up": Mayor Marion Barry's administration began with great promise and activity, but was marred by mismanagement and corruption and ended with his conviction on drug charges.

1991: Sharon Pratt Kelly was inaugurated as Washington's first female mayor.

1994: "Mayor for Life" Marion Barry back in office.

1995: Korean War Veterans Memorial is dedicated.

Who's Who

Everyone seems to pass through here sooner or later, and it would be an impossible task to list here all the famous people, politicians included, associated with Washington. The following is a selection of those who have contributed to the history of the city.

Adams, Henry (1838–1918). Historian and philosopher. Grandson of President John Quincy Adams and son of the diplomat Charles Francis Adams. Although his best-known book is his autobiographical work *The Education of Henry Adams,* he also wrote a monumental *History of the United States.* He settled in Washington in 1877 in a house on the site of the present Hay-Adams Hotel.

Barry, Marion S., Jr. (b. 1936). Mayor of Washington 1979–1991, second holder of the office, former civil rights activist. Clouded by allegations of official and private misbehavior, his first administration culminated in his conviction on drug charges in 1991. He achieved a stunning comeback when he was re-elected to office in 1994.

Bradlee, Benjamin (b. 1921). Executive Editor emeritus of the *Washington Post.* He steered the *Post* through the period of the Watergate investigation (1972–4), conducted by journalists Carl Bernstein and Bob Woodward.

Buchwald, Art (b. 1925). Syndicated newspaper columnist living in Washington who writes with mischievous wit and humor about life and politics in the capital. His column appears in some 500 newspapers in countries all over the world, and several collections of his articles have been published as books.

Douglass, Frederick (c.1817–95). Pioneer advocate of black liberation. His real name was Frederick Augustus Washington Bailey, but he assumed the alias Douglass after escaping from the slavery into which he was born. He dedicated his life to writing, lecturing, and campaigning for the cause of black freedom and equality. See Frederick Douglass House in "Sights and Attractions."

Ellicott, Andrew (1754–1820). Surveyor who helped L'Enfant lay out the area that is now the District of Columbia. He took over after L'Enfant's dismissal, and the map of the territory published in 1793 was in his name, although it was mostly L'Enfant's work.

Ellington, Duke (1899–1974). Seminal jazz composer, band leader, and pianist, born in Washington. His real name was Edward Kennedy Ellington.

Graham, Katharine (b. 1917). Chairman and Chief executive officer of the Washington Post Company. Her son, Donald E. Graham, is publisher of the *Washington Post* newspaper. See also Benjamin Bradlee above.

Hayes, Helen (1900–93). Actress, born in Washington. Helen Hayes became a star after appearing in James Barrie's play *Dear Brutus* in 1918. Probably her most famous role was as Queen Victoria in the play *Victoria Regina* (1935). Namesake of the annual Washington theater awards, D.C.'s glittery equivalent of the Tony Awards.

Hoban, James (1762–1831). Irish-born architect who designed and supervised the construction of the White House.

Hooker, General Joseph (1814–79). A name that achieved a dubious immortality. Hooker was a Union general during the Civil War who tried to restrict prostitution in the capital by confining camp-followers (nearly 4,000) to one part of the city. Hence the term "hooker."

Hoover, J. Edgar (1895–1972). Director of the Federal Bureau of Investigation for 48 years from 1924 until his death. Born in Washington and a graduate of George Washington University Law School, Hoover built the FBI into the powerful organization that it is today. A tough, combative figure, he was both widely respected and greatly disliked. For 20 years he lunched regularly at the Mayflower Hotel, and after his death his customary table was draped in red, white, and blue for a week, in mourning.

Jolson, Al (1886–1950). Popular singer and actor. Originally named Asa Yoelson, he was born in Russia and raised in southwest Washington, where his father was a rabbi.

Latrobe, Benjamin Henry (1764–1820). English-born architect. He came to America in 1796 and designed a number of buildings in Washington including Decatur House and parts of the Capitol and the White House.

L'Enfant, Pierre Charles (1754–1825). The brilliant, temperamental French engineer and architect who, more than anyone else, is responsible for Washington's design and layout. Having come to America to fight in George Washington's army against the British, he was commissioned in 1791 to prepare a plan for the federal capitol. The following year he was dismissed after quarreling with the commissioners of the District of Columbia. He spent the latter part of his life fighting for greater compensation and died in poverty. Posthumous recognition came in 1909 when his remains were moved to Arlington National Cemetery and a monument to him was erected there.

Pope, John Russell (1874–1937). Architect whose serene neoclassical buildings are a major feature of Washington. They include the National Archives, the West Building of the National Gallery of Art, the Jefferson Memorial, and the House of the Temple. (See "Sights and Attractions.")

Shepherd, Alexander Robey ("Boss") (1835–1902). Shepherd was to Washington what Haussmann was to Paris. He became head of the Board of Public Works in 1871 and governor of the District of Columbia in 1873. Under his regime a vast program of public works was undertaken, which bankrupted Washington but at last gave it adequate sidewalks, water mains, sewerage, and lighting.

Smith, Captain John (1580–1631). English adventurer who, in 1608, with "7 souldiers and 7 gentlemen," sailed up the Potomac. Where Washington now stands he discovered a settlement of Algonquin Indians. Charmed, he encouraged colonists to settle there.

Smithson, James (1765–1829). Smithson never came to Washington, but it would have been a very different place without him. He was a British scientist whose bequest of $500,000 to the United States resulted in the creation of the Smithsonian Institution, the nation's largest and most comprehensive collection of museums.

Sousa, John Philip (1854–1932). Bandmaster and composer. Born in a house on Capitol Hill, Sousa was for many years leader of the U.S. Marine Band before forming his own. Composer of many styles of music, he is most famous for his rousing marches which include "Liberty Bell," "Semper Fidelis," "The Stars and Stripes Forever," and the "Washington Post March," played every time a band passes the newspaper's offices. He also wrote 5 novels and an autobiography, *Marching Along.* Of Polish parentage, his real name was So, to which he later added the letters USA.

Thornton, William (1759–1828). Scottish-born doctor, architect, and inventor. He emigrated to the United States in 1787, won the competition for the design of the Capitol in 1792, and supervised its construction until he was replaced by Latrobe.

Washington, George (1732–99). First president of the United States, he chose the location of the city that was named in his honor. He selected a site far enough inland to be safe from surprise naval attack yet at the same time accessible to ocean-going vessels. His own home was nearby at Mount Vernon (see "Excursions").

Washington, Walter E. (b. 1915). What more appropriate name for the man who became the first mayor of Washington in 1975? An African-American, and a lawyer by profession, he held the office for 4 years.

INDEX

WASHINGTON, D.C.

1-12 Washington, D.C. Street Atlas
13-14 District of Columbia & Vicinity
15 Washington, D.C. Transit Map

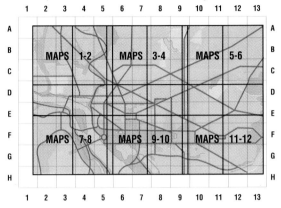

KEY TO MAP SYMBOLS

City Maps

Major Place of Interest	P Parking
Park	M Metro
Built-up Area	—— Railroad
Divided highway	←— One way street
Primary road	*i* Information
Secondary road	**7** Adjoining Page No.
Other road	

Area Maps

ROADS

Freeway

Tollway

Road under construction

Other divided highway

Primary road

Secondary road

Other road

CITY

☐   City

■   Point of Interest

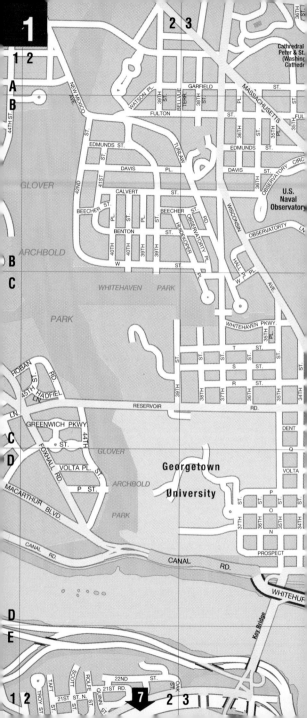

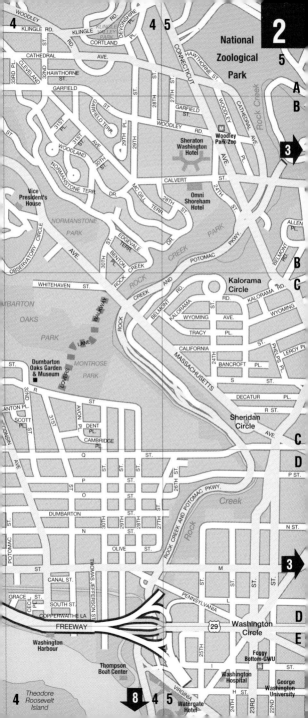

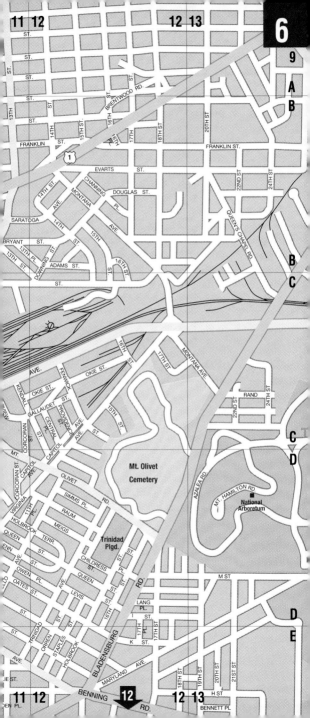

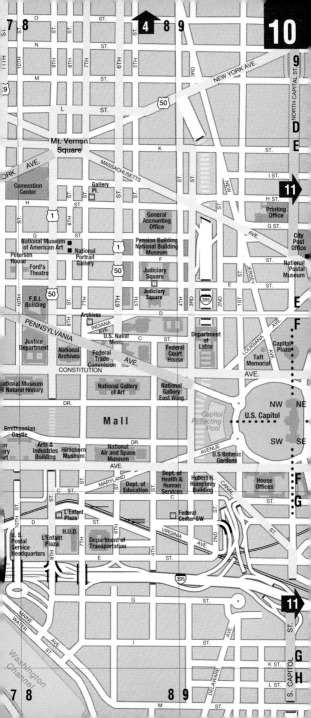

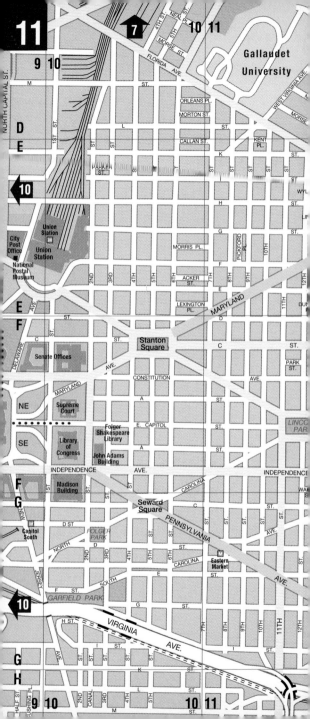

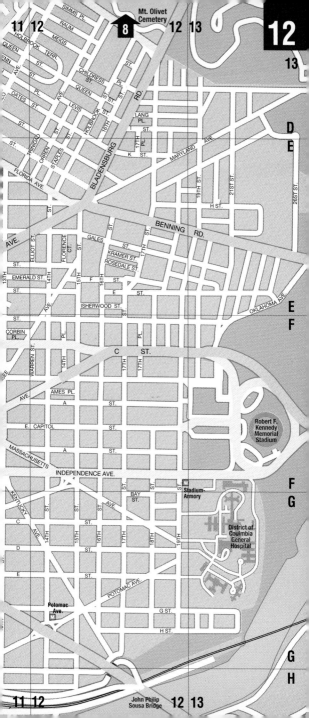

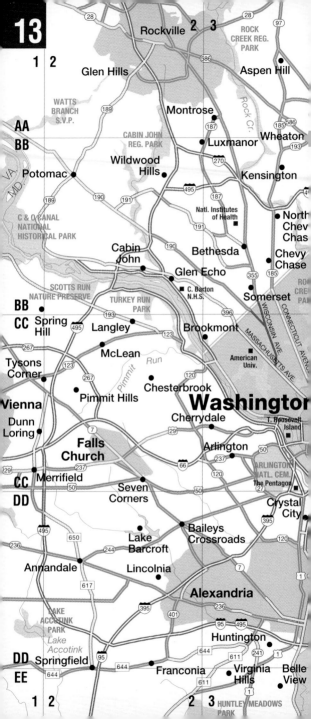

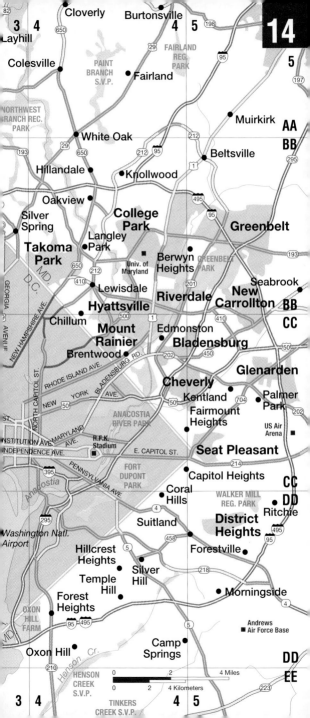

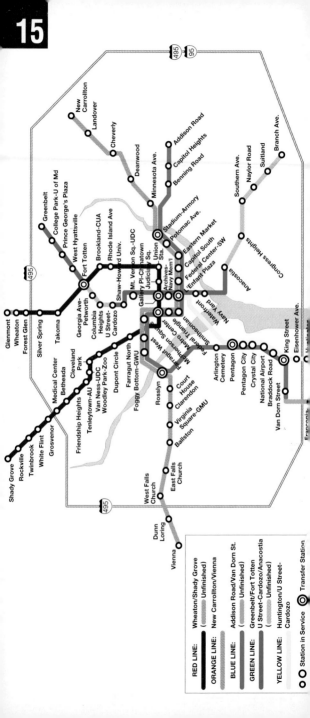